FamilyFun VACATION GUIDE
Great Lakes

By Pamela Hill Nettleton
and the experts
at FamilyFun Magazine

New York

Editorial Director
Lois Spritzer

Design & Production
Impress, Inc.
Hans Teensma
Pam Glaven
Katie Craig
Lisa Newman
James McDonald
Katie Winger

Disney Editions and *FamilyFun*

Book Editors
Alexandra Kennedy
Wendy Lefkon
Lisa Stiepock

Research Editor
Beth Honeyman

Contributing Editors
Jon Adolph
Rani Arbo
Duryan Bhagat
Jodi Butler
Jaqueline Cappuccio
Deanna Cook
Tony Cuen
Ann Hallock
Jessica Hinds
Martha Jenkins
Heather Johnson
Rich Mintzer
Jody Revenson
David Sokol
Deborah Way

Copy Editors
Diane Hodges
Jenny Langsam
Monica Mayper
Jill Newman

Editorial Assistants
Laura Gomes
Jean Graham

Production
Janet Castiglione
Sue Cole

This book is dedicated to our *FamilyFun* readers, and contributors, and to traveling families everywhere.

Pamela Hill Nettleton is editorial director of *Minnesota Monthly* magazine, author of *Getting Married When It's Not Your First Time* (Quill, 2001), and lives with her husband and three children in Minneapolis.

Illustrations by **Kandy Littrell**

For information address Disney Editions,
114 Fifth Avenue, New York, New York 10011-5690.

Printed in the United States of America

First Edition
1 3 5 7 9 8 6 4 2
Library of Congress Cataloging-in-Publication Data on File
ISBN: 0-7868-5302-6

Visit www.disneyeditions.com

CONTENTS

Dear Parents,

A FRIEND OF MINE—a dad—said something recently that rang true to me. "A great childhood," he said, thinking aloud, "is really made up of a thousand small good moments." His comment prompted me to step back and take stock of what those moments might be for my own two young sons. What will be their happiest memories? Topping the list in my mind are the simple but extraordinary pleasures we've had traveling together: the hermit crabs we discovered at a Maine beach, the afternoon spent playing catch on the Mall in Washington, the thrill of a first flight, a first train ride, a first hike to a mountaintop.

As parents, we all work incredibly hard to find the time and money to take our children on vacation. We want to show them the remarkably varied American landscape and introduce them to its many cultures and histories. We want to get away from jobs, homework, and household chores long enough to enjoy one another's company uninterrupted. And most of all, we want to have fun.

The editors at *FamilyFun* and I take great pride in this book and others in the series. They are a culmination of ten years worth of gathering for our readers' the best vacation advice out there. Traveling with children is an art—and our charge is to help with your decisions every step of the way so that you can make the most of every minute of your time away.

Alexandra Kennedy

Alexandra Kennedy
Editorial Director,
FamilyFun magazine

How to Use This Guide

WELCOME TO THE world of *FamilyFun* magazine's new travel guide series. In our effort to present you with the finest in vacation options, we called on the best experts we know: our hardy group of writers. All are parents who travel with their kids, and all live and work in the area(s) about which they're writing. These are the people who can tell you where to find that teddy bear shop that isn't in the main mall, which restaurant has the best milk shakes, which museum will invite your toddler to roll up his sleeves and create art, and which theme park will give your preteen a good return on the price of admission. With all their recommendations comes the endorsement of their kids: our traveling children have been our best critics.

Since all of the guides in this series cover more than one state, we have divided them into easy-to-use sections. So here's a guide to the guide.

READY, SET, GO!—is a mini-encyclopedia of handy facts, practical advice, what to do/where to go/when to go/how to travel: in other words, all you need to know about planning a successful family vacation.

INTRODUCTION—will give you an overview of the states being covered in this guidebook. Read it—it will whet your appetite, and perhaps give you some new ideas for family activities.

CHAPTERS—States and chapters are presented in geographical order. Chapters represent the regions we think your family will enjoy most. We have omitted those places that we feel would not be family-friendly or are too expensive for what you get in return. We also make note of attractions that appeal only to a certain age range.

FamilyFun has given each entry a rating—stars (★) that range from one to four—to guide you to our favorites. Remember, however, that this guidebook contains nothing that we do not recommend—it's just that we liked some things better than others. We've also assigned a dollar sign rating ($)—in high season for a family of four, also ranging from one to four. Check the price range at the start of each chapter as the key changes. We hope that this will help you to decide whether a hotel, restaurant, or attraction will fit in with your budget.

Typically, we start each chapter with an introduction, followed by *FamilyFun*'s Must-See List of up to ten things to try to do while visiting. We've divided attractions into two categories: "Cultural Attractions" (museums, historic sites, and so on) and "Just for Fun" (water parks, zoos, aquariums, roller coasters, and the like). Wherever possible, we've included Website information.

What more can we say? We hope that this guide helps you to fashion the best possible vacation for your family, one that is a pleasure in the planning, a delight in the doing, and one that will leave every member of your clan with memories that will last a lifetime—or at least until ninth grade.

Bon Voyage!

Great Lakes

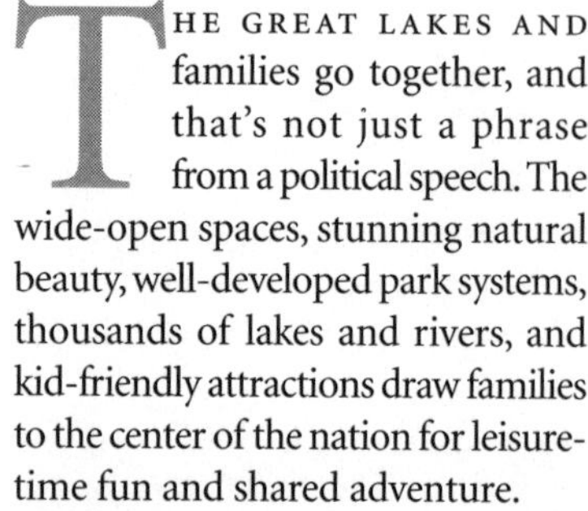

THE GREAT LAKES AND families go together, and that's not just a phrase from a political speech. The wide-open spaces, stunning natural beauty, well-developed park systems, thousands of lakes and rivers, and kid-friendly attractions draw families to the center of the nation for leisure-time fun and shared adventure.

Midwesterners love the outdoors and make the most of each season with swimming, boating, canoeing, fishing (even in winter!), camping, hiking, biking, cross-country skiing, snowmobiling, snowshoeing, and ice-skating. The ski resorts of northern Minnesota and Michigan and the winter carnival of St. Paul count the snowy months as their high season. Minnesota, Wisconsin, and Michigan northwoods family resorts—filled with boaters and swimmers all summer long—hunker down in winter, becoming cozy, fireside retreats for cross-country and downhill skiers.

In summer, the evergreens get competition from hardwood trees

leafing out in lighter shades of green, and even a highway drive becomes a scenic adventure. Gardens, both private and public, are brilliant with color, and a stroll through a Chicago neighborhood is a visual treat. Summers here can be very warm, and families head for the lakes and beaches, resorts and parks, picnic grounds and outdoor cafés.

The beaches at Lake Superior, Lake Michigan, Lake Huron, and Lake Erie are wide and long enough to give visitors the feel of being at the eastern seashore—you truly can't see the other side of these lakes, and a day playing in the sand feels like a day at the ocean. A simple stroll along a Great Lakes beach is an adventure: enormous oar boats are easily spotted making their way into port, sea birds scour the waves for lunch, and the prevalence of agates and lake-polished rocks please young treasure hunters.

In addition to their natural treasures, Great Lakes cities offer educational and fun experiences like the Adler Planetarium & Astronomy Museum and the Shedd Aquarium in Chicago, the Great Lakes Science Center in Cleveland, and the peerless Center of Science and Industry museums in Columbus and Toledo.

Where there are families and children, there are amusement parks. The Great Lakes offer plenty of chances to get soaked on water rides, get scared on roller coasters, and get tired from a whole day of too much fun: the indoor Knott's Camp Snoopy in the Mall of America, Valley Fair south of the Twin Cities, Ohio's Paramount's Kings Island, Six Flags Ohio, Wyandot Lake Wet and Dry Adventure Park Six Flags in Columbus, Cedar Point Water Park and Soak City in Sandusky on the shores of Lake Erie, and Six Flags Great America, near Chicago.

However you like your family fun, it's here: sophisticated and educational, outdoor and natural, or wild and wacky.

Let the fun begin!

Pack up and get going.
You're on vacation!

Ready, Set, Go!

JUST TEN YEARS AGO, *FamilyFun* was a fledgling magazine, and the family travel "industry"—now a booming, $100 billion annual trade—was as much a newcomer as we were. In a way, you could say we have grown up together.

FamilyFun was one of the first national magazines to actively research and publicize travel ideas for families with school-age children (a fun job, we must add). Over the last decade, as the numbers of traveling families increased, so did the business of family travel. These days, there are more resources, opportunities, and means for the vacationing family than ever before —which, in turn, gives *FamilyFun* the chance to be an even more valuable clearinghouse of ideas for you.

Through the years, we have been privileged to work with veteran travel writers and editors who have gone around the world with their kids. We've also taken time to listen to our readers—insightful, creative families from across the United States—and to note (and sometimes publish) their stories, recommendations, and tips on traveling as a family. A combination of those two wisdoms is what awaits you on the following pages.

Although it may not be readily apparent, a lot of trial and error underlies these pages. Each destination, before it reaches this book, undergoes a rigorous investigation, and not all make the grade.

We know that family vacations are a big investment, and we know that's why you're here. You're hoping to sidestep the pitfalls of experimentation and to locate destinations that will be a real hit with your family. Congratulations! You've come to the right place.

FIRST STEPS

At the outset, organizing a family vacation can seem as daunting as landing a probe on Mars. Better to stay home and watch the Discovery Channel, you think—maybe toast a few marshmallows in the fireplace.

The truth is that planning an adventurous vacation can be fun, especially if you prepare for it in advance and involve your kids. The onerous part is remembering all the things you have to think about.

That's where we come in. This introductory chapter covers family travel from A to Z, from deciding where to go, to getting there and making the most of your vacation. Some of this may seem like old news to you, but we want to make sure you don't forget a thing.

HAVE MODEM, WILL TRAVEL
For information on how to research and book travel plans on the Web, turn to page 31.

How much do we spend?

Chances are, you already know approximately what you have to spend on a vacation—and you've already got a modus operandi when it comes to money matters. Maybe you're a family that carefully figures a budget, then finds a vacation to fit it. Or maybe you're the type to set your heart on a once-in-a-lifetime trip, then scrimp and save until you can make it happen.

Determine the type of trip you will take. Before you even start your planning, take a moment to consider: what kind of trip are you taking? Are you splurging on a dream vacation, or conserving on a semiannual getaway? What aspects of this trip are most important to you?

Budget carefully. Once you know what those broad parameters are, the next step is to think through your vacation budget in detail—if not at the outset of planning, then at an opportune point along the way. When you know what you have to spend, you'll make quicker and less stressful decisions en route and you'll be able to pay the bills without a grimace once you get home. You'll find lots of budget-saving tips in this introductory chapter.

When can we go?

Scheduling your vacation well can make a big difference in everyone's experience of the trip.

Consider each individual. Most likely, tight school and work schedules will decide when you travel — but if possible, aim for a time slot that allows everyone to relax. For instance, an action-packed road trip sounds exciting, but it might be just the wrong medicine for a parent who's squeezing it into a packed work schedule. End-of-summer trips may be tough for kids with back-to-school anxieties, and midyear trips that snatch kids from school sometimes cause more trouble than they're worth.

Where do we go?

In this book (and the others in this travel series), you'll find scores of winning family destinations. By all means, though, don't stop here. Doing your own research is half the fun, and these days, you have a wealth of resources at your disposal.

Make a list of destinations. What hot spots intrigue your clan? What adventures would you like to try? Draw up a big list, and don't worry about coming up with too many ideas—you can return to this list year after year. Here are a few trails you can follow: relatives, friends, and coworkers (who love to report on their own successful trips), a professional travel agent, local chambers of commerce and state tourism boards, and magazines, the Internet (see page 34 for some good family travel sites), and local hotels and outfitters in the geographic areas you're interested in.

Evaluate your family. A good vacation has to accommodate *everyone* in the family, no matter what their ages, limitations, or interests. While no destination will make everyone happy all the time, you should search vigilantly for those that offer a niche for each family member.

Involve your kids. The more involved your kids are in planning—especially during these early, brainstorming stages — the more likely they are to work to make the trip a success.

Experiment wisely. While experimentation can add spice to a trip, too much may overwhelm your kids (and you). If your child has her heart set on horseback riding, for example, make sure she tries it out at home before you put down a deposit on a dude ranch vacation.

Check the season. Be informed about travel conditions for the time of your trip and make sure you're not heading for trouble (hurricane season in Florida, for example, or black-fly season in the Adirondacks). This is especially important if you're cashing in on off-season deals.

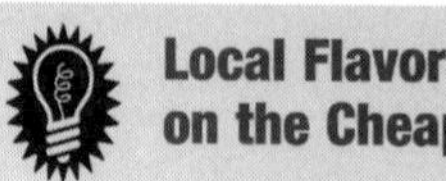

Local Flavor on the Cheap

Don't wait till you arrive at your destination to investigate opportunities for local fun—research a few in advance:

- **Check out a regional festival or agricultural fair. For fairs in the western U.S., visit www.fairsnet.org and for festivals nationwide, visit www.festivals.com**
- **Explore a college campus (which may offer green space, bike paths, museums, observatories, and more). To find a list, go to a general Internet search engine like www.yahoo.com, click on education, and search for colleges by state. Then, call the school's information office for a map and a roster of special events.**
- **Visit a farmers' market. For a list of markets around the U.S., log on to www.ams.usda.gov/farmersmarkets/**
- **Take in an air show (they're usually free at military bases). For a list of air shows by region, see www.airshows.org**
- **Find a local nature center or Audubon preserve.**

Schedule appropriately. How much time do you need to give this particular destination its due? You don't want to feel like you're rushing through things—but neither do you want to run out of activities that will interest your kids.

Should we have an itinerary?

Drawing up a travel itinerary, whether it's rough or detailed, will ensure that you travel wisely, hit the hot spots, and give everyone in your group a say in what you'll see.

Include something for everyone. No doubt, each member of your family will have his or her own list of must-sees. If a unanimous vote on itinerary stops is out of the question, ask everyone to write down top choices, then create a schedule that guarantees each person at least one or two favorites. If your children span a wide age range, remind them that there will be some patient standing by while siblings (and Mom and Dad) have their moments in the sun.

Involve the kids (again). Once you've got the basic stops down, kids can help research destinations, plan driving routes, locate pit stops, and help plan rainy-day alternatives.

Make a plan, then break it. Don't let your preplanned schedule get in the way of spontaneous delights. What if your kids want to ride that water slide for an extra three hours? One fun moment in hand is usually worth at least two on the itinerary.

Beat the crowds. Remember to head for popular attractions first thing in the morning or in late afternoon and early evening. Save the middle of the day for poolside fun or activities that take you off the beaten path and away from crowds.

Travel in tune with your family's natural rhythms. Preschoolers tend to be at their best early in the day—a good time for structured activities. Many teens, on the other hand, are pictures of grogginess before noon. Adapt your itinerary to suit ingrained family habits—including your usual meal and nap times—and you'll have smoother sailing. When visiting very popular destinations, take the time to find out in advance when their slowest periods are.

Train Your Own Tour Guides

Guided tours at historic sites and museums are often a snooze (or too sophisticated) for young kids. Instead, create your own tour—have each family member study up on a different attraction by writing or calling for brochures, surfing the Web, and visiting the library. Then, when you arrive, you'll have an expert guide on board.

GETTING THERE

As we all know, the experience of taking kids from point A to point B runs the gamut from uneventful (read: bliss) to miserable. Knowing the ins and outs of your travel options will speed you toward a sane trip.

FamilyFun READER'S TIP

Hire Some Junior Travel Agents

When we were planning a summer trip to Louisiana, I overheard one of my kids tell another that they were going to have to do everything Mom and Dad wanted to do. That's when I decided that each family member would get to plan a full day of our trip. I purchased a regional travel guide and told everyone they had $200 for one day's activities, meals, and accommodations, so they would have to budget (a useful exercise for my 10- and 12-year olds). Every night, any money left over from that day was given to the next planner. I am proud to say that everything went well, and the kids proclaimed it the best vacation ever!

Cindy Long, Spring, Texas

By Plane

PROS: It's fast. And if you land a good deal, air travel can actually be affordable.

CONS: If you don't land a good deal, air travel can be prohibitively expensive, especially for a big family. Other pitfalls include flight delays, mounting claustrophobia on long trips, and strict baggage restrictions.

Look for deals. Traveling in off-peak season and taking off-peak flights (very early or very late in the day) may save you money; flying midweek and staying over Saturday night almost always will. You may also wish to research deals at different airports (for instance, T. F. Green Airport in Providence, Rhode Island, often offers cheaper fares than Boston's Logan Airport 45 minutes away). Also, remember that most sale tickets have a cutoff date—you'll have to book two, three, or four weeks ahead of your departure date to get the deal.

Consider using an agent. Booking your own airline reservations on the Web is a cinch these days (see pages 35 and 36), but there are still advantages to using a professional travel agent who knows your family's needs. First of all, for the $10 or $20 per-ticket surcharge you may pay, you'll save Web-surfing time, and you'll be spared the stress of babysitting the fickle airline market. Also, an agent may be able to suggest a Plan B (such as using a smaller airport to get a better deal)—something the Web search engines can't do for you. Try to get a good agent recommendation through friends, coworkers, or relatives; if you need further help, the American Society of Travel Agents (703-739-2782, www.astanet.com) provides a list of members, as well as brochures on travel topics (including one on how to choose a travel agent).

By Car

PROS: Road trips are the cheapest way to get from here to there, and they can also be real adventures. In addition, the car is familiar territory for your kids, so they'll feel right at home (for better or worse) during the trip. And, of course, a road trip affords you priceless flexibility.

CONS: You're in for major advance planning, from making sure your car is in good condition to scheduling regular rest stops and having a dependable cache of road snacks, games, and other diversions. Even with those, the hours of close confinement may quickly erode your family's wanderlust.

Get a good map. If you belong to AAA, request a free "TripTik" map. Otherwise, you can map your route and download printed driving directions on Websites like www.mapquest.com, www.freetrip.com, and www.mapsonus.com

CHECKLIST

Flying with Kids

WHEN YOU BOOK

- Try first for a nonstop flight. If that's not available, fly "direct," which means you'll stop at least once but won't switch planes.
- Book flights that depart early in the day, if possible. If your flight is delayed, you—and the airline—will have time to make other arrangements.
- Specify your ticketing preferences, whether paper or electronic.
- Check to see if a meal will be served in flight. If so, order meals your kids like. Many airlines offer kids' meals or a vegetarian choice that may be pasta. If not, plan accordingly.
- Ask for the seats you'd like, whether they're a window, an aisle, or the bulkhead for legroom.

PACKING TIPS

- Stuff your carry-on for every contingency. Pack all medications, extra clothes for little kids, diapers, baby food, formula, wet wipes, and snacks (they'll also help kids swallow to relieve ear pressure).
- Have each child carry a small backpack with travel toys, a light sweatshirt, and a pair of socks for the flight.

ON THE DAY OF YOUR TRIP

- Call ahead to check for delays.
- Have all photo IDs within easy reach (not necessary for kids under age 18 traveling with their parents on domestic flights; on most international flights, even infants will need a passport).
- If you have heavy bags, check your luggage first and then park.
- If you are early for the flight or run into long delays, don't go straight to the gate. Instead, meander through the airport's diversions: windows onto the runways, children's play areas (many major airports now have these), Web access computers, and, of course, stores where kids can find a treat to tide them over.
- Carry on extra bottled water. It's easy to get dehydrated on a plane, and the drink service may be slow in reaching you.

ON THE PLANE

- Ask if your child can view the cockpit (the best time may be after the flight is over).
- Secure pillows and blankets for family members who may want to nap.
- Take breaks from sitting; occasionally walk the aisles and switch seats.

FLYING FEARS

Most children are fearless fliers—and those who are afraid often can trace their concerns to adults who unintentionally transmit their own fears. If you need help answering your children's questions, you can ask them on-line at www.wic-kid. com

FamilyFun TIP

Bookworms

When you're on the road, there's nothing like a good story to pass the time. For night drives, audio books can be a lifesaver. Try borrowing or renting one from your local library, or visit www.storytapes.com, the Website for Village StoryTapes (800-238-8273). You can either rent or purchase from their excellent selection; three- to four-week tape rentals cost $6 to $17 (for *Harry Potter IV*); to buy, tapes cost $12 to $60.

Be prepared for emergencies, large and small. It goes without saying that your car should be in prime working order before you depart. You should have supplies for road emergencies on board, as well as a good first-aid kit (see page 33 for a list of what to include), and, if you have one, bring a cell phone.

Keep things orderly. We all know what happens to our cars within minutes of the time the kids buckle in; on long road trips, expect the chaos to rise by a factor of ten. In an effort to keep things in check, bring containers to hold trash and toys; pack the children's luggage so it's easiest to reach; divvy up the back-seat space so kids know where their boundaries are; and go over basic behavior rules before you leave.

Drive in time with your family's rhythm. Night driving offers less traffic and a chance that young kids will sleep (you can let them ride in their pj's). Alternatively, an early start may avoid late-afternoon, kid-cranky hours. When possible, go with your family's natural flow.

Help prevent motion sickness. Have frequent, small meals during your trip (symptoms are more likely to occur on an empty stomach). Over-the-counter medications such as Dramamine, as well as ginger ale, ginger tea, or ginger candy also can help, but once symptoms begin, it's usually too late for oral medications. Make sure the car is well ventilated, and have sickness-prone travelers take a window seat, which offers

WEATHER WATCHERS Before you leave, assign forecaster duties to one of your kids. Using the Internet, he or she can research and predict the type of weather you'll encounter (and advise everyone on what to pack). Try www.weather.com

fresh air and a view of the road. If a child feels nauseated, have him look straight in front of the car or focus attention on the horizon. If your child becomes carsick, stop the car to give him a break from the motion; having him lie down with his head perfectly still also may help.

By Train

PROS: First of all, trains are just plain cool, for kids and adults alike. Second, there's room to explore, and everyone can kick back and enjoy the view. And third, if you are headed to a major metropolitan area with a good public transit system, you'll avoid the expenses and hassles of city driving and parking.

CONS: There's only one national passenger rail service, Amtrak, and at press time its future was in question. Also, Amtrak's limited network may not be convenient to your destination (ask about connector trains and rental car agencies when you call). In some regions of the United States, Amtrak's city-to-city service rivals car, bus, and plane travel for efficiency; on cross-country hauls, this is not the case. If you're investing in a long train trip, you're in it more for the experience of train travel.

Inquire about special deals. Children ages 2 to 15 usually ride for half fare when accompanied by an adult who pays full fare. Each adult can bring two children at this discounted rate. Amtrak also offers

A Road Trip Survival Kit

A BAG OF TRICKS

- mini-puzzles with a backboard
- video games, cassette or CD player (with headphones)
- paper, pens, pencils, markers
- travel versions of board games
- stuffed animals
- Etch A Sketch
- colored pipe cleaners
- deck of cards
- cookie sheet (a good lap tray)
- word puzzles
- small action figures or dolls
- stickers
- Trivial Pursuit cards
- cotton string (for cat's cradle games)

A COOLER OF SNACKS

Bring lots of drinks and a cache of snacks like granola bars, trail mix, grapes, carrot sticks, roll-up sandwiches, fruit leather, and popcorn.

Keeping 'Em Busy: 60-Second Solutions

SQUABBLE SOLUTIONS

Give your kids 25 cents in pennies at the start of the trip. Each time they fight or whine, charge them a penny. Offer a reward, such as doubling or tripling their money, if they haven't lost a cent during the ride.

WAGER AND WIN

Kids are natural wagerers—they love to bet how much, how long, how far, how many. If you're in a bind for a moment's entertainment, ask them to guess the number of French fries on your plate or to estimate how many steps it will take to walk to your airport gate. The key here is to be able to verify the guesses—you'll need to wear a watch with a second hand and carry a calculator.

CREATIVE COMPETITION

Kids love challenges. Need to get rid of the trash in the car? See who can smash the trash into the smallest paper ball, then toss it in the wastepaper bag. Want quiet time? Hold a five-minute silence contest. Need to get through errands in a hurry? Challenge your kids to a race against time. You may feel that your motives are transparent, but your kids won't care.

special seasonal rates, other family deals, and Web-only deals.

How to find them. Amtrak's Website, www.amtrak.com, provides information on fares, schedules, reservations, routes and services, station locations, and special offers. You can also call Amtrak at 800-872-7245 for information and reservations. When you book, ask if there is a full-service dining car and ask whether you can reserve a block of seats for your family.

Consider a sleeper car. For overnight trips, sleep-in-your-seat fares are the cheapest, but first-class bedrooms are much more comfortable.

Arrive early. If your train seats are unassigned, get to the station early for the best chance of eveyone's sitting together. You can even have one parent run ahead to grab a group of seats while the other shepherds children and luggage to the platform.

By RV

PROS: It's a home away from home, which means you can eat, sleep, and use the indoor plumbing (as everyone will agree, one of the finest features of RV travel) whenever you want. In an RV, you are free to explore with independence, self-sufficiency, and freedom—three assets that can be priceless when you're traveling with kids.

CONS: It's a home away from home,

FamilyFun READER'S TIP

Patchwork Pillows

I am 10 years old, and every year my family goes camping. I collect patches from each place we visit, including the Grand Canyon, Yellowstone and Yosemite National Parks; San Francisco; Las Vegas; and, most recently, Santa Fe, New Mexico. I put all the patches I've collected during each year on separate pillows. I keep the pillows on my bed to remind me of our great trips.

Alex Smythe, Tucson, Arizona

which means you face dishes, cooking, and maintenance (generators, water pumps, waste tanks, and the engine, for starters). In addition, RV rentals are not cheap, although they can compare favorably to the cost of a week's lodging, food, and travel (especially for big families).

What they cost. Expect to pay rental fees between $500 and $1,500 per week, depending on location, model, and time of year you'll be traveling, and the luxury factor (RVs can get pretty posh). Gasoline costs will be high, but you'll save considerably on food and accommodations (campground fees average $20 to $40 per night).

How to find them. Rental information is available through auto clubs and through Go RVing (888-GO-RVING, ask for the free video and literature; www.gorving.com). Cruise America (800- 327-7799) offers 150 rental centers across the United States and Canada. The RV America Website (www.rvamerica.com) has listings of dealers, clubs, and resources.

Be a savvy renter. Choose an RV that's big enough for your family, but know that many campgrounds only permit vehicles less than 30 feet long. Before you rent, ask how many people fit comfortably in the RV, what powers the appliances, how much insurance is required, and whether supplies such as linens and kitchen utensils are included in the rental price. Get a demonstration of how to work everything in the vehicle, read the manual, practice a little ahead of time, and you'll be ready to take the plunge.

By Bus

PROS: The major advantages of bus travel are that it's cheap, that it spares you the stress of driving, and that tickets usually can be purchased on the day of your trip, at the station. **CONS:** Unfortunately, traveling by bus often takes longer than by car. What's more, bus travel offers little opportunity for diversion for your

Thinking of Skipping School?

If you are, then according to a recent Travel Industry Association of America poll, you're in lots of company. The TIA survey found that one in five parents allows a child to miss school to gain travel experience (of these, 72 percent, however, missed only one or two days). If you're planning to play hooky on vacation, start by keeping the school well informed of your plans. Discuss with the teachers what work your kids will have to keep up with, and create a regular routine during your vacation when they can do so. To help kids stay in touch with their classmates and to broaden their learning experience, establish a way for them to share their travel adventures with the class, either while they're en route (by e-mailing or posting letters) or once they return to school.

children. And since you're sitting close to other passengers, many lively family games are off-limits (some buses offer a TV movie; ask when you call).

How to find them: Greyhound Lines (800-229-9424) offers service across the United States. In the Northeast, between New Hampshire and Washington, D.C., Peter Pan Bus Lines (800-237-8747) is another option. Both have Websites, www.greyhound.com and www.peterpanbus.com, complete with fare and schedule information. To locate smaller local or regional bus lines, try the local Yellow Pages or the department of travel and tourism in the region you'll be visiting.

By Rental Car

PROS: This isn't exactly a pro, but if you've flown or trained into an area without a safe and dependable public transport system, you'll need a rental to get around. Plus, a rental car is cost-efficient for families (as opposed to solo travelers). Best of all, you won't be putting miles on your own car—and if you rent a minivan, you can have drink-cup slots and elbowroom for every single kid.

CONS: None, really, save the expense and a list of rental and insurance decisions that can be as daunting as a Starbucks menu.

How to find them: Your travel agent can book a car for you, but if you want to do it yourself, you'll find all the major agencies in the 800 directory.

Compare costs. Whether you shop on-line or over the phone, compare costs for as many companies as you can (no one company has the best deals in every city or state). In general, weeklong and weekend rentals are a better deal than per-day rentals. In your research, you may wish to inquire about companies' service records, especially if you're going with a local budget chain.

Ask about discounts. Membership in AAA or other associations, credit cards, entertainment book coupons, and package-deal reservations may net you bargains: ask about potential discounts when you make your reservation.

Ask about services and charges. Rental car companies put a lot of information in fine print. So, before you pay (and before you drive away), ask lots of questions. What are the mileage and one-way drop fees? Is there a fee for early or late car returns? Should you bring the car back with an empty gas tank or a full one to get the best refueling price? Does the company offer 24-hour breakdown service? Do the cars have air-conditioning, a jack, and a spare tire? Is there a fee for extra drivers (married couples are often exempt, but you should check). Are car seats available at no extra charge? (Even if the answer is yes, your own car seat may be cleaner, and, because it's familiar, more comfortable for your child.)

Pay only for the insurance you need. The car, and any damage to it, will be your responsibility for the duration of your trip. Before you purchase insurance from the rental agency, check to see whether your own auto or liability insurance provides adequate coverage. Some credit card agreements may also include rental protection; call the customer service

FamilyFun TIP

Compare Quotes

When you book a room at a major hotel chain, call both the hotel's local number as well as the toll-free reservation number; the rates you'll be quoted may differ.

FamilyFun READER'S TIP

Tabletop Scrapbook

Here's a fun project my family has long enjoyed while traveling. After we have mapped out our vacation, my kids, and now grandchildren, use a laundry pen to draw our route on a cotton tablecloth. We pack up the cloth along with colored markers, and while on the road, family members take turns marking the name of towns and rivers and noting funny signs. When we stop for picnic lunches, we not only use the cloth but also continue adding drawings of sights we've seen and things we've done. After the trip is over, we have a memory-filled tablecloth to use for years to come.

Janet Askew, Adair, Iowa

number on the back of your card to inquire.

Where to Stay

Where you tuck your kids in at night depends entirely on your family's traveling style and budget—and, of course, on what's available in the area to which you're traveling. There are so many options—hotels, motels, inns, cottages, cabins, condominiums, resorts, time-shares, campgrounds—it can be hard to know where to start.

Lists of local accommodations can be found through tourism boards, the Web, travel books, and the 800 numbers or published directories of major franchises. However, finding the places that really go the extra mile for families isn't easy. This book—and other family travel publications—will be your best bets, as will the time-tested recommendations of friends and acquaintances. Always, always ask your own questions as well: see our checklist on page 25 for some basics.

Hotels, Motels & Lodges

From generic chains, to mom-and-pop operations bursting with character, to ritzy palaces, this category really runs the gamut. If you don't have a dependable recommendation (from a friend, trusted travel agent, or guidebook like this one), you may wish to place your trust in the major chains (budget or no) where you at least know what you're getting.

How to find them: Most major chains can be found in the 800 directory (as well as on the Web) and can provide a list of property locations. Alternatively, you can contact regional travel bureaus or consult a national rating system, such as those in Mobil Travel Guides (available in bookstores or the on-line store at www.mobil.com) or the Automobile Association of America (call your local AAA office to order regional TourBook guides).

PICKY EATERS? If you have picky eaters in the family (or if you suspect a child may not enjoy the food at a certain restaurant), feed them ahead of time—and let them enjoy an appetizer or dessert during your meal.

Inns, B&Bs, and Farm Stays

These have traditionally been the domain of honeymooning couples and retirees. Increasingly, though, they are accommodating a growing family travel market. There are certainly gems out there for your discovery—but do your research rigorously (speak with the owner, if possible) to find out whether kids are *truly* welcome at the destination of your choice. The last thing you want to be doing on vacation is shushing your kids and shooing them away from pricey antiques. Look for inns and B&Bs attached to a working farm—these tend to be more kid-friendly, with animals to watch and feed and plenty of outdoor play space.

How to find them: Try travel magazines, regional chambers of commerce, and two excellent Websites, www.bedandbreakfeast.com and www.bbgetaways.com

Condos and Cottages

These are ideal if your group is staying put for the length of your vacation, since they offer room to spread out and cook your own meals. When you book, ask about amenities: does the condo come with linens, pots and pans, a television, phone, dishwasher, and washer/dryer? Are there extra tax and/or booking fees? If you rent directly from the owner, be even more rigorous in your questioning. Is there

WHAT TO ASK BEFORE YOU BOOK

1 ACCOMMODATIONS: What rooms (or condos or cabins) are available? How many beds are there and what size are they? Are the rooms nonsmoking? What amenities are included (laundry, phone, cable TV, refrigerator, balcony, coffee service, cots, cribs, minibar)? Are the rooms located in the main building? What specific views are available? Is there a charge for kids staying in the same room with parents? Are there family packages? Can guests upgrade rooms upon arrival?

2 DINING: Are there dining facilities on the property? If so, are there restrictions for kids? What are some menu items, and what does the average meal cost? Is there a kids' menu? Is there a complimentary breakfast offered? Are there snack and/or drink machines? If there are no dining facilities on-site, is there a family restaurant nearby?

3 RECREATION: What recreational facilities are available (game rooms, pool, tennis courts, equipment rental, and so on)? At what hours are they available? Are there additional charges for their use? Are there age or time restrictions for any recreation? What recreational options are available in the nearby community (movie theater, minigolf, bowling, and the like)?

a cancellation policy if the place is not up to your standards?

How to find them: The Internet has made it easy to connect potential renters with homeowners and rental brokers. Unfortunately, that means there are literally thousands of sites to sift through. Luckily, most sites offer very detailed information on properties, so you can actually make an informed decision on-line to pursue a place.

For starters, here are the Website addresses for a number of national and international vacation rental clearinghouses: www.eLeisure Link.com (888-801-8808); Barclay International Group (800-845-6636; www.bar clayweb.com); and 10,000 Vacation Rentals, Inc. (888-369-7245; www. 10kvacationrentals.com).

To rent directly from a property owner, try Vacation Rentals by Owner at www.vrbo.com You also can locate condos and cottages by inquiring at local tourism bureaus, local realtors (especially for seaside properties), and major resorts, which often keep lists of rentals on property or nearby.

Family Hostels

A CHEAP SLEEP

If you think hostels are the exclusive domain of students and backpackers, think again: many of the neatest have private family rooms that can be reserved in advance. Some also offer special programs, such as historic walking tours, natural history programs, and sports activities. Hostels in the Hostelling International/ American Youth Hostels system are as varied as their locations and include registered historic buildings, lighthouses, and a former dude ranch. For the latest edition of *Hostelling Experience North America*, call *202-783-6161* or visit www.hiayh.org

Campgrounds

These range from the extremely rustic—grassy knolls with fabulous views to the luxurious—complexes with video games, sports areas, and fax and modem hookups.

Depending on where and how you prefer to camp, you'll have your pick of sites in state or national parks, national forests, or private campgrounds. (See "Happy Campers," pages 38-39.)

When you book a site, inquire: What are the nightly fees? Does the campground accept reservations? If no, how early should you arrive in order to claim a site? Is there a pool or lake? Lifeguards? Equipment rentals? Laundry facilities, rest rooms, and hot showers? A grocery store nearby? Remember that campgrounds near major tourist attractions fill up early, so make reservations in advance (choice spots in some national parks, for example, fill up months ahead).

How to find them: In addition to the campgrounds recommended in this book, you can find lists of campgrounds on the Internet: check out About.com's camping section at www.camping.about.com, www.camping-usa.com, and the National Association of RV Parks & Campgrounds at www.gocampingamerica.com For campgrounds in national parks, visit www.nps.gov and state. For a national directory of KOA campgrounds, visit www.koa kampgrounds.com

Resorts

A resort vacation is a big investment, and up-front research is essential to ensure you get your money's worth. When you are making inquiries, don't be shy about taking up the resort staff's time with questions. Be sure to grill them with the entire housing quiz on page 25. Ask, too, about programming for kids and families. If there is a children's program, what days and times does it run? Is it canceled if not enough kids sign up? What is the ratio of counselors to children? What are the age divisions? What activities does the program offer? What are the facilities? What, if any, is the additional cost? Are there games, programs, or organized recreation especially for families? Baby-sitting services? Assistance for kids who get sick? What are the terms for these? If the resort is "all-inclusive," find out

FamilyFun TIP

Walk it through

When you're booking a room or condo over the phone, ask the reservation specialist to "walk" you through the place, virtually, from the front door to the balcony view (if there is one!). They may think you're going overboard — but you'll really know what you're getting.

FamilyFun READER'S TIP

Invent a Travel Kit

When our family flies, I make travel kits for my two sons, Noah, 8, and Paul, 4. I fill old wipes boxes with a variety of treats: chocolate kisses, fruit snacks, a sealed envelope with a love note inside, stickers, and a small wrapped package such as a pencil sharpener, pencils, and a blank book (I staple together scratch paper). I write the boys' names on the front with a permanent marker, and then, in flight, they decorate the boxes with stickers. The trick is not to give them the travel kits until we're on the plane. After they exhaust their supply of goodies inside, they can refill it with things they collect during the trip.

Kathy Detzer, White River Junction, Vermont

Travel Insurance

It's not for everyone, but some travelers like to invest in this just-in-case insurance. Cancellation policies cover losses if you can't make your trip due to illness or a death in the family (you may wish to consider this if you have to put down a hefty deposit or prepay for your vacation in full). Medical policies provide for some emergency procedures. You can buy travel insurance from a specialty broker (see below), from your travel agent, or directly from an insurance company. Do not buy insurance from the tour operator or cruise line you will be traveling with.

Travel Guard International (800-826-1300; www.travel-guard.com)

CSA Travel Protection (www.csatravelprotection.com)

Travel Assistance International (800-821-2828; www.travelassistance.com)

Access America (866-807-3982; www.accessamerica.com)

exactly what is covered. If you will be taking advantage of the services included in the price, it may mean a good deal for your family; if not, you might be better off elsewhere.

How to find them: Travel magazines, travel agents, and family travel Websites (see page 34) will all be able to offer recommendations on family resorts. Also, the Globe Pequot Press (www.globepequot.com) has two good resource books: *100 Best Family Resorts in North America* and *100 Best All-Inclusive Resorts of the World.*

SAVING MONEY

A great vacation balances moments of extravagance with activities that are as enjoyable as they are affordable. The key, then, is to find painless ways to cut costs so that you can feel good about indulging. Here's a host of secrets from budget-savvy travelers.

Stock up at home. Specialty items, such as sunscreen, film, batteries, over-the-counter medications, and first-aid supplies can be outrageously expensive in vacation spots. Buy them in bulk at home and bring them with you.

Travel off-peak. Whether it's a ski resort town in the summertime, or Yosemite National Park in the spring, or the Adirondacks in the winter, off-peak travel is one of the best ways to save, as long as you're primed to enjoy the unique flavor of an off-season trip. Rates for travel and lodging are often slashed considerably—and you can enjoy a different perspective (and fewer crowds) at the destination of your choice.

Don't delay. The sooner you begin planning and booking your vacation (six months to a year or more in advance is not too early), the more deals will be available to you.

Shop around. This is the cardinal rule of vacation planning. Take time to compare prices for every service that you'll be buying, from airfares, hotels, and rental cars to tickets for attractions.

Ask for discounts. Don't be shy about asking for discounts. Call ahead to the attractions that you plan to visit and ask where one finds discount coupons. When making hotel reservations, ask if discounts are available—if not on the room alone, then on a package that may include the room and tickets to a nearby attraction. Coupons are also available on-line: a good place to start is the coupon link at www.about.com

Guided Tours

WHEN DO YOU NEED ONE?

For certain types of specialty travel (technically challenging outdoor adventures, for example), an expert guide is a necessary aid for a safe and enjoyable trip. In addition, using a local guide for day trips (say, fishing or snowmobiling) can be a wonderful way to connect with local lore and culture in the region you're visiting. In general, however, guided tours (especially group tours that include full itineraries and meals) tend to be pricey, tightly scheduled, and lacking the freedom most families value highly.

STRAP A SHOE BAG to the back of the front seat and stuff it with your small kid-entertainment supplies: crayons and coloring books; kids' magazines; craft supplies, such as pipe cleaners, markers, glue sticks, and construction paper; songbooks; paper doll kits; a deck of cards; and a cassette player with story tapes. And don't forget a Frisbee, jump rope, and chalk (to draw hopscotch grids) for rest stops.

FamilyFun READER'S TIP

Make Your Own Postcards

While traveling by car or plane, my kids entertain themselves by creating their own postcards. Before the trip, I buy blank, prestamped postcards from the post office. Once we are under way, the kids draw pictures on the cards — usually of things they have done on vacation or are looking forward to doing. We address the cards to relatives and friends and drop them in the mail, making sure we send a few home for our own travel journal. This activity has been so successful, we now give friends travel kits of the prestamped cards and crayons as a bon voyage gift.

Lynette Smith, Lake Mills, Wisconsin

Look at package deals. At first blush, packages can seem outrageously expensive. But before you pass them up, compare them carefully to what you'd pay if you bought all the pieces of your vacation separately. Rates for airfare, lodging, and car rentals can be substantially lower when purchased together, especially for popular destinations. Contact your travel agent for information or research deals from travel clubs like AAA (call your local chapter or visit www.aaa.com), American Express Travel Services (800-346-3607; www.americanexpress.com), and from tour agencies affiliated with major airlines.

Use member benefits. Membership in an auto club, professional organization, or Entertainment book club may score you discounts on travel bills—ask before you book. Your credit card company, as well, may offer free services, such as collision-damage and travel-accident insurance, if you use the card to pay for travel expenses (call to request a copy of the company's travel benefits policy). If you travel regularly, the savings you'd garner from Web-saver clubs like www.bestfares.com can be well worth the $50 to $70 annual fee.

Tickets to attractions. Buying tickets to attractions in advance through an association or organization or at the hotel desk often will save you money. Equally important, you'll avoid the ticket line itself. On-line, try www.citypass.com for discount tickets in major metropolitan areas.

Keep your distance. Unless on-site housing offers necessary convenience for your family, consider lodging that's outside the major tourist area or city you're visiting. An extra 15 minutes of travel can considerably reduce lodging expenses, especially if you're staying more than a few days.

Check out kids' deals. Look for hotel deals where kids eat and/or stay free with their parents.

Consider cooking. Dining out is certainly part of the vacation experience, but three meals per person, per day add up quickly. Cooking your own meals can save you lots of money, even if you factor in the expense of a room with a kitchenette. In a regular hotel room, you can probably manage breakfast and/or lunch with a well-stocked cooler.

Pack your own minibar. Those high-priced hotel minibars are magnets for kids. Make a list of your kids' favorite treats, then purchase them in bulk as individually wrapped items. Pack a selection in a separate box or bag that can double as the designated minibar once you arrive at the hotel.

Let's do lunch. If you have a yen to try a particular fancy restaurant, head there during lunch. The atmosphere will be the same, and the menu will be similar, but smaller lunchtime portions will be accompanied by lower prices.

Revel in free fun. Remember the birthday when your child spent more time playing with the wrapping paper than with the actual toy? Vacations are filled with similar, low-cost but memorable moments, including hours at the beach, hiking trails, parks, and playgrounds. If you're in a new area, scan the local paper for listings, or call a local travel bureau or chamber of commerce for ideas.

Be savvy about souvenirs. Decide ahead of time how much you're willing to spend on souvenirs. Depending on the age of your kids, give each child his or her own spending money (they'll be stingier with their own funds than they are with yours). As an added incentive, let them keep a portion of any money they don't spend.

Using the Web

With the advent of the World Wide Web, individuals now have access to all the tools that travel agents use (and then some). The trick is to know how to use them well.

PROS: Researching travel ideas on the Web may draw in your kids more readily than a guidebook would.

Packing With—And For—Kids

Like so much of your family vacation, packing is a balancing act—in this case between including everything you need and making sure you can actually lift your bags. No matter where you're headed, this checklist should cover most of the essentials.

Give the kids a role. Every child has favorite outfits as well as clothing that he or she won't wear (and that you shouldn't bother packing). Young children can select the clothes they'd like to bring and set them aside for you. Older kids can do much of their own packing, especially if you help them write up a checklist of their own.

Don't worry about wrinkles. Like aging, this happens even with the best of precautions. Suggest some folding methods, but don't insist on your kids' finessing this. One surprisingly effective technique for kids is simply to roll everything up.

Make each child responsible for his or her own luggage. A backpack and a soft-sided suitcase for each child will do the trick. Let your kids decorate their bags with stencils and stickers — and remember to attach a name tag.

Separate toiletries in sealed, waterproof bags. Lids on toiletries often pop off or open during travel.

Take precautions in case of lost luggage. If you're flying to your vacation destination, pack at least one complete outfit for each family member in each suitcase. That way, if a piece of luggage is lost, everyone still has a change of clothes. Also, pack medications, eyeglasses, and contact lens solution in carry-ons.

Clothing

Include an outfit for each day of the week, plus extra shirts or blouses in case of spills. If your children are younger, encourage them to choose brightly colored outfits that will make them easier to spot in the crowd.

- ♦ Comfortable shoes or sneakers
- ♦ Socks and undergarments
- ♦ Sleepwear
- ♦ Light jackets, sweaters, or sweatshirts for cool weather
- ♦ Bathing suits
- ♦ Sandals or slip-on shoes for the pool
- ♦ Hats or sun visors
- ♦ Rain gear, including umbrellas

Toiletries

- ♦ Toothbrushes, toothpaste, dental floss, and mouthwash
- ♦ Deodorant
- ♦ Combs, brushes, hair accessories, blow-dryer
- ♦ Soap
- ♦ Shampoo and conditioner
- ♦ Shaving gear
- ♦ Feminine-hygiene items

- Lotions
- Cosmetics
- Nail care kit
- Tweezers
- Cotton balls and/or swabs
- Antibacterial gel for hand washing
- Sunscreens and lip balm
- Insect repellent

Miscellaneous "must-haves"

- Essential papers: identification for adults, health insurance cards, tickets, traveler's checks
- Wallet and/or purse, including cash and credit cards
- Car and house keys (with duplicate set packed in a different bag)
- Eyeglasses and/or contact lenses, plus lens cleaner
- Medications
- Watch
- Camera and film (pack film in your carry-on bag)
- Tote bag or book bag for day use
- Books and magazines for kids and adults
- Toys, playing cards, small games
- Flashlight
- Extra batteries
- Large plastic bags for laundry
- Small plastic bags
- Disposable wipes
- First-aid kit
- Travel alarm
- Sewing kit

Keep Your First-Aid Kit Handy

There's no such thing as a vacation from minor injuries and ailments, so a well-stocked first-aid kit is essential to have on hand. You can buy a prepackaged kit or make your own by packing the following items in an old lunch box:

- **Adhesive bandages in various sizes, adhesive tape, and gauze pads**
- **Antacid**
- **Antibacterial gel for washing hands without water**
- **Antibacterial ointment**
- **Antidiarrheal medicine**
- **Antihistamine or allergy medicine**
- **Antiseptic**
- **Antiseptic soap**
- **Pain relief medicine—for children and adults**
- **Cotton balls and/or swabs**
- **Cough medicine and/or throat lozenges**
- **Motion sickness medicine**
- **Fingernail clippers**
- **First-aid book or manual**
- **Ipecac**
- **Moleskin for blisters**
- **Ointment for insect bites and sunburn**
- **Premoistened towelettes**
- **Thermometer**
- **Tissues**
- **Tweezers and needle**

FamilyFun TIP

The Internet Travel Bible

If you're serious about researching (and especially booking) travel plans yourself, consult *Online Travel* by Ed Perkins (Microsoft Press, $19.95). This paperback tome is an invaluable resource on getting the best deals available and navigating the benefits and pitfalls of today's travel market, both on- and off-line.

Plus, when it comes time to book reservations, the Web can be a treasure trove of bargains—if you know how to hunt for them (see "The Internet Travel Bible" above). Why is that so? In essence, the Internet allows travel service providers to change their bargain pricing structures and unload unsold seats and rooms at a moment's notice. Of course, agents are still out to make as much money as they can—but you often can reap the benefits of their last-minute sales. In fact, many of these sales are available only on-line.

CONS: Keeping tabs on the travel market on-line can be extremely time-consuming if you are determined to find the best deal possible. In addition, since Web search engines can't read your mind and ask you questions, they can't ferret out all your options—just the ones that fall within the parameters you specify. So if you aren't a savvy searcher, you might miss the best deals (or the best destinations) even after hours of research.

Family travel Websites. It's a challenge to locate truly family-friendly sites among the hundreds available. For researching travel ideas and gathering travel tips, here are some of the best sites. Try our own Website too—www.familyfun.com—it too has a lot of travel ideas.

- ♦ www.vacationtogether.com is a searchable database of family vacation ideas, reprinted from various publications (including *FamilyFun* magazine). You'll also find packing checklists and links to reservation sites here.
- ♦ www.travelwithkids.about.com is a terrific clearinghouse for family vacation ideas, package deals, current bargains, lists of accommodations, packing checklists, travel tips and games, downloadable maps, and more.
- ♦ www.thefamilytravelfiles.com is a well-organized family travel Website that showcases a range of trip ideas and offers a free travel e-zine.
- ♦ www.familytravelforum.com is a monthly on-line newsletter specializing in well-screened links to family-friendly accommodations, airfare deals, seasonal events, and more.

General travel sites. In addition to family-specific sites such as the ones listed above, there are literally thousands of useful Websites that can help you plan and book your vacation. They are too numerous to list here! We have included many of our favorites throughout this chapter; in addition to those, here are a few you may find useful.

♦ www.officialtravelinfo.com lists contacts for travel and tourism bureaus worldwide (you can search the United States by state).

♦ www.fodors.com, www.frommers.com, and www.nationalgeographic.com are sites related to travel magazines. Often, they'll post selections from current issues, as well as other travel-related articles.

♦ www.travel-library.com (a wide range of travel topics, travelogues, and destination information) and www. about.com (a general site with good travel links) are sites that can lead you to travel information that you may (or may not!) be looking for.

Book your own airline reservations. Using the same databases as travel agents use, the leading travel sites have made booking your own flight as simple as typing in when you'd like to leave, when you'd like to return, your origin and destination, and airline choice. They kick back a list of flights that most closely match

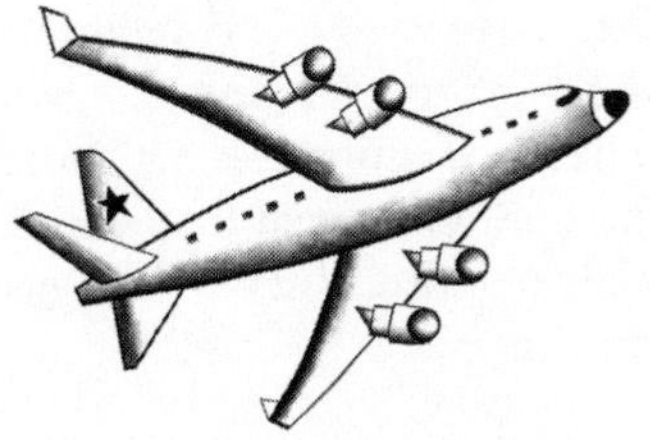

Broker a Hotel Deal

Great deals at major hotels usually turn up off-season or at the last minute, but here's another tactic families can try: work with a hotel consolidator (also called a hotel broker or discounter).

Consolidators work by securing blocks of hotel rooms at wholesale prices, then reselling them at rates that are—in theory, at least—lower than the published "rack" rate. Some consolidators will only reserve your room; you pay the hotel directly. Others require a prepaid voucher that you present to the hotel upon arrival. Many consolidators claim savings of 10 to 50 percent (some even more), but as with any bargain, it pays to know what you're getting into.

SOME TIPS:

- **Ask about service charges. Is there a user fee for the consolidator?**
- **Are there financial penalties for trip cancellation or rescheduling?**
- **Compare rates. The consolidator may not beat a hotel's special offers.**

With those caveats, try:

Quikbook: Good selection and easy to use, with hotels in 33 cities. Call 800-789-9887 or see www.quikbook.com

Central Reservation Service: Lists hotel deals in ten major cities. Call 800-555-7555 or visit www.roomconnection.com

Gumshoe Games

The detectives in your group will just love these tests of their sleuthing ability.

Secret highway messages: Pass out the pencils and paper, and keep your eyes peeled for official road signs. Each time you spot one, write down the first letter. When you've passed five to seven signs—and have five to seven letters—you're ready to crack the code. Here's how: each letter stands for a word. So the letters D, S, C, S, and A could stand for the secret message "Drive slowly, construction starts ahead." Of course, others in your family may interpret it as "Dad, stop, candy store ahead."

Two truths and one lie: The first person makes three statements about himself or herself. Two are true; the other is a lie. For example, you could say, "I had a dog named Puddles. My sister cut off my hair once when I was asleep. I won the school spelling bee when I was in third grade." Everybody then holds up one, two, or three fingers to show which statement they think is the lie. Reveal the answer and let the next person fib away.

your specifications and then let you choose the flights you want. After confirming your choices, you pay with a credit card, print your itinerary, and either receive your paper tickets in the mail or, more likely, pick up your tickets when you check in at the airport. **NOTE:** Some people prefer paper tickets because if a flight is missed or cancelled an e-ticket may not be exchangable at a different airline's counter.

Our favorite flight sites are Expedia (www.expedia.com), Travelocity (www.travelocity.com), and Trip.com (www.trip.com). Don't assume that all offer the same flights or the same prices; the important thing is to shop around, even among these sites.

Before you pay for your tickets, you should double-check with two other sources. First, look at your chosen airline's home site to see if they offer extra miles for booking flights on-line, or special, unadvertised Web deals. And call your travel agent, tell her the flight you're interested in, and see if she can beat the price. Lastly, be sure you're aware of the taxes, airport surcharges, and possible site use fees that may be added to your ticket price.

For more information about airlines, airports, and on-line reservations, go to www.iecc.com/airline/. Also, check out Ed Perkins' *Online Travel* (Microsoft Press, $19.95). To find out more about frequent flier mile programs, visit www.frequent flier.com

Book hotel and rental car reservations. In general, hotel and rental car reservations work the same way that airfare reservations do. The Web is an excellent source of hotel deals (especially for vacation packages, if you're a savvy shopper); rental car companies, on the other hand, generally offer little in the way of discounts above what you can get at the desk.

FREE ATLAS
Best Western offers free road atlases with Best Western sites: call 800-528-1234.

Sign up for e-mail newsletters. If you find a good travel Website that offers a free newsletter, it doesn't hurt to sign up—you may receive timely notice of travel deals that you otherwise would miss. Just be sure that you save any information on how to cancel the subscription in case you want to opt out.

Are Internet travel arrangements foolproof? No, unfortunately. The Internet is prime territory for scams, although you can guard against most of them with a few protective strategies. First, deal with major sites (like the ones listed in this book) or directly with brand-name company sites (like Avis or Holiday Inn) whenever possible. When you're transmitting your credit card information, make sure your connection is secure (your browser should tell you when one has been established). Also, you should double-check to see that the service provider's Website has a secure server. (Look for a locked padlock in the corner of your browser's window or "https"—the "s" stands for "secure"—in the URL.) If a site doesn't seem completely aboveboard, it may not be. Finally, when in doubt, back out. As long as you don't give a company your credit card number, they can't charge you anything.

FamilyFun READER'S TIP

A Colorful Road Game

This homemade road game is a big hit with my 4-year-old son, Tommy. I clip cards out of colored construction paper and print a different letter of the alphabet on each. During a car ride, each of us picks a card and searches for an object or a structure that matches the color and begins with the letter on our card. For example, a player with a *B* on a yellow card might spot a school bus. Since we began playing this game, my son tends to remember many more details about our travels. Instead of hearing, "Are we there yet?" we hear, "Oh no, I haven't found mine yet!"

Susan Robins, Cottage Grove, Oregon

CHECKLIST

Happy Campers

If your family's idea of a vacation involves nightly campfires, sleeping bags, and potential wildlife sightings near (or in!) your living space, check out these great resources for tent and RV camping.

The Trailer Life Directory provides travelers with a list of several thousand campgrounds and RV parks throughout the United States and Canada. Each location is rated on a three-step scale that assesses the park's facilities, cleanliness, and overall appeal; ratings are updated on an annual basis. You can register at www.tldirectory.com to search the directory for free or order your own copy for the road on-line or at bookstores.

Woodall's campground directories also rate a large number of parks—more than 14,000 locations throughout the United States and Canada are scored on their facilities and recreation. You can purchase a directory which covers the entire area, or shorter versions of the guide are available for the western and eastern regions. Woodall's also publishes a directory exclusively for tent campers. Again, you can register to access campground listings for free at www.woodalls.com, but the on-line directory does not include Woodall's convenient rating system. The complete directories can be purchased at Woodall's Website or bookstores.

There's no centralized reservation system for every campsite within the **National Park system**, so your best bet is to contact each individual park. Campground reservations here usually must be made several months in advance since the sites are so popular, so don't count on finding a space unless you've planned ahead. Contact information for the National Parks can be found at their Website, www.nps.gov Policies for state parks also vary from place to place, so you'll have to contact individual campgrounds for camping information.

Veteran car campers recognize **KOA Kampgrounds** by their familiar yellow, red, and black signs. KOAs allow your family to rough it while enjoying many of the amenities of home. Novice campers will be thrilled to have access to hot showers, flush toilets, laundry facilities, and convenience stores. All KOA locations have both tent and RV sites, and some even have cabins that your family can rent. If you plan to stay multiple nights at one or more KOA Kampgrounds, consider purchasing a Value Kard. You'll get a 10 percent discount on your registration fees and a free copy of the KOA directory (you'll still pay for shipping). You can also research KOA locations for free at www.koakampgrounds.com or purchase your own directory on-line or by calling 406-248-7444.

If you're looking for campgrounds where your family can pitch a tent in peace and quiet, check out *The Best in Tent Camping* series (published by Menasha Ridge Press). The books detail the best in scenic, tent-only sites without all of the bells and whistles.

One key to a great camping trip is remembering all of your supplies. If your family is RV or car camping, you can usually purchase any forgotten items on the road. However, if you're traveling far off the beaten path, you'll need to be careful to double-check your belongings.

Here's a checklist of supplies to make your camping experience go smoothly. If you're renting an RV, be aware that you may be able to rent your bedding and cooking supplies for an additional fee and save the trouble of bringing your own.

- Tent(s) and tent stakes
- Plastic ground cloth/tarp
- Sleeping bags (or bedding, for an RV)
- Sleeping pads
- Camp stove (with extra fuel)
- Pots, plastic dishes, mugs, and utensils
- Water bottle or canteen
- Lantern and/or candles
- Bottle and/or can openers
- Sharp knife (parents should hold on to this)
- Plethora of plastic/trash bags
- Dish soap (preferably biodegradable)
- Stocked coolers
- Water (or a portable filter or purifying tablets)
- Waterproof matches or lighter(s)
- Flashlights (and extra batteries)
- Bandanna (for use as a head covering, pot holder, and napkin)
- Trowel
- Folding saw
- First-aid kit, medications
- Sunscreen
- Insect repellent
- Toilet paper
- Day packs
- Child carriers (for little ones)
- Compass and area map
- Clothing (make sure to pack many layers)
- Two pairs of shoes (in case one gets wet)
- A hat
- Sunglasses
- Toiletries (try to take only necessary items)
- Camera
- Binoculars
- Kid supplies (toys, books, favorite stuffed animal)

Ohio

THE MULTITUDE OF Ohio's family-friendly vacation opportunities includes a stop at the Rock and Roll Hall of Fame, a visit to a community of Amish farm families, and to the beautiful Cuyahoga Valley Recreation Area, where you and your children can bike, hike, boat, and otherwise enjoy the great outdoors. For stimulating young minds, there are such super museums as the COSI (Center of Science and Industry) in Toledo and Columbus, the Great Lakes Center in Cleveland, and the Cinergy Children's Museum in Cincinnati. Ohio boasts four

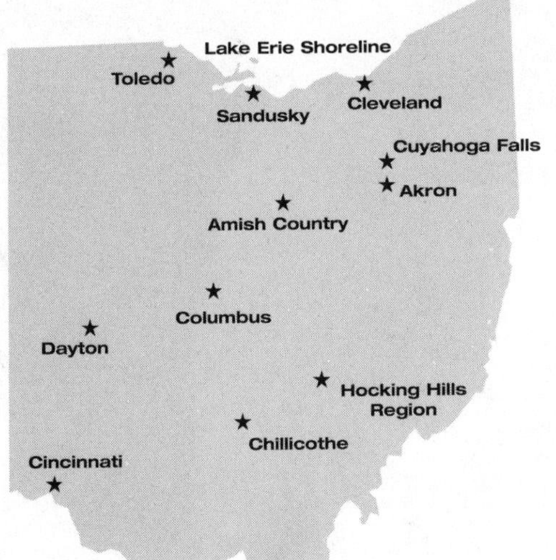

world-class zoos: Toledo, Cleveland, Columbus, and Cincinnati. Not to be outdone, the theme parks are legendary, too: there's Cedar Point, Camp Snoopy, and Soak City in Sandusky; Six Flags Ohio in Aurora; Water Works Family Aquatic in Cuyahoga Falls; Coney Island in Cincinnati; Paramount's Kings Island and WaterWorks at Kings Island; and Wyandot Six Flags in Columbus.

Add to this an outstanding system of state parks with organized activities and do-it-yourself fun for both day visitors and overnight guests (see "Ohio State Park Resorts" on page 58) and you have the makings of a memorable trip.

ATTRACTIONS

$	under $5
$$	$5 - $15
$$$	$15 - $25
$$$$	$25 +

HOTELS/MOTELS/CAMPGROUNDS

$	under $75
$$	$75 - $100
$$$	$100 - $140
$$$$	$140 +

RESTAURANTS

$	under $10
$$	$10 - $20
$$$	$20 - $30
$$$$	$30 +

***FAMILYFUN* RATED**

★	Fine
★★	Good
★★★	Very Good
★★★★	*FamilyFun* Recommended

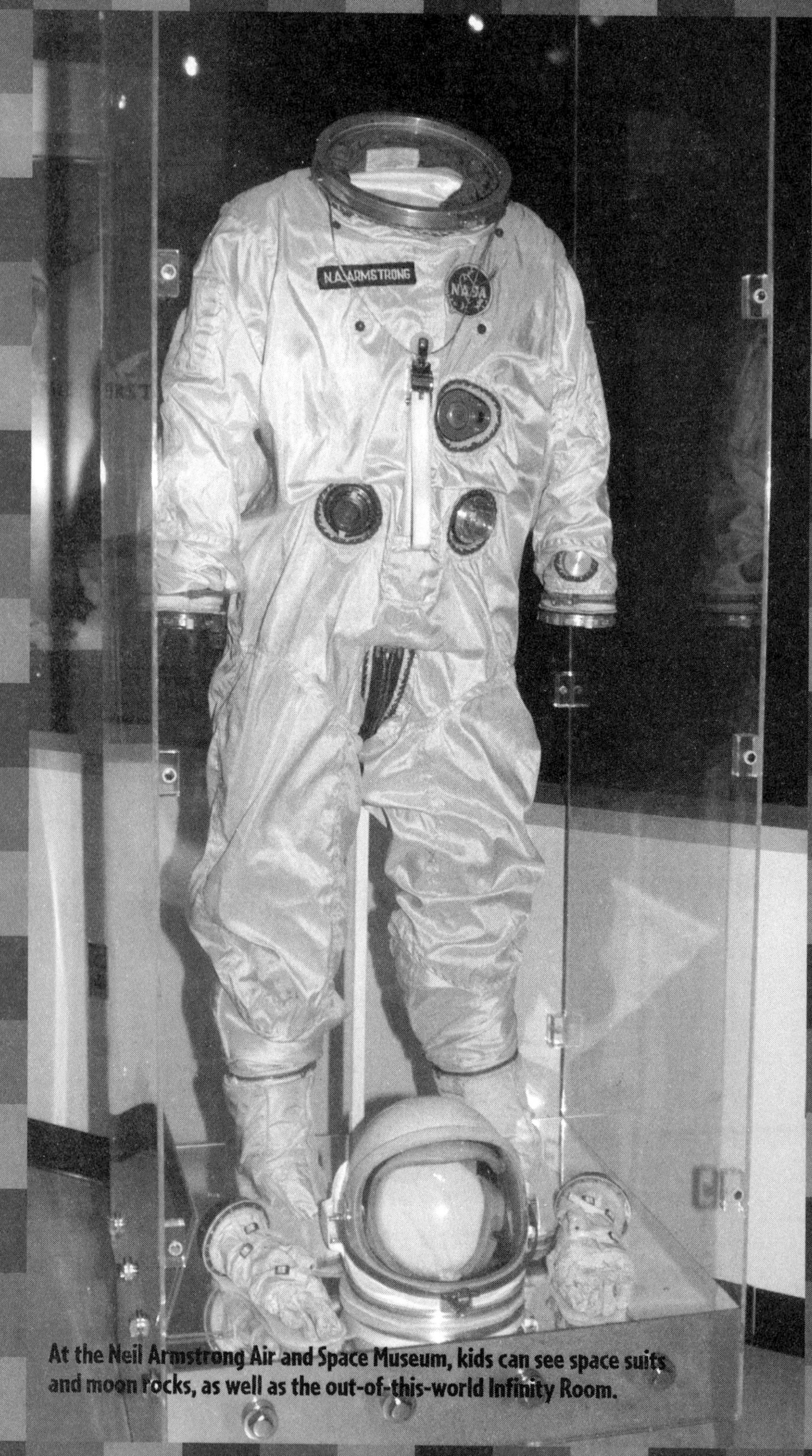

At the Neil Armstrong Air and Space Museum, kids can see space suits and moon rocks, as well as the out-of-this-world Infinity Room.

Toledo

THE THIRD-BUSIEST PORT on the Great Lakes, Toledo is a city that embraces the water. Waterfront along the Maumee River has been reclaimed as a dining and entertainment hot spot called International Parkway, and the views alone—of the more than 100 remarkable bridges and the steady river traffic—provide hours of activity for both kids and adults. A Golden Gate–style suspension bridge links downtown to the new restaurant complex and the *Willis B. Boyer*, a huge freighter-turned-museum, across the river; lift bridges are regularly raised and lowered to allow ships to pass under. You and your kids can also get a look at the city from the water by taking a river cruise aboard an old-fashioned sternwheeler, the *Awanna Belle.*

Beyond the water, the COSI (Center of Science and Industry) in Toledo is a great way to spend the day with children, who will have so much fun they'll never suspect that they've learned a lot about the laws of physics. Another educational-yet-enjoyable spot is the Neil Armstrong Air and Space Museum, which lets

COSI: Toledo (page 44)

Neil Armstrong Air and Space Museum (page 45)

Toledo Zoo (page 46)

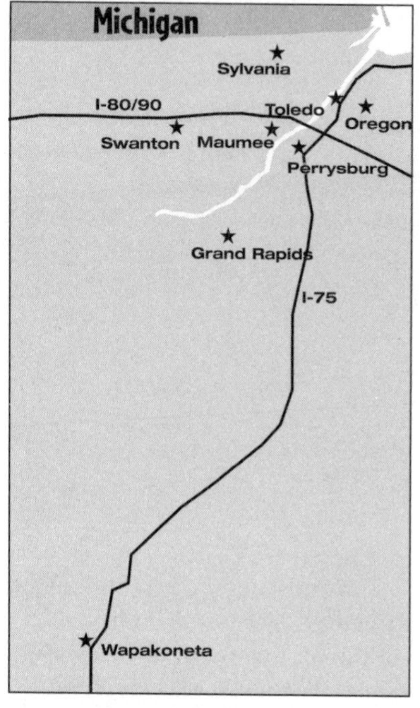

kids get a close-up look at a real space capsule and genuine moon rocks. Meanwhile, the Toledo Zoo provides lovingly landscaped and shady grounds, plus the requisite roster of animals large and small for still more quality family time.

CULTURAL ADVENTURES

COSI: Toledo

MUST-SEE FamilyFun MUST-SEE ★★★★/$$

The Center of Science and Industry is a rather staid title for such a totally cool, kid-focused place. Just call it the COSI (ko-sigh) for short. Your kids won't want to leave this cross between a children's museum and a science center—when they finally do, they'll insist on coming back the next day. Each exhibit teaches a principle of physics or a law of science in a highly imaginative and completely fun way.

Pitch fast balls and learn how the structure of various sports balls affects speed, arch, and curve. Play virtual volleyball against a special screen that plays back moves and teaches lads how to spike at the proper angle to win. Or be a camera operator and tape other kids jumping, hooping, and spiking. Your son can be a TV meteorologist in front of a "blue" screen; your daughter can direct a television show from a console filled with TV screens (or vice versa).

Look up—there's a high-wire act going on, and your kids can join in! The High Wire Cycle is a unicycle that rides a wire suspended 20 feet up. It looks scary, but is actually an illustration of the laws of physics; because of how the cycle is weighted, it can't tip or fall. Your kids can also safely indulge their urge to scale mountainsides on the center's climbing wall; have water fights inside a plastic-enclosed pond (they'll get a little wet, but not soaked); build sand castles; engineer bridges; and experiment with how loading a boat improperly can make it sink. With the periscope, they can look up and out to the waterfront from inside the building.

For toddlers and preschoolers there's Kidspace, where they can play hospital and ambulance, build with the gigantic building blocks, and hang out in rooms where they're actually encouraged to make noise. Kidspace also has special activities (bug hunts, storytelling, sing-alongs, and arts and crafts) from time to time.

Before you leave, stop at the COSI store for fun and funky toys with a scientific bent. The Atomic Cafe has a patio overlooking the river, and kid-friendly fare. Strollers are available. *1 Discovery Way, Toledo; (419) 244-2674;* www.cositoledo.org

Miami and Erie Canal Restoration ★★★/$

The year 1876 comes to life at this living-history museum. Historical reenactors give a talk, then guests board a 60-foot-long replica canal boat pulled by mule team for a 45-minute ride down one mile of the original Miami and Erie Canal, including two passes through a working original lock. After the ride, you can see how a water-powered sawmill works and visit an old-time general store. Closed November through April. *The restoration is located in Providence Metropark in Grand Rapids, about 12 miles southwest of Toledo. U.S. Route 24 at State Route 578, Grand Rapids; (419) 832-6006.*

MUST-SEE FamilyFun MUST-SEE Neil Armstrong Air and Space Museum ★★★★/Free-$$$$

Neil Armstrong is a native of Wapakoneta, a town that's an hour and a half south of Toledo. The astronaut's hometown museum looks almost like an underground bunker, with its earth-sheltered, modern architecture. It houses artifacts from his space voyages and those of other astronauts, including John Glenn, another Ohio native. Kids like seeing footage of the moon landing, plus real moon rocks and space suits, but what they really love is the Infinity Room, 18 square feet of mirrored surfaces. Walk in and get the

FamilyFun **READER'S TIP**

Time in a Bottle

Our kids (Kiersten, 12, Nicolai, 10, Jarin, 4, and Micah, 1) love to collect rocks, so whenever we go someplace special, we choose one to mark the trip. We write on them—where we went, the date, the initials of those who were there, and other notes, if there is room—and save them in glass jars. Memories of Sunday drives, camping trips, fairs, birthday parties, and family vacations are all recorded and "bottled."

Ron and Marci Clawson, Sandy, Utah

awesome, limitless feeling of being in outer space. The *Gemini VIII* spacecraft and *Apollo 11* artifacts are also on display. Closed December through February. *From Toledo, take Highway 75 to exit 111, and watch for signs. 500 South Apollo Dr., Wapakoneta; (800) 860-0142; (419) 738-8811;* www.ohiohistory.org

SS *Willis B. Boyer*

★★★/$$

Launched in 1911, this was once the largest freighter on the Great Lakes. Today the restored ship is a museum, with a massive engine room and very swanky officers' dining room. Everyone in the family can have his or her photo taken at the wheel of the big ship. Volunteers lead regular tours, but you can also explore yourself. Even if you don't have time to go inside, drive up under the lighted bridge at night and get a close-up view of the massive hulk of the ship. It's very impressive. *International Park, 26 Main St., Toledo; (419) 936-3070.*

Toledo Museum of Art

★★/Free

This museum is considered one of the country's top ten art museums. The collections are exceptional: you can introduce your kids to the works of Rubens, Gainsborough, Rembrandt, Van Gogh, Picasso, Matisse, and many other great masters. The museum holds children's programs regularly—call to see what's up during your visit. There's a café and gift shop, too. *2445 Monroe St., at Collingwood Ave., Toledo; (800) 644-6862; (419) 255-8000;* www.toledomuseum.org

JUST FOR FUN

Maumee Bay State Park Resort

★★★/Free

This is a perfect place for roughing it in style—complete with cable TV and an indoor pool. For more information, see "Ohio State Park Resorts" on page 58.

Toledo Mud Hens

★★★/$-$$

Remember Corporal Klinger on *M*A*S*H*? This was his favorite team, and it's a favorite attraction in Toledo still. The season runs April through September, but the Hens Souvenir Shop is open all year. Game tickets are relatively inexpensive (compared to those for major league games), making this a great way to take everyone out to the ball game. *Fifth Third Field, 406 Washington St., Toledo; (419) 897-4367.*

MUST-SEE FamilyFun MUST-SEE Toledo Zoo

★★★★/$$

Founded in 1900, this well-established zoo has lovely landscaping, lots of shade, playgrounds, and picnic areas, all of which make it a great family spot. Oh yes, there are animals too—some 4,700 in all, representing 700 different species. The Aviary has more than 500 birds from 175 species, flying free and walking around.

One of the newer zoo attractions is the Arctic Encounter, which lets you look underwater where polar bears and seals swim. There's also a new gray wolf exhibit here.

Elsewhere, the aquarium holds more than 40,000 gallons of display tanks of fish from the coral reef, the rain forest, and other ecosystems, plus an inky octopus. And look up—there's a model of a huge shark on the ceiling.

The Primate Forest has three outdoor exhibits and an indoor viewing area where you can spy black-and-white Colobus monkeys, plus five other species. In Kingdom of the Apes, three generations of the same gorilla family play. Brilliantly colored tree frogs live in the Reptile House with turtles and crocodiles and snakes, and Frogtown, USA, is home to toads, frogs, and other hopping and creeping critters. In the Hippoquarium, tots can get right up to the window and see a half-submerged hippo take a swim.

In the Aviary, preschoolers can pretend to be baby birds and snuggle into oversized nests.

The most interesting lunch stop is at Carnivore Cafe, where kids get to eat in cages and pretend they're the animals. **NOTE:** The one negative about this zoo is that the concession staff seems to be consistently crabby and unhelpful, and lines for food and drink can be long. Bring along some water and snacks for your kids to keep them from getting too hungry, and get in line for burgers and drinks before anyone says they're starving. Additional parking fee. *2700 Broadway, Toledo;* (419) 385-5721; www.toledozoo.org

The Zoo Deal

If you'll be visiting several zoos in Ohio, it pays to buy a family zoo membership. Members get free admission to more than 100 zoos in the country, including Ohio's African Safari Wildlife Park, Akron Zoo, Cincinnati Zoo, Cleveland Metroparks Zoo, Columbus Zoo, and The Wilds. Pay for the family membership at the first zoo you visit, and you won't have to pay another zoo admission fee for the rest of your trip.

Bunking Down

Hilton Toledo ★★/$$

Located on the 350-acre campus of the Medical College of Ohio, this luxury hotel is a bit out of the way, but has lots of conveniences. The 213 oversize rooms have microwaves, refrigerators, VCRs, and cable TV. There's an indoor pool, plus a sauna, indoor track, and basketball, volleyball, racquetball, and tennis courts. And when hunger strikes, there's also a restaurant on-site. *3100 Glendale Ave., Toledo; (800) 445-8667; (419) 381-6800;* www.hilton.com

Holiday Inn French Quarter

★★★★/$$$

The atrium at this 299-room hotel has a New Orleans theme. And kids love spotting goldfish in the pond. The newly renovated rooms aren't decorated in a discernibly French Quarter style, but they are clean and nicely furnished. Some two-bedroom suites are available. Kids love the two "holidomes," with two indoor/outdoor pools, a sauna, a whirlpool, a fitness center, and more. The nine-hole putting green, pool tables, Ping-Pong tables, and game room round out the fun. You can sample the free continental breakfast and evening hors d'oeuvres. Ask about family packages and the Sunday brunch. *The hotel is in Perrysburg, about 15 miles south of Toledo off I-75 (193/Perrysburg/Fremont exit). 10630 Fremont Pike, Perrysburg; (888) 874-2592; (419) 874-3111;* www.hifq.com

Ohio has the only state flag that is not rectangular. Instead, the flag is a **burgee**, shaped like a swallow's tail.

Maumee Bay State Park Resort

★★/$$$$

Private balconies that overlook Lake Erie are nice touches at this 120-room resort hotel. It's perfect for an active family who plays tennis and racquetball, likes to rent boats and bikes, loves the beach, cross-country skis and sleds in winter, or plays golf in summer (see "Ohio State Park Resorts" on page 58). *Ten miles east of Toledo, 1750 Park Rd., #2, Oregon; (800) 282-7275; (419) 836-1466;* www.maumeebayresort.com

Radisson Hotel Toledo

★/$$

Connected to the SeaGate Centre entertainment complex and convention center, this 400-room hotel is across the street from Promenade Park and the Maumee River. Some suites are available, and there's a hotel restaurant and an on-site exercise room. *101 N. Summit St., Toledo; (800) 333-3333; (419) 241-3000;* www.radisson.com

Wyndham Hotel

★★★/$$

The location could hardly be better. This 241-room hotel is connected to the COSI (Center of Science and Industry); it faces the waterfront, and has pretty room views and glorious walks day and night. The walkways and overlooks are paved and, except for an occasional staircase, allow easy stroller access. Eat breakfast or lunch at the restaurant overlooking the water and watch the lift bridge rise and lower to let ships come through. Another plus: the hotel has a deli, café, and pizza shop. Kids like the indoor pool; there's also a fitness center and a whirlpool. *2 Seagate Summit St., Toledo; (800) 996-3426; (419) 241-1411;* www.wyndham.com

Good Eats

American Plaza Café
★★/$

On the first floor of the Wyndham Hotel, this place offers great views of the bridge, the river, and passing boats, plus a solid breakfast, lunch, and dinner menu of kids' favorites. *Wyndham Hotel, 2 Seagate on Summit St., Toledo; (419) 241-1411.*

International Parkway

Across the river from downtown and the COSI, this complex of restaurants includes something for everyone; our favorites are the Italian food at **Zia's** (***$$, *20 Main Street; 419/697-4559*) and the seafood at the **Real Seafood Co.** (****$$$, *22 Main Street; 419/697-4400*).

Panera Bread Co. ★★★/$

This bakery–coffeehouse–bagel stand chain produces heavenly breads, muffins, cookies, and bagels. Try the cinnamon crunch bagel—it's better than a sweet roll. *791 Dussel Dr., Suffolk Square, Maumee; (419) 897-7800.*

Tony Packo's Cafe
★★★/$

The specialty here is near and dear to any kid's heart: hot dogs. Celebrities come here for the chili dogs and the big, plump hot dogs that locals call coneys, then sign their name to a hot dog bun before they go. Really—the walls are lined with the autographed rolls. *1902 Front St., Toledo; (419) 691-6054. Also at 5827 Monroe St., Sylvania; (419) 885-4500.*

Green Spaces:

TOLEDO'S METROPARKS

THE TOLEDO AREA is home to nine Metroparks, natural preserves where you and your kids can hike, bike, picnic, and more. *For additional information, call (419) 535-3050.*

Bend View and Farnsworth Metroparks

Visit these two contiguous stretches of green along the banks of the Maumee River for the views—particularly the dramatic view of a 90-degree bend in the river at the Bend View patio overlook. The parks have natural areas, walking and skiing trails, and picnic areas. Farnsworth also has shelters, biking, fishing, playground equipment, and a boat launch. *Access to both parks is gained through Farnsworth Metropark, south of Toledo and of Side Cut Metropark, at the intersection of Neowash Road and Highway 24. Visitors to Bend View must hike in via the Towpath Trail; (419) 878-7641.*

Oak Openings Preserve

A large preserve west of Toledo, Oak Openings has a natural area, 27 miles of walking and skiing trails, 20 miles of trails for horseback riding, picnic areas, playground equipment, fishing, and ice-skating. This is also the site of Ohio's only "living" sand dune. *It is (roughly) bordered by Highway 20, Highway 295, and Highway 64, in Swanton; (419) 826-6463.*

Pearson Metropark

This is Toledo's most popular metropark. The Packer-Hammersmith Center, with exhibits on wildlife and the Black Swamp, is here. The park also has a natural area, walking and skiing trails, ice skating, picnic shelters, a bike trail, pedalboat rentals, tennis courts, and playground equipment. *East of Toledo, it is bordered by Starr Avenue, Wynn Road, Navarre Avenue, and Lallendorf Road; (419) 691-3997.*

Providence Metropark

This is the site of the authentic Miami and Erie Canal Restoration (see page 45) where you and the kids can take a narrated trip on a mule-drawn canal boat ($) through the working original lock. You can also visit Isaac Ludwig Mill, a water-powered sawmill and gristmill that dates back to 1846. Demonstrations of log sawing and flour grinding are given throughout the day. During the summer, Fridays are Family Days, and include one-hour programs such as candle dipping, kite or toy making, cane pole fishing, or nature walks. Call for details: *(419) 832-6006.* Blacksmithing, coopering, and tinsmithing demonstrations are given on Sunday afternoons. The park also has a natural area, walking and skiing trails, picnic sites, a general store, fishing, and ice-skating. *It is south of Toledo and of Bend View Metropark, along the Maumee River and Towpath Trail at Jeffers Road; (419) 832-6004.*

Secor Metropark

The park features walking and ski trails, picnic areas and shelters, and playground equipment. *West of Toledo, the park is bordered by Central Avenue, Wolfinger Road, Irwin Road, and Miller Road; (419) 829-2761.*

Side Cut Metropark

Toledo's first metropark is named for the "side cut" made to connect the main branch of the Erie Canal to the Maumee River. This is the site of the historic Miami and Erie Canal limestone locks, and Fallen Timbers State Memorial and monument. It also has a natural area, walking and skiing trails, picnic areas, tennis, ice-skating, fishing, and playground equipment. *South of Toledo along the Maumee River, the park includes the Audubon Islands; most of it is south of Highway 80/90 and east and west of Highway 23; (419) 893-2789.*

Swan Creek Preserve

There's a natural area, walking and skiing trails, picnic areas, a wildlife display, and playground equipment. Watch little ones closely, as the creek embankments are often steep. *Within Toledo proper, the park is bordered by Airport Highway, Byrne Road, Glendale Avenue, and Eastgate Road; (419) 382-4664.*

Wildwood Preserve

In addition to a natural area, walking and skiing trails, picnic sites, a wildlife exhibit, and playground equipment, the preserve features a Manor House and 100-year-old schoolhouse that are open to the public. *It is on the west-central edge of Toledo, bordered by I-475, Talmadge Road, Highway 250, and Hollan-Sylvania Road; (419) 535-3050.*

Soak City's got wavepools, waterslides, a "sprayground," and tube rivers.

Sandusky and the Lake Erie Shoreline

THE WHOLE POINT of coming to this part of Ohio is Cedar Point Amusement Park, with roller coasters so high you can see them from miles away. The park is in Sandusky, on the shores of Lake Erie, midway between Toledo and Cleveland (about an hour's drive from each).

First the bad news: the drive along the northern border of Ohio isn't very scenic. You can't always see the water, because the roads don't often follow the shoreline closely, turning inland here and there. In places, the lakeshore drive is almost grubby.

The good news is that there are worthy attractions all along the way from Cleveland, because Cedar Point draws so many drivers doing exactly what you're doing: following the lake to Sandusky and the big roller coasters. It seems an improbable

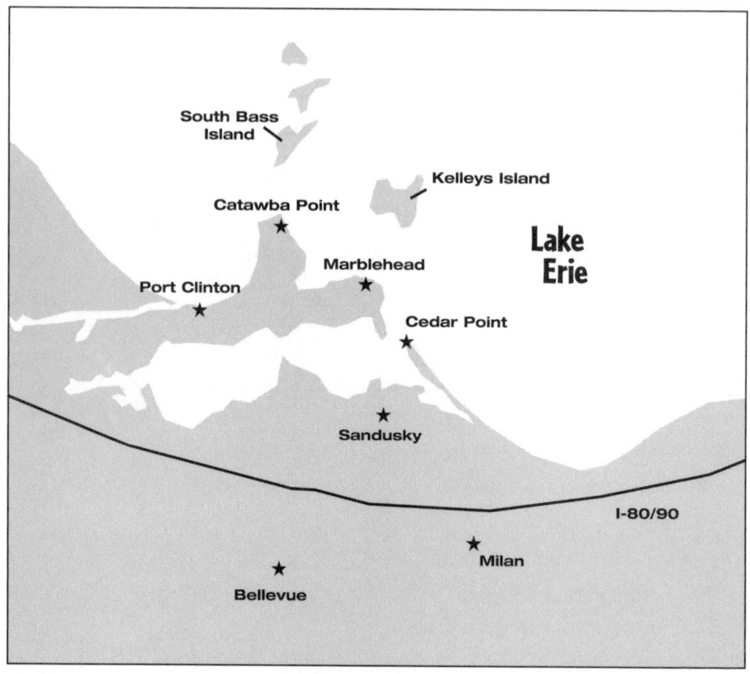

place to see African wildlife, but that's just what you'll find at the African Safari Wildlife Park. Goofy Golf and Sports City offer sophisticated miniature-golf courses and go-cart fun. Many of the small shore towns have ferries that will take you out to the Lake Erie islands (see "Lake Erie Islands" on page 61); or arrange a fishing excursion (see "Go Fish" on page 60). The lake's influence is felt on area restaurant menus: perch, perch, and more perch.

Many families spend more than a day at Cedar Point, so you can pick from many hotels and motels clustered along the roads that lead to Sandusky. To be even closer to the action, you and your roller-coaster aficionados can stay in a hotel right on the amusement park grounds.

CULTURAL ADVENTURES

Museum of Carousel Art and History ★★/$

It's hard to say what's more fun: watching wood-carvers create fanciful carousel animals or taking a ride on the working merry-go-round. *On the Square, 301 Jackson St., at W. Washington St., Sandusky; (419) 626-6111;* www.merrygoroundmuseum.org

JUST FOR FUN

African Safari Wildlife Park

★★★★/$$$

Giant antelope, giraffes, and zebras come right up to your car as you drive through this park. Your children can even feed them with food the park provides. Expect squeals of excitement as the huge creatures take the treats from your little ones' hands. There are also camel and pony rides, pig races, and a playground. *The park is northwest of Sandusky and 15 miles west of Cedar Point. 267 Lightner Rd., Port Clinton; (800) 521-2660; (419) 732-3606;* www.africansafariwildlifepark.com

Cedar Point/Soak City/Challenge Park

★★★★/$$$$

An enormous and famous 364-acre, 129-year-old theme park, Cedar Point sits on a point of land on the shores of Lake Erie. Boasting more than 150 rides and attractions, including 14 roller coasters, this is the home of Millennium Force, which claims to be the world's tallest, fastest roller coaster. Vital statistics: it is 310 feet tall, hits speeds of 92 mph, and has 80-degree drops (for those who have forgotten their geometry, that's nearly straight down). The rest of the park is pretty exciting, too. The Power Tower is an astounding 300 feet high, and

Sandusky Side Trips

Peel the kids away from the amusement park long enough to give them a little history and culture.

Got a science nut or a junior inventor in the family? Drive to Milan (south of Sandusky on Rte. 250, just across I-80/90) to visit the **Edison Birthplace Museum** *(9 Edison Dr., Milan; 419/499-2135)*, a walk-through home furnished just as it was when the great inventor was born in 1847. The low-key guided tour takes an hour, and if your children are in the middle grades, it will be particularly interesting.

While you're in town, check out the **Milan Historical Museum** *(10 Edison Dr., Milan; 419/499-2135)*, adjacent to the Edison birthplace. Here, seven buildings share one acre of beautiful gardens. Most interesting to kids are the 1840 Sayles Home, carriage shed, and blacksmith shop, which offer a glimpse of life in the mid-1800s.

Then head south and west on Rte. 20/18 to Bellevue, and the **Mad River and NKP Railroad Museum** *(253 Southwest St., Bellevue; 419/483-2222)*, where you'll see locomotives, cabooses, passenger trains, and freight trains.

For an underground adventure, proceed south on Highway 269, to **Seneca Caverns** *(15248 Township Rd. 178, Bellevue; 419/483-6711)*. Take the hour-long tour of the cavern's seven levels, see the underground river, then try mining for gemstones. Caverns: open May to mid-October; other attractions: open April through October.

has two rides. One shoots riders up, while the other drops them down. Go up to 240 feet, hit negative gravity, and bounce back down—or do it in reverse. Before you have lunch. The Mantis is a 3,900-foot-long twister and turner visible from outlooks along the Lake Erie shoreline miles away. Maybe it's called Mantis because riders begin to pray?

When you've all had your fill of (or if you'd just as soon skip) the screaming, spinning, power-packed drops and coasters, move on to the carousels, boats, antique cars, and a steam-powered train ride. Camp Snoopy is an amusement park especially for younger children, and your smaller kids will also like the Kiddy Kingdom, which has scaled-down water rides, miniature bumper cars, and small-scale trucks to drive. The Jr. Gemini is a kid-size and not-too-scary roller coaster. If the day is hot, cool off inside one of the three air-conditioned theaters while you take in a song-and-dance show. There's the high-dive show *Splash!*, and at the end of the day, a big laser and music show.

Soak City and Challenge Park are two attractions next to Cedar Point, under the same management but each with separate entrance fees. Soak City offers 18 acres of wave pools, slides, tube rivers, and pools. The "spraygrounds" are just for little kids, while body slides are for older thrill seekers. Totally cool: a swim-up concession stand.

Challenge Park offers bungee-style rides, a Triple Challenge Raceway go-cart track, and miniature golf. **NOTE:** Traffic to this very popular park can get so dense that signs along the road advise you which route to take and give you a call-ahead number to check traffic. Here's a tip—come in the evening, pay special moonlight rates, and enjoy lighter crowds. You can rent a stroller. Closed November through April. 1 *Cedar Point Dr., Sandusky; (800) 237-8386; (419) 627-2350.* www.cedarpoint.com

Goofy Golf ★★★/$-$$$

This is a very big miniature-golf course! The two separate 18-hole layouts have hills, doglegs, and tricky bits of business that will challenge any duffer. There are also three go-cart tracks for various skill levels and ages, bumper boats, and an arcade. Closed November through April. Separate fees for each activity; packages available. *3020 Milan Rd., Sandusky; (419) 625-9935.*

CEDAR POINT'S FIRST RIDE thrilled the public back in the 1880s. The water trapeze threw daring visitors into Lake Erie.

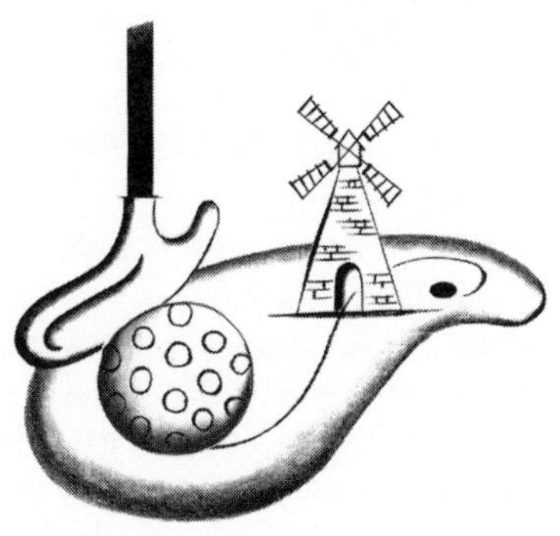

Prehistoric Forest

★★/$$

Learn more about dinosaurs at this pretend prehistoric forest. Children can dig for bones or track dino footprints. The Reptile House is home to modern-day descendants of the dinos, such as pythons, alligators, and lizards. Closed October through April. *8232 East Harbor Rd., Marblehead; (419) 798-5230;* www.mysteryhill.com

Sports City

MUST-SEE FamilyFun MUST-SEE ★★★★/$$

It's loud, it's raucous, and it's exactly what your kids like. There's an arcade game room, plus chances to be way more active: 36 holes of miniature golf, bumper boats, four go-cart tracks, batting cages, and amusement park rides. The menu offers what kids like, too: pizza. Closed November through March. *5205 Milan Rd., Sandusky; (800) 733-3353; (419) 627-1716;* www.sportscity.com

Bunking Down

At or Near Cedar Point

There are four places to stay overnight in or very close to the Cedar Point amusement park, three of them waterfront resort hotels.

Breakers Express

★★/$$$

Economy hotel this may be, but each of the 350 rooms is furnished with two queen-size beds and a television. Mom and Dad will appreciate the quick and courteous service, the clean and large rooms, the outdoor spa, and the on-site laundry facilities. Kids will head for the arcade and smile-inducing Snoopy-shaped outdoor pool. *1201 Cedar Point Dr., Sandusky; (419) 626-0830.*

Hotel Breakers

★★★/$$$$

Built in 1905, this grand hotel has the most luxurious accommodations near Cedar Point, and is only a two-minute walk to the park. The hotel has 650 well-appointed rooms and suites and three family-friendly dining options—the Coffee Shop serves a casual breakfast buffet, lunch, and dinner; Dominic's offers sizable-portion Italian dinners; and Beaches and Cream is a '50s-style ice-cream parlor located by the outdoor pool. (There's an indoor pool, too.)

OHIO STATE PARK RESORTS

THE OHIO state parks system is recognized for its excellence, and most of the state parks have a resort facility operated by Amfac Parks & Resorts. In addition to accommodations in lodges and cabins, the resorts have recreational facilities and organized activities for both day visitors (for a fee) and overnight guests. Your family can swim, fish, boat, canoe, and golf, as well as participate in scavenger hunts, guided hikes, bonfires, movie nights, nature presentations, crafts workshops, sand castle contests, kids' karaoke, and other fun programs.

Burr Oak State Park Resort

★★★/$$

Getting away in the woods is the name of the game here. There are 30 cabins and a 60-room lodge (all have TVs), plus an indoor pool. *Glouster; (800) 282-7275; (740) 384-3060.*

Hueston Woods State Park Resort

★★★/$$-$$$

The park is pristine at this Southwest Ohio resort. In addition to 37 rustic cabins and a 92-room lodge (all with TVs), the resort has indoor and outdoor pools, a golf course, tennis courts, and a game room. *College Corner; (800) 282-7275; (513) 523-6381.*

Maumee Bay State Park Resort

★★★/$$$$

Set on the shore of Lake Erie, this is an ideal spot for a family retreat. Children's activities, organized on the weekends and most weekdays in the summer, include games, arts and crafts, hayrides, and hikes. The 16 two-bedroom and 4 four-bedroom cabins and the 120-room lodge all have cable TV, and the kids will be happy to see the outdoor and indoor pools. For Mom and Dad, there's a whirlpool/sauna, and an 18-hole golf course. *Fifteen minutes from Toledo via Rte. 2. E. Oregon; (800) 282-7275; (419) 836-1466.*

Mohican State Park Resort

★★★/$$-$$$

Six thousand acres of state park surround this resort on the banks of Pleasant Hill Lake. Choose between the 25 cabins and a lodge building with 96 recently renovated rooms. Cabins have local TV, lodge rooms have cable; all have coffeemakers. Kid pleasers include outdoor and indoor pools, boating, golf, tennis, fishing, and hiking. There's a game room, too. *Perrysville; (800) 282-7275; (419) 938-5411.*

Punderson Manor State Park Resort ★★★/$$-$$$

This resort is touted as one of the

most romantic getaways in the Midwest, but don't let that stop you from bringing your family here to wade at the sandy beach, play tennis, volleyball, or basketball, or go hiking. The 26 cabins (with TV) sleep five comfortably; the English Tudor–style lodge has 31 rooms (with local TV) and a restaurant. There are outdoor and indoor pools. *Rte. 87, Newbury; (800) 282-7275; (440) 564-9144.*

Salt Fork State Park Resort

★★★★/$$-$$$

The grand stone lodge is set in the rolling hills of Ohio's state park, within view of the state's largest park lake. Kids will like the outdoor and indoor pools, the game room, and the volleyball, basketball, and tennis courts—plus, for Mom and Dad, a golf course. There are 148 rooms in the lodge and 54 cabins; all have satellite TV. *Off I-77 exit 47 on Hwy. 22 E., Cambridge; (800) 282-7275; (740) 439-2751.*

Shawnee State Park Resort

★★★/$$

Outdoor and indoor pools, a (nearby) golf course that hugs the Ohio River, 25 cabins, and a lodge with 50 rooms make this a family-friendly spot. All cabins have TVs. *Friendship; (800) 282-7275; (740) 858-6621.*

Attached to the main hotel is the Breakers Towers with another 230 rooms and suites, including a floor reserved for families, and decorated with your family's favorite characters from *Peanuts.* A TGI Friday's restaurant is located in the towers. *1 Cedar Point Dr., Sandusky; (419) 626-0830;* www.cedarpoint.com

The Radisson Harbour Inn

★★/$$$

A little less convenient and a lot less charming than Hotel Breakers, this long, three- and four-story resort hugs the waterfront. Guests have access to Cedar Point Beach. All 237 rooms have balconies and coffeemakers; some have refrigerators, too. The kids will go for the indoor pool and game room. There's also a TGI Friday's Restaurant and a deli/bakery. The inn provides water taxi service to the park. *2001 Cleveland Rd., Sandusky; (800) 333-3333; (419) 627-2500;* www.radisson.com

Elsewhere in the Area

Holiday Inn Cedar Point

★/$$

Family-friendly facilities are good here: indoor and outdoor pools, an indoor miniature-golf course, a large video arcade, and a restaurant. Two Jacuzzis, an exercise room, and a sports bar complete the picture. See if you can land one of the 175 rooms equipped with a refrigerator and

Go Fish

If you and your kids want to try to catch the big one out on Lake Erie, it's best to book a professional charter boat. Do it far in advance, if possible, so you won't be disappointed. For a recorded fishing report, call *(419) 625-3187*; For charters, contact Captain Hook *(800/453-4803* or *419/433-5421)*, Spearfish Charters *(800/735-1218* or *419/627-8340)*, or Captain's Park *(888/306-7835* or *419/433-4536)*.

Certain species of fish, such as walleye, trout, bass, and perch, run in particular areas of the lake at specific times of the year—ask the charter company for advice about the best time to visit. You'll need a valid Ohio fishing license; your charter captain can help you get one.

microwave. *5513 Milan Rd., Sandusky; (419) 626-6671;* www.holiday-inn.com

Ramada Inn of Cedar Point ★/$$

The Sports City complex is across the street, and you can walk to the movie theater. Other pluses: the 100 rooms have free cable TV; there's an outdoor pool and a restaurant; and kids 17 and under stay free with parents. Ask about the Cedar Point packages, available in May and June. *5608 Milan Rd., Sandusky; (800) 228-2828; (419) 626-9890;* www.sanduskyhotels.com

Good Eats

Graham's ★★/$$

Right outside Cedar Point amusement park, this place gives grown-ups a little relaxation while still being laid-back enough for children to enjoy. The style is casual-dressy, not fussy, and the dining room has contemporary chandeliers and lots of plants. You can also sit outside on a brick patio. The adult menu includes perch from the lake, but the surf and turf, chicken tarragon, and veal piccata are reliable, too. If you've got a child who's a light eater, share an entrée—they're generously sized. Hungry kids can select spaghetti and meatballs, chicken fingers, or pizza from the children's menu. Oddly enough, you can't get lunch, as they're only open for breakfast and dinner. *2047 Cleveland Rd., Sandusky; (419) 627-0011.*

Mon Ami Restaurant ★★/$$$

This historic 1872 winery is now a restaurant serving walleye, perch, and steaks. There's a children's menu, too. For dessert, order the pie. *3845 E. Wine Cellar Rd., Port Clinton; (419) 797-4445.*

DAY TRIP

Lake Erie Islands

North of Sandusky, a peninsula of Ohio land juts into Lake Erie. The towns of Catawba Point and Marblehead are here, east of Port Clinton. Both towns are jumping-off points for ferries that head out into the lake, stopping at a handful of islands.

Kelleys Island

This largest of the Lake Erie islands measures 2,800 acres, all of it on the National Register of Historic Places. Travel is by foot, bike, or golf cart. For grown-ups, the charming homes surrounded by white picket fences make simply taking a walk an enjoyable way to spend time. Kids will be more interested in Inscription Rock, where they can see prehistoric Native American pictographs from the Erie tribe, which lived here 300 years ago, and the 400-foot-long Glacial Grooves at Kelleys Island State Park, giant ruts cut into the rock by glaciers. *Ferries depart Marblehead for Kelleys Island every 20 minutes from March through December.*

South Bass Island

The island's main town, Put-in-Bay, is a popular day trip with shopping—and a bit of a history lesson. During the War of 1812, the Battle of Lake Erie was fought 10 miles offshore. The Victory and International Peace Memorial in Put-in-Bay is a tribute to those lost in that battle. If you want a great view and the kids aren't afraid of heights, ride the elevator up the memorial to the observation platform, 317 feet above the water. Other Put-in-Bay kid pleasers are the 20-minute tour of **Perry's Cave** *(979 Catawba Ave., Put-In-Bay; 419/285-2405)*, with an underground lake, and the **Alaskan Wildlife Museum** *(Meechen Rd., Put-In-Bay; 419/285-9736)*, with more than 200 animals. A park facing the lake is across the street from a large wooden carousel that kids can ride for a dollar. There are swimming beaches, too. Only those staying overnight may bring a car onto the island. Day trippers can rent a golf cart or bikes or take a bus (**Island Bike Rental and Transportation;** *419/285-4855*), or take a cab (**Put-In-Bay Cab Co.;** *419/285-6161*). If you'd like to spend the night, or get more information about the island, call the **Put-In-Bay Chamber of Commerce** *(419/285-2832)* for a list of accommodations. **Miller Boat Line** *(800/500-2421)* runs a ferry to Put-In-Bay from Catawba Point; the trip takes less than 20 minutes. You can ride the ***Goodtime I***, which departs from Jackson Street Pier in Sandusky *(800/446-3140; 419/625-9692)*, or the ***Jet Express***, departing from Port Clinton *(800/245-1538)*.

Kids and parents will be wowed by the I. M. Pei–designed Rock and Roll Hall of Fame–inside and out.

Cleveland

As recently as 1980, Cleveland would be the last place we'd recommend for a family vacation. Well, you know what families are saying about this city on Lake Erie's shore now? "Cleveland rocks!" In the last two decades, the city has turned itself around to become a model of urban revitalization and reengineering. It now boasts a revived waterfront, new baseball and football stadiums, and the world-renowned Rock and Roll Hall of Fame.

A ride on Lolly the Trolley provides a wonderful introduction to the city. A one-hour narrated tour will help to orient your family, and you just might learn something about Cleveland's history. (Two-hour tours are also available, but are generally longer than kids can tolerate.) Reservations are required for all tours

Cleveland Metroparks Zoo & RainForest (page 68)

Great Lakes Science Center (page 66)

Pro Football Hall of Fame (page 69)

Rock and Roll Hall of Fame (page 70)

Six Flags Worlds of Adventure (page 71)

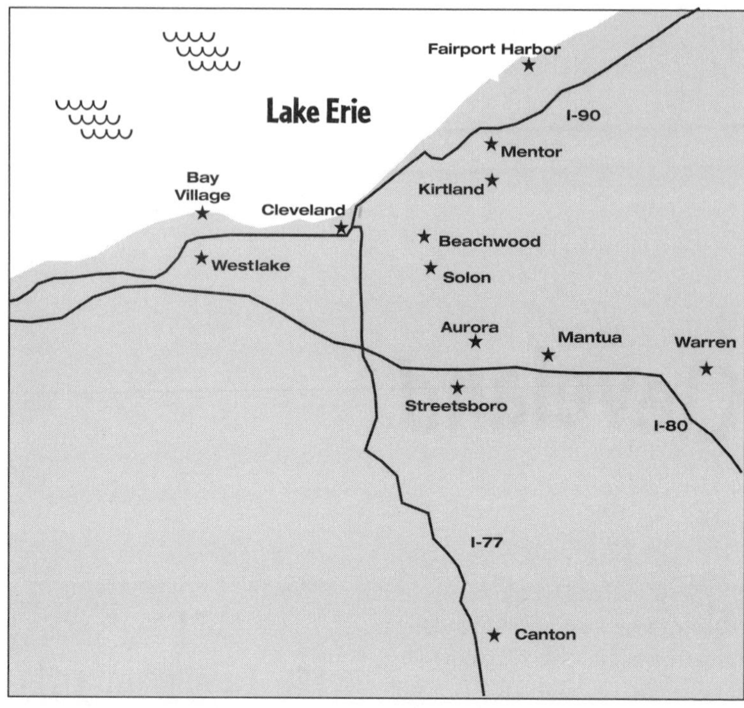

that depart from the Trolley Tours station at the Powerhouse at Nautica on the west bank of the Cuyahoga River in Cleveland Flats (*216/771-4484* or *800/848-0173*). Once you have your bearings, the options for family fun are endless. The Rock and Roll Hall of Fame is a one-of-a-kind stop with more than just pop culture to offer: noted architect I. M. Pei designed the striking building. Spend a day at the Cleveland Metroparks Zoo, and hang around in the RainForest exhibit long enough (about 12 minutes) to see a real rainstorm, complete with lightning and thunder. Genuflect before entering the Pro Football Hall of Fame and sit in a movie theater where the seats rotate so that you seem to be right in the center of the action of an NFL game and probably closer to a running back than you ever wanted to get. Head for a Cleveland Indians baseball game or a professional soccer match for real-life sports action. If your kids complain that they haven't done anything, hit the roller coasters, water park, and other fun stuff at Six Flags Worlds of Adventure. **NOTE:** In addition to Cleveland proper, the attractions listed below are in neighboring communities.

CULTURAL ADVENTURES

Children's Museum of Cleveland ★★★/$$

Interactive exhibits give your kids a chance to explore their world in imaginative, creative ways. The Splish Splash attraction lets them play with a working lock, at a large water table, or in the bubble area. They can also see how weather is recorded and understood, learn about bridges, work at an airline ticket counter, or go shopping at a supermarket. An infant and toddler area called the Big Red Barn provides all sorts of barnyard fun and activities, but no real animals. *10730 Euclid Ave., University Circle, Cleveland; (216) 791-5437;* www. museum4kids.com

Cleveland Museum of Natural History ★★★/$$

Among the awesome "folks" on display here are a 150-million-year-old, 70-foot-long skeleton of a Haplocanthosaurus delfsi, nicknamed Happy, prehistoric fish, a 40-foot allosaurus, and another dinosaur called a nonottyrannus. The oldest hominid fossil is here, too, and is also improbably named: Lucy. Young rockhounds like the Wade Gallery of Gems and Jewels. And if you visit during the non-summer months, you can look through the observatory's telescope. Additional fee for the planetarium shows. *1 Wade Oval, University Circle, Cleveland; (800) 317-9155; (216) 231-4600;* www.cmnh.org

Fairport Harbor Marine Museum ★★/$

Tour an 1871 lighthouse tower, check out the pilothouse, and take a look at Great Lakes marine artifacts. Kids over 8 like this more than the younger ones. From the top of the lighthouse, you can see Canada. There's also a nautical gift shop. Open Wednesday, Saturday, and Sunday from Memorial Day through

FamilyFun READER'S TIP

Reward Good Backseat Behavior

Backseat squabbles were a big problem for the Niehues family of Red Wing, Minnesota, on long car trips. "Four kids can find a lot to fight about!" says mom Mary. Now, though, Mom and Dad give each of the kids a roll of quarters at the beginning of the trip. Every time they have to correct a child's behavior, the culprit forfeits a quarter. But any quarters still remaining at the trip's end are the child's to keep. "My husband and I came out even the first time," Mary says, "but we never have again!"

Mary Niehues, Red Wing, Minnesota

the weekend after Labor Day. *The museum is on Lake Erie, about 30 miles northeast of Cleveland. 129 Second St., Fairport Harbor; (440) 354-4825.*

Great Lakes Science Center ★★★★/$$

More than 330 hands-on science and technology exhibits give curious youngsters plenty to do—and think about. Your kids' hair is sure to stand on end when the Bridge of Fire's static electricity generator gets crackling. Plastic is put to work in the Polymer Funhouse, where kids can shape and mold polymers into imaginative objects. They can also explore giant outdoor mazes, pretend they are microbes invading a huge body, pilot a blimp, or just play in the sports area. There's also an Omnimax theater with a giant domed screen (additional fee). Any family architecture buffs should take in the view of I. M. Pei's remarkable Rock and Roll Hall of Fame next door through the floor-to-ceiling windows of the science center. If hunger strikes, there is a Pizza Hut and a deli on the premises. *601 Erieside Ave., Cleveland; (216) 694-2000;* www.greatscience.com

> **FamilyFun SNACK**
>
> **Cereal Solution**
>
> Before you leave on vacation, empty all your cereal boxes and create this snack mix.
>
> In a large bowl, combine 3 cups of assorted cereals with ⅓ cup each of raisins, peanuts, and pretzels. Melt 4 ounces of white chocolate according to package directions and stir it into the cereal mixture until the bits are well coated. Chill for 20 to 30 minutes. Place in ziplock bags.

Lake Erie Nature and Science Center ★★/Free

Take a walk on the wildlife side to see the many creatures that call this center home—opossums, red-tailed hawks, water and land turtles, turkey vultures, and owls to name a few. A saltwater tank holds ocean fish, a freshwater tank is full of fish found in Lake Erie, and resident reptiles include boa constrictors, pythons, and iguanas. Family pets like rabbits and guinea pigs round out the population. Best of all, some of the animals are in open-roofed pens so kids can get up close for a good look. *From Cleveland, take Highway 90 west to the Clague exit. 28728 Wolf Rd., Bay Village; (440) 871-2900.*

JUST FOR FUN

Cleveland Browns ★★★/$$$$

Cleveland sports fans suffered a major blow in the 1990s when their team, a huge source of local pride, was snatched away to Baltimore by its owner. Thankfully, the NFL recognized what residents knew all along—Cleveland is football! The league granted a new franchise, and a new Browns team started kicking off at a new stadium in 1999. *1085 West 3rd St., Cleveland; Stadium: (440) 891-5050; tickets: (216) 241-5555;* www.clevelandbrowns.com

Cleveland Cavaliers
★★/$$

Swish! Young hoops fans love watching the city's professional basketball NBA team in action, especially if your home team is in town. *Gund Arena, One Center Court, Cleveland; (216) 420-2287;* www.cavs.com

Cleveland Crunch ★★/$$-$$$

This championship professional soccer team sometimes tosses miniature soccer balls to their fans, and team members are kind about giving autographs. Youth league players may imagine themselves on the field in a few short years. *Convocation Center, Cleveland State University, 2000 Prospect Ave., Cleveland; (216) 687-5082.*

Cleveland Indians
★★★/$$

Even if they're not big baseball fans, kids generally get a kick out of seeing a game at open-air Jacobs Field, "the Jake." The crowd, the snacks, and the souvenirs, are as much a part of the festive experience as the game itself. Look for the kids' concession stand, which sells PB&Js, juice boxes, and snow cones. For a special memento, stop at the booth in the concourse where kids are photographed and their pictures turned into their very own baseball cards. Cool! If you're visiting in summer with avid baseball fans, take the ballpark tour—it's free. Offered May through September, it lasts about an hour and includes behind-the-scenes views of the press box, dugout, and batting cages, and a stop at Little Tikes Kids Land, the play area for young fans. Cameras are welcome. *Jacobs Field, 2401 Ontario St., Cleveland; tickets; (216) 420-4200; tours: (216) 420-4385;* www.indians.com

Cleveland Metroparks
★★★/Free

Ohio's parks system is known for its excellence, and Cleveland is no exception. Metroparks surround the city, preserving 19,000 acres of rivers, gorges, and scenic valleys. Your family can use the 60 miles of trails for biking, walking, and in-line skating. In winter, all of the parks' unpaved hiking trails are also open to cross-country skiers. You can also ski at the CrossCountry Ski Center in the River Grove Winter Recreation Area, and toboggan down a 1,000-foot chute at Mill Stream Run. Pick up maps and brochures of the trails and parks at various points around the city—call the office for the location nearest you; *(216) 351-6300.*

Kangaroos, Koalas, and Kookaburras, Oh My!

More than 3,000 animals from all the continents on earth live at the Cleveland Metroparks Zoo & RainForest, a 168-acre park of rolling hills and shady groves. The RainForest exhibit alone has more than 600 insects (including the giant hissing cockroach), reptiles, and animals; kids especially love the orangutans that swing overhead. The indoor RainForest also boasts its own waterfall—and its own weather. It actually rains in here, about once every 12 minutes.

In the Australian Adventure, your kids can walk among the kangaroos, see koalas, climb the improbably named Yagga tree, and learn what the heck a kookaburra is.

The Northern Trek is home to cold-climate creatures like polar bears, Siberian tigers, reindeer, grizzlies, and wolves.

The Primate, Cat, and Aquatics building houses red pandas, snow leopards, and gorillas, lemurs, and chimps—among other interesting creatures.

The aquariums house stingrays, sharks, and piranhas. Walk through the exhibits or take the complimentary zoo trams. Picnic areas are plentiful, and it's easy to find a spot to stop, get the kids a snack, and refuel for more exploring. *3900 Wildlife Way, Cleveland; (216) 661-6500;* www.clemetzoo.com

Cleveland Metroparks Zoo & RainForest
★★★★/$$

This way-cool zoo has it all—and then some. For more information see "Kangaroos, Koalas, and Kookaburras, Oh My!" at left. *3900 Wildlife Way, Cleveland; (216) 661-6500;* www.clemetzoo.com

Cleveland Rockers
★★/$$

If you and your kids are among the growing number of women's professional basketball fans, a Rockers game will be a treat. *Gund Arena, corner of Huron Rd. and Ontario St., Cleveland; (216) 263-ROCK;* www.rockers.com

Goodtime III
★★★/$$$

Board this sleek, modern ship for an enjoyable two-hour cruise through Cleveland Harbor and up the Cuyahoga River. Along the way you'll see 19 bridges and many shoreline landmarks, including the Lorenzo Carter Cabin, a replica of the home where the first man to settle Cleveland lived. An interesting recorded narration covers the lively history of the city. Kids like being on a boat and grown-ups appreciate the sights and the scenery; everyone should have a good time on the *Goodtime III. 825 E. Ninth Street Pier, North Coast Harbor, Cleveland; (216) 861-5110;* www.goodtimeiii.com

Headlands Dunes State Nature Preserve ★★★/$

The scenic preserve on Lake Erie is a good place to see migrating birds and monarch butterflies, along with a great view of Fairport Harbor Lighthouse. Headlands Beach State Park, part of the preserve, has the longest beachfront on Lake Erie. *From Cleveland, take I-90 east to Route 2, east to Route 44, north to the park, Mentor; (440) 632-3010.*

Holden Arboretum ★★/$

This fact may not impress the kids much, but nevertheless, this is the nation's largest arboretum, with more than 3,100 acres of gardens, flower and plant displays, hiking trails, and a gift shop. *It's in Kirtland, about ten miles from Cleveland via I-90 east and Route 306 south. 9500 Sperry Rd., Kirtland; (440) 946-4400;* www.holdenarb.org

Lake Farmpark ★★/$$

Imagine a theme park about farming, and you've got the gist of this place. Kids will leave knowing where their breakfast, lunch, and dinner come from, and how a real farm works. They can watch tractors at work, ice cream being made, and sheep being shorn. They can also take a horse-drawn wagon ride, milk a real cow, and eat great country food. Educational exhibits include a fun model of a tomato vine with six-foot tomatoes and 12-foot leaves. They can see more than 60 breeds of livestock, including some rare and endangered species. The whole family will enjoy strolling through the orchards, vineyards, gardens, greenhouses, and fields of the 19th-century farm. *From Cleveland, take Highway 90 east to Route 306, south to Route 6. 8800 Chardon Rd., Kirtland; (440) 256-2122; (800) 366-3276;* www.lakemetroparks.com

MUST-SEE FamilyFun MUST-SEE Pro Football Hall of Fame ★★★★/$$

Gridiron fans of all ages love this five-building museum, with its centerpiece designed, appropriately enough, to look like a giant football. The Hall of Fame proper is a series of wide hallways with a bronze bust of each Hall of Famer and a history of his contribution to the game. The photo gallery features some of the most riveting and suspenseful moments of the game, captured by top sports photographers. Memorabilia and artifacts from players and teams are displayed, and Super Bowls have their own special place. A favorite among kids is the QB-1 Call-the-Play theater, where 10 visitors can compete simultaneously in a football video game. Game Day Stadium is a two-sided, rotating movie theater; the film starts in the locker room, then the entire seating area rotates and moviegoers find themselves in the thick of the action of an NFL game (possibly scary to very young children). There's also a video theater featuring great moments in football, and you'll have a chance to play sports trivia games on a television monitor. The museum store is filled with football toys and souvenirs. On Enshrinement Day each summer, thousands of spectators flock here for the free outdoor ceremonies, during which new members are inducted in the Hall of Fame. *From Cleveland, take 77 south, exit 107A at Fulton Rd. 2121 George Halas Drive N.W., Canton; (800) 282-5393; (330) 456-8207;* www.profootballhof.com

Punderson Manor State Park Resort ★★★/$$

Romantic? Yes. Family-friendly? Absolutely. See how this place does it all in "Ohio State Park Resorts" on page 58.

MUST-SEE FamilyFun MUST-SEE Rock and Roll Hall of Fame ★★★★/$$$

Kids think of this as a museum of musical history. Mom and Dad get to take a trip down memory lane—and a chance to introduce their kids to the music they grew up with. Both generations should have a blast at this bright, colorful, lively—and loud—monument to modern music. The glass pyramids designed by I. M. Pei might remind grown-ups of the Louvre, but this 150,000-square-foot joint ain't no stuffy museum. The instruments, clothes, records, and other possessions of rock's greatest stars are on eye-catching display, and there's music, music everywhere.

Check out exhibits, films, and interactive displays about rock icons like Elvis, Aretha, and Mick. (If your kids don't know who they are, it's about time they learned! That said, children under 12 are likely to be bored pretty quickly, unless they are real rock-and-roll aficionados.) See Elvis's first guitar, Jim Morrison's Cub Scout uniform, Janis Joplin's Porsche, John Lennon's 1964 Rickenbacker guitar, Madonna's gold bustier, the original manuscript of "Hey Jude," and Jimi Hendrix's hand-written lyrics to "Purple Haze." Push buttons to view videos of rockers being inducted into the Hall of Fame, and watch a rock-and-roll movie in one of the three theaters. The Hall of Fame also hosts special limited-engagement exhibits like "Roots, Rhymes, and Rage: The Hip-Hop Story." *1 Key Plaza, Cleveland; (888) 764-7625; (216) 515-8444;* www.rockhall.com

Six Flags Worlds of Adventure

MUST-SEE FamilyFun MUST-SEE

★★★★/$$$$

This mega complex combines three exciting worlds of fun into one. Experience a thrill park featuring ten roller coasters—including the new X-Flight flying coaster and the mammoth Batman Knight Flight. Meet Bugs Bunny at the all-time kids' favorite, Looney Tunes BoomTown.

On the marine side, watch spectacular shows starring dolphins, walruses, otters, and a cast of crazy cats and dogs.

And at Hurricane Harbor water park, make a splash in the 25,000-square-foot wave pool, 21 water slides, lazy river, or Turtle Beach for tiny tots. *Six Flags is about 45 minutes from Cleveland; take either 480 east or 271 south to 422 east; get off at the Solon exit and turn right onto S.O.M. Center Road to Highway 43; follow signs. 1060 N. Aurora Rd., Aurora; (330) 562-8303;* www.sixflags.com

Artists are eligible for induction into the **Rock and Roll Hall of Fame** 25 years after the release of their first album.

S.S. *William G. Mather* Museum ★★/$$

From 1925 to 1980, this 618-foot-long steamship carried loads of grain and ore through the Great Lakes. The sheer scale of the vessel is amazing—the engine room is four stories high. Children can try out their sailors' knots, turn the ship's wheel, and see how sailors lived, worked, ate, and slept. **NOTE:** Some of the climbing up and down would be difficult while carrying a toddler; this tour is best for kids 5 and older. Closed November through April. *1001 E. 9th St. Pier, North Coast Harbor, Cleveland; (216) 574-6262;* www.little.nhlink.net

BUNKING DOWN

Aurora Inn ★★/$$$$

Close to Six Flags, this 69-room white-clapboard and black-shuttered inn is homey and welcoming, if a bit pricey. The charge is per room, not per person, which gives families a break. Gregory's is an on-site restaurant with family fare. There's plenty on the premises to keep everyone busy: indoor and outdoor pools, an exercise room, tennis courts, whirlpool, and saunas. *30 Shawnee Trail, Aurora; (800) 444-6121; (330) 562-6121.*

Hilton Garden Inn, Cleveland Airport ★★★/$$

The location is convenient—six miles to Six Flags and 12 miles to downtown—and the 168 rooms have such handy extras as a microwave, refrigerator, and coffeemaker. The kids will welcome the

A Golden Golden Arches

The town of Warren is about 30 miles east of Cleveland, but a meal at the local **McDonald's** *(162 North Rd., Warren; 330/856-3611)* here is worth the drive. This is one fancy-schmancy Mickey D's: two stories high, trimmed in brass, tiled in marble, and adorned with an indoor waterfall. Down your Big Mac while listening to piano music played on a baby grand, and ride up and down the levels in a glass elevator. *Très* chic.

indoor pool (hurrah!), along with a whirlpool, fitness center, and restaurant, Great American Grill. The front desk has small LCD games, Lincoln Logs, Legos, and board games for young guests' use. *4900 Emerald Court SW, Cleveland; (800) 445-8667; (216) 898-1898;* www.hilton.com

Mar-Lynn Lake Park

★★★/$$

This camping spot, 30 miles from Cleveland and 10 miles from Six Flags, has rustic log cabins along with pull-throughs, full hookups, and 30/50-amp outlets. The swimming area has a soft sandy beach, slide, and diving board. Toddlers create hours of fun at the play camp, while older kids enjoy the Ping-Pong, volleyball, basketball, and horseshoes. Kids love the activities planned for them, including pancake breakfasts, hayrides, and kid Olympics. Homemade fudge and hand-dipped ice cream sold at the General Store are not to be missed. Reservations advised. *Take Ohio Turnpike (I-80) to exit 187 to Rte. 303, Streetsboro; (888) 627-5966; (330) 650-2552.*

Yogi Bear's Jellystone Park

★★★/$$

About 35 miles from Cleveland, this campground has a lot of pluses, including a pool, lake access, boating, and fishing. Kids can play in the game room, watch cartoons in the theater, compete on the miniature-golf course, and see Yogi in person. Reservations advised. *3392 Rte. 82, Mantua; (800) 344-9644; (330) 562-9100;* www.jellystoneohio.com

GOOD EATS

Aurora's Amish Style Restaurant and Bakery ★/$

An Amish community doesn't really run this spot, but the hearty menu recalls Amish roots with home-baked breads and sweets and home-made comfort food that ignores all cholesterol concerns. For breakfast, you can try waffles, pancakes, cinnamon rolls, croissants, biscuits and gravy, and muffins. Lunches are sandwiches, including hot roast beef and meat loaf with mashed potatoes. The dinner menu includes steak, roast beef, and pork chops. The children's menu offers the usual. *The restaurant is in the Aurora Premium Outlets, about 40 miles southeast of Cleveland. 549 S. Chillicothe Rd./Rte. 43, Aurora; (330) 562-3554.*

Cooker Bar & Grille ★★/$

With several Cleveland-area branches, this chain restaurant is a great family dining choice. You can eat your meat loaf, pot roast, sandwiches, and desserts in a relaxed, casual atmosphere. Kids' table manners (or lack thereof) are not a problem here. *2101 Richmond Rd., Beachwood; (216) 831-6656.* Also at *6150 S.O.M. Center Rd., Solon, (440) 519-9800; 7787 Reynolds Rd., Mentor, (440) 269-8480; I-90 at Columbia Rd., Westlake, (440) 899-9494.*

Hard Rock Cafe ★★/$$

Take a peek at the guitars, clothes, and memorabilia of rock-and-roll stars while you order up familiar favorites: burgers, sandwiches, and gooey desserts. Get a T-shirt, too. *The Avenue at Tower City Mall, W. Second and Huron Aves., Cleveland; (216) 830-7625;* www. hardrock.com

Max and Erma's ★★/$$

Yummy hamburgers (you order the gourmet version—get the kids a cheeseburger), plus diner fare, pasta, and sandwiches are the options. Kids won't leave before a trip through the build-your-own sundae bar. *Detroit St. at Crocker Rd., Westlake; (440) 899-8686.*

The Stables ★★/$$

After visiting the Pro Football Hall of Fame in Canton, come here for lunch or dinner. The building, once a stable, is now filled with football paraphernalia. Kids like watching games on big-screen TV sets, and can keep busy during the wait for your meal by playing trivia games at the table. On the menu are sandwiches, burgers, steak, seafood, ribs, and chicken, plus a children's menu of smaller portions. *2317 13th St. N.W., Canton; (330) 452-1230.*

After taking in the zoo and museums in Akron, take a quiet stroll through Cuyahoga Falls.

INTRODUCTION

Akron and Cuyahoga Falls

THE FIRST THING most people think of when they think of Akron is a tire. This association is certainly justified, as it is where the B.F. Goodrich and Goodyear companies once manufactured the wheels on which the world turns. (In, fact, Akron still produces half of the nation's tire supply.) But how did this once small town in northern Ohio become the rubber capital of the world? Location. Location. Location.

The opening of the Erie and Ohio Canals in 1832 immediately attracted industry to the area, and Akron boomed. But, there's more to Akron than tires. . . .we promise. The Hale Farm and Village provides visitors with an education about the history of the region, and the Goodyear World of Rubber to learn more about, well, rubber—which is more interesting than you may think (to everyone except preschoolers). Your family can also check out the zoo, a water park, and an imaginative museum devoted to inventors and

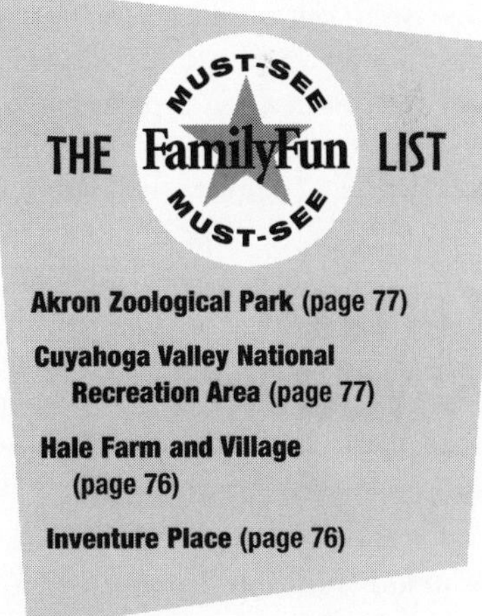

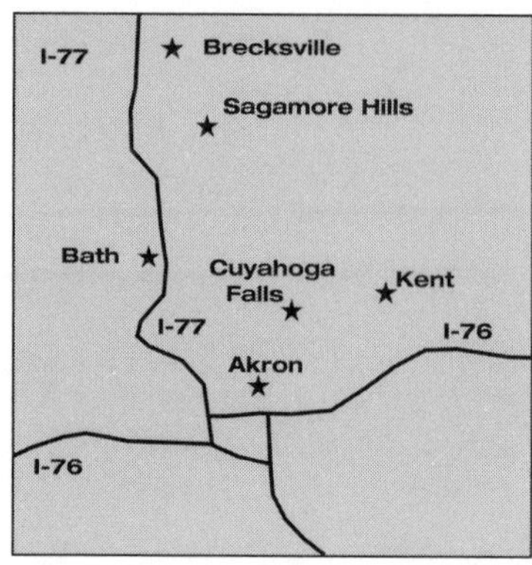

inventing, including Ohio-born Thomas Alva Edison.

Nearby Cuyahoga Falls, just four miles north of Akron via Route 8, is a picturesque town built around the Cuyahoga River (and its noted falls). Many visitors use it as a home base for exploring the stunning natural beauty of the Cuyahoga Valley. The Colonial New England architecture may seem out of place here, but it gives the area a village feel. A pleasant river tour, a water park, and a riverfront entertainment area with a boardwalk complete the picture.

CULTURAL ADVENTURES

Goodyear World of Rubber
★★★/Free

Your kids, probably like you, tend to take rubber for granted. After you visit this museum, you'll have a different view. See a mock rubber plantation and a movie about manufacturing tires. Learn how Charles Goodyear stumbled onto the vulcanization process and how tires are produced. There's not much here for tiny tots—but grade-schoolers will like the Indianapolis 500 race cars and the tire taken from the all-terrain vehicle that was used on the moon. *1144 E. Market St., Akron; (330) 796-7117.*

MUST-SEE FamilyFun MUST-SEE Hale Farm and Village
★★★★/$$

What was life like in these parts back in 1848? Visit Hale Farm and Village and find out. This restored and operational village is a must-see. Historical reenactors serve as glassblowers, blacksmiths, and other village residents, and will answer your kids' questions about how families worked, played, ate, and subsisted before video games, or even radios, existed. Some of the reenactors have pretty saucy opinions—your kids will get a history lesson that actually entertains them. They'll also get a kick out of the spinning, candlemaking, cooking, and preserving food. Closed November through April. *2686 Oak Hill Rd., Bath; (330) 666-3711;* www.wrhs.org

MUST-SEE FamilyFun MUST-SEE Inventure Place
★★★★/$$

How do inventors think? Where do they get their ideas? Your kids—mostly the 8-and-older set—

can learn more about the power of the mind here—and learn to foster their own daydreamy, imaginative thoughts. At the Inventor's Workshop, kids can create new machines on the spot, using tools and parts provided; hammer together a wooden toy boat; take apart a broken appliance to see how it works (though Mom and Dad might want to make it clear that this isn't something they should try at home); create their own animated movies; and use magnets to make a metal sculpture dance. The National Inventors Hall of Fame is here too, a celebration of people who imagined the unimaginable, inventing stuff like air-conditioning, television, and Velcro. One exhibit traces Thomas Edison's inventions from idea to reality. *221 S. Broadway at University Ave., Akron; (800) 968-4332; (330) 762-4463.*

JUST FOR FUN

MUST-SEE FamilyFun MUST-SEE Akron Zoological Park ★★★/$$

Red pandas, barking deer, tigers, bears, penguins, rare Chinese alligators, and lions are among the 400 animals that reside at this modest but fun zoo. Be sure to see the river otter exhibit—these guys are real acrobatic rascals. Kids can take a pony ride and a train ride around the grounds. Additional parking fee. Closed November through March. *500 Edgewood Ave., Akron; (330) 375-2550; (330) 375-2525;* www.akronzoo.com

MUST-SEE FamilyFun MUST-SEE Cuyahoga Valley National Recreation Area ★★★★/$

Your family can wind through the 33,000-acre wooded valley of the Cuyahoga ("crooked") River while hiking, biking, golfing, and skiing—all in season. The magnificent park is 22 miles long and follows the path of the old Ohio and Erie Canal between Cleveland and Akron. The flat Towpath Trail, once traveled by mules and horses as they pulled boats through the canal, past an old stone lock, now serves as a wonderful trail for walking and biking. Another good trek for children is the Ledges Trail, passing through shifted glacial rock formations. It's just over two miles long, but you can walk part of it and turn around. Two area ski resorts cater to downhill skiers and snowboarders: **Boston**

ORIGINALLY, RUBBER WAS made from plants native to India and Malaysia. The bark, leaves, and stems of rubber plants produce a sticky sap when they are cut into, and this substance can be used to create erasers, balls, etc....

Mills *(7100 Riverview Rd., Peninsula; 330/657-2334)* and **Brandywine** *(91146 W. Highland Rd., Sagamore Hills; 330/657-2334)*. The national recreation area has four visitors' centers. The **Canal Visitor Center** *(7104 Canal Rd., Valleyview; 216/524-1497)*, by the Towpath Trail, is open daily year-round; take the kids for a canal lock demonstration. The **Happy Days Visitor Center** *(500 W. SR 303, Boston Heights)*, near the Ledges Trail, is closest to Cuyahoga Falls; take Route 8 north to Route 303, west one and one half miles. *Park headquarters: 15610 Vaughn Rd., Brecksville; (800) 445-9667 within Ohio.*

Cuyahoga Valley Scenic Railroad
★★★/$$-$$$

Travel on 26 miles of track through the Cuyahoga Valley National Recreation Area in a nostalgic passenger train with cars dating from the 1930s and 1940s. You can get an all-day excursion ticket, which lets you get off and explore. Stop in the historic town of Peninsula to shop or to rent bikes and check out the scenic Ohio and Erie Canal Towpath Trail. You can also visit the Canal Visitor Center *(see above)*. The round-trip takes just over 90 minutes, or get the all-day excursion ticket. **NOTE:** The ride is particularly stunning in mid-October with the fall foliage. *Board at Old Rockside Road for the 26-mile trip. (800) 468-4070 within Ohio; (330) 657-2000.*

FamilyFun GAME

Geography

Start with anyplace in the world: Kansas, say. The next person has to think of a place that begins with the last letter of Kansas, such as South Africa. Whoever goes next needs a place that starts with A. It has to be a real place—and no using a map!

Dover Lake Waterpark
★★/$$

Seven water slides, three tube rides, a water-whirl ride, two speed slides, and a wave pool will give your kids summer thrills. And after the slides and water rides, there are amusement park rides, a train ride, and a swimming lake with sand beach. Older kids can head to the miniature-golf course, and batting cages, free video arcade, and horseshoe pits add to the fun. There's a parking fee. Closed September through May. *From Akron, take Route 8 into Macedonia, left at Highland Road, and follow the signs. 1150 W. Highland Rd., Sagamore Hills; (330) 655-7946;* www.doverlake.com

Falls River Tours ★★/$$$

Take the *Front Runner* or the *Cuyahoga Cruiser* pontoon boat (each holds about 20 people) on an hour-long trip up and down the Cuyahoga River. A narrator fills you in on the geology and wildlife of the area, as well as some of the colorful river history. You can take longer tours, but this is just about the right length for children. Tours operate May to late October (weekends only in October) and depart Cuyahoga Falls on the hour. *Riverfront Center Pkwy., North Pier, Cuyahoga Falls; (330) 971-8225.*

Riverfront Centre ★★/Free

The boardwalk area, or "town square" of Cuyahoga Falls, hosts activities and events. Spring through fall, you can take boat rides and view the falls. The nonwinter months also have kid pleasers like a rubber-duck race, ice cream on Thursday afternoon, and Friday night concerts. *2100-2200 Front St., Cuyahoga Falls; (330) 971-8135.*

Water Works Family Aquatic Center ★★★/$$$

The slow-moving lazy river offers a dreamy float in an inner tube for kids 3 and up. Older thrill seekers go for the 158-foot steeply winding tunnel slide and the even less relaxing Drop Slide, 23 feet of what feels like a wet free fall. This water park is not as stupendously sized as some, which is rather nice. Preschoolers and toddlers like the sand play area and small toddler slide. Closed between Labor Day and Memorial Day. *2025 Monroe Falls Ave., Cuyahoga Falls; (330) 971-8299.*

Bunking Down

Crown Plaza Quaker Square ★★★★/$$$

Your kids won't forget this hotel stay. They'll sleep in grain silos. The hotel is part of Quaker Square, a one-of-a-kind hotel/restaurant/ shopping complex set in the historic Quaker Oats cereal factory. The factory's 19th-century 120-foot silos—which stored grain until 1970—have been converted into 196 modern hotel rooms that are round, 24 feet in diameter. The conversion took more than seven years and many creative construction solutions—sawing through six-inch walls of concrete to create windows, doors, and balconies for starters. Each room has Nintendo and in-room movies. Executive suites are equipped with refrigerators. The hotel now sports an enclosed pool. Be sure the kids check out the murals of local artist Don Drumm that cover the curved lobby walls—they incorporate the enormous original gears and machinery of the mill and factory. The adjacent grain mill now holds period-theme restaurants and shops. *135 S. Broadway, Akron; (330) 253-5970;* www.quakersquare.com

Ramada Inn ★★/$

Kids stay and eat free at this typical but comfortable inn. There's an on-site restaurant, an outdoor heated pool, and a fitness and game room.

Other welcome amenitites: coffeemakers, irons and ironing boards, and free HBO. *4363 State Rte. 43, Kent; (330) 678-0101.*

Sheraton Suites Akron/ Cuyahoga Falls
★★★★/$$$

The suites at this all-suite lodging are perfect for families. The 149-room hotel is directly on the Cuyahoga River and Falls. Kids love the immense cedar deck that overlooks the river, and the "Rock Elevator" that lets them walk along the edge of the gorge in complete safety. The bedrooms are separated from the sitting rooms (with a pullout queen-size sofa bed) by louvered doors. Other family-friendly amenities include two televisions, a VCR, and a kitchen with refrigerator, microwave, and minibar. Kids will like the indoor pool, while Mom and Dad try the sauna and whirlpool. Plan on at least one meal at the hotel's RiverFront restaurant, dramatically perched above the falls *(opposite page). 1989 Front St., Cuyahoga Falls; (800) 325-5788; (330) 929-3000;* www.sheratonakron.com

EASY AS PIE

If a trip to The Pie Factory brings out the chef in your children, give them a hand with this quick ice-cream pie recipe.

Place 1 1/2 cups finely crushed graham crackers or chocolate wafers into a 9-inch pie pan. Stir in 5 tablespoons of melted butter, then press the mixture into the bottom and sides of the pan. Freeze for 30 minutes. Fill with one quart of mint chocolate-chip or peanut butter ice cream, layer on 1/2 cup hot fudge sauce, top with 2 cups whipped cream, and top with colorful sprinkles. Freeze before slicing and serving.

GOOD EATS

The Pie Factory ★★/$

Set in the Quaker Square complex, this place is just what its name says. Bring home an entire pie, or sit down for a slice of apple, peach, berry, or banana cream with coffee or a glass of milk. If you insist on protein, try pizza, a homemade pot-pie, soup, or salad. Kids can look through the window into the glassed-in bakery and see how pastry chefs make these delightful concoctions. *Quaker Square, 135 S. Broadway, Akron; (330) 252-0552.*

RiverFront ★★★/$$

This restaurant in the Sheraton Suites hotel literally hangs out over the falls and, thanks to floor-to-ceiling windows, has a remarkable view that kids love. The unexceptional though varied menu has decent food with lots of kid-friendly choices, such as spaghetti marinara. Have the breakfast buffet, lunch, or an early dinner here (while it's still light) and watch the water gush over the falls. *1989 Front St., Cuyahoga Falls; (330) 929-3000.*

Native Americans used the word **cuyahoga,** which means crooked, to describe the twisted shape of the local river.

Trackside Grill ★★/$

When historic Quaker Square was still a mill and factory producing Quaker Oats, the railroad that passed right by the building was the company's lifeline. This restaurant honors the railroad's history, decorated with authentic train memorabilia and three 80-ton *Broadway Limited* railroad cars. Kids love dining on family fare in a real Pullman car. Before you leave, stroll through the restaurant to learn more railroad history. *Quaker Square, 135 S. Broadway, Akron; (330) 253-4541.*

Souvenir Hunting

Quaker Square

Once home to the Quaker Oats cereal factory and mill, Quaker Square is now a hotel, restaurant, and shopping complex. Because it sits on the old mill's train tracks, the complex has a railroad theme. **My Little Red Wagon** *(330/384-1644)* sells educational toys, including many trains and train-related items; **J. Marco Galleries** *(330/376-2188)* on the second floor features Native American jewelry and artifacts; **The News Stand** *(330/253-6467)* sells comic books and magazines; and the **Mill St. Noodle Co.** *(330/253-3233)* sells kitchen gadgets, including children's bake sets and novelty sprinkles (some are shaped like barnyard animals). When you need a break, stop at the **Mill St. Candy Co.** *(330/535-6502)*, which serves up warm oatmeal cookies; the Quaker Oats tins sold here make nice souvenirs. **Quaker Square,** *135 S. Broadway, Akron;* http://www.quakersquare.com/shop_fr.htm

Introduce your kids to Amish customs (and proper tourist etiquette) at the Mennonite Information Center.

Amish Country

OHIO IS HOME TO THE densest concentration of Amish and Mennonite communities in the country. Driven from their homelands by religious persecution, they immigrated to the United States (primarily from Switzerland and Germany) over a period of 125 years, starting about 1720. The Amish believe that the Bible teaches a life of simplicity and the separation of church and state, so they reject technology and contemporary cultural changes that most people regard as progress. No phones, no cars, no Nintendo. No electricity, and no zippers, even.

If you are traveling between Columbus and Cleveland around the town of Wooster; in Holmes and Tuscarawas Counties in East-Central Ohio; or in Southern Ohio, along the Ohio River in Adams County, you may see Amish people driving horse-drawn buggies, farming in the fields, or working outdoors.

Though the Amish do not welcome visits to their farms and homes, a visit to the Mennonite Information Center in Berlin will introduce your kids to these groups and their beliefs. The Holmes County Amish Flea Market, while far from representative of typical Amish life, sells many types of Amish handicrafts and is a

The Mennonite Information Center (page 85)

Roscoe Village/Canal Boat Rides (page 86)

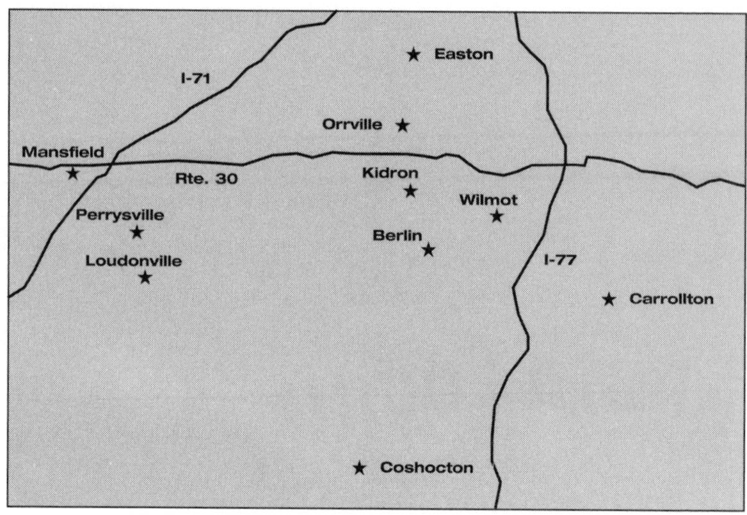

good stop if you want to bring home a quilt or jars of homemade preserves. Throughout the area, restaurants and lodging trade on the Amish reputation for home-grown, home-cooked food—but don't expect to find Amish waitresses and gregarious Amish hosts. The Amish aren't rude, but are generally shy of modern "English" (non-Amish) people.

FamilyFun TIP

Personal Adventures

Take turns sharing the memorable events of your lives. What was the scariest thing that ever happened to you? The funniest? The best? The worst? The most embarrassing? What have you done that you are most proud of?

A few tips for an Amish Country trip: along highways, watch out for horse-drawn buggies (marked with triangular, glow-in-the-dark, "slow-moving vehicle" signs). The horses are accustomed to traffic, but give them a wide berth anyway, to be on the safe side. If you'd like to buy an authentic Amish souvenir, be on the lookout for a brown-painted refrigerator or box standing at the end of a driveway at an Amish farm. It's actually a sort of self-service shop. Many Amish would rather not speak with "the English" but will leave out homemade breads and jams and handcrafted items for sale in a box or nonworking appliance. It's the honor system: leave your money on the shelf (there's usually a box or cup provided) and take what you want. Be respectful: although their old-fashioned dress and conveyances are picturesque, don't start snapping away with your camera—Amish and Mennonite people prefer not to be photographed. Also, bear in mind that many shops and attractions are closed on Sunday.

CULTURAL ADVENTURES

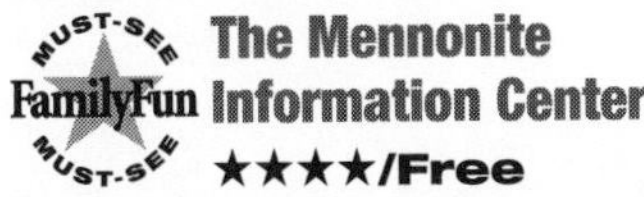

The Mennonite Information Center ★★★★/Free

Begin your family's Amish country tour here. View the video and take a look at the 265-foot cycloramic mural-in-the-round, which depicts Mennonite and Amish history. The center will give you and your children an understanding of why the Amish and the Mennonites live as they do. *5798 County Rd. 77, Berlin; (330) 893-3192.*

JUST FOR FUN

Mohican Canoe Livery and Fun Center ★★/$$-$$$

Rent canoes, kayaks, and rafts and explore the Mohican River from a site about an hour's drive from Columbus. Kids can also ride go-carts and play miniature golf. You can spend the night in cabins or a lodge. Closed in winter. *3045 State Rte. 3S, Loudonville; (419) 994-4097.*

WHEN TO WED

Amish weddings are usually held in November and December because harvest season is complete and the harsh winter weather is still to come. Weddings typically take place on Tuesday and Thursday because those are the least busy days of the week.

Mohican State Park Resort ★★/Free

Choose to swim,hike, fish, play golf or tennis at this 6,000 acre park. For more information, see "Ohio State Park Resorts" on page 58.

Richland Carousel Park and Carousel Magic Factory ★★★/$

Ride a hand-carved wooden carousel that has 52 animals and two chariots. Then take your kids to see how wood-carvers carve the beasts you've ridden. The carousel is in the center of the town of Mansfield, the factory is at 44 West Fourth St., less than half a block away. *75 N. Main St., Mansfield; (419) 522-4223.* (The factory is closed on Sunday and Monday.)

Roscoe Village/ Canal Boat Rides

★★★★/$-$$

This restored 1800s canal town is complete with a winery and pottery and basket factories. There's lots of history here, plus some super stops for gifts and souvenirs. Kids can take a horse-drawn boat ride in the canal. (No, the horses don't swim—they walk along the shore and pull the boat through the water.) *White Woman St., Coshocton; (800) 877-1830; (740) 622-9310.*

Salt Fork State Park Resort

★★★/Free

Pools, a game room, and acres of sports options please kids of all ages. For more information, see "Ohio State Park Resorts" on page 58.

BUNKING DOWN

Amish Country Inn and Hannahs House B&B

★★/$$$

Operated by the same owners, the inn and the bed-and-breakfast are about a quarter mile apart in the heart of Amish Country. The 50-room inn is tucked into the hills of Holmes County. It features a pool, whirlpool, and sauna. Located in a beautifully restored Victorian mansion, the B&B has six rooms, two of which share a bath, and two with whirlpools. The rooms in both sites have satellite TV, and telephones. You can take your kids on guided Amish home tours, for buggy rides, and to pet animals at the Schrocks Farm (same owners) about three miles away. You are also minutes away from the shops on Berlin's Main Street. *Berlin; (800) 935-5218; (330) 893-3232.*

The Inn at Amish Door

★/$$

Kids will head for the indoor pool at this 50-room hotel, which also has a bakery and gift shops. The Amish Door Restaurant serves traditional Amish fare. *1210 Winesburg St., Wilmot; (800) 891-6142; (330) 359-7996.*

Mohican State Park Resort

★★/$$-$$$

See "Ohio State Park Resorts" on page 58.

Salt Fork State Park Resort

★★★/$$-$$$$

See "Ohio State Park Resorts" on page 58.

THE J.M. SMUCKER COMPANY started in 1897 when Jerome Monroe Smucker made apple cider from trees originally planted by Johnny Appleseed.

SOUVENIR HUNTING

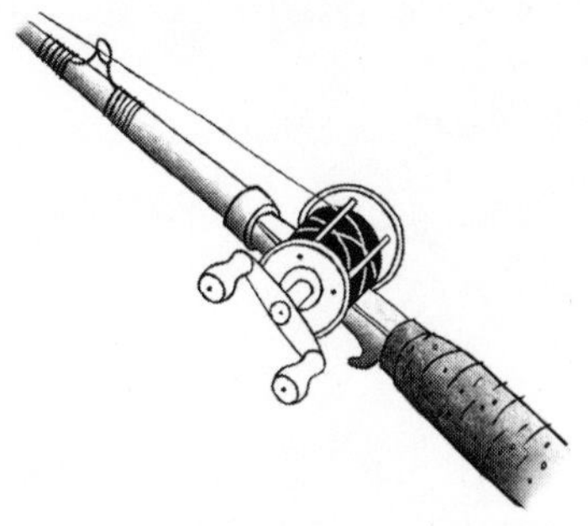

Galyan's

What's fun here is that you and your kids can try out the fishing gear, kayaks, and canoes in the 300-by-250-foot pond behind the store. *Easton Town Center, off I-270 at the Easton Way exit;* www.galyans.com

Lehman's

Here's where the Amish and other self-sufficient local folk shop, and it's a trip back in time. The store sells newly made but old-fashioned tools, kettles, farm implements, and household equipment. After they see the wonderful antiques display, the kids will leave with a new appreciation for the family car and air-conditioning. *1 Lehman Circle, Kidron; (330) 857-5757.*

Simply Smucker's

Add Smucker's jams, jellies, and other goodies to your roadside picnic or state park campout. *333 Wadsworth Rd., Orrville; (330) 684-1500.*

Otters and others at the Columbus Zoo and Aquarium frolic at kid's-eye level.

Columbus

JUST ABOUT smack-dab in the center of the state, Columbus is Ohio's largest city—a fact that surprises many visitors struck by the city's quiet charm. The attractive, lively state capital is distinguished by historic neighborhoods (like German Village) as well as very modern architecture (like COSI: Center for Science and Industry, and the downtown skyscrapers). The lighted skyline is a wonder at night; you don't need another excuse to take the kids downtown for a drive or a walk at twilight. And be sure to take a walk along the riverfront. It won't be busy, and it will be beautiful and paved for an easy go with a stroller.

Columbus also has lots that the kids will find fun and that is, whether they realize it or not, educational. The renowned Columbus Zoo and Aquarium is an ideal daylong outing, as is the truly remarkable COSI, one of the liveliest and most imaginative children's museums you've ever seen. The goofy Field of Corn in nearby Dublin is a work of art

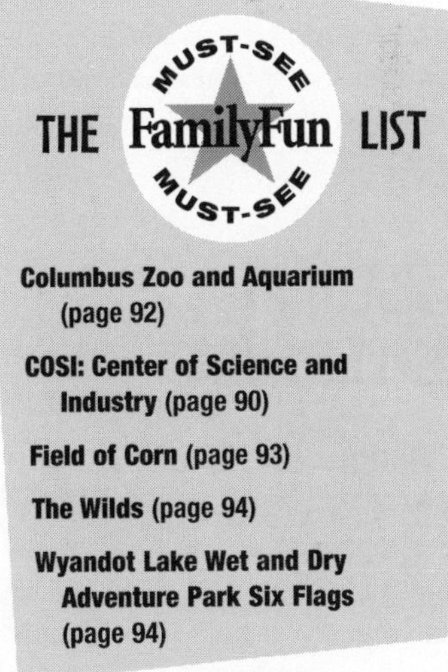

Columbus Zoo and Aquarium (page 92)

COSI: Center of Science and Industry (page 90)

Field of Corn (page 93)

The Wilds (page 94)

Wyandot Lake Wet and Dry Adventure Park Six Flags (page 94)

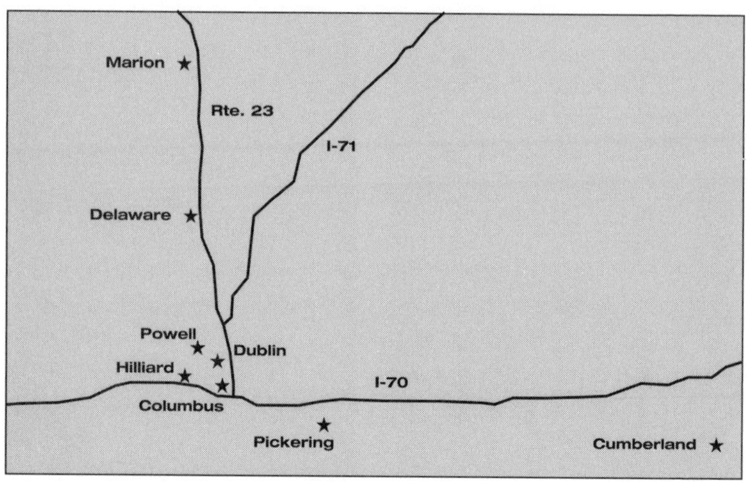

your kids won't forget, and a drive through The Wilds lets children see wildlife they'll never spot on a normal family drive: rhinos, giraffes, and bison. The least educational outing may also be the most fun: a visit to the Wyandot Lake Wet and Dry Adventure Park Six Flags.

Columbus parks hold outdoor concerts and performances in the summer. *To find out what's planned during your visit, call (614) 645-3800 or (614) 645-7995.*

Cultural Adventures

Columbus Museum of Art ★★/$

The impressive art and photography collections here aren't particularly aimed at children. Kids will, however, like the sculpture garden. The museum often holds children's programs; call for a schedule. There's a café and a museum shop. *480 E. Broad St., Columbus; (614) 221-6801;* www.columbusmuseum.org

MUST-SEE FamilyFun COSI: Center of Science and Industry ★★★★/$$

Even though you're on vacation, there's no harm in giving your kids some brain food—and this world-class educational center fills the bill. For more information, see "Think About It. . ." on page 96. *353 W. Broad St., Columbus; (877) 257-2674.*

Ohio Historical Center and Village ★★★/$$

Visit this 1860s-style village and get a taste of life "way back when." The 18 buildings are authentic reproductions and include a stable, shops, a schoolhouse, and a church. Reenactors play period characters. The village men's baseball team has the not-very-manly name of the Muffins, and the women's baseball team, the Lady Diamonds, plays in bloomers. Rooting in the Victorian manner is great fun: be polite, no hooting, no spitting. The teams play regularly April through Labor Day, but not every weekend; call for current schedule. *I-71 North at 17th Ave., Columbus; (800) 653-6446; (614) 297-2300;* www.ohiohistory.org

Olentangy Indian Caverns ★★★/$$

These caverns were formed millions of years ago by an underground river. Many are quite large, tall enough to stand in, and spacious enough to walk through comfortably. The Wyandot tribe used the caverns for shelter and ceremonies. An 1821 inscription in the entrance was likely the work of the first white man to come here, J. M. Adams, a member of a wagon train. The Cave House is at the entrance and is the starting point of the half-hour self-guided tour or 40-minute guided tours (summer only). **NOTE:** Participants travel 55 feet down, descending on concrete stairs. Strollers are impossible and carting toddlers is exhausting; the tour is not recommended for preschoolers. Your older kids will like the fossils and rock strata they'll see along the way, as well as displays of the many artifacts that were discovered when these caverns were first explored. Temperatures are about 54°F underground, so bring along a jacket or sweater. Afterward, stop at the rock shop and try mining for gemstones at the water sluice. Kids can also play miniature golf and shop at a miniature frontier land, a re-creation of a historic fort. The epitaphs in the mock cemetery make for fun reading. Closed November through March. *The caverns are about 35 minutes from Columbus via Route 315 north. 1779 Home Road, Delaware; (740) 548-7917;* www.olentangyindiancaverns.com

Santa Maria Replica ★★★/$

After all, the city is named for Christopher Columbus. Gradeschoolers who have studied the voyages of the *Nina*, *Pinta*, and *Santa Maria* enjoy touring this museum-quality, full-scale replica of the explorer's flagship. Part of the appeal here is learning what life was like for a 15th-century shipmate. Open spring and summer only. *Battelle Riverfront Park, Columbus; (614) 645-8760.*

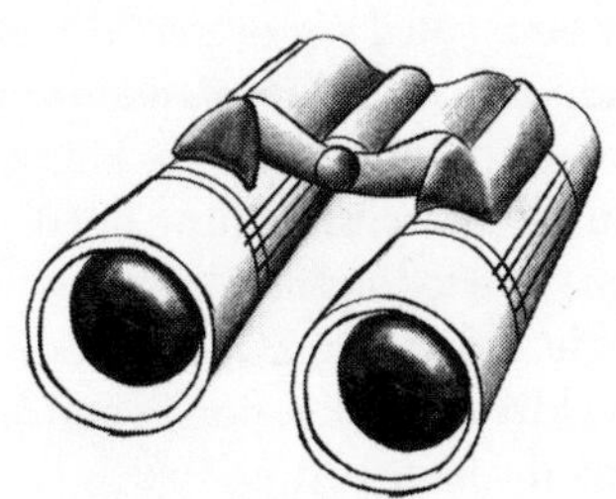

Just for Fun

MUST-SEE FamilyFun MUST-SEE Columbus Zoo and Aquarium ★★★★/$$

The zoo shares an enormous parking lot with the Wyandot Six Flags (see page 94). On a hot, sunny day, especially on a weekend, this means you may have to park pretty far away and walk in the sun for quite a while to get to the zoo. The parking lot is unpaved, so making your way with a stroller is tough going. Load up on the sunscreen and have everybody wear hats. Note that the zoo has some amusement park rides, so if your children are too young to feel they've missed something by not going to the water park, skip Six Flags and just head for the zoo.

Once you do get there, the zoo itself is shady and beautifully landscaped. Grab a newsletter when you enter and check out the Meet the Keeper schedule. These are especially interesting times to view the exhibits, as the keepers will be feeding or otherwise tending to the animals. Plan your route accordingly.

As you make your way around the zoo, you'll see oversized metal sculptures of alligators and tortoises here and there that the kids can climb. Beware, though: on hot days, don't set a toddler in shorts down on the hot metal! Your little ones will also love riding live ponies and visiting the large petting zoo.

The zoo encompasses 485 acres and holds more than 10,000 animals, including the sea creatures in the aquarium. Your bug lovers will want to make a beeline for the arthropod house, site of fascinating insect exhibits. A staff member does demonstrations, and you may be lucky enough to feel a gigantic millipede walk across your hand or to see a giant cockroach or hairy spider up close. Real close.

The cheetah pen is another must-see. It's a large, simulated natural environment, and you need to take the walkway above the pen to look down and see the big cats. **TIP:** On hot days, they lie in the shade under the trees in the far corners, and you might have better luck walking around to that side of the pen.

On the far side of the cheetah pen is a dock overlooking the O'Shaughnessy Reservoir. Buy a handful or two of the food sold in dispensers there and toss it down. You'll be rewarded by a flurry of pink-mouthed carp, rolling and thrashing around, hoping to catch a mouthful. Look for the manatee exhibit, with live mangrove trees surrounding a 200,000-gallon tank representing a Florida inlet, where three manatees live. Children can walk right up to the glass walls and see the lumpy-looking manatees swimming behind it. Then give your kids a ride on the carousel, while parents rest in the the ring of rocking chairs surrounding it. If you see a black-and-white Border collie zipping around the grounds barking at the plentiful geese, it's not an unruly pet of a visiting family. This is Sweep, a trained zoo "employee," whose job it is to herd geese away from certain spots in the zoo and back into the water.

The zoo has several concession stands and picnic shelters, plus plenty of shady spots to simply sit down on the grass and let the kids play for a while. Additional parking fee. *The zoo is in Powell, 17 miles northwest from downtown Columbus. 9990 Riverside Dr., Powell; (800) 666-5397; (614) 645-3550;* www.columbuszoo.org

Field of Corn

MUST-SEE FamilyFun MUST-SEE

★★★★/Free

Now this will get the youngsters giggling. In Dublin, just northwest of Columbus, there's an amusing work of public art that depicts a one-of-a-kind cornfield: 109 enormous ears of corn, five to six feet tall and made of cement, stand in rigid formation. *From Columbus, take Highway 270 to the 161 Dublin exit, go east and turn right on Frantz Road; the field is about half a mile down on the right. Rings and Frantz Rds., Dublin.*

Homestead Park

★★/Free

Bring a picnic and let everyone enjoy this imaginative playground, outfitted with bridges, towers, cranes, and tunnels. The nearby play waterfort has built-in squirt guns that in summer never run out of water. Bring a towel. There's also a biking track and trails for hiking. *About 25 minutes from Columbus; take Route 33 to the Plain City exit. 4675 Cosgray Rd., Hilliard; (614) 876-9554.*

Magic Mountain

★★/$$$

Let your kids play indoors and out. Facilities include a miniature-golf course, a KidsGym, go-carts, an arcade, and giant play structures to climb on, crawl through, and slide down. There are two locations, one on the east side of Columbus and one north of town in Polaris. *8350*

Pop! Pop! Pop!

Things are a-poppin' at the Wyandot Popcorn Museum in Marion, about 30 miles north of Columbus. The world's largest collection of popcorn antiques (poppers of all kinds) is here, proving that families have craved the salty munchy for centuries. The museum is open Wednesday through Sunday year-round. *It's just west of Highway 23 at 169 East Church St., Marion; for additional details, call (800) 992-6368; (740) 387-4255.*

Lyra Dr., Columbus; (614) 844-4386. Also at 5890 Scarborough Blvd., Columbus; (614) 863-6400; www.magicmountainonline.com

Motorcycle Hall of Fame ★★/$$

Ogle 100 bikes and view exhibits on the men and women who designed them and gave them their cool reputation. *On the southeastern edge of Columbus. 13515 Yarmouth Dr., Pickering; (614) 856-2222;* www.motorcyclemuseum.org

MUST-SEE FamilyFun MUST-SEE

The Wilds ★★★★/$$

The 9,000 acres of woods, wetlands, lakes, and prairie help create a protected habitat for 20 species of American, Asian, and African animals. In this zoo, the wildlife roams free and the humans are in the cages—in this case, safari buses. Your family will see rhinoceroses, zebras, giraffes, antelope, bison, camels, and wild horses during the one-hour guided tour. What kid wouldn't go wild? There's a café and picnic area, too. Closed November through April. *14000 International Dr., Cumberland; (740) 638-5030;* www.thewilds.org

MUST-SEE FamilyFun MUST-SEE

Wyandot Lake Wet and Dry Adventure Park Six Flags ★★★★/$$

Looking for a good way to beat the dog days of summer in Columbus? This amusement park is next to Columbus Zoo and shares the same giant, unpaved parking lot where it's easy to lose your car and hard to find any shade. Slather the sunscreen on the kids and try not to despair if you're pushing a stroller across the gravel—it's easier going once you get to the entrance. The park has more than 60 rides and slides, plus a variety of live shows (they might feature magic, ice-skating, or circus acts). There's a generous-size wave pool, the Canoochee Creek lazy river ride, and Christopher's Island, a fantasy land of "abandoned ships," lagoons, and a tree house, where the water in the 99 water-squirting gadgets is thoughtfully heated. Warn skittish kids about the 1,000-gallon dump of water that occurs every few minutes. The dry adventures include an antique carousel, the Starfish Ferris wheel and the Sea Dragon wooden roller coaster. Toddlers have their own mini-parks in Tadpool Kiddie Pool and Kiddieland. And when the troops

THE OHIO BUCKEYE—also known as the American horse chestnut—received its name from its large two-toned seeds. The seeds of the state tree look similar to the eyes of the eastern white-tailed deer.

get hungry, there are plenty of options—pizza, hamburgers, spaghetti, funnel cakes, and ice cream to name a few. Closed November through April. *10101 Riverside Dr., Powell; (800) 328-9283; (614) 889-9283;* www.sixflags.com

BUNKING DOWN

AmeriSuites Columbus Dublin

★★/$$$

The major draw here is the location, especially for families with very small children who would love a visit to the zoo, Wyandot Lake, and the Field of Corn. Each of the 124 rooms is a suite with lots of the stuff that make Moms and Dads smile: cable TV, a microwave, and a refrigerator. The kids will like the outdoor pool, and the deluxe complimentary continental breakfast buffet will fortify everyone for a day of sight-seeing. *6161 Park Center Cir., Columbus; (800) 747-8483; (614) 799-1913;* www.amerisuites.com

Doubletree Guest Suites ★/$$

Stay in the heart of downtown and have suite comfort. Your kids will enjoy the glass elevator, which offers a view of the Scioto River (as do some premium rooms). Suites are especially large, and all have two telephones, two TVs, a refrigerator, and coffeemaker. *50 S Front St., Columbus; (561) 989-9717.*

GO PLAY OUTSIDE!

The city of Columbus has some 13,000 acres of public parkland, so visiting (and local) families are never at a loss for a place to get some fresh air and exercise. A couple of favorite spots:

FRANKLIN PARK

A great place for a picnic, the park has fishponds, a formal Japanese garden, and a playground. *1777 East Broad St., Columbus; (614) 645-8733; (614) 645-3000.*

INNISWOOD METRO GARDENS

This 92-acre park has nine gardens, all wonderful for walking and letting the kids stretch. *940 S. Hempstead Rd., off Dempsey Rd., Columbus; (614) 895-6216.*

The Westin Great Southern Columbus

★★★★/$$$

Theodore Roosevelt and Sarah Bernhardt once stayed here—not together, of course. The wedding-cake-pretty downtown hotel was built more than a century ago and has been restored to Victorian splendor. The kids will "ooh" and "aah" when they see the lobby, which is white and gold and glorious: soaring skylights, stunning chandeliers, and marble-lined expanses. Each of

THINK ABOUT IT...

EVERY EXHIBIT AT COSI: **Center for Science and Industry**, part children's museum, part science museum, part fun house, is aimed at getting kids of all ages to participate, discover, sample, and solve. Next door to Columbus's impressive high school, the COSI (pronounced ko-sigh) itself is an architectural wonder. It hugs the Scioto riverfront and at 300,000 square feet is longer than three football fields.

The Ocean exhibit lets children try on an underwater helmet and explore a sunken-ship exhibit (it's not really under water). Your kids can also see what life is like on a submersible, watch how flowing water deposits and rearranges sand and silt, and try to engineer a bridge to hold back the tide. In the "i/o" area, the world of electronics is almost magical; the kids can explode laser fireworks or play virtual volleyball.

The Sim Zone beckons your electronic-game-playing wizards. The exhibits explain how arcade games were invented and how the evolution of computer technology led to more complex and ever-cooler games. A nice thing: the games featured here are nonviolent and suitable for kids of all ages. Take a ride on the 30-seat SimEx Motion Simulator to really feel "in the game."

Gadgets gives the kids a chance to explore gears, pulleys, and giant propellers. Progress lets you walk through time, from 1898 to 1962, learning what everyday folks thought of newfangled inventions like the horseless carriage, the lightbulb, and television. Toddlers and preschoolers will like **Little Kidspace**, where they can play in a soft playground designed to keep them safe and stimulate their imaginations.

There's also the **John Glenn Theater**, where you can watch an adventure documentary on the seven-story Extreme Screen, and a modern planetarium with computer-generated images of the universe and an incredible sound system. **NOTE:** Before entering, tell the little ones that it will be very dark inside, and hold on tight to prevent wanderers from escaping.

Don't forget to look up! COSI features a high-wire act that your kids can try: riding a unicycle along a cable stretched over the lobby. Scientific principles are being demonstrated here. Don't worry, Mom, your child can't tip or fall: you can't change the laws of physics.

The gift shop stocks great science kits, books, gizmos, and the Atomicafe keeps everyone fueled with sandwiches and yummy desserts. *333 W. Broad St., Columbus; (888) 819-2674; (614) 228-2674;* www.cosi.org

the 196 rooms is a modern two-room suite equipped with a minibar, cable TV, and a marble bath. Some rooms are small—ask for a space that best fits your family. Cribs and rollaway beds are available. The Theatre Café offers breakfast, lunch, and dinner. *310 S. High St., Columbus; (614) 228-3800;* www.westin.com

Good Eats

Buckeye Hall of Fame Café ★★/$

Wherever you turn in this sports bar, you'll see red, and the Ohio State University Buckeye logo. The place has a sporting energy that kids enjoy and a menu that includes burgers and peanut-butter-and-jelly sandwiches. Adults can orders steak, pasta, lobster, burgers, and salads. But come early—after the game this place is filled with grown-up, beer-drinking fans. *1421 Olentangy River Rd., Columbus; (614) 291-2233;* www.buckeyehalloffamecafe.com

Hamburger Inn ★★/$

A real 1950s-style diner, it serves sodas, burgers, shakes, and fries like soda fountains used to do. Need we say more? *16 N. Sandusky St., Delaware; (740) 369-3850.*

94th Aero Squadron ★★/$$

Here's a place for your flight-fixated offspring. This airport eatery has a great view of planes taking off and landing. The restaurant itself has a "World War I flying ace" theme, with country French decor and an American menu heavy on chicken and steak dishes. There's a children's menu, too. *Port Columbus International Airport, 5030 Sawyer Rd., Columbus; (614) 237-8887.*

Panera Bread ★★★★/$

Part of a chain, this bakery and bagel shop serves fresh baked breads and bagels, along with soups, salads, plus sandwiches. *Olentangy Plaza, 875 Bethel Rd., Columbus; (614) 457-6800.*

Souvenir Hunting

Anthony-Thomas Candy Company

Stop in to buy made-on-the-premises chocolate treats. Your kids will go for the guided tour that shows how the candy is created by hand; reservations required. *1777 Arlingate Lane, Columbus; (614) 274-8405.*

The Book Loft of German Village

This old-fashioned, independent bookseller houses more than 500,000 discount volumes for readers of all ages. Kids can spend hours in the children's sections, and looking for the store's mascot, a calico named Winky! *631 S. Third St., Columbus; (614) 464-1774;* www.bookloft.com

Let the sight of Cincinnati's Roebling Suspension Bridge inspire your kids to do some engineering of their own at the Cinergy Children's Museum.

Cincinnati and Dayton

SETTLED IN the 19th century, primarily by German immigrants, Cincinnati is a pristine city with an easy pace. Its position in the center of the Tri-State area (Indiana, Ohio, and Kentucky) provides a unique blend of Midwest hospitality and southern charm. Set on the winding shores of the Ohio River, it is both beautiful and rich in cultural, family-friendly resources. North of downtown, the Over-the-Rhine district retains the city's 19th-century architecture and appeal. A visit during the day gives a glimpse of the one-time German enclave and Findlay Market, a people-watcher's paradise. The Harriet Beecher Stowe House is northeast of downtown. During the mid-1800s, Cincinnati served as an important station for slaves on the road to freedom. For now, the house of the abolitionist and author of *Uncle Tom's Cabin (2950 Gilbert Ave., Walnut Hills; 513/632-5120)* is the sole reminder of the city's role in the

Cincinnati Museum Center at Union Terminal (page 102)

Cincinnati Zoo and Botanical Gardens (page 105)

Paramount's Kings Island (page 106)

United States Air Force Museum/IMAX Theatre (page 104)

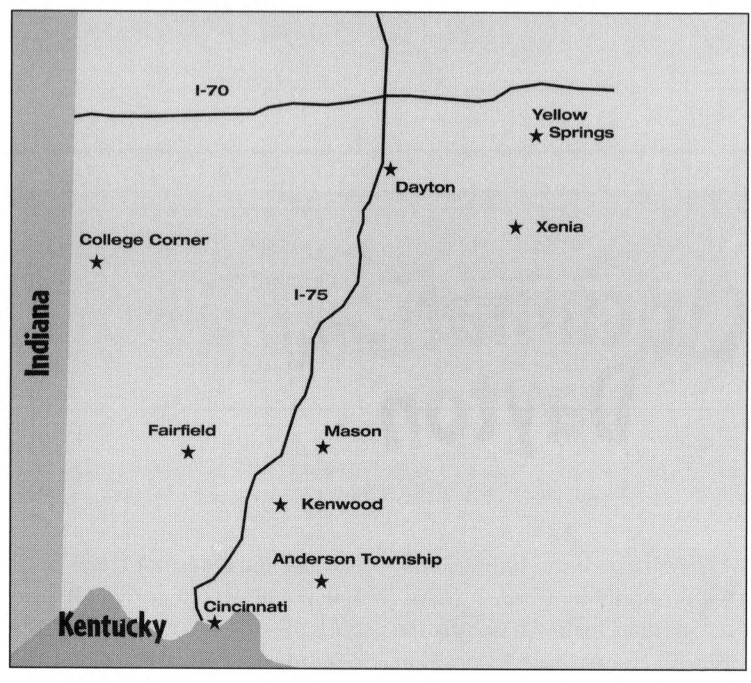

abolition of slavery. Construction on the National Underground Railroad Freedom Center was scheduled to begin as we went to press. The museum will be located on Elm Street, at the foot of the Roebling Suspension Bridge (the 1876 predecessor of Roebling's masterpiece, the Brooklyn Bridge in New York City). The Cincinnati Museum Center at Union Terminal is a historic railroad building that now houses three museums (children's, history, and natural history and science), and there are wonderful art and fire fighting museums, too. When your kids get tired of culture, visit the Coney Island water park and Paramount's Kings Island, the big, mother-of-all theme parks with more than a dozen roller coasters and its own water park. The 125-year-old Cincinnati Zoo is well worth a visit, too.

On their way to or from Cincinnati, many travelers visit Dayton, 55 miles to the north. Dayton is where the Wright brothers, inventors of the airplane, created their first successful design. If your kids aren't airplane buffs now, they probably will be after a trip here. Among the sites that commemorate Orville and Wilbur's contributions to flight are the Wright Cycle Company shop, Carillon Historical Park, and the

Huffman Prairie Flying Field. The U.S. Air Force Museum at nearby Wright-Patterson Air Force Base covers the history of aviation from the Wright brothers to the present, and even displays an *Apollo 15* space module.

Cultural Adventures

Blue Jacket ★★/$$

Performed in a 1,500-seat amphitheater, this play tells the story of the Shawnees' fight for freedom, complete with firing cannons, live horses, and shooting arrows. Skip it if you have kids under 5—the sound effects will likely frighten them and they'd probably be too squirmy to last through the show, anyway. Dinner shows include a buffet. Performances are held Tuesday through Sunday from early June to the first weekend in September. Ask about family rates. *The theater is in the town of Xenia, 10 miles east of Dayton (take Route 35 east, exit at Bickett). 520 S. Stringtown Rd., Xenia; (877) 465-2583; (937) 376-4318.*

Boonshaft Museum of Discovery ★★★/$

Part children's museum, part science museum, and part zoo, this is a place kids are sure to like. The building is interesting in itself: a silvery, sleek structure with the planetarium

High-Flying Games

Games that use a pen or pencil are perfect to play on airplanes, since you can lean on the tray top. The following ideas are especially enjoyed by players who are sitting in a row. Unlike backseat games, which can get fairly boisterous, these plane pastimes are a bit quieter, so you won't make enemies of your fellow fliers.

CRAZY CREATURES

Create strange-looking people, beasts, or any combination of both by folding a piece of paper into three equal sections. One person draws the face in the top section, then folds down the paper so the next person can't see it. That person then draws the midsection of the body, folds down the paper, and passes it to the third person, who sketches the legs in the bottom section. Finally, unfold the paper and name your creature.

TOUCHY TELEPHONE

This is a good game for people sitting in a row. Player 1, on one end, thinks of a word. Player 2, next to 1, closes his or her eyes and holds out an arm. Using a finger, Player 1 "writes" the word on Player 2's arm. The word gets passed down the row—and maybe across the aisle—until it reaches the last person in your party. That person says the word he thinks was written on his arm out loud, and Player 1 says the original word. Let Player 2 start the next round, and so on.

Heads, I Fly

The pilot of the first flight in history was almost determined by a coin toss. Wilbur Wright won the toss, but he stalled the plane on his first flight attempt. Orville made the second attempt and went into history as the first person to fly a machine-powered, heavier-than-air vehicle.

dome on one end. The many hands-on, interactive exhibits focus on the natural sciences and environmental studies. There's also a planetarium and laser show, and the Wild Ohio and EcoTrek sections showcase more than 100 live animals, including bobcat Van Cleve. Don't leave without seeing the 3,000-year-old mummy. Your kids will talk about it for weeks. *2600 DeWeese Pkwy., Dayton; (937) 275-7431.*

Carillon Historical Park

★★★/$$

If your family includes two squabbling brothers, show them what a little creative friction can accomplish at a re-creation of the workshop of Orville and Wilbur Wright. This historical museum is a complex of 20 buildings on a 65-acre campus. It includes the Wright Cycle Company's original building and the *1905 Wright Flyer III. 1000 Carillon Blvd., Dayton; (937) 293-2841.*

Cincinnati Art Museum

★★★/$$

This is a first-rate art museum, but you be the judge as to whether your children are in the mood—or at the age—to view Impressionist paintings, ancient Egyptian art, antique musical instruments, and period rooms. Eat at the café and shop at the museum shop; both offer kid-friendly fare. *953 Eden Park Dr., Cincinnati; (513) 721-2787;* www.cincinnatiartmuseum.org

Cincinnati Fire Museum

★★★/$

Set in a restored fire station, the museum is filled with exhibits about how fires have been fought through history. Totally cool: a real fire engine where kids can push buttons, ring bells, and make the lights flash. Kids will get some useful lessons about fire safety, too, although younger ones might be upset by the video about the dangers of fire fighting. Not to worry: a slide down the fire pole will brighten any mood. *315 W. Court St., Cincinnati; (513) 621-5553;* www.cincyfiremuseum.com

MUST-SEE FamilyFun MUST-SEE

Cincinnati Museum Center at Union Terminal ★★★★/$$

This Art Deco railroad terminal is now a complex of three museums, each with a separate admission charge. *301 Western Ave., Cincinnati; (800) 733-2077; (513) 287-7000;* www.cincymuseum.org

The Cincinnati History Museum ★★/$$

The subject—the history of this city—might sound like a yawner for kids. But the exhibits are done so imaginatively that even 4- and 5-year-olds are likely to surprise you by enjoying themselves. Walk into the World War II living room of the Flynn family and listen to them talk about the 1940s. Board a streetcar and hear war news. Plant and harvest pretend vegetables in a victory garden. Go farther back in time and visit shops of the early 1900s, try on clothes and hats, and walk down re-created early streets of Cincinnati; *(513) 287-7000.*

Cinergy Children's Museum ★★★★/$$

Hands-on exhibits let your kids conduct experiments and explore the scientific properties of water, learn to observe animal behavior the way real scientists do, engineer structures that actually bear weight and stand strong, and more. Toddlers (under 5) head for the Little Sprouts Farm, with hands-on farm scenes that play music or recorded messages when touched. The Robert D. Lindner Family Omnimax Theater shows nature, travel, and science movies on a five-story wraparound screen; *(513) 287-7000.*

The Museum of Natural History & Science ★★★★/$$

Learning by doing is the approach here. Explore an underground bat cave in a simulated limestone cavern. Walk through "glaciers" that trace the Ice Age in the Ohio Valley. (**TIP:** One route requires climbing and will be fun for school-age kids; the other route is stroller accessible.) Dig up dinosaur bones with paleontologists' tools in a big sandbox. See how much garbage an average family produces (a lot!). Pretend to be a doctor or a dentist in an office, and play a goofy game of pinball where the game is your gastrointestinal tract and the ball is food. Sorta gross, but interesting; *(513) 287-7000.*

Dayton Art Institute

★★/Free

Mom and Dad will like this beautiful museum—one of the country's finest midsize art institutes, and Dayton's top attraction—for galleries of fine art treasures, but kids will be most drawn to Experience Center, the hands-on family education center with activities and special events. Jazz, classical, and gospel concerts are held regularly; call for a schedule. *456 Belmonte Park N., Dayton; (800) 296-4426; (937) 223-5277;* www.daytonartinstitute.com

SunWatch Indian Village

★★★/$$

The Fort Ancient tribe settled here in about A.D. 1200, leaving behind a giant sundial secured in the earth. A Native American village has been reconstructed at the site, where your kids can see how our country's first inhabitants lived, worked, and played together. *2301 W. River Rd., Dayton; (937) 268-8199;* www.sunwatch.org

United States Air Force Museum/IMAX Theatre

★★★★/$$

More than 300 aircraft and missiles, including the *Air Force One* used by presidents John Kennedy and Dwight Eisenhower, and the 1909 *Wright Military Flyer*, can be viewed at the world's oldest and biggest military aviation museum, just outside of Dayton. The entire history of aviation is covered here, from the Wright brothers' artifacts (they first tried to fly here on Huffman Prairie Field) to the *Stealth* fighter and the *Apollo 15* space module. The 40-minute films on flight and flying (fee) shown every hour on the six-story-high IMAX Theatre screen are the closest you'll get to flying these high-powered planes yourself. Be prepared for an adrenaline rush—your kids will be supercharged after this experience! (The movies may be too intense for little ones—and are not a good idea for those who suffer from motion sickness.) *The base is at the northeast border of Dayton; take Hwy. 4NE to Harshman Road; then head south to Springfield and east to the entrance on the right. 1100 Spaatz St., Wright-Patterson Air Force Base, Dayton; (937) 255-3286; (937) 253-4629;* www.wpafb.af.mil/museum/

JUST FOR FUN

The Beach Waterpark

★★★/$$$

Real sand sets this water park apart from the rest. Among the more than 30 water slides and attractions are: the Aztec Adventure, a water coaster set in faux Aztec ruins; the Cliff, a five-story free-fall slide; Thunder Beach Wavepool, a 750,000-gallon "ocean" with four-foot-high crashing surf; The Banzai, a twin speed slide; and Hidden Rapids, a whitewater inner-tubing adventure. Take younger children on a calmer cruise on the Lazy Miami River, or let them gently splash in the Pearl, a lagoon pool, or play on Splash Mountain. Open from Memorial Day through Labor Day; also open November 24 to December 31 for a Holiday Fest of ice-skating, horse-drawn carriage rides, craft sales, and visits from Santa. *The water park is approximately*

15 miles northeast of Cincinnati (take I-71 north to exit 25). 2590 Waterpark Dr., Mason; (800) 886-7946; (513) 398-7946; www.thebeachwaterpark.com

Carew Tower Observatory ★★★/$

Your kids, like most, will jump at the chance to go way up high. Take the elevator to the tower's 49th floor for a great view of downtown and the surrounding area. *Fifth and Vine Sts., Cincinnati; (513) 579-9735.*

Cincinnati Zoo and Botanical Gardens ★★★★/$$

FamilyFun MUST-SEE

If your kids love dinosaurs and other reptiles, they'll go nuts when they see the remarkable Komodo dragons, ten feet long and up to 300 pounds. The Insectarium—a zoo within the 125-year-old main zoo and home to critters that crawl and creep with multiple feet—is another kid pleaser. Jumbo-size attractions include the red panda, the Bengal tiger, and the polar bears. The manatee exhibit is a very popular ecology lesson—kids learn how humans and their motorboats are endangering these lumpy, dumpy, gentle creatures. There are elephant, camel, and train rides, too, plus a children's zoo (small additional fee) with pygmy goats, potbellied pigs, zebu cattle, and exhibits (not hands-on) of a Tasmanian devil, otter, and walrus. Several fast-food stands are open, weather permitting. *3400 Vine St., Cincinnati; (800) 944-4776; (513) 281-4700;* www.cincyzoo.org

> **FamilyFun TIP**
>
> **Cool It**
>
> Whether you use a cooler, an insulated bag or box, or Tupperware, here's how to keep snacks cool without messy, melting ice: add frozen juice boxes; make sandwiches on frozen bread; pack some frozen grapes; include a smoothie frozen in a tightly sealed container; use sealed ice packs.

Coney Island ★★/$$

Zip down the Zoom Flume on a water toboggan! Slip through the Pipeline Plunge tube water slide! This water park has 22 rides and attractions, including Sunlite Pool, which has seven diving boards and one enormous water slide. There are bumper boats, pedal boats, kiddie rides, and miniature golf, too. Reduced rate for children; kids under 4 free. Open Memorial Day to Labor Day. *6201 Kellogg Ave., Cincinnati; (513) 232-8230;* www.coneyislandpark.com

Hueston Woods State Park Resort ★★/$-$$

Here you can hunt for fossils and stay in a golf resort. For more information, see "Ohio State Park Resorts" on page 58.

FamilyFun Must-See Paramount's Kings Island ★★★★/$$$$

You'll see what's exciting about this theme park from quite a distance. Yes, up there in the treetops, just grazing the topmost branches, is a roller coaster. Yikes. And it's only one of many at this 300-acre theme park with more than 80 rides and attractions. The friendly and helpful staffers are wonderfully patient with children.

Among the wicked coasters is Beast, the longest wooden roller coaster in the world, which reaches 64 mph racing down a 135-foot hill at a nearly impossible 45-degree angle. The Son of Beast is the tallest, fastest, only looping wooden coaster in the world. Flight of Fear propels riders from zero to 54 mph in four seconds and shoots them through four complete loops, all in total darkness. Face/Off is an inverted roller coaster (the tops of the ski-lift-style seats are attached to the track and your legs swing free). Riders sit face-to-face as they race up a 138-foot hill and through a 72-foot loop—and then do the same thing all over again, backward. Drop Zone delivers the unique sensation of being lifted 26 stories in the air, then dropped in a free fall. Some crazy kids—and grown-ups—think all of the above are just swell.

Take younger kids to the park's two themed areas designed for them. Favorite cartoon characters stroll around, ready to shake a hand and pose for a picture. The WaterWorks 30-acre water park, included in the general admission fee, has a young children's play area, a lazy river, a heated wave pool, and plenty of different rides and slides. Kids can try bodysurfing at WipeOut Beach, or head for Nickelodeon Splat City's fun maze, where they can make great slimy messes and then clean them up with water sprays. Closed November through March. *The park is about 15 miles northeast of Cincinnati off Hwy. I-71. 5688 Kings Island Dr., King's Island (in Mason); (800) 288-0808; (513) 754-5700;* www.pki.com

Young's Jersey Dairy Farm ★★★/$$

The miniature-golf course is named Udders and Putters, and that pretty much sums up this fun stop. Play

CINCINNATI-STYLE CHILI is quite different than its southwestern counterpart. The Ohio version is served as a topping to spaghetti and hot dogs and often contains one unexpected ingredient—chocolate! For a taste of this local favorite, stop by one of the Skyline Chili restaurants.

miniature golf, visit the petting farm, and have a scoop of homemade ice cream in a cone. If your kids like such things, take a tour of the dairy farm. For a sit-down, family friendly meal of farm cooking (pot roast, pork chops, mashed potatoes, plus kids meals), try the **Golden Jersey Inn**, set inside a big, red barn. The **Dairy Store** offers homemade ice cream, sandwiches, breakfasts, and bakery treats. Closed November through March. *The farm is about 25 miles east of Dayton; take Highway 70 east to R/68, exit 52A. 6880 Springfield-Xenia Rd., Yellow Springs; (937) 325-0629;* www.youngsdairy.com

BUNKING DOWN

Holiday Inn Cincinnati Downtown ★★/$-$$

If you like being close to everything, without the headaches of being "in" downtown, this is the spot for you. Less than a mile from downtown, and 15 minutes from the airport, the 243-room hotel is very comfortable for families. The decent-size rooms were recently renovated, and include such amenities as in-room movies, cable, and a refrigerator. Kids also love the swimming pool. The Simmering Pot Restaurant is open for breakfast, lunch, and dinner, and offers home-style cooking in a relaxed atmosphere. *800 W. 8th St., Cincinnati; (513) 241-8660;* www.holiday-inn.com

Hueston Woods State Park Resort

★★/$$

This lodge boasts pools, golf, and cable TV. For more information, see "Ohio State Park Resorts" on page 58.

Kings Island Campground

★★/$

This campground is just a short walk/shuttle ride to the Paramount theme park. The site's three price ranges are $20 for no hookups, $32 for water and electricity, and $36 for water, electricity, and sewer. The cabins with air-conditioning and heat sleep four and cost about $60 a night. The campground features special events and activities that change frequently (call for information), plus a camp store, bike trail, volleyball and basketball, shower, and laundry. Pets are allowed if leashed. Closed November through March. Reservations required. *6300 Kings Island Dr., Kings Island (in Mason); (800) 832-1133.*

GOOD EATS

Montgomery Inn at the Boathouse

★★/$$

Kids are welcome at this relaxed eatery. The entire place is decorated with sports and entertainment memorabilia. Try the delicious ribs, duck, or pork chops; kids have a menu with burgers and sandwiches. The

Saratoga chips are divine. Skip the unremarkable fried shrimp, crab cakes, and grilled salmon. *925 Eastern Ave., Cincinnati; (513) 721-7427.*

Panera Bread ★★★★/$
The smell of freshly baked bread emanating from this bakery and bagel shop will stop you in your tracks. In addition to their signature breads and bagels, they serve delicious soups, salads, sandwiches, and desserts. The cinnamon crunch bagels are as good as sweet rolls; the mild Asiago cheese ones are marvelous, too (rather like pizza). The Oriental chicken salad, Sierra turkey sandwich, and vegetarian gumbo are all top favorites. It's in Kenwood, at the northeast edge of the Cincinnati border on Hwy. 22. *Kenwood Pavilion, 8115 Montgomery Rd., Kenwood; (513) 891-5401.* Also at: *Festival Market, 7711 Beechmont Ave., Anderson Township, (513) 232-8300;* and *500 Kolb Ave., Fairfield, (513) 874-3400.*

Skyline Chili ★★★★/$
This is the place to sample Cincinnati's local specialty: five-way chili. What makes it different from Texas-style chili, you might ask? The meat sauce is spiced with cumin, bay leaf, allspice, cinnamon, and chocolate. . . yes, chocolate. The sauce is then ladled over spaghetti noodles (and sometimes beans), and topped with grated cheddar and onions. The restaurant has franchises all over the state. Try the Vine Street location downtown. *1007 Vine St., Cincinnati; (513) 721-4715;* www.skylinechili.com

Waffle House ★★★/$
Half fast-food restaurant, half diner, this place about 45 minutes from Cincinnati is as unfussy as they come.

FamilyFun READER'S TIP

Travel Trivia

My husband and I wanted our family trip to be both educational and fun for our 9- and 11-year-old boys. To engage their interest, we devised a game to play while sight-seeing. Every morning I would give my sons three questions pertaining to the places we would visit that day. If they answered all three they could order the dessert of their choice at dinner. They could use any resource, including a plaque at the site, a tour guide, brochures, and the like. They thought it was great fun to win a dessert off Mom and Dad, and they were so successful that we bought a round every night. Websites and guidebooks were our sources for the questions. With that little bit of preparation, our kids ended up not only having a great time but learning a lot, too.

Kathy Davis, Charlotte, North Carolina

But the food arrives quickly and is good, which is all that matters when you have hungry kids in tow. Order the specialty of the house, waffles, grilled cheese, or burgers. And don't forget the hash browns, served seven ways. The pie, especially the chocolate cream, is pretty darn good, too. You're near Jungle Jim's International Farmer's Market (see Souvenir Hunting). *Take Highway 75 to 275 west; get off at exit 41 go five miles north to 5141 Dixie Hwy., Fairfield; (513) 829-8542.*

Souvenir Hunting

Jungle Jim's International Farmer's Market

Hungry? You will be after seeing this four-acre market filled with treats from around the world: bread, cheese, produce, and candy. Fill a basket for a family picnic. The market is in Fairfield, about 45 minutes from Cincinnati. *Take Highway 75 to 275 west, get off at exit 39. 5440 Dixie Hwy., Fairfield; (513) 829-1919;* www.junglejims.com

Wolf Gallery of Photography

Books, posters, and notecards feature beautiful modern and historical images of the Queen City. Closed Sunday. *41 W. Fifth St., Carew Tower, Cincinnati; (513) 241-2004.*

This area, rich in state parks and memorials, offers loads of picnicking and hiking opportunities.

INTRODUCTION

Chillicothe and the Hocking Hills Region

THE REGION SURROUNDING Ohio's first capital, Chillicothe, is distinguished by rich cultural history and dramatic natural beauty. The Hopewell, Shawnee, and, of course, Chillicothe all made their homes here, and many of their historic treasures remain—most notably the country's longest effigy mound, crafted in prehistoric times into the shape of an uncoiling snake, at Serpent Mount State Memorial in Locust Grove and a Hopewell ceremonial site built more than 2,000 years ago at Fort Hill State Memorial in Hillsboro. The outdoor theater presentation of *Tecumseh!* continues to be the area's largest attraction in the summer. For nature lovers, the experience of discovering Hocking Hills State Park's streams, waterfalls, sandstone cliffs, caves, and varied flora and fauna can't be beat. The Hocking Valley Scenic Railway in Nelsonville offers historic rides by rail, including special holiday season rides with Santa. Noah's Ark Animal Farm in Jackson mixes zoo-style

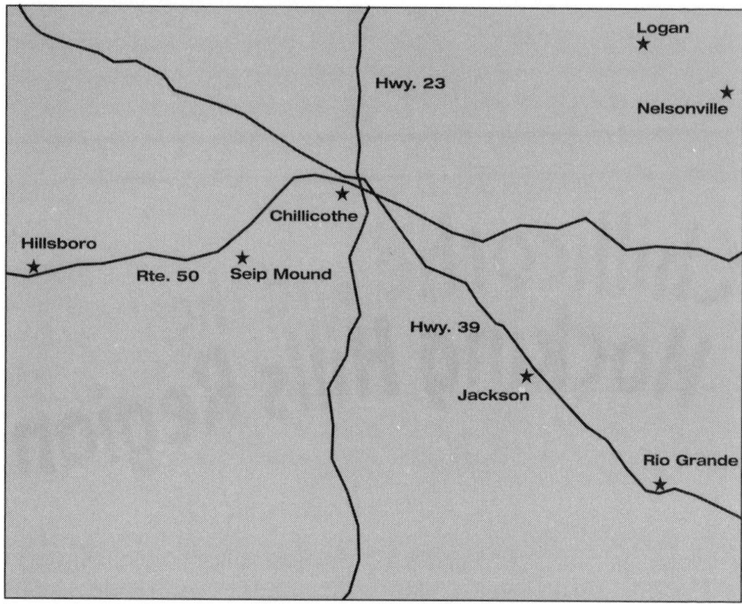

attractions (100 animals and birds) with miniature golf, train rides, and even a pay-to-fish lake. Bob Evans Farm in Rio Grande serves meals in the home-style fashion of the restaurant chain, but also gives kids the run of the old family farm, where they can ride a hay wagon and see barnyard animals.

FamilyFun TIP

A Tougher Tic-tac-toe

Make the classic game of tic-tac-toe a little more lively and a bit tougher with this one basic change: with each turn, *each* player can fill in the empty space of his choice with either an X or an O.

CULTURAL ADVENTURES

Fort Hill State Memorial
★★★/$

Fort Hill is home to one of the best-preserved Native American hilltop enclosures in North America. The Hopewell people built the mile-and-a-half-long earth enclosure and two ceremonial buildings here more than two millennia ago! Bring a picnic and spend the day exploring this historic treasure, as well as the 11 miles of hiking trails that run through the 1,200-acre nature preserve. The preserve is home to some of Ohio's most rare flora and fauna. Pick up a map at the museum before setting out on your hike, and have your kids pick a few plants and animals from the displays to identify on your journey. As you hike the gorge, look for the many natural bridges and arches including Keyhole Bridge and Natural Y Bridge. No admission charge for children under age 5. Closed Monday and Tuesday in the summer and Monday to Friday from Labor Day through Memorial Day. *Off St. Rte. 41 on Twp. Rd. 256. 13614 Fort Hill Rd., Hillsboro; (800) 283-8905; (937) 588-3221.*

Robbins Crossing at Hocking College ★★/$

If your children enjoy historical reenactors, they'll like visiting this 1850s log cabin village. Hocking College students and volunteers operate a blacksmith shop, make candles, and spin yarn while dressed in period costume. Kids are encouraged to ask questions and especially to interact with the staff. Open weekends Memorial Day through October. *3301 Hocking Pkwy., Nelsonville; (740) 753-3591, ext. 2555.*

Seip Mound ★★/Free

There is no museum here—a landmark plaque created by the Ohio Historical Society provides some information to visitors of this Hopewell burial mound. The mound is the central structure in a group of geometric earthworks

TECUMSEH!

The life of the legendary Shawnee leader Tecumseh is the subject of an outdoor play performed in summer at Sugarloaf Mountain Amphitheatre in the town of Chillicothe, 40 miles south of Columbus. The huge outdoor stages and setting heightens the *Tecumseh!* experience, and the action is pretty cool: live horses galloping down from the hills, arrows flying overhead, and artillery off in the woods. Curtain time is 8 P.M., but arrive in the afternoon if you would like to take the backstage tour (tours are offered at 4 and 5 P.M., Monday through Saturday). Check out the exhibits on prehistoric Indians at the free mini museum, too. See the performance alone, or add a buffet dinner for an additional fee. Sugarloaf Mountain Amphitheatre *(740/702-7677; 740/775-0700) is off U.S. 23N to Dalano Road; follow highway signs marked Outdoor Drama.*

degraded by farming and erosion. However, the central mound is impressive at 240 feet long, 130 feet wide, and 30 feet high. Excavations have revealed evidence of prehistoric dwellings that surrounded the central mound. Ground markers outline the suspected sites of the dwellings. *Seip Mound is 14 miles southwest of Chillicothe on U.S. Rte. 50; (614) 297-2630;* www.ohiohistory.org

Serpent Mound State Memorial

★★★★/$

This gigantic serpent shape was formed of earth by the prehistoric Adena people. It is the longest effigy mound in the country, measuring about five feet high and nearly a quarter of a mile long. It resembles an uncoiling snake; an oval doughnut shape at one end is thought to be the head. (You can see this from the car along State Rte. 770, east of the mound.) The mound, along with other cone-shaped mounds, is on a plateau overlooking the Brush Creek Valley. Archaeologists are still debating the exact purpose and meaning of the mound, but whatever its original purpose it's an awesome sight, and one that kids over 6 will likely remember. Stop at the on-site museum to learn some possible explanations for the mound and have a picnic. An observation tower also provides an interesting perspective of the mounds. Closed November through March. Parking fee. *Twenty miles south of Bainbridge, six miles north of State Rte. 32. to 41 to 73, Locust Grove; (800) 752-2757; (937) 587-2796.*

MUST-SEE FamilyFun MUST-SEE

Tecumseh!

★★★★/Free-$$$

This not-to-be-missed spectacle is theater/history lesson/shoot 'em ups/and dinner—all in one memorable afternoon. For more information, see "*Tecumseh!*" on page 113.

JUST FOR FUN

Bob Evans Farm

★★★/$$

The ubiquitous (more than 400, and counting) Bob Evans family restaurants throughout the mid-Atlantic and eastern midwestern United States got their start here at what was originally called the Sausage Shop. You can still get home-style meals here (see Good Eats), but you

can also have some down-on-the-farm fun: horseback riding, hayrides, canoeing, and meeting the resident barnyard animals. Take your kids to tour the historic log cabin village, too. The company founder, Bob Evans, lived on this farm for nearly 20 years. Once a stagecoach stop, the homestead is on the National Register of Historic Places. Open from Memorial Day through Labor Day. *Take U.S. 35 to St. Rte. 325 S. to State Rte. 588, Rio Grande; (800) 994-3276; (740) 245-5305;* www.bobevans.com

Burr Oak State Park Resort

★★/Free

This resort in the woods has something for everybody. For more information, see "Ohio State Park Resorts" on page 58.

MUST-SEE FamilyFun MUST-SEE Hocking Hills State Park ★★★★/Free

Part of Hocking State Forest, this 2,000-acre state park is home to numerous indigenous plants and animals, including more than 100 different types of birds. The trail to Old Man's Cave is a good nature walk for children. About two miles long, it leads through a forested ravine past waterfalls, rock formations, and the entrances to two caves. Head into the caves if you have sturdy shoes and the kids have sweaters or jackets. Other highlights: Rock House, built right into a cliff; the picturesque and rugged Cantwell Cliffs; and Ash Cave, carved from a huge rock, with its own waterfall. Parking fee. *20160 State Route 664, ten miles southwest of U.S. 33, Logan; (740) 385-6841;* www.hockinghillspark.com

Hocking Valley Scenic Railway

★★★/$$

Ride an old-fashioned train through scenic southeastern Ohio. Trains depart from the Nelsonville depot for the 22-mile, two-hour trip to Logan and back on weekends from Memorial Day to mid-November. On weekends from late November to mid-December, "Santa Train" rides include on-board narration of holiday poems and stories, plus music and a visit with Santa and his elves. **NOTE:** Be advised that though there is a 30-minute pit stop at Robbin's Crossing (a re-created 1850s pioneer village) there are no rest rooms on the train. *133 Canal St., Nelsonville; (800) 967-7834;* (740) 753-9531; www.hvsr.com

MUST-SEE FamilyFun MUST-SEE Noah's Ark Animal Farm

★★★★/$

This spot is particularly interesting to the 8-and-under crowd. Kids can see more than 100 exotic animals and birds here. There are also train rides, miniature golf, picnic areas, a pay-to-fish lake, and concessions. Closed November to March. *1527 McGiffins Rd., Jackson; (800) 282-2167; (740) 384-3060.*

Shawnee State Park Resort

★★/Free

Golf, pools (indoor and out), and lots more are good reasons to stop here. Also see "Ohio State Park Resorts" on page 58.

BUNKING DOWN

Ash Cave Cabins and Conference Center

★★★★/$$$-$$$$

In the scenic Hocking Hills, this resort offers nine cabins for families. Each comes with a hot tub, fireplace, charcoal grill, and other niceties. There is a nearby hiking trail and a restaurant on-site. Weekend rates include breakfast. Reduced rates are given for families staying three nights or more. *25780 Liberty Hill Rd., Logan; (800) 222-4655; (740) 332-1902;* www.ashcave.com

Burr Oak State Park Resort

★★/$$

There are 30 cabins and a 60-room lodge at this woodsy resort. For more information, see "Ohio State Park Resorts" on page 58.

Inn at Cedar Falls

★★/$$

What kid wouldn't want to stay in an 1840s log cabin? The inn also has 15 hotel rooms inside a barnlike structure, some with kitchens and refrigerators. There aren't many child-focused amenities—not even a pool—but the inn is less than two miles from Old Man Cave, and steps away from hiking, biking, and cross-country skiing trails. **NOTE:** The single cabin has one bathroom that is not totally private. *In Hocking Hills, 21190 State Rte. 374, Logan; (800) 653-2557; (740) 385-7489.*

FamilyFun READER'S TIP

Taste-testers

While traveling cross-country on vacation a few years ago, my husband and I grew tired of our children's requests to visit the same old fast-food places for the latest kids'-meal prize. So we instituted the no-fast-food rule: when our family hits the road on vacation, we only stop at restaurants we can't visit back home. In other words, no nationally franchised restaurants or fast-food joints. The idea is to find some regional flavor. As it gets closer to lunch or dinner, we hit the side roads looking for one-of-a-kind diners, rib joints, custard shops, and the like. Thanks to this rule, we have eaten Indian fry bread in the Badlands, great sloppy ribs in Tennessee, sensational seafood in South Carolina, and more. Dylan, age 7, and Ryan, 10, enjoy being on the lookout for the quirkiest place and don't even miss the "prize inside" scene.

Lisa Tepp, Milwaukee, Wisconsin

Shawnee State Park Resort ★★/$$

This family-friendly spot features 25 cabins and a lodge. For more information, see "Ohio State Park Resorts" on page 58.

GOOD EATS

Bob Evans Farm ★★/$

The first in what has become a long chain of family restaurants serves typical homestyle meals for breakfast, lunch, and dinner. Sausage gravy and biscuits, chicken and mashed potatoes, burgers, and sandwiches are the specialties here (see Bob Evans Farm on page 114). *Take U.S. 35 to St. Rte. 325 South to State Rte. 588, Rio Grande; (800) 944-3276; (740) 245-5305.*

Lewis Family Restaurant ★/$

If your children like Thanksgiving dinner, they'll like the menu here, which makes much use of turkey grown on the Lewis farm. Burgers, sandwiches, and steak are available, too. *966 E. Main St., Jackson; (740) 286-5413.*

The Olde Dutch Restaurant ★/$

Stick-to-your-ribs helpings of chicken and potatoes, turkey and dressing, and meat loaf and gravy are served here. They're filling, but try to leave room for the yummy desserts. There's a children's menu and an ice-cream shop. On Sunday, try the hearty brunch. *12791 State Rte. 664 S., at U.S. 33; (740) 385-1000.*

Homemade Travel Desks

Laps are great for lots of things, but writing and drawing are not among them. Keep art projects from collapsing all over your child by making a custom-fitted travel desk out of a sturdy cardboard box. First, while she is seated, measure the height and width of her lap. Now, cut a half-moon big enough to comfortably fit over her legs on two opposite sides of the box and remove the bottom flaps.

If you have time, you can paint the box to dress it up and staple or glue smaller accessory boxes or envelopes to the sides for storage. You can also flip it over to store paper and other travel games inside when it's not in use.

Michigan

MICHIGAN, A STATE shaped like a big mitten, with a "hat" called the Upper Peninsula (or "U.P." by the locals), has 3,200 miles of gorgeous Great Lakes shoreline. And folks around here take advantage of every inch. What natives love about Michigan are the same things that make vacationing families flock to this state: the remarkable beauty and the many opportunities to play outdoors.

In summer, kids love playing on the sugar-sand beaches, wading in the water (Lake Michigan is almost always too cold for real swimming), boating, and fishing.

Come fall, colors are luscious. Walk a golden aspen-lined country road. Look down on brilliant red maples from a high, rocky ridge. Stop and have your own mini harvest at an orchard and drink freshly pressed apple cider.

In winter, the cross-country skiing is legendary. Any kid who's big enough to stay upright on skis will get a real charge out of a nighttime ski excursion along nicely groomed trails. And although you may not see any genuine mountains on the map, Michigan boasts some pretty high hills, thanks to some helpful glaciers. Rest assured, you'll find plenty of excellent downhill skiing.

So, whatever the season, bring the family to Michigan.

ATTRACTIONS

$	under $5
$$	$5 - $15
$$$	$15 - $25
$$$$	$25 +

HOTELS/MOTELS/CAMPGROUNDS

$	under $75
$$	$75 - $100
$$$	$100 - $140
$$$$	$140 +

RESTAURANTS

$	under $10
$$	$10 - $20
$$$	$20 - $30
$$$$	$30 +

***FAMILYFUN* RATED**

★	Fine
★★	Good
★★★	Very Good
★★★★	*FamilyFun* Recommended

All the history in the Henry Ford Museum is in one room – all 12 acres of it!

Detroit and Dearborn

THEY DON'T CALL THIS Motor City for nothing. The operative word here is cars. Detroit and nearby Dearborn love their cars, their car manufacturers, and their car designers, and they celebrate them in museums, billboards, and attractions. Where else would you find the World's Largest Tire? Your kids will like the Automotive Hall of Fame and the Spirit of Ford in Dearborn, about 15 minutes southwest of Detroit. And right next door are two more must-see attractions in one: the Henry Ford Museum (more cars) and Greenfield Village. Packed with fascinating, kid-friendly things to do and learn, they merit at least a full day of your family's trip to this area. **TIP:** If you buy a ticket for both the Hall of Fame and the Henry Ford Museum, you get a discount.

You'll also want to drive to and around Belle Isle, the island park in downtown Detroit, and stop at the zoo, aquarium, and museum. The park has wide, landscaped, walkways that were made for strollers.

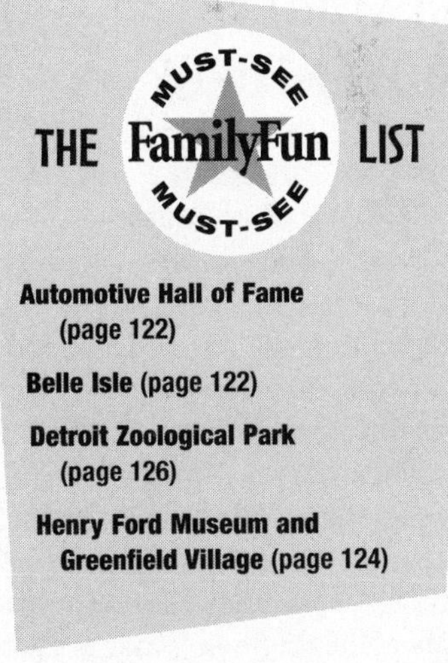

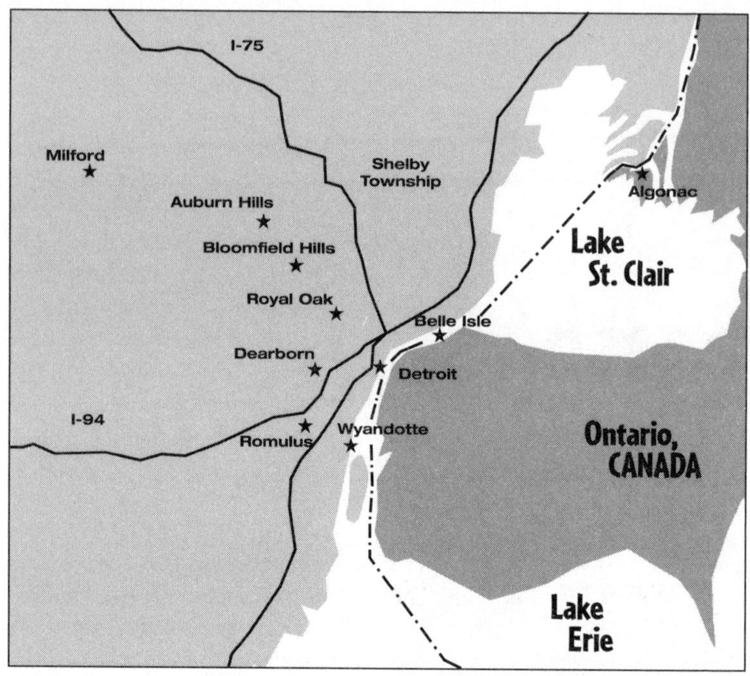

CULTURAL ADVENTURES

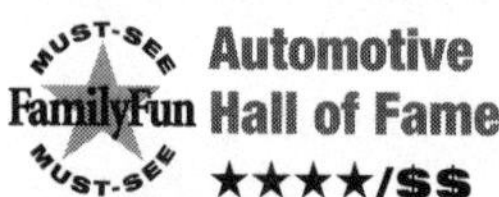

Automotive Hall of Fame

★★★★/$$

Any car nuts in your family will think this is one terrific place. Kids can start up a replica of the first gasoline-powered car, apply for a job at General Motors in 1920, crank-start a Model T Ford, and design their own futuristic vehicle. Along the way they'll learn the history of the automobile industry and of the designers who created innovative cars. Half price for children 5 to 12; under 5 free. *21400 Oakwood Blvd., Dearborn; (313) 240-4000;* www.automotivehalloffame.org

Belle Isle

★★★★/Free

Just south of Detroit, this 981-acre paramecium-shaped island in the Detroit River is now being reclaimed after years of lying fallow. You'll need a car to tour—the attractions are too far apart to walk, and the roads around the island offer great views of the Ambassador Bridge and the freighter traffic moving through the country's busiest inland waterway. While on the island, stop at the aquarium and the conservatory *(see below)*. Parents will appreciate the Conservatory's gardens, while kids enjoy the playground. The Nature Center *(313/852-4056)* has educational nature trails. Belle Isle Beach has a big water slide and a bathhouse, and you can fish from piers at four points around the island. If you're here in summer, come after dark to see the colored light and water shows at the gorgeous Scott Memorial Fountain. *To get to Belle Isle, take I-75 south to East Jefferson exit; follow Jefferson to Bridge St. and follow the signs; (313) 852-4075.*

The Anna Scripps Whitcomb Conservatory ★/Free
Your young gardeners might be interested in seeing the orchid collection here, one of the country's largest. This is a pretty diversion, but not a must-see for kids. The building was patterned after Thomas Jefferson's Monticello home. *Inselruhe and Central Aves., Belle Isle; (313) 852-4065.*

Belle Isle Aquarium ★★/$
This is the country's oldest aquarium (opened in 1904). Stop in if you're on Belle Isle, but don't come to the island just to see the place, particularly if your vacation has already included some supersnazzy aquariums—but the stingrays, electric eels, and coral-reef fish are pretty cool. *Off Central Ave., Belle Isle.*

Cranbrook Institute of Science ★★★/$$
A life-size Tyrannosaurus rex (and those guys were larger than life!) stands right in the center of an exhibit exploring the connection between dinosaurs and birds. A full-size mastodon model adorns a display that traces the mastodon's disappearance from the earth. Rock

A BIG WHEEL

Billed as the world's largest tire, this Uniroyal tire began life as a Ferris wheel at the 1964 World's Fair in New York. The drive-by attraction, 80 feet tall and weighing ten tons, is on the main drag—alert your kids so they can look for it. Coming into Detroit from the airport on I-94, look on the right (south) side of the road. As you approach the Schaefer Highway exit, there it is. You can't really get up close, but it's fun to see.

African American History

Around 1910, African Americans began migrating north in the hope of finding work in the nation's new industrial center—it was known as the Great Migration. With a large African American population, Detroit also has some extraordinary resources in which to learn about African American culture and heritage.

The Detroit Institute of the Arts ***(5200 Woodward Ave., Detroit; 313/833-7900)*****—regarded as one of the top six museums in the nation—has collections of art from ancient Egypt and Africa.**

Greenfield Village in Dearborn (see page 127) includes slave quarters on a "plantation," where reenactors tell tales of the pre-Civil War days in the South.

The Motown Historical Museum at Hitsville USA ***(2648 W. Grand Blvd., Detroit; 313/875-2264)*** **lets kids see Studio A, the original Motown recording studio (1959 to 1972), plus memorabilia from the Jackson Five, the Supremes, and other famous Motown groups (famous to Mom and Dad, anyway, if not the kids).**

The Charles W. Wright Museum of African American History ***(315 East Warren Ave., Detroit; 313/494-5800)*** **is the largest African American museum in the country. You can walk through a reconstructed slave ship and read the letters of Booker T. Washington and Frederick Douglass.**

hounds should see the minerals and rocks, and a new Bat Zone will interest bat lovers. Kids also get a chance to hatch their own storm, do experiments, and play with the laws of physics. The planetarium has traditional constellation presentations and a laser light show (additional fees for both). Getting hungry? Stop at the cafe, then hit the gift shop for toys, books, and gadgets. *From Detroit, take I-75 to the Square Lake exit. 39221 N. Woodward Ave., Bloomfield Hills; (877) 462-7262;* www.cranbrook.edu

Detroit Children's Museum

★★★/Free

Silverbolt, the museum mascot out front, is true to his hometown—a horse made from nearly half a ton of chrome automobile bumpers. The major focuses here are the natural sciences, world cultures, and fine arts. In the Discovery Room, toddlers can play with blocks and educational toys, while the older kids (4 to 12 or so) tackle a treasure-hunt map that sends them all over the museum looking for interactive attractions. Call for hours, as they change by the season. Open Saturday only October through May. *6134 Second Ave., Detroit; (313) 873-8100.*

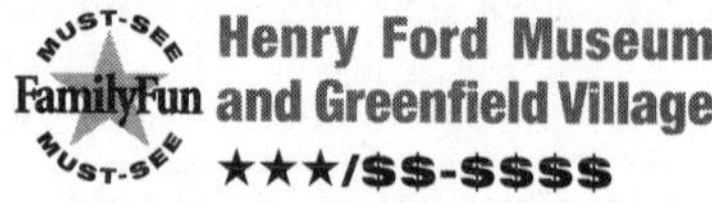

Henry Ford Museum and Greenfield Village

★★★/$$-$$$$

There's so much to do at this fascinating museum and historic village site that we've decided to dedicate an entire sidebar to it. You'll find it on page 127; www.hfmgv.org

The Walter P. Chrysler Museum

★★★/$$

If you plan on seeing just one car museum, make it the Henry Ford Museum. For interactive car-related fun, the Automotive Hall of Fame is the best choice for kids. But if your family really, really likes cars, add this museum to your list of must-sees. Kids will get a kick out of seeing the more than 70 rare models of Chrysler, Dodge, Plymouth, Jeep, Hudson, Rambler, Nash, DeSoto, and Willys cars and trucks on display here. Interactive modules teach kids about automotive technology and how cars affected everyday life in this country. The museum gift shop has car models, books, T-shirts, and more. Stop in the lower-level snack bar—it's designed to look like a Chrysler dealer showroom from the 1930s. About 30 miles north of Detroit. *Take I-75 north to exit 78; turn right at first traffic light to Chrysler Dr. One Chrysler Dr., at Squirrel and Featherstone Rds., Auburn Hills; (888) 456-1924;* www.chryslerheritage.com

Just for Fun

Comerica Park

★★★/Free-$$

The Detroit Tigers baseball team plays here. The park also has a Ferris wheel and carousel to keep young fans amused during long games, and a great view of the Detroit skyline. Your kids will also get a kick out of the dancing-water fountain in center field. In 2002, Ford Field opened next door as the new home for the

FamilyFun **READER'S TIP**

Box Cars

My kids and I found boxes big enough to sit in and spent the afternoon turning them into play cars. First we cut the bottoms out, then we painted the boxes, added windshields (from the boxes' top flaps), rearview mirrors (cardboard covered with aluminum foil), wheels (paper plates), and license plates. The cars were such a big hit!

Cindy Gwozdz, Taunton, Massachusetts

Detroit Lions. If you have any pro ball fans in the family, try to get tickets for a game. **NOTE:** The restaurants, bars, and parking facilities around Comerica fill up quickly on game days. To find parking and decent restaurant seating, arrive early and allocate enough extra time to keep everyone in a happy mood. *Brush and Adams Sts., Detroit; (313) 962-4000;* www.detroittigers.com

Detroit Zoological Park ★★★★/$$

MUST-SEE FamilyFun MUST-SEE

This well-known and attractive new zoo is designed for a comfortable family outing. Rent a stroller for your little ones at the entrance, and take the smooth, paved paths around the 125-acre park, where cageless habitats are arranged according to the animals' continent of origin. Inside the front door of the National Amphibian Conservation Center, the life cycle of a frog from egg through tadpole to adult is rendered in three-dimensional ceramic. The center houses enormous, 50-pound salamanders; big, fat frogs; exotic rain forest creatures; and more, all exhibited in natural surroundings behind glass. The Holden Museum of Living Reptiles houses lizards, crocodilians, turtles, and lots of snakes. Take the underwater tunnel through the new Arctic Ring of Life exhibit and see polar bears and seals swimming in chilly waters. Arctic foxes, snowy owls, harbor seals, and other tundra-dwellers also live here. You can board a miniature train for a ride around the zoo, and the kids will go for the wonderful playground. *From Detroit, take Hwy. 75 N to I-696 W; take exit 16 off I-696 and follow the signs. 8450 W. 10 Mile Rd., at Woodward Ave., Royal Oak; (248) 398-0900;* www.detroitzoo.org

FamilyFun GAME

Thumb Wrestling

When you crave an active car game, pack up the books and puzzles and thumb wrestle. Two players sitting next to each other hook the four fingers of their right hands together so both of their right thumbs are sticking straight up. The object is to pin down your opponent's right thumb using your right thumb.

Diamond Jack's River Tours ★★★/$$

Taking a tour of the Detroit River by charter boat lets your family see Detroit from the water, but your kids will probably be more excited about getting an up-close look at some of the huge freighters they've glimpsed from a distance. If your kids are old enough to manage two hours afloat, they'll enjoy this trip. You can buy snacks and beverages on board. *Departs from Hart Plaza in Detroit or Bishop Park in Wyandotte; (313) 843-9376;* www.diamondjack.com

HENRY FORD MUSEUM AND GREENFIELD VILLAGE

THE KIDS WILL LOVE IT here—and so will you. Worth setting aside two days to see, this isn't an industrial museum of cars and assembly lines, but a chronicle of how the automobile changed our culture, and how technology affected agriculture—one of Ford's personal passions. The museum and the village are two attractions in one. You can pay to enter just one or the other, but both are well worth seeing. Plan on lots of walking, so wear comfy shoes and bring or rent a stroller. You'll have to leave the stroller outside the village buildings, but the sites are far apart and there's a lot of outside walking, so it's worth it.

The **Henry Ford Museum** measures 12 acres—and it's all one room! Ford himself wanted to have all the exhibits on one floor, and the single, high-ceiling room and airy, pleasant design were his ideas. Enter through a replica of Philadelphia's Independence Hall. Inside, you'll see Ford's first car, the Model T; an entire 1946 diner (it'll make you hungry, but it doesn't serve food). Moving on through the decades, there's a 1940s Texaco service station, a 1950s drive-in movie theater, a 1960s Holiday Inn room, and hundreds of historic and experimental cars, planes, and trains. An original McDonald's sign (remember the real Golden Arches?) gives you a chance to talk to the kids about the world before fast food. The presidential limousine in which John F. Kennedy was shot is here, as well as the chair Lincoln sat in at Ford's Theatre, and George Washington's camp bed (which looks very uncomfortable). The Tower of Power lets kids try to hand crank enough energy to power lightbulbs. It's tough! Made in America is an exhibit of how factories and assembly lines produce goods. A large furniture and housewares collection chronicles the changing face of American home life during the last century. The kitchen displays—appliances and products from 1790, 1840, 1890, and 1930—are a hoot. Hungry? Head for the Oscar Mayer Wienermobile (you can't miss it—it's the enormous hot dog car) and the hot dog stand next to it. Or dine in the Michigan Cafe.

Greenfield Village was also a brainchild of Henry Ford. (Greenfield Village is currently undergoing underground restoration efforts and will reopen to the public in June 2003.) He bought up some 80 historic buildings—including the home of Noah Webster, the

continued on next page

Wright brothers' cycle shop, and Thomas Edison's Menlo Park laboratory—and moved them to this 81-acre site. It's a short drive (in a Model T) or long walk from one cluster of buildings to another. Riding in a Model T is a great way to see the village, and if you get the driver talking, you'll learn a lot.

Historical reenactments make things more interesting. Drive by the garage where Henry Ford built his first car, and young Henry may jump in the car and ride with you for a few blocks. Stand outside of the Wright brothers' home and cycle shop long enough, and the brothers themselves appear, in a heated argument about whether flight is possible and how their newfangled airplane might be improved.

Children can try out or watch demonstrations of all types of industry and production, including textile weaving, wool carding, printing, machining, tinsmithing, and glassblowing. The whole family can ride the *Suwanee Steamboat* paddle wheeler through the little lagoon or take a locomotive ride around the village. The train makes several stops and is a good way to get from one point to another. Don't miss the railroad turntable, an ingenious invention that allows one person to turn a 25-ton locomotive around with ease. There's the 1913 Herschell–Spillman carousel that kids young and old can ride.

When the troops get hungry, stop at the Eagle Tavern, styled like an 1850s stagecoach stop, complete with authentically costumed servers. Or try A Taste of History cafeteria, where your kids can try Abraham Lincoln's chicken fricassee or a peanut recipe from George Washington Carver. For munchies, there are also a few snack and beverage stops throughout the village.

In the gift shops, you'll find great toys, books, plus all kinds of fun icons of American automobile travel: license plates, road signs, retro photos, and magazine ads of gas companies and gas stations, and more. Ask the staff for the best package for your family. The museum is open year-round; the village is closed January through March. *20900 Oakwood, Dearborn; (800) 835 5237; for tickets and general information (313) 982-6100; IMAX theater, (313) 271-1570;* www.hfmgv.org

BUNKING DOWN

The Best Western Greenfield Inn

★★★★/$$$

TVs in the bathrooms and an indoor pool will make your kids remember the night they stayed here. The inn is conveniently close to the Henry Ford Museum and Greenfield Village, and its architecture is delightful. The sprawling campus is like a Victorian village, trimmed in period detail. The gardens have a gazebo, and a family-friendly restaurant inside a Victorian-style mansion. Each of the 209 guest rooms and suites has handy extras: refrigerator, three phones, a clothesline, TV, and a VCR. Guest laundry is another welcome amenity. *3000 Enterprise Dr., Allen Park/Dearborn; (800) 528-1234; (313) 271-1600.*

The Dearborn Inn

★★★★/$$$

Kids are welcome at this elegant, historic inn that's right across the street from the Henry Ford Museum and Greenfield Village. In summer, a weekend package for a family of four includes room, tickets to Greenfield Village or the Henry Ford Museum, and breakfast, all for less than $200. The 222 rooms include nine two-bedroom units. An outdoor pool and three restaurants complete the picture. *20301 Oakwood Blvd., Dearborn; (800) 228-9290; (313) 271-2700;* www.marriott.com

Hilton Garden Inn, Detroit Metro Airport

★★/$$$$

Stay at this pricey but convenient hotel, and you'll be in your room minutes after you get off the plane. Considered a luxury hotel, this spot has lots of features that make traveling with kids easier: refrigerator, microwave, coffeemaker, TV, two phone lines, and voice mail. There's an indoor pool and room service, too. *31800 Smith Rd., Romulus; (800) 445-8667; (734) 727-6000;* www.hilton.com

A Sporting Chance

Pro sports are big in Detroit. No matter what the season, you can almost always find a game to go to. The Detroit Tigers play in the new **Comerica Park** baseball stadium (see Just for Fun on page 125). The city's other baseball team, the Detroit Lions, now has a brand-new stadium, too. **Ford Field** *(2000 Brush St.; 313/962-4285)* sits right next door to Comerica Park. The Detroit Pistons play basketball at the **Palace of Auburn Hills** *(2 Championship Dr., Auburn Hills; 248/377-0100)*. The Detroit Red Wings play hockey in the **Joe Louis Arena** *(600 Civic Center Dr.; 313/396-7444)*.

Hyatt Regency Dearborn

★★/$$$$

Do your preteens love to shop? This 772-room hotel is in a mall. Kids who aren't shoppers will enjoy the indoor pool. Some of the rooms are very pricey. There are several restaurants on the premises; try Bistro, which has a children's menu. *Fairlane Town Center, 18900 Michigan Ave., Dearborn; (800) 233-1234; (313) 593-1234;* www.hyatt.com

GOOD EATS

Eat at Joe's

★★★★/$$

Like the name says, this eatery is at Joe's—more specifically, Joe Dumars' Fieldhouse, a 70,000-square-foot sports and exercise complex with seven basketball courts plus volleyball courts. Who plays on those courts? Well, sometimes the guys you're used to seeing on ESPN, including Detroit Piston Joe Dumars himself. Stars and amateurs alike come here to play. You can toss the ball around a little, or just eat and watch the live action overlooking the basketball court and roller-hockey rinks. The menu is kid-pleasing, with burgers, nachos, subs, and other stuff sports fans of all ages like. *It's 30 to 45 minutes from Detroit; take I-75 north to M-59 east to Mound Road north. 45300 Mound Rd., Shelby Township; (586) 731-3080;* www.joedumarsfieldhouse.com

Hockey Town Cafe

★★★/$$

If you're at Comerica Park, keep the sports theme going by taking the kids here for a meal before or after the game. It's just across the street from the ballpark, and they'll love the over-the-top hockey decor. A menu with sandwiches, pastas, salads, steaks, and chops has something for everyone. Come for lunch; this is a sports bar, so the evening crowd can get raucous. Do look in at the street-level saloon, though—it has a ring of ice around the bar! The rooftop café gives you a great view of the city. *2301 Woodward Ave., Detroit; (313) 965-9500.*

Rainforest Cafe

★★★★/$$

Part of the popular chain of theme restaurants, this enormous, 325-seat eatery serves up burgers and sandwiches in a drippy overgrown rain forest atmosphere that your kids will like. There are live and mechanical animals, real rainstorms with thunder and lightning, and a talking tree that feeds kids facts about threatened rain forests. *About 45 minutes from Detroit; take I-75 north to exit 84B. Great Lakes Crossing Mall, 4310 Baldwin Rd., Auburn Hills; (248) 333-0280.*

SOUVENIR HUNTING

Great Lakes Crossing

If you're looking for a great big mall and entertainment center, this is the one. The mall has an oval racetrack design, with stores lining both sides of the track, or aisle.

Jeepers! *(800/533-7377)* is an indoor amusement park with bumper cars, a roller coaster, and four other rides, plus video games and equipment to climb on. **GameWorks** *(248/745-9675)* is an entertainment center aimed at kids and grown-ups, with plenty of big-screen simulator games and some amazing rides. The big **Bass Pro Shops Outdoor World** store *(248/209-4200)* almost qualifies as a wildlife center. There's a 30,000-gallon aquarium with its own waterfall, and the mounted animal dioramas throughout the store are like those you'd find at a natural history museum. Some area hotels have packages that include a mall trip; contact the mall for information. *About 30 minutes/30 miles from Detroit; take I-75 north to exit 84. 4000 Baldwin Rd., Auburn Hills; (877) 746-7452.*

Water Toys

If you'd like an outdoor adventure while visiting this very urban place, take a kayak or canoe out on a river outside Detroit. The following outfitters, each about an hour from Detroit, can set you up with everything you need.

Great Lakes Docks and Decks
Rents canoes and kayaks. Open year-round. *Take I-94 East to exit 243. 7427 Dyke Rd., Algonac; 800) 292-DOCK; (586) 725-0009.*

Heavner Canoe Rental
Rents canoes and kayaks and offers guided tours. Open April through November. *2775 Garden Rd., Milford; (248) 685-2379.*

Wolynski Canoe Rental
Rents canoes and kayaks. Open May through October. *2300 Wixom Trail, Milford; (248) 685-1851.*

Lansing's got a lot of nature to explore, from the bugs at the Minibeast Zooseum to the skies at Planet Walk to the hiking trails at Riverbend Nature Area.

INTRODUCTION

Lansing

LANSING, IN THE CENTER OF southern Michigan, is the state capital and home to Michigan State University (MSU). When the legislature chose Lansing as the capital—in 1847—the site was just one cabin and a sawmill! But by the early 1900s, the town was home to Oldsmobile—and considerably more established. Even if your kids are far from college age, they'll find lots to do and learn here. There's the entertaining Impression 5 Science Center; the unique Planet Walk, where kids can stroll through the solar system; and the Potter Park Zoo. The "bug zoo" is either fascinating or creepy, depending on how you feel about bugs. MSU itself has a butterfly house and a special children's garden, plus special holiday displays and presentations.

Impression 5 Science Center (page 134)

Michigan State University Butterfly House, Children's Garden, Farms, and Museum (page 136)

Minibeast Zooseum and Education Center (page 137)

Planet Walk (page 137)

Potter Park Zoo (page 137)

William B. Burchfield Park/Riverbend Nature Area (page 138)

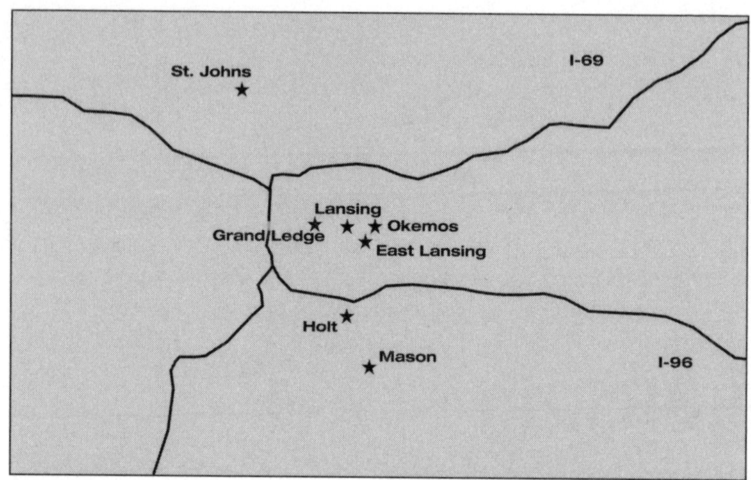

CULTURAL ADVENTURES

Abrams Planetarium
★★★/$

State-of-the-art computer graphics at this sky theater introduce your kids to the worlds above. *MSU campus, Shaw La. and Science Rd., East Lansing; (517) 355-4672.*

Impression 5 Science Center
★★★★/$

This hands-on science center, built in an attractive, historic building, invites children to engage all five senses as they explore exhibits on holograms, computers, physics, and even types of local fish. *200 Museum Dr., Lansing; (517) 485-8116;* www.impression5.org

JUST FOR FUN

Andy T's Farms ★★/$

Most youngsters like seeing the cows and horses, but city and suburban kids in particular will enjoy visiting the petting barn, picking produce, taking a hayride, and sampling home-baked goods. *3131 S. Business U.S. 27, St. Johns; (989) 224-7674.*

FunTyme Adventure Parks
★★★/$$

Dad or Mom can hit a bucket of balls at the driving range. Older kids can play miniature golf, ride go-carts, slip down the water slide, visit the arcade, or hit baseballs in the batting cages. Everyone (even the little guys) can splash around in the pool. There are three of these entertainment complexes in the Lansing area (only the Mason location has the water slide). *800 N. Hogsback Rd., Mason (517/676-1942); 3384 James Phillips Dr., Okemos (517/627-6607); 6295 E. Saginaw Hwy., Grand Ledge; (517/627-6607).*

J & K Steamboat Line

★★★/$$

Take an old-fashioned riverboat cruise on a paddle wheeler. The *Princess Laura* has tours (no dining) and the *Michigan Princess* offers lunch, dinner, and themed cruises, such as Kids Spectacular complete with clowns, games, music, punch, and cookies (call ahead for schedule). Captain John points out shoreline attractions and some of the natural details of the area. The *Princess* is especially elegant, with three levels and crystal chandeliers. Lunch cruises last 90 minutes; dinner cruises are two hours. *Cruises depart from Grand River Park in Grand Ledge, about ten miles west of downtown Lansing; (517) 627-2154;* www.michiganprincess.com

Lake Lansing Parks North and South

★★★/Free

A tricycle track—known as the tyke track—will thrill family members who aren't quite big enough to do the really exciting stuff (big-wheeled bicycles and tricycles are available at no charge). These two rustic parks have a total of 440 acres to let off some steam when your family needs a break from being tourists. Both

Fruits and Labors

City kids tend to think fruits and veggies grow in plastic bags in the freezer. Michigan's a great spot to teach them about nature by letting them pick their own food right off the vine, bush, or tree. You'll find roadside orchards and farms throughout the state—just follow the signs along the highway. Here's what's in season when:

APPLES: September
ASPARAGUS: April and early May
BLUEBERRIES: July through September
CHERRIES: July
PEACHES: August
RASPBERRIES: July
STRAWBERRIES: June

have picnic areas, playgrounds, volleyball and basketball courts, horseshoe pits, and a ball field. Lake Lansing Park North has five miles of trails and boardwalks for hiking; in winter, they become cross-country ski trails. The smaller of the two (30 acres), Lake Lansing Park South has a beach with a swimming area and pedal boats to rent, a snack bar, and a bathhouse. *North: Lake Dr., Lansing; (517) 676-2233. South: Marsh Rd., Lansing; (517) 676-2233.*

The Ledges in Grand Ledge and Fitzgerald Park ★★★/Free

These 60-foot-high, 300-million-year-old rock formations extend from the Grand River shore in the city of Grand Ledge, ten miles west of Lansing. Along the two and a half miles of wooded trails on the Ledges in Fitzgerald Park, you can picnic and, in winter, cross-country ski. Water buffs can canoe and fish along the river. *133 Fitzgerald Park Dr., Grand Ledge; (517) 627-7351.*

Michigan State University Butterfly House, Children's Garden, Farms, and Museum ★★★★/Free

Spend a day showing your kids the cool sights at the MSU Lansing campus. The **Butterfly House** in the Plant and Soil Science Building *(Boque and Wilson Rds.; 517/355-0348)* has numerous species of butterflies flying freely among the plants; tours are by appointment only. At the **4H Children's Garden** *(517/353-6692)*, behind the Plant and Soil Science Building, your kids can check out the twig tree house, garden house, and 60 tiny gardens, including one with a pizza theme and one with a Peter Rabbit theme. The place is handicapped (and stroller) accessible, and was designed especially for kids. They'll also go for the miniature Monet's Giverny, a frog fountain that spits water, an Alice in Wonderland maze, and a Secret Garden. If you've got city kids, don't

FamilyFun READER'S TIP

Scenic Views

I am always trying to make car travel more fun for my kids and easier on me. One idea that has worked very well is a picture scavenger hunt. I cut pictures out of old picture books, magazines, and catalogs and paste them on a piece of poster board. Then I punch holes in the two top corners of the poster, tie a piece of elastic between them, and hang the poster from the back of the front seat. Each time they see one of the items—an airplane, tractor, bicycle, or horse, for example—they place a sticker on that picture. My kids love this game so much that it entertained them throughout a recent 13-hour trip.

Lisa Reynolds, San Antonio, Texas

miss every afternoon's milking of the cows at the university's **Dairy Farm** *(College Rd., between Jolly Rd. and Collins Rd.; 517/355-7473)*. Kids can see sheep, horses, and pigs, too. The **MSU Museum** *(West Circle Dr., east of Beaumont Tower; 517/355-2370)* has three floors devoted to the cultural and natural history of this Great Lakes region—best for children 5 to 12. The museum store is a great spot to shop for educational (hey, they're still fun) toys. *For general MSU information, call (517) 355-1855;* www.ent.msu.edu

Minibeast Zooseum and Education Center

★★★★/$

It's got a great name outside, and what's inside is pretty terrific, too. Think "zoo," but for smaller beasts—insects, worms, and critters kids have personal experience with (and can get eye-to-milli-eyes with). There are hands-on activities, programs, outdoor exploring, and more. *6907 W. Grand River Ave., Lansing; (517) 886-0630.*

Planet Walk

★★★★/Free

If you have grade-schoolers who are scientists in the making, taking the Planet Walk is one of the coolest things to do in Lansing. Every step equals about one million miles. You begin at the sun (to scale, about 20 inches in diameter), walk past the Earth (about the size of a pen-

cil eraser), to Jupiter, 932 feet away, and on out to Pluto. It takes less than an hour to travel five billion scale miles. *The walk starts outside the science center (200 Museum Dr.) and ends near the Potter Park Zoo; (517) 371-6730.*

Potter Park Zoo

★★★★/$$

This pretty zoo is set in a 100-acre park of gardens and oak forest along the Red Cedar River. More than 400 animals live here, including a rare black rhinoceros, red pandas, snow leopards, Siberian tigers, lemurs, penguins, and kangaroos. See if your kids can spot the bald eagles in the sky. There's a farmyard petting zoo, too. *1301 Pennsylvania Ave., Lansing; (517) 483-4222;* www.potterparkzoo.com

Uncle John's Cider Mill

★★/Free

Fall's the season to be here. Your family can ride a tractor-drawn wagon, walk the nature trail, take a train ride, have a cup of cider and a doughnut, and leave with a home-

Vacation Rewards

Set up a Souvenir Budget

***FamilyFun* readers, *the Howells of Morgan Hill, California,* aren't the only ones who swear by giving their two kids a set amount of money for vacation souvenirs and letting the kids choose how to spend it. Putting them in charge has not only eliminated those grating requests to Mom and Dad, but has also put the kids in touch with how much things cost. "They're more inclined to pinch pennies," mom Cindy says, "when it's their pennies."**

Institute a Good Deed Bank

A trip to see Mickey Mouse inspired the *Mohan family of Eden Prairie, Minnesota,* to start a Good Deed Bank. "We knew that after paying for the trip we would have little money left for extras at the park," recalls Marci Mohan. So she had her kids decorate a coffee-can bank to look like Mickey Mouse. In the weeks leading up to the trip, whenever Hannah, age 9, or Dylan, 6, got caught doing something helpful, their parents dropped a coin in the bank. The kids' good deeds earned them a chunk of change to spend on vacation. And, says Marci, "We had a more considerate household."

made caramel apple. Special events are held in September and October. Closed January through April. *About 22 miles from Lansing; take U.S. Rte. 27 north past the town of St. Johns. 8614 U.S. 27 N, St. Johns; (989) 224-3686.*

William M. Burchfield Park/Riverbend Nature Area ★★★★/Free

A park naturalist conducts day camps for kids during the summer. In winter, your whole family can slide down one of the two 700-foot-long toboggan runs (the toboggans are free). Together, the park and nature area cover more than 500 acres along the scenic Grand River. Among the kid-pleasing aspects: a supervised swimming area, a fishing pond, pedal boat rentals, horseshoe pits, ball field, and playgrounds. In May through October, you can rent canoes and kayaks and hike the more than six miles of trails. There's an entrance fee for vehicles. *About 20 minutes from Lansing; take U.S. 127 to Holt Road to Grovenburg Road. 881 Grovenberg Rd., southwest of Holt; (517) 676-2233.*

BUNKING DOWN

Best Western Governor's Inn and Conference Center ★/$$

The indoor pool is enough of a reason for families to stop at this place with 131 rooms and suites. There's an outdoor pool, too. *6133 S. Pennsylvania Ave., Lansing; (517) 393-5500.*

Residence Inn by Marriott ★★/$$$

Traveling families will appreciate this all-suite lodging. Among the 78 rooms are a dozen two-bedroom units. Some suites have fireplaces, and each room has a handy refrigerator, coffeemaker, microwave, and cable TV; there's also an indoor pool on the premises and access to basketball and tennis courts. *922 Delta Commerce Dr., Lansing; (517) 886-5030;* www.marriott.com

GOOD EATS

Great Lakes Diner ★★/$

You can't really go wrong with this kid-friendly classic diner, with its old-fashioned, black-and-white-tile and shiny stainless steel. *2211 S. Cedar St., Lansing; (517) 482-0300.*

Melting Moments Homemade Ice Creams ★★★/$

Homemade, hand-packed, hometown ice cream. Yum. *313 E. Grand River Ave., East Lansing; (517) 332-0110.*

You'll get big hugs for spending a day with your kids at Full Blast Family Entertainment Center.

Battle Creek and Kalamazoo

THESE TWO TOWNS IN THE southwestern portion of Michigan are about 22 miles apart (via I-940). Kalamazoo is westernmost, and has an exciting air museum, an award-winning nature center with a butterfly house, and an interactive museum with a fascinating Challenger Space Center exhibit.

In Battle Creek, to the east, breakfast really is the most important meal of the day. This is the home of cereal-producing giant Kellogg, and cereal rules. Stop at Kellogg's Cereal City USA to pretend you're a cornflake on its way through a production line and learn what the world was like before cereal. Imagine. If you happen to be in Battle Creek on the second Saturday in June, head downtown for Cereal Fest. The World's Longest Breakfast Table is set with cereal and milk, and festivalgoers can pull up a chair. Kellogg's Binder Park Zoo is here in Battle Creek, too.

Binder Park Zoo (page 143)

Full Blast Family Entertainment Center (page 143)

Kalamazoo Valley Museum (page 142)

Kellogg's Cereal City USA (page 143)

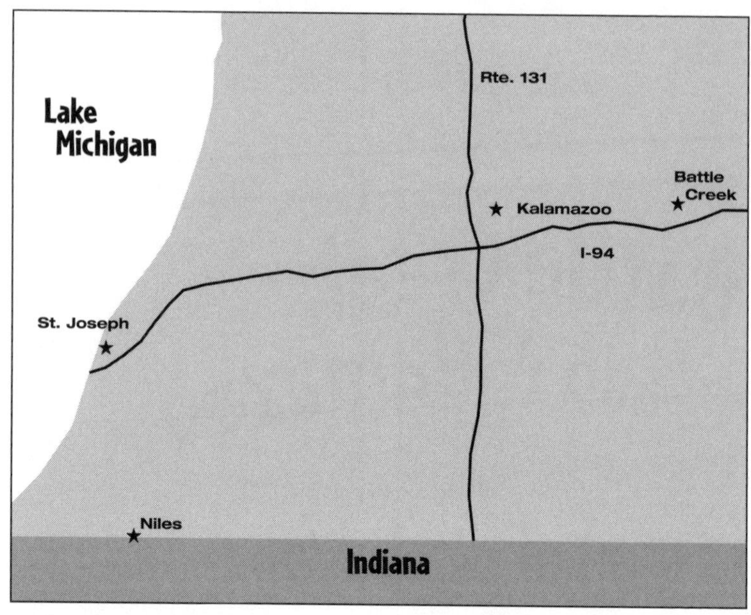

Cultural Adventures

Kalamazoo Aviation History Museum

★★★/$$

More than 50 restored aircraft are on display here. If your kids are model builders, they'll be blown away, but even if they aren't, they'll be impressed by the fierce faces, painted on the World War II fighter planes. Kids love hopping into the cockpit of the on-site trainer plane. You can also take a virtual-reality flight into outer space on a simulator. *3101 E. Milham Rd., Kalamazoo; (616) 382-6555;* www.airzoo.org

Kalamazoo Valley Museum

★★★★/Free

Visit the totally cool Challenger Learning Center at this interactive museum and planetarium. Your kids will feel like Captain Picard on the *Star Ship Enterprise* when they enter the "bridge" exhibit here. The Interactive Learning hall is like a movie theater, but on the back of the seat in front of you is a computer touch screen. A robot emcee asks questions, and you and your kids register your answers on your screens. The subjects and some of the content of what happens next—which science and nature topics are discussed, for example—are based on this interaction. *230 N. Rose St., Kalamazoo; (800) 772-3370 or (616) 373-7990;* http://kvm. kvcc.edu

JUST FOR FUN

Binder Park Zoo ★★★★/$

More than 250 animals live here, and that's not counting the bugs. The insect exhibits have some big bugs. You can walk elevated boardwalks to see exotic animals in their natural environments below (the walkways are stroller-friendly). The giraffe herd here is one of the largest in the country, and there's an African savanna environment that showcases more than 60 animals, including zebras. Closed mid-October to mid-April. *7400 Division Dr., Battle Creek; (616) 979-1351;* www.binderparkzoo.org

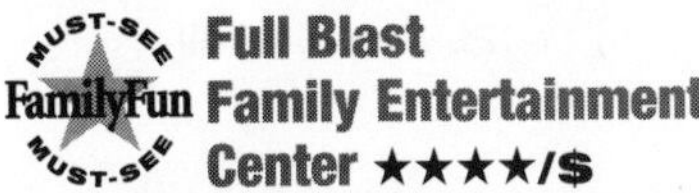

Full Blast Family Entertainment Center ★★★★/$

The indoor/outdoor water park has two 100-foot water slides, two 200-foot water slides, a zero-depth entry pool, a lazy river, a jet spa, and water play areas. There's also a three-story indoor play area for preschoolers, a virtual-reality video arcade, a computerized rock-climbing wall that simulates real climbs like Devil's Tower (but you're never actually very far off the ground), three full-size gyms, and a running track. Everyone will sleep well after a visit here. *35 Hamblin Ave., Battle Creek; (616) 966-3667;* www.fullblast.org

Kalamazoo Nature Center ★★/$

The big draw here is the butterfly house, where children can see how caterpillars become butterflies (a useful lesson to learn right before adolescence sets in). In the hummingbird garden, kids will be delighted to realize that those thimble-size bits of buzzing fluff are actually birds. Eight miles of hiking trails, and an interpretive center that lets you walk right through trees will please your nature buffs. *700 N. Westnedge, Kalamazoo; (616) 381-1574;* www.naturecenter.org

Kellogg's Cereal City USA ★★★★/$$

Yes, children, there was a time before breakfast came in a box, when kids ate grains that didn't come in funky

> **FamilyFun TIP**
>
> **Water Play**
>
> If you want to spend some time on the water, **Niles Canoe Rental** can set you up with everything you need—and more.
>
> This outfitter rents canoes, kayaks, and tubes. Closed October through April. *1430 N. Old U.S. 31, Niles; (616) 683-5110.*

IT'S THE BERRIES!

South Haven, a shore town west of Kalamazoo, is known for its blueberries. In fact, the town produces a five-foot-wide pie each August as part of its National Blueberry Festival. Even if it's not August, head for South Haven and visit the Blueberry Store *(525 Phoenix St., South Haven; 616/637-6322)* for pies, muffins, preserves, butters, sauces, and toppings, plus books about berries, berry-scented candles, and other things that will put your family in a berry, berry good mood.

shapes and bright colors. This 45,000-square-foot entertainment center proves it, tracing the development of breakfast cereal. It also illustrates the production process. Your family can follow the cereal as it moves through a copper mixing tank, see an overhead railroad drop corn kernels into cooking tanks, and think more about breakfast than you ever have before. Tony the Tiger leads kids through an interactive exhibit about daily nutrition, and young visitors can see how cereal characters like Tony get invented by playing an interactive computer game. Look up for the Tony the Tiger hot-air balloon. The coolest part of all: kids can help manufacture a cereal box with their own picture on the front. There's a restaurant on site that looks and cooks like a 1930s diner, and there's more than cereal on the menu. It's grrrrreat! *171 W. Michigan Ave., Battle Creek; (616) 962-6230;* www.kelloggscerealcityusa.org

BUNKING DOWN

Battle Creek Inn

★★/$$

There's lots to like at this 211-room inn: an indoor pool with a spa, an outdoor pool, a game room, a putting green, a fitness center, and a restaurant. You can fuel up on the complimentary hot breakfast bar or continental breakfast before setting

out for the day. *5050 Beckley Rd., Battle Creek; (800) 232-3405; (616) 979-1100;* www.battlecreekinn.com

McCamly Plaza Hotel

★★/$$$

Next door to Kellogg's Cereal City USA and within walking distance of the Full Blast Family Entertainment Center, this 244-room hotel offers an indoor pool, sauna, and a steak house. Your preteens will be pleased to find that the hotel is connected to McCamly Place Mall. *50 Capital Ave. SW, Battle Creek; (616) 963-7050.*

GOOD EATS

Clara's on the River

★★/$$

Set in a refurbished train depot, this family-friendly place has a children's menu as well as steaks, seafood, and the like for the grown-ups. *44 N. McCamly St., Battle Creek; (616) 963-0966.*

Waterfront Seafood Restaurant

★★/$$$

The lake views here are wonderful, so ask for a table near the window. Grown-up meals are inventive, and the children's menu offers the usual kid pleasers. *315 W. Columbia Ave., Battle Creek; (616) 962-7622.*

DAY TRIP

For Inquisitive Kids Only

If you're traveling up from Indiana along the Lake Michigan shoreline, stop in the city of St. Joseph, Michigan (about 90 minutes from Battle Creek, and an hour from Kalamazoo), to see the **Curious Kids' Museum** *(415 Lake Blvd., St. Joseph; 616/983-2543)*. The 6,000-square-foot hands-on, interactive discovery center focuses on science, technology, history, and culture. Among other activities, your kids will get a chance to navigate "Lake Michigan" and work on a cargo ship, and to see how an apple orchard works (they can pick their own plastic apples and make "cider"). Each year there's a new exhibit on what it's like to be a child in a selected country and culture. A cool science demonstration lets kids encase themselves in a giant soap bubble.

Plan to visit Holland, Michigan, during the May Tulip Festival.

INTRODUCTION

Grand Rapids and the Muskegon Area

GRAND RAPIDS is in the southwestern quarter of Michigan, near the west coast of the "mitten." Muskegon is even farther west (39 miles), nearly on the coast. Stop at the four terrific children's attractions if you're just passing through, and explore more if you're staying overnight.

Michigan's Adventure Amusement Park has fun on a grand scale—the Shivering Timbers roller coaster is one of the longest wooden coasters in the world. There's also a children's museum where kids can pull on waders and build a river bridge; a Fish Ladder Sculpture, where kids watch salmon travel upriver; and the Higher Ground Rock Climbing Centre.

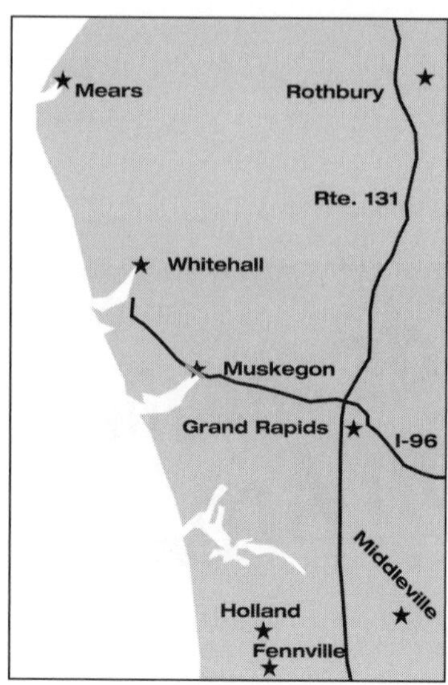

CULTURAL ADVENTURES

Grand Rapids Children's Museum ★★★/$

The 35-or-so exhibits here are certain to please your kids. Kids can become builders and engineers of giant towers made of plastic blocks and creators of giant sculptures made with about-to-burst bubbles. With a nod to the origins of the city, another area lets kids design a river-crossing bridge or pull on hip boots and wade right in. Thursday is Family Night, with a reduced admission fee; children under 2 free. *11 Sheldon Ave. NE, Grand Rapids; (616) 235-4726;* www.grcm.org

JUST FOR FUN

MUST-SEE FamilyFun MUST-SEE Fish Ladder Sculpture ★★★/Free

Can fish climb? Pose the question to your youngsters before stopping here. They may be surprised to learn that the answer is yes. It's exciting to watch salmon making their way upriver by climbing this "ladder"—a sculpture designed and built by a local artist to help the salmon scale a six-foot dam to get to their spawning grounds. Fish can be seen jumping up the sculpture at any time of year, but you'll see the most in September and October. *It's north of Grand Rapids, along Grand River at the junction of Leonard and Front sts.*

Frederik Meijer Gardens ★★/Free

Even if your kids aren't botanists, they'll still enjoy a walk through this lovely garden and sculpture park. The 100 bronze sculptures include a 24-foot bronze horse in the style of Leonardo da Vinci. A tropical conservatory, indoor specialty gardens, and both a garden shop and gift shop are also here. *1000 E. Beltline NE, Grand Rapids; (616) 957-1580;* www.meijergardens.org

Higher Ground Rock Climbing Centre ★★/$$

More athletic 10- to 12-year-olds enjoy the challenge of climbing more than 5,600 square feet of overhangs, roofs, slabs, and verticals—ranked for sheer novices or sheer terror. *851 Bond St. NW, Grand Rapids; (616) 774-3100.*

John Ball Park Zoo ★★★/$

More than 1,000 animals live in this zoo, including incredibly ugly warthogs (well, they're probably cute to their mothers). Other animals include big cats (lions and tigers) and farm animals that kids can pet. Also here is Living Shores Aquarium, offering underwater views of penguins and local fish. *1300 W. Fulton St., Grand Rapids; (616) 336-4300.*

Michigan's Adventure Amusement Park ★★★★/$$$

This water and amusement park is home to Shivering Timbers, one of the world's longest wooden roller coasters, made of one million feet of lumber. During the two-minute ride (it feels like a lifetime!), you go up, up, up ten stories above the ground, and then come down at a rate of about 65 mph. If that doesn't satisfy their thrill quota, there are five more roller coasters, plus thrill rides and kiddie rides.The water park has three wave pools, and no fewer than 24 water slides—no kidding. Smaller fry can float down the lazy river on tubes. Closed after Labor Day to Memorial Day. *U.S. 31 off Russell Rd., enter on Riley Thompson St., Muskegon; (231) 766-3377;* www.miadventure.com

DAY TRIP

This Holland Loves Tulips, Too

If you're in the Grand Rapids area in May, take a ride out to Holland for the **Tulip Festival.** The 30-minute drive (I-196 to the Holland exit) feels like it lands your family in the Netherlands. The annual event celebrates the Dutch heritage of the community and the blooming of millions of tulips across town. Kids go for the parades, dancers, music, and Dutch things to eat. Call for this year's dates (*800/822-2770;* www.tuliptime.org).

Appropriately enough, Holland also is the site of a **Dutch Village Theme Park and Wooden Shoe Factory** *(12350 James St.; 616/396-1475)*, styled after a 100-year-old Dutch town. Open mid-April to mid-October, it features kiddie rides, historic exhibits, and folk dancing in the streets. Still more things Dutch can be found at the **Veldheer Tulip Gardens, DeKlomp Wooden Shoe & Delftware Factory** *(12755 Quincy St.; 616/399-1900).* Kids won't care about the Delftware, but might be interested to see how wooden shoes are carved.

Before leaving the Holland of the Midwest, visit **Windmill Island Park** *(Seventh and Lincoln Aves.; 616/355-1030)*, with a real working Dutch windmill and an antique carousel to ride; it's open May through October.

DAY TRIP

Silver Lake Sand Dunes

Some of the most beautiful dunes in Michigan—about 2,000 acres of them—are found in Silver Lake State Park, 80 miles north of Grand Rapids along the state's east coastline. Your family will have a memorable adventure exploring these constantly but very slowly shifting sand mountains on a special dune-worthy vehicle.

Mac Wood's Dune Rides *(629 N. 18th Ave., Mears; 231/873-2817)* load 18 riders into a sort of elongated red-and-white, open-air SUV with wide tires. Kids will think it's great to drive off the road and right onto the sand. You'll travel up the hills, down into the valleys, and along the beach, where you can stop, get out, and wade. The tours cover seven miles and last about 40 minutes; they're offered from mid-May to early October. Don't forget to wear caps, sunglasses, and sunscreen.

BUNKING DOWN

Amway Grand Plaza Hotel

★★★/$$$$

A good, if pricey, choice for families, this 682-room, 30-story hotel is *the* elegant address in Grand Rapids. All rooms have cable TV, and some have refrigerators, microwaves, and VCRs. There's a heated pool, tennis courts, racquetball courts, a whirlpool, saunas, a gift shop, and three restaurants. *187 Monroe NW, Grand Rapids; (616) 774-2000;* www.amwaygrand.com

Double JJ Resort

★★★/$$$$

Leave your fussy clothes at home. This ranch lets your kids get good and trail-dusty while horseback riding, watching the rodeo, and rustling up some grub at cowboy cookouts. Best of all, there's a special children's dude resort for youngsters ages 7 to 17 (additional fee). Drop the kids off for the day, or let them stay overnight and sleep out in a tepee, Conestoga wagon, or log cabin. Accommodations for families include 45 log cabins. There's no television, but each cabin has a mini fridge, microwave, and coffeemaker—plus a two-person whirlpool. During the summer, you must buy a package that includes all meals. *About an hour from Grand Rapids. Rothbury; (800) 368-2535; (231) 894-4444;* www.doublejj.com

Grand Inn & Conference Center

★★/$$

Parents will appreciate the one-, two-, and three-bedroom suites with some with kitchenettes. Cribs and rollaway beds are available. Kids will go for the indoor pool, and the family can fuel up for the morning with the complimentary continental breakfast. *3221 Plainfield Ave. NE, Grand Rapids; (800) 445-5004; (616) 363-0800;* www.grandinngr.com

Michillinda Beach Lodge

★★★/$$$$

Part of this family resort looks like a charming country inn; the other part is in a two-story modern building. Families have been coming here for 30 years, and most stay a week or more in the summer. The 49 units are all on Lake Michigan. This is a classic resort retreat, with no phones, cable, microwave, or fridge—just lots of water play in the lake and on the beach, and hanging out with the family. Rates include breakfast and dinner, served in the lakefront dining room. You'll all have a great time playing tennis and miniature golf, swimming in the heated pool (your toddlers can use the wading pool), and enjoying the private beach. Guests have golf privileges at a private course nearby. Each evening, there are family-oriented activities like sing-alongs around a western campfire. Closed after Labor Day to Memorial Day. *About an hour from Grand Rapids. 5207 Scenic Drive, Whitehall; (231) 893-1895;* www.michillindalodge.com

GOOD EATS

Doo Drop Inn ★★/$

If your kids like fish, treat them to lake perch—a beloved dish in these parts. If they'll eat nothing but chicken nuggets, you can still drop in—the kids' menu offers nuggets and other favorites. (The place's name will tickle the funny bones of knock-knock joke fans.) *2410 Henry St., Grand Rapids; (231) 755-3791.*

Frosty Oasis ★★★/$

You can get sundaes, floats, malts, shakes—and burgers, if you really want protein. *2181 W. Sherman, Grand Rapids; (231) 755-2903.*

Canoes, Kayaks, Rafts, and Tubes

All you need for an afternoon of water fun can be rented from these Grand Rapids area outfitters:

Indian Valley

Open April through November. ***8200 108th, Middleville; (616) 891-8579.***

Old Allegan Canoe Rental

Open May through mid-October. ***2722 Old Allegan Rd., Fennville; (616) 561-5481.***

The cherry capital of the world is also home to the famously fun Sleeping Bear Dunes.

Northern Lake Michigan Shore

THIS AREA OF NORTHWEST lower Michigan is known as the Cherry Capital of the World. Orchards line the roadsides and fruit stands, and pick-your-own sites come in season during the summer. The rest of Michigan comes here to swim, boat, and fish along Lake Michigan and hike and bike along the wooded trails, like those at Sleeping Bear Dunes National Lakeshore. The sugar-sand beaches are great for building castles; you may swim at the beaches, but often, the lake is too cold (though it warms some at the most shallow beaches during the hot summer months). Traverse City is home to a zoo, a nature reserve, a museum, and an adventure park.

Tell your kids to watch the trees and campsites for black squirrels. The dark marauders aren't seen elsewhere in Michigan, but in and around Traverse City, the squirrels are pitch-black. And at night, look up in the sky for aurora borealis—the northern lights.

Clinch Park Zoo (page 155)

Dennos Museum Center (page 154)

Fun Country (page 155)

Grand Traverse Lighthouse Museum (page 154)

Pirate's Cove Adventure Park (page 155)

Sleeping Bear Dunes National Lakeshore (page 156)

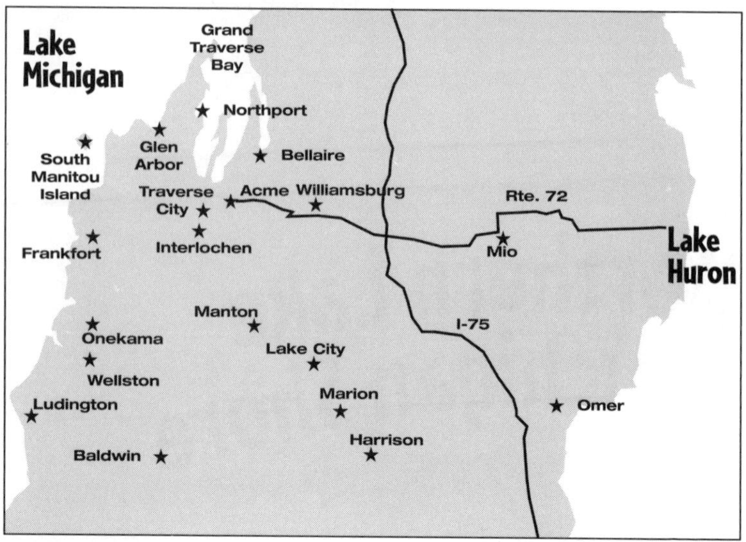

CULTURAL ADVENTURES

Dennos Museum Center ★★★★/$

This museum, at the entrance to Northwestern Michigan College, contains the largest collection of Inuit art in the world. Changing exhibits like historic clothing, sculptures, and paintings are of little interest to most kids. But for kids 3 and up, the place to be is the Discovery Room. Interactive exhibits include an antigravity mirror that makes it look like you're floating, a wall of wood panels that makes musical sounds when touched, and a video area that remembers how your body moves and then "replays" it in wildly colored images. *1701 E. Front St., Traverse City; (800) 748-0566; (231) 995-1055;* www.dennosmuseum.org

Grand Traverse Lighthouse Museum ★★★★/$

One of the oldest lighthouses on the Great Lakes has been converted into a fantastic museum! It's all in the family as your kids get a tour from the museum's curator, the son of a former lighthouse keeper. Young and old enjoy climbing to the top of the lighthouse for the view. (You'll need to buy a Michigan State Park vehicle permit to enter the grounds.) Closed November to mid-May. *Leelanau State Park, 15500 N. Lighthouse Pt. Rd., Northport; (231) 386-9145;* www.grandtraverselighthouse.com

Interlochen Center for the Arts

★★★/$$

This famous arts school hosts summer camps and a boarding high school for students from around the world. Luckily for locals and visitors, the young artists-in-training regularly present programs in music, dance, visual arts, and theater. Call ahead for a schedule of events. *M-37, Interlochen; (231) 276-6230.*

JUST FOR FUN

Amon Orchards and Farm Market ★★★/Free

Your family can visit the petting zoo, see how cider is made, and pick your own apples. In fall, kids can try to find their way through the corn maze, then choose a pumpkin (the maze is probably too confusing for kids under 5). Closed December through May. *8066 Hwy. 31 N., Acme; (800) 937-1644; (231) 938-9160;* www.amonorchards.com

MUST-SEE FamilyFun MUST-SEE

Clinch Park Zoo

★★★/$$

See Northern Michigan wildlife, such as beavers and otters, bear, bison, and native game fish. The turtle pond is fun, but it's the otters who steal the show. There's also a 1,500-foot sandy beach here, with lifeguards, rest rooms, and snack bar. Closed after Labor Day to Memorial Day. *Grandview Parkway at Cass, Traverse City; (231) 922-4904.*

MUST-SEE FamilyFun MUST-SEE

Fun Country

★★★★/$$

Your preteens and older kids will head immediately for Big Blue Betsie, a dauntingly high (more than 300 feet) water slide. Steer your young kids toward Little Blue Betsie or the Little Beaver splashing pond. The water/amusement park lets kids buzz around in go-carts, hit 18 holes of miniature golf, or work out sibling rivalries in the aquatic playground with squirt guns (where they can also cool off during the summer). Closed Labor Day to Memorial Day. *9320 Hwy. 31 S., Interlochen; (231) 276-6360.*

Grand Traverse Nature Education Reserve ★★/Free

Boardwalks and trails make it easy for families to make their way through this 400-acre reserve. Resident animals like black squirrels, birds, chipmunks, and skunks can be seen from viewing platforms. *Two miles south of the airport between Cass St. and Keystone Rd., Traverse City; (231) 941-0960;* www.gted.org

MUST-SEE FamilyFun MUST-SEE

Pirate's Cove Adventure Park

★★★★/$$

Ahoy, maties! The two miniature-golf courses here have a pirate theme that makes 18 holes unusually adventurous. Tiger Woods–wannabes will like shooting through caves, waterfalls, and over bridges. This is

Beaching It

- **Traverse City State Park** *(U.S. 31 along Grand Traverse Bay)* has a long sandy beach, fishing in the bay, and a trout stream.
- **West End Beach** *(Grandview Pkwy. and Division St., Traverse City; 231/922-4910)* has a roped-off swimming area.
- **Clinch Park** *(Grandview Pkwy., Traverse City; 231/922-4910)*, where the zoo is, has a 1,500-foot sandy beach and lifeguards during park hours.
- **Bryant Park Beach** *(Garfield and Peninsula Dr., Traverse City; 231/922-4910)* is an especially good beach for toddlers. It's wide and deep, with shade here and there, and it's less crowded than Clinch Park. The water is shallow enough for wading without fear of drop-offs, plus there are rest rooms, a playground, and picnic areas.
- **East Bay Park** *(Front St. and East Bay Blvd.; 231/922-4910)* has a shallow sandy beach with a playground, grills, and rest rooms.
- **Elmwood Township Park** *(off M-22, one mile N of M-72)* has a playground and rest rooms.
- **Interlochen State Park** *(on M-137, 16 miles southwest of Traverse City; 231/276-9511)* has two lakes, Duck and Green, with swimming, fishing, a beach house, and a boat launch.

also a water park, with a Water Coaster you can ride even in street clothes—you may be a little damp, but won't get soaked. When the munchies strike, order fast food from familiar national chains. Combination packages are available. Closed November to mid-May. *1710 Hwy. 31 N., Traverse City; (231) 938-9599;* www.piratescove.net

Ranch Rudolf

★★★/$$-$$$

Your 8-and-older kids can ride solo here, and even younger sibs can sit on a horse that Mom or Dad leads. If your family isn't into riding, you can canoe and go tubing in warm weather and cross-country ski and snowshoe in winter. The 195-acre ranch is in the midst of the Pere Marquette Forest. All rides have guides. Open for horseback riding, canoeing, and tubing May through October; for skiing and snowshoeing when weather permits. *6841 Brown Bridge Rd., Traverse City; (231) 947-9529;* www.ranchrudolf.com

Sleeping Bear Dunes National Lakeshore

★★★★/$

This park edges more than 30 miles of Lake Michigan, with lots of beaches, South Manitou Island *(see page 157)*, and water fun galore. The dunes are great to climb and play on, but don't plan on walking to the lake. It's a long, hot way in the sum-

BUT, MOM, I DIDN'T BRING MY . . . Then rent it. Bikes, in-line skates, ice skates, jogging strollers, downhill and cross-country skis, snowshoes, and snowboards can be rented at **Brick Wheels,** *736 E. 8th St., Traverse City; (231) 947-4274;* www.brickwheels.com

mer, and slogging through the sand makes it tough going anytime. You can see many of the dunes from the car if you take the seven-mile Pierce Stocking Scenic Drive (open mid-May through November). If your kids (and your spouse) are up for long hikes, try the 35 miles of marked trails; in the winter they become cross-country ski trails. In the two rivers, the Platte to the south and the Crystal to the north, you can fish and canoe. There are two campgrounds, too (see Bunking Down). *The park is 30 miles west of Traverse City on M72; (888) 334-8499; (231) 326-5134.*

South Manitou Island

★★/$

You can get to this island, part of Sleeping Bear Dunes National Lakeshore, only once a day by a ferry *(231/256-9061)* that departs from the fishing village of Leland, north of the park every day at 10 A.M. and returns from the island at 4:30 P.M.This is a place for families who like to rough it. No cars are allowed on the island, and neither food nor water is sold. After the 90-minute ferry ride, you follow the trail from the dock to the visitors' center, where you can see displays about park resources and learn about park wildlife. Kids will like the one-hour guided tour of the island by pickup truck *(231/326-5134)* and the chance to play on a sandy beach near the 100-foot-tall 1871 South Manitou Island Lighthouse. Unless you have a family of divers, though, you won't be able to see most of the 25 to 50 shipwrecks around the island. See if you can spot one wreck, the Liberian freighter *Francisco Morazon*, from the South Manitou Island shore.

Tall Ship Cruises

★★★/$$$$

Young sailors will get a real thrill when your family cruises the lake on a replica of an 18th-century topsail, gaff-rigged tall ship. The *Malabar* offers afternoon and sunset cruises that last about two hours. If you're really hard-core sailors, consider the two- or five-day cruises aboard the *Manitou. 13390 W. Bay Shore Dr., Traverse City; (800) 678-0383; (231) 941-2000;* www.tallshipsailing.com

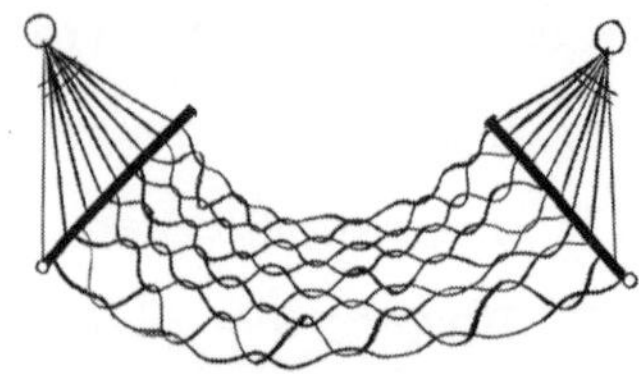

BUNKING DOWN

Most resorts in the area cater to golfers in the summer and skiers in the winter. When you call, ask about packages—special promotions can mean significant savings.

Arbutus Campground
★/$$
There are 50 sites, boating, fishing, and a beach. *Ten miles southeast of Traverse City; (231) 775-9727.*

Grand Beach Resort Hotel
★★★/$$$$
This 95-room modern hotel has rooms with varied layouts, so tell the reception clerk what you want when booking your room. Some accommodations are suites; one has a kitchen. Kids will appreciate the 300-foot sandy beach and parents will like the view of East Grand Traverse Bay. *1683 Hwy. 31 N, Traverse City; (800) 968-1992; (231) 938-4455;* www.grandbeach.com

Grand Traverse Resort and Spa
★★★/$$$-$$$$
This family-oriented resort has a day camp for 7- to 12-year-olds daily in summer and weekends the rest of the year, with half- and full-day sessions. The 1,400 stunning acres of forests and orchards, with half a mile of shoreline on East Grand Traverse Bay, also has four swimming pools, nine tennis courts, three championship golf courses, and a playground. Your kids can take part in other supervised activities, such as games, swimming, hiking, and arts and crafts—some require a fee, some don't. The Cub House provides day care for younger children.

The resort has some 660 guest units: some hotel rooms and suites, and some condominiums. There is also a deluxe tower with 186 suites (each with a two-person whirlpool), two lounges, a restaurant, and 20 boutiques. All units offer views of the bay or the golf course; some have fireplaces. Cribs and rollaway beds are available. There are several restaurants with children's menus. *100 Grand Traverse Village Blvd., Acme; (800) 748-0303; (231) 938-2100.*

The Homestead
★★★★/$$-$$$$
This is one of the few resorts that pays attention to teens, setting up a loose schedule of social activities during the summer, including canoe races, volleyball games, tennis, and pizza parties. Some are free; some have a fee. Year-round children's programs (half- and full-day) also make this an attractive spot for family vacations, along with tennis, bik-

ing, swimming, and hiking. This 500-acre resort is surrounded by the rolling hills of Sleeping Bear Dunes National Lakeshore, a national preserve. It has one mile of Lake Michigan beach and six miles of shore along the Crystal River. You can choose a room, suite, or condo in two hotels, Fiddler's Pond and Little Belle. Condominium units have full kitchens and one to four bedrooms. The resort's "village" has restaurants, shops, a child-care center, and a heated pool. The river and lake merge at the Beach Club. In winter, you can ski the cross-country trails and downhill slopes. Any time of year, parents can get babysitters at a reasonable hourly rate. Closed in April and in November. *1 Wood Ridge Rd., Glen Arbor; (231) 334-5000;* www.thehomesteadresort.com

Interlochen State Park

★★★/$$

Take your pick between modern and rustic sites among the more than 500 lakeside and wooded campsites here. *M-137, 16 miles southwest of Traverse City; (231) 276-9511.*

Portage Point Inn

★★★/$$$$

Kids are welcome at this exceptionally pretty 1903 inn, situated on a narrow peninsula with Lake Michigan on one side and Portage Lake on the other. Listed in the National Register of Historic Places,

Biking Through Michigan

Hit the bike trails with just the right bike for each of you and all the planning already done. Call **Michigan Bicycle Touring** *(231/263-5885).* They rent trail bikes for kids ages 5 to 8 that attach to the back of a parent's bike. They also have Burleys, which are pull-behind chariotlike rides for tots. And, if your children want to pedal on their own, they have plenty of kids' bikes, too. They'll also set you up with a scenic route that avoids traffic and, if you like, will provide a guide to help with flats and navigating.

More biking fun can be had on the many Traverse City area trails. **Lost Lake Trail** *(One Wildwood Rd., Interlochen State Park; 231/922-5280)* is a six-mile route through relatively flat woods that even children could manage. **Sand Lakes Quiet Area** *(3 miles south of Williamsburg on Broomhead Rd.; 231/775-9727)* is a 3,000-acre preserve with 12 miles of bike trails. **Traverse Area Recreational Trail** offers class-one biking, plus Rollerblading.

FLOAT YOUR BOATS

Northwest Outfitters
These folks will meet you at your destination with kayaks and equipment, then give you basic instructions and send you out on your own. If you prefer, you can hire a guide at an hourly rate; *(231) 946-4841.*

The following places rent canoes and kayaks; some rent rafts and tubes, too.

Alvina's Canoes and Boat
Open May through September. *6470 Betsie River Rd. S., Interlochen; (231) 276-9514.*

Baldwin Canoe Rental
Open April through October. *Baldwin; (800) 272-3642; (231) 745-4669.*

Chippewa Landing
Open May through October. *Four miles north of Manton; (231) 824-3627.*

Duggan's Canoe Livery & Campground
Open May through October. *Harrison; (989) 539-7149.*

Famous Jarolim Canoe Rental
Open May through October. *Wellston; (231) 862-3475.*

Gotts Landing Canoes/Kayaks
Open April through October. *Mio; (989) 826-3411.*

Hinchman Acres Canoe Rental
Open April through October. *Mio; (989) 826-3267.*

Old Log Resort
Open May through December. *Marion; (231) 743-2775.*

Pine Creek Lodge
Open year-round. *13544 Caberfae Hwy., Wellston; (231) 848-4431.*

Pine River Paddlesport Center
Open April through November. *9590 S M-37, Wellston; (800) 71-RIVER; (231) 862-3471.*

Rainbow Resort
Open April through October. *731 Camp Ten Rd., Mio; (989) 826-3423;* www.rainbowresortmio.com

Riverbend Campground
Open May through September. Canoe Rental, *864 N. Main St., Omer; (517) 653-2576.*

Smithville Landing
Open May through September. *Lake City; (231) 839-4579.*

it has a beautiful white-columned porch fronting on Portage Lake—but don't expect your kids to linger there. They'll be too busy boating, sailing, and fishing; playing tennis, shuffleboard, badminton, volleyball, softball, and golf; and frolicking on the two sandy beaches. The property consists of 14 buildings on 18 acres, including the 296-room hotel, ten cottages set in the woods, and modern condominium buildings. The main hotel has basic rooms with no refrigerator or microwave, but you can purchase an American plan for meals; the condominiums have full kitchens with TVs and VCRs. *8513 S. Portage Point Dr., Onekama; (800) 878-7248; (231) 889-4222;* www.portagepointinn.com

Scheck's Place ★★★/$$

This is a good stopping place if your kids like to ride; there's a horse camp and 30 campsites (but no electricity or water at the sites, so be ready to rough it) along the shore-to-shore hiking trail. You can't stable your own horse, though. *Brown Bridge Rd., 12 miles southwest of Williamsburg; (231) 775-9727.*

Shanty Creek ★★★/$$-$$$$

There's something for every family's budget at this 4,500-acre resort made up of two villages, Summit Village and the Alpine-style Schuss Village. They're three and a half miles apart, and you travel between them on a shuttle. Accommodations range from hotel rooms, studios, condos, and chalets, to the Lodge at Cedar River, an all-suite luxury hotel overlooking the golf course and the ski runs of the Schuss. Some of the 600 guest units have fireplaces, whirlpools, and decks. In summer, you can golf, water-ski, play tennis, bike on mountain trails, boat, play racquetball, and swim in the indoor or heated outdoor pools. Also during the summer months Camp Gandy is a place where kids ages 6 to 12 can swim, hike, and enjoy other supervised activities. In winter, your snowboarders will be glad to know that there are two terrain parks for snowboarding. If you're beginners or intermediate skiers, try the Summit Village ski area; the steeper vertical drop of Schuss Village makes it more fun for experienced skiers. Skiing and snowboard lessons for children are available. Daily child-care programs for all ages (newborn to 12) are offered during ski and golf seasons only; baby-sitters are available year-round. Of the three on-site restaurants, the most casual and kid-friendly is Ivan's. Ask about package plans. *1 Shanty Creek Rd., Bellaire; (800) 678-4111; (231) 533-8621;* www.shantycreek.com

Sleeping Bear Dunes National Lakeshore ★★/$

There are also two campgrounds here—**Glen Arbor** *(231/334-4634)* and **Platt River** *(231/325-5881).*

Traverse City State Park
★★★/$

A beach, a picnic area, and more than 300 campsites are here. *On U.S. 31 along east Grand Traverse Bay, Traverse City; (231) 922-5270. Call (800) 44-PARKS for reservations.*

GOOD EATS

A & W Drive-In ★★★★/$

You can eat inside, but c'mon, Mom—it's way more fun to eat in the car. Burgers, coneys, root-beer floats—you know the drill. *Hwy. 115 and Hwy. 22, Frankfort; (231) 352-9021.*

Don's Drive-In ★★★/$

Drive in and order from the car in this 1950s (really, it actually existed back in the '50s) drive-in. A real carhop comes to the car to take your order. Or go inside to sit in a booth and work the jukebox. Burgers, coneys, shakes—what else could you ask for? How about kids' meals that arrive in a paper pink Cadillac. *2030 Hwy. 31 N., Traverse City; (231) 938-1860.*

Gordie Howe's Tavern & Eatery
★★/$$

Mementos, jerseys, photos, and gear decorate this hockey legend's restaurant. There's even a penalty box kids can sit in! *851 S. Garfield St., Traverse City; (231) 929-4693.*

House of Flavors Restaurant
★★★★/$

It's the 1950s here, no question: a jukebox, waitresses wearing uniforms and bad beehive hairdos, and rock-and-roll music. The menu predates the era of cholesterol concerns, offering creamy malts, burgers, and great, greasy-in-a-good-way breakfasts. The wallpaper's a hoot—it's a montage of historic photos of the area. Kids won't fidget while waiting for dinner to arrive: they can look through the windows into the ice-cream factory next door. *402 W. Ludington Ave., Ludington; (231) 845-5785.*

J & S Hamburg ★★★/$

Burgers and shakes, plus a fish fry on Thursday through Saturday night should fill everyone up with little fuss. *1083 S. Airport Rd., Traverse City; (231) 941-8844.*

Omelette Shoppe and Bakery
★★★/$

Get breakfast until 3 P.M. here, when the place closes down for the day. It's

When It Snows

The Traverse City area is ski country, and when the flakes fly, Michigan folks know what to do with them. Both cross-country and Alpine skiing are very big here, and resorts and outfitters will set your family up with all the equipment and instruction you want. **Hickory Hills** *(2000 Randolph St., Traverse City; 231/947-8566)* is a city-operated ski hill with six lighted downhill runs, five rope tows, and 2½ kilometers of cross-country trails. **Mt. Holiday Ski Area** *(3100 Holiday Rd., Traverse City; 231/938-2500)* has 12 slopes and two chair lifts, a T-bar, and rope tows. **Grand Traverse Resort Nordic Center** *(Traverse City; 800/748-0303)* offers eight kilometers of cross-country trails, about 1⅓ kilometers of them lit at night. The **VASA Pathway** *(Bratlett Rd., Acme; 231/938-4400)* has groomed trails and hosts an annual cross-country ski race.

perfect for the kid who loves scrambled eggs. *124 Cass St., Traverse City (231/946-0912); Campus Plaza, 1209 E. Front St., Traverse City (231/946-0590).*

SOUVENIR HUNTING

Children's World

You won't find any Barbie dolls at this delightful toy store. Instead, the owners of 30 years have amassed a huge collection of traditional toys: stacking dolls, old games, wood and tin toys, bears of all sizes, stick horses, tea sets, doll cases and clothing, Radio Flyers, wood airplanes, trains, and more, all within 500 square feet! *140 E. Front St., Old Town Traverse City; (231) 946-3450.*

Grand Bay Kite Company

Choose from among hundreds of kites—simple to sophisticated. *121 E. Front St., Old Town Traverse City; (231) 929-0607.*

Hocus Pocus

Gags, games, costumes, and, of course, magic tricks are the draw here. The store owner will also give kids a demonstration of how a trick works before they decide to buy. *140 E. Front St., Old Town Traverse City; (231) 941-0556.*

Horizon Books

This family-owned bookstore regularly hosts children's book author and illustrator readings and signings. *243 E. Front St., Old Town Traverse City; (231) 946-7290.*

At the Great Lakes Teddy Bear Factory in Mackinaw Crossings, kids can create their own stuffed teddies.

Mackinaw City and Petoskey

MACKINAW CITY is at the northernmost point of the "mitten" of Michigan, south of Mackinac Island. The French built a fort, Michilimackinac, in 1715; today the fort is the country's longest ongoing archaeological dig. Part of an attraction called Colonial Michilimackinac, the dig is open to the public and is a great way to get your kids excited about history. Families also like Mill Creek Historic State Park, where reenactors bring the 18th century to life. While you're in town, take in a free concert at Conkling Heritage Park (in summer) and visit Mackinaw Crossings, a seven-acre mall with a butterfly store and a teddy bear factory. Then cross the extraordinary Mackinac Bridge, which reaches north and links the lower part of Michigan to the state's Upper Peninsula.

Some 35 miles southwest of Mackinaw City is the city of Petoskey. The 300-acre state park and nature preserve here has a mile-long beach where you can hunt for the state "rock," a fossil called a Petoskey stone.

Colonial Michilimackinac (page 166)

Mackinac Bridge (page 167)

Mackinaw Crossings (page 167)

Straits of Mackinac Vesper Cruise (page 168)

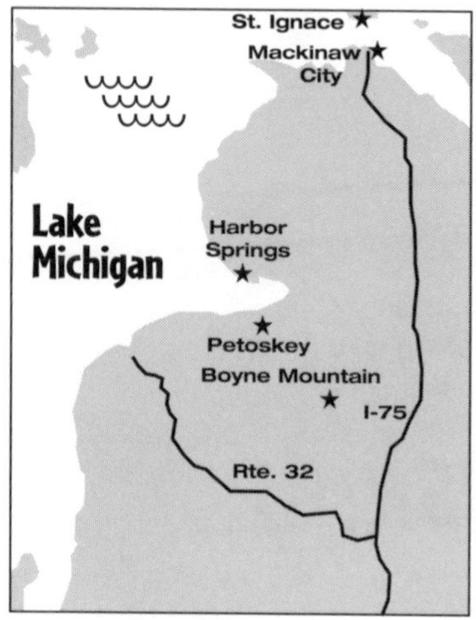

CULTURAL ADVENTURES

Colonial Michilimackinac ★★★★/$$

In 1715, the French settled this fur-trading village and military outpost. The British occupied it from 1761 to 1781. Today, the historic landmark is the site of the longest ongoing archaeological dig in the United States and a reconstruction (on the original site) of a working colonial village. Take the kids underground to see the archaeological tunnel exhibit for a firsthand view of how archaeologists work and a look at the artifacts they've found at the fort. Then take the walking tour and watch the cooking and craft demonstrations. The cannon firings are usually a hit—just warn preschoolers that a big boom is coming (on summer days, firings are every hour; less frequent at other times of year). *At the foot of the Mackinac Bridge, Mackinaw City; (231) 436-5563;* www.mackinacparks.com

Historic Mill Creek State Park ★★★/$$

In the late 1700s, a water-powered sawmill here provided the area with lumber. Today, at the reconstructed mill, costumed interpreters and demonstrations teach kids (and adults) where wood comes from. Kids will think it's cool to stand inside the mill and feel the waterfall thunder alongside. When you've had enough history you can take a nature walk (there are 6,405 acres and about four miles of wooded trails), have a picnic, or eat lunch at the Mill Creek Cookhouse. *Three miles southeast of downtown Mackinaw City on U.S. 23; (231) 436-5563;* www.mackinacparks.com

SPELL THAT AGAIN?

Mackinaw City, Mackinac Bridge, Mackinac Island: same pronunciation (mack-in-awe), different spellings. No one knows why it happened, but, hey, at least you're saying it right.

Mackinaw City Walk of History ★★/Free

This one-and-a-half-mile walk along the lakeshore follows a trail of sculptures and historical markers that point out locations of special interest and explain their history. Some big kids appreciate the historical info; little kids like the walk. Do it at sunset if everyone still has the energy. *It starts in Maritime Park at the foot of the Mackinac Bridge.*

JUST FOR FUN

MUST-SEE FamilyFun Mackinac Bridge ★★★★/$

This five-mile-long bridge is known to the locals as Mighty Mac and is the largest expansion bridge in the country. Stretching from Mackinaw City to St. Ignace, it connects Michigan's Lower and Upper Peninsulas. It cost $96 million to build in 1957, and now costs $1.50 to cross (the view is worth the toll). If you're around on Labor Day, join the natives in their annual walk across the bridge. Check out the bridge history in the city's **Mackinac Bridge Museum** *(231 E. Central Ave., Mackinaw City; 231/436-5276). Take I-75 north to the bridge.*

MUST-SEE FamilyFun Mackinaw Crossings ★★★★/$$

This seven-acre entertainment, restaurant, and shopping complex is modeled after a Victorian

Winter Fun

Just south of Petoskey and Mackinaw City is a haven for skiers, snowboarders, and other folks who enjoy sliding around on the cold white stuff in winter. Together, the region's two major ski areas—**Boyne Mountain** and **Boyne Highlands** *(800/462-6963 for both)*—have more than 100 downhill runs and nearly 30 lifts. The area gets plenty of natural snow—about 12 feet a year—and the resorts have snowmaking equipment as well. You'll also find sledding hills and tubing, ice-skating, snowmobile trails, and 350 kilometers of cross-country ski trails. Boyne Mountain is the better choice for beginners.

village, with shop fronts painted in whimsical colors and a walkway lined by dancing fountains. Kids get a kick out of the oversize cartoon characters walking around the 40-plus shops and attractions. Don't miss **A-Maze-N-Mirrors**, a maze of mirrors and glass. Teddy bear fanatics will immediately note the paw prints on the sidewalk, which lead to the **Great Lakes Teddy Bear Factory**. Kids can create a teddy bear to their own specifications; youngsters select the parts, and watch as someone sews them together. From May through October, there's a free laser-light show each night at dusk. *248 S. Huron Ave., Mackinaw City; (231) 436-5030;* www.mackinawcrossings.com

Petoskey State Park

★★★/$

Brief your kids on Michigan's official state rock, the Petoskey "stone," before you stop at the milelong beach, one of several at this 300-acre nature preserve. They'll be ready to join the other people sifting through the sand looking for the stones. The Petoskey stone is actually a fossil coral, recognizable by the hexagonal patterns on its surface; get it wet and you can see the patterns more clearly. (If your treasure hunters come up empty-handed, don't despair. The rocks are sold in local shops.) For a great view of the bay, hike the Old Baldy Trail to the top of a dune (but only if your children are 10 or older—the set of 100 stairs at the top of the hill makes this a tough climb for little ones). *M119, Petoskey; (231) 347-2311;* www.michigan.gov/dnr

Straits of Mackinac Vesper Cruise

★★★★/Free

How bridges stay up is one of the great mysteries of childhood. Your kids can learn all about it on a narrated 90-minute cruise under the Mackinac Bridge that describes the construction. Cruises run on Sunday at 8 P.M. from Father's Day through Labor Day. *Old State Ferry Dock on S. Huron Ave., Mackinaw City; (800) 666-0160.*

BUNKING DOWN

Apple Tree Inn

★/$$

The 40 rooms here all have views of Little Traverse Bay. Your kids will appreciate the family-friendly features like a VCR and refrigerator. Parents might opt for a suite or a room with a whirlpool. The indoor pool will accommodate swimmers, and the continental breakfast is free. *915 Spring St., Petoskey; (800) 348-2901; (231) 348-2900.*

Bay Winds Inn ★★/$$

This 50-room Victorian inn is truly charming. Better yet, it offers lots of extras that make kids (and their Moms and Dads) happy: an indoor pool and spa, cable TV and HBO, in-room refrigerators, and complimentary continental breakfast. *909 Spring St., Petoskey; (800) 204-1748; (231) 347-4193.*

Best Western Dockside ★★/$$

Right on the beach, and with a large indoor heated pool, this hotel has 70 rooms with balconies and water views. Each unit has a refrigerator, and you can rent VCRs. One real plus is the complimentary hot breakfast. *505 S. Huron, Mackinaw City; (800) 774-1794; (231) 436-5001;* www.bestwestern.com

Best Western of Harbor Springs ★/$$

If you're traveling with a larger family, check out the 4 two-room suites among the 46 guest rooms here. They have fireplaces, kitchens, and, in some cases, whirlpools. All rooms have cable TV and refrigerators. Get off to an early start after the complimentary continental breakfast. There's an indoor pool and hot tub, too. *8514 M-119, Harbor Springs; (800) 528-1234; (231) 347-9050;* www.bestwestern.com

Petoskey State Park ★/$

Stay at the **Dunes Campground** (one of two in the park) if you want to be close to the beach house and the main beach. The **Tannery Creek Campground** has wooded sites. Each has electrical hookups and a dumping station. *Petoskey State Park, M119, Petoskey; (231) 347-2311.*

GOOD EATS

Darrow's Family Restaurant ★★/$

Everything is made from scratch at this casual, family-owned restaurant. Burgers, whitefish, and fresh-baked bread and pie are the highlights here. *301 Louvingny St., Mackinaw City; (231) 436-5514.*

Why Are Those Trees Out on the Ice?

The kids are bound to ask, so here's the answer: when the strait between Mackinac Island and St. Ignace freezes solid, islanders pull their old Christmas trees out on the ice and mark the route where ice is most solid, island-to-shore. That way they know the safest place to drive their snowmobiles (until the ice thins and thaws).

Let your kids bike, walk, and blade freely around the no-cars-allowed Mackinac Island.

INTRODUCTION

Mackinac Island

EVER WISH YOU COULD transport your family back in time, to simpler days without video games, without frantic kids' sport schedules and due-tomorrow book reports, without the honking and clanking of traffic noise? Come to Mackinac Island. The pace is leisurely, the atmosphere historic. No cars are allowed—the main means of transport are walking, bikes, in-line skates, and horse-drawn conveyances (you and your kids will learn the difference between a dray and a buggy). You can relax and let your kids bike, walk, and Rollerblade on paths and roads—there's no car traffic to worry about.

Mackinac Island is in the Straits of Mackinac, between the "mitten" of Michigan and the Upper Peninsula. Long a destination for wealthy vacationers from Chicago and Detroit, the island feels as though it's caught in a time warp (grown-ups might want to watch the Christopher Reeve–Jane Seymour film *Somewhere in Time* before visiting here). The architecture is Victorian and colonial, and some of the oldest buildings in America stand here. The small stone churches are popular

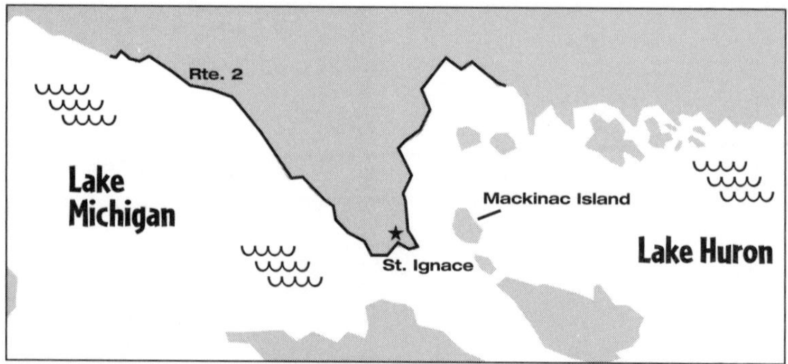

for weddings, and the island is a honeymoon haven, too, but families are very welcome and will find plenty for kids to do. They'll like the ferries, the horse-drawn vehicles—and the parent-drawn vehicles, too (rent a pull-behind cart for little ones and head out on a bike trip).

Most of Mackinac—85 percent—is a state park, preserving the island's history (Fort Mackinac was built during the Revolutionary War) and natural beauty (the limestone formations are extraordinary, and the hiking and biking paths plentiful). Have your kids look for bald eagles, take a sailing cruise, fish for perch, whitefish, and Chinook. Visit Fort Mackinac and take a narrated carriage tour. Explore caves and hiking trails. Visit the famous Butterfly House, where the greenhouse is as full of as many butterflies as flowers. And be sure to sample the local fudge. It's delicious, and fudge vendors are everywhere.

Leave your car at Mackinaw City at the northern point of the "mitten," or in St. Ignace at the southern point of the Upper Peninsula, and take the passenger ferry to the island (see "Mackinac Island Ferries," page 173). Horse-drawn carriages wait at the dock to take you to town or to your hotel.

Cultural Adventures

Fort Mackinac

MUST-SEE FamilyFun MUST-SEE

★★★★/$$

This fort has quite a history. In 1715, the original Fort Michilimackinac was built on the mainland overlooking the Straits of Mackinac by French soldiers and fur traders. The British took over that strategically situated fort in 1761, at the end of the French and Indian wars. Native Americans charged and won the fort in 1763 as part of a larger plan to drive the British out of the Great Lakes. When that plan failed, the British returned and peacefully reclaimed the fort. As the Revolutionary War began, the British moved the fort to a 150-foot-high limestone bluff on Mackinac Island overlooking the harbor, where it now stands. The British gave up the fort in 1796, only to recapture it during the War of 1812. From 1815 to 1895 the fort served as a U.S. military outpost; in 1895, the area was designated a national park.

The view from the fort is spectacular. You can see Lake Huron, Lake Michigan, and the Mackinac Bridge from the limestone heights. Watch the horses clip-clop through the town below, and see the ships move through the straits. The fort has 14 original buildings staffed with costumed interpreters (tour guides) who play period Victorian games with children, set off cannons, play military tunes, and otherwise demonstrate and explain what life was like in the fort in 1780. You might even see a court martial reenactment.

The oldest building on the island is the Officers' Stone Quarters, built in 1781. Inside, there is a Kid's Quarters, with hands-on stuff for kids to do: try on old uniforms, stroke a furry animal pelt, for example. The shop stocks replicas of the kinds of toys children used to play with in the late 1700s. Stay for lunch at the Fort Mackinac Tea Room. Closed mid-October to mid-May. Overlooking the harbor, *Mackinac Island; (906) 847-3328; (231) 436-4100;* www.mackinacparks.com

Mackinac Island Ferries

Three companies offer ferry service across the Straits of Mackinac between St. Ignace and Mackinaw City and Mackinac Island.

ARNOLD TRANSIT CO. provides smooth, fast catamaran transport. One day of free parking is included in the rate. *Mackinac Island; (906) 847-3351.*

SHEPLER'S MACKINAC ISLAND FERRY runs a tram from the parking lots to their dock. The company provides free overnight and daily parking. Enjoy coffee or feed the kids a snack at the Capt. Bill's Espresso Bar until the ferry arrives. Schedules are available at both docks. Ferries run from May to early November. *Mackinaw City Dock: (231) 436-5023. St. Ignace Dock: (800) 828-6157 or (906) 643-9440;* www.shepIerswww.com.

STAR LINE MACKINAC ISLAND FERRY offers perhaps the most kid-pleasing and exciting ride, aboard hydrojet ferries. Free daily parking, shuttle service to hotels and campgrounds, and indoor and valet parking are available. *587 N. State St., St. Ignace; (800) 638-9892.*

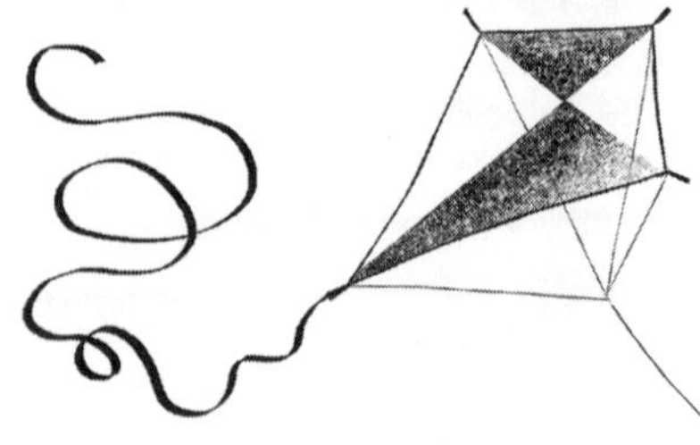

Just for Fun

MUST-SEE FamilyFun MUST-SEE

Arch Rock

★★★★/Free

It looks like a rough-hewn man-made bridge. So kids may be surprised to learn that nature made this rock bridge, which arches gracefully over the water. Over thousands of years, erosion wore away the soft lower rock, leaving the harder breccia rock as the arch. *Along the northern shoreline, Mackinac Island.*

MUST-SEE FamilyFun MUST-SEE

Butterfly House

★★★★/$

The flowers in this greenhouse are pretty, but they are mere backdrop for the real stars: butterflies from all around the world. Kids can see the colorful creatures flit from flower to flower, then learn about the development of butterflies (they started out with lots of legs and a bad habit of eating gardens, not decorating them). *Behind St. Anne's Church, Mackinac Island; (906) 847-3972;* www.mackinac.com/butterflyhouse

MUST-SEE FamilyFun MUST-SEE

Mackinac Island Carriage Tours

★★★★/$$

Take a ride in a horse-drawn carriage through Mackinac Island. It's a fun way to get to Fort Mackinac, and a great way to see the historic homes and avenues of the island. Mackinac Island Carriage Tours—run by the Chambers family for six generations—is the world's largest horse-and-buggy livery. Kids love the narrated tour that lasts one and three quarter hours. Look for the carriages across from the Arnold Boat Dock; tours return here, but you can also get out at the fort. (Also see "Drive Your Own Buggy" on page 175.) *Huron St., Mackinac Island; (906) 847-3307.*

Skull Cave

★★★/Free

Kids will like this spooky story: English trader Alexander Henry was one of only a few British survivors of a 1763 Michilimackinac Indian uprising. A friendly Michilimackinac named Wawatam hid Henry in Skull Cave, where he spent the night. At daylight, he realized he had slept on a bed of human skulls—the cave was a burial ground for a local tribe. *To get to Skull Cave, take the Garrison Road pathway and bicycle trail.* There are no tours or admission fee—it's just a local point of interest and a good reason for a walk. From the cave you can take a narrow trail up to the island's highest point, Fort

Holmes. The British landed here in 1812 and captured Fort Mackinac.

BUNKING DOWN

Accommodations on the island tend to be fussy and Victorian, something your kids may or may not adjust to. Air-conditioning, television, and video games are not the rule here, so ask specific questions when you book a room. To get your kids into the spirit of the place, have them pretend they've traveled back in time. Who knew Dad could drive a horse? And who knew afternoon tea could be so much fun?

The Grand Hotel

★★★/$$$

This is *the* address on Mackinac Island, at least for families who don't mind the lack of electronic amenities. Television in the rooms is a new thing here, although you can request a VCR. You'll have to judge if this place is right for your kids. It attracts a lot of senior citizens and people who enjoy the old-fashioned rules of dressing for dinner (Dad, you have to wear a jacket), and there are no video games anywhere on the premises. But who knows? Your children may grow to love afternoon tea, and may even develop a taste for the chamber music played at dinner. In summer, there are free, supervised children's activities daily. Families can bike, swim in the 250-foot pool, and play croquet, golf, and tennis. Breakfast and a five-course dinner are included in the rate. There are 343 rooms, and all can accommodate up to six people.

Built in 1887, Grand Hotel is one of the few remaining grand summer resort hotels of the 19th centu-

Drive Your Own Buggy

While Mackinac Island Carriage Tours are a popular way to see the island (see Just For Fun on page 174), you can also rent your own carriage and handle the horses yourself. Don't worry if you don't know much about horses. The horses know their way around town and can certainly make it back to the livery—one leisurely clip-clop at a time. Rent a horse and carriage at:

CHAMBERS RIDING STABLE (only has pony rides for kids) *Market St., Mackinac Island; (906) 847-6231*

CINDY'S RIDING STABLE *Market St., Mackinac Island; (906) 847-3572*

JACK'S LIVERY STABLE *Mahoney St., Mackinac Island; (906) 847-3391*

ry. (The hotel was featured in the film *Somewhere in Time.*) If you decide not to stay here—and your kids are into this kind of thing—you may want to stop by for the $10 tour and see the great architecture, the lobby, and the 660-foot-long porch, said to be the longest in the country. Your $10 will count toward lunch. (A percentage of the tour fees are donated to the American Paralysis Association in Christopher Reeve's honor.) Closed November through April. *Cadotte Ave., Mackinac Island; (800) 334-7263; (906) 847-3331;* www.grandhotel.com

So much **fudge** is made on Mackinac Island that **100 tons of sugar** is transported here each year.

Island Bike Rentals

Bicycles are a favorite form of transportation on the island. Many hotels and bed-and-breakfast inns lend or rent bikes to guests, including both Mission Point and Grand Hotel. Or you can rent bikes at the places listed below.

- **IROQUOIS BIKE RENTAL** *(906) 847-3321*
- **ISLAND BICYCLE RENTALS** *(906) 847-6288*
- **ORR KIDS BIKES** Also has strollers and Burley carts. *(906) 847-3211*
- **RYBA'S BICYCLE RENTAL** *(906) 847-6261*

Harbour View Inn
★★★/$$$-$$$$

This delightful Victorian manor was built in 1820 by a Great Lakes fur trader and his wife, the granddaughter of Returning Cloud, Chief of the Ottawa Indian Nation. There are 65 rooms in all. Those in the main house are elegant (probably too fussy for some younger kids), and offer lovely views of the harbor or the gardens. Families will be most comfortable in the main house's studio-style suites, in the carriage house, or the guest house. Amenities include whirlpools and balconies, and a complimentary deluxe continental breakfast. *Huron St., Mackinac Island; (906) 847-0101;* www.harbourviewinn.com

The Island House
★★★/$$$$

This is the oldest hotel on the island, built in 1852. The 97 rooms include some two-bedroom suites that particularly suit families. There's a playground, an indoor swimming pool, and a staff baby-sitter (hurray!). *Huron St., Mackinac Island; (800) 626-6304; (906) 847-3347;* www.theislandhouse.com

Lilac Tree Hotel ★★★/$$$$

The 39 suites in this hotel have some nice family-friendly features. Each unit has a bedroom with one king- or two queen-size beds, plus a parlor with a sleeper sofa; a door separates the two rooms. In-suite extras include a wet bar, refrigerator, microwave, and two TV sets with cable. Many units have balconies and some even feature two-person whirlpools. *Huron St., Mackinac Island; (906) 847-6575;* www.lilactree.com

Mission Point Resort

★★★/$$$$

This resort is on 18 acres of Mackinac Island lakefront, with beautiful views of Lake Huron and the Straits of Mackinac. The hotel has 242 rooms, including some suites. Resort facilities include a heated outdoor swimming pool, hot tubs, tennis, lawn bowling, and croquet. The Children's Discovery Club for ages for 4 to 10 has a 3,000-square-foot play area with special rooms for preschoolers, and even a 12-foot tepee. Club counselors also take kids outside to play and on field trips to island attractions. *One Lakeshore Dr., Mackinac Island; (800) 833-7711; (906) 847-3312;* www.missionpoint.com

Good Eats

The Fort Mackinac Tea Room

★★★★/$$

Tea and deli-style snacks are accompanied by a stunning view of the bridge and the lake. Children are welcome, and the atmosphere, while being far from that of a fast-food joint, is fine for young children. Closed December to mid-May. *Fort Mackinac, Mackinac Island; (906) 847-3331.*

Mustang Lounge ★★/$

It's a very kid-friendly spot, serving hot dogs, peanut butter sandwiches, burgers, and other comfort food. *On Astor St. across form the shoe store, Mackinac Island; (906) 847-9916.*

Salle à Manger

★★★★/$$$$

Dining is a fussy five-course affair at this Grand Hotel restaurant, but if your children are older and have good table manners, the historic architecture and great food are worth the extra effort. Guests are required to dress for dinner: jacket and tie for men, boys 8 and older must wear a coat and tie, and women and girls wear dresses. *Grand Hotel, Mackinac Island; (906) 847-3331.*

FamilyFun TIP

State Park Bargain

Visit all the Mackinac State Historic Parks—Fort Mackinac, Colonial Michilimackinac, and Historic Mill Creek—once or as many times as you like during the season for a reduced rate of $8.25 for adults and teens, $5.25 for children 6 to 12, and $49 for a family. *For information, call (231) 436-4100;* www.mackinacparks.com

The Round Island lighthouse is one of more than 115 such beacons on Lake Michigan's Circle Tour *(see page 183)*.

Upper Peninsula

THE UPPER PENINSULA OF Michigan tops Wisconsin and reaches east over to almost touch Mackinac City. The northern part of the Michigan "mitten" is woodsy and natural, but the U.P. (pronouncing it yoo-pee), as resident Yoopers call it, is true wilderness. Here there are 4,300 inland lakes (not counting the three Great Lakes it borders), more than 150 waterfalls, and seven million acres of forestland. Drive the U.P. and expect one gorgeous sight after the other. The Great Lakes shorelines are edged with strikingly dramatic rock formations, and lighthouses dot the coast. Families can enjoy all kinds of outdoor activities here: skiing and snowmobiling in the winter, swimming, fishing, and boating in the summer.

Agawa Canyon Tour Train (page 181)

Glass-bottom Boat Shipwreck Tour (page 182)

Palms Book State Park (page 183)

Soo Locks (page 184)

Upper Peninsula Children's Museum (page 181)

Whitefish Point–Great Lakes Shipwreck Museum (page 181)

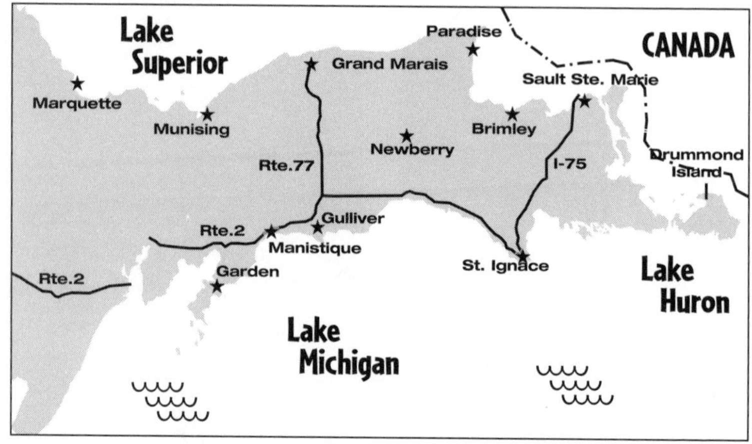

A good way to tour the U.P. is to start at St. Ignace, the point that nearly touches the tip of the mitten, and trace a rough circle counterclockwise around the peninsula, back to where the Mighty Mac bridge touches down on land again. In St. Ignace, the gateway to the peninsula, take a walk along the waterfront boardwalk. From Cedarville and Hessel, look out to the lake and see the 36 islands of St. Martin Bay. Camp at the state park in Brimley. See the Great Lakes Shipwreck Museum in Whitefish Point. Stop at the shops of Paradise and take your kids' pictures in the historic village.

Near Grand Marais, drive along the Pictured Rocks National Lakeshore to see the remarkable sandstone rock formations edging the Great Lakes. At the state park in Fayette, your family can explore the dozen buildings that remain of an abandoned iron-smelting town of the 1800s, then have a swim at Roger's Beach. Afterward, see the lighthouse at Manistique and tour the lonely-looking Seul Choix lighthouse out on the point.

Cultural Adventures

Seul Choix Point Light

★★/$

Climb the stairs of this lighthouse to the beacon, tour the rooms of the keeper's house, and try to get your kids to imagine what it must have been like to live in this isolated spot. The French name (pronounced *suhl schwa*) means "only choice." When French sailors came in on a stormy night, this was their only choice and hope. *In Gulliver, 11 miles east of Manistique; (906) 283-3169.*

S.S. *Valley Camp* Museum Ship ★★★/$$

This retired ore freighter is now permanently docked at Mariner's Park on the St. Mary's River. Take your kids on a tour of the immense ship and learn what traveling the Great Lakes is like for sailors. Reduced rates for children 6 to 12; kids under 6 free. *Sault Ste. Marie; (906) 632-3658;* www.thevalleycamp.com

Upper Peninsula Children's Museum ★★★/$

This museum was designed by kids. The Incredible Journey takes children on a tour of the human body. Also here: a mini city street with stores (a grocery store, a beauty salon); a puppet theater; and a music room with instruments. The gift shop, called Dino-Store-Us, has great keep-'em-busy-in-the-car toys. *123 W. Baraga Ave., Marquette; (906) 226-3911;* www.upcmkids.org

MUST-SEE FamilyFun MUST-SEE

Whitefish Point–Great Lakes Shipwreck Museum ★★★★/$$

The shoreline here is known as Shipwreck Coast—and for good reason. This is where the shipwreck of the *Edmund Fitzgerald*, immortalized in Gordon Lightfoot's hit ballad, took place. The ship's bell was raised from the lake and is displayed here to honor the 29 men lost in that wreck on November 10, 1975, as well as the 30,000 men, women, and children lost in shipwrecks on the Great Lakes since 1679. Fixating on the shipwrecks might make some kids too nervous to even ride a ferry—if you have anxious offspring, steer them to the less ominous maritime artifacts here. They can also watch the video presentation and take a tour of the Whitefish Point Light Station, the oldest active lighthouse on Lake Superior. Closed mid-October to mid-May. *18335 North Whitefish Pt. Rd., Paradise; (877) SHIPWRECK; (906) 635-1742;* www.shipwreckmuseum.com

JUST FOR FUN

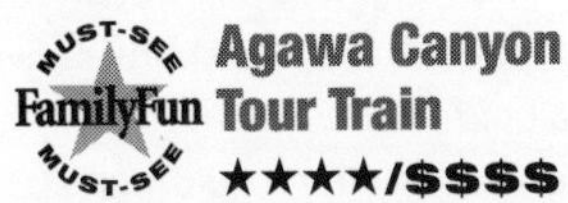

Agawa Canyon Tour Train ★★★★/$$$$

Travel by rail through the Laurentian wilderness into Agawa Canyon Park. Your kids will be fascinated as you *chug-chug-chug* through forests, past granite rock formations of the

Canadian Shield, and over brilliant blue lakes. The train departs from Sault Ste. Marie at 8 A.M. and returns at 5 P.M.; you spend two hours at Agawa Canyon Park. The trip takes 3½ hours each way, which is long for younger kids; *(800) 242-9287;* www.agawacanyontourtrain.com

Drummond Island

★★★/Free

Still a wilderness, this 136-square-mile island is one of the largest in the Great Lakes. At the easternmost tip of the U.P., it's one mile offshore from Detour Village. An inexpensive car ferry runs 24 hours a day, leaving Detour 40 minutes after the hour. There's but one village on the island, and it's seven miles away from the ferry dock. Go figure. Discover one of the island's many little beaches, and you're likely to have it all to yourself. You can also rent a bike at **Yacht Haven** *(at the end of Water Street; 906/493-5232).*

1848 Point Iroquois Light Station and Museum

★★★/Free

Bend. Stretch. Warm up. Your kids will be up the 72 steps in a flash; Mom and Dad might take a little longer. The view is worth the climb. *On Lakeshore Dr., west of Brimley; (800) 647-2858.*

Fayette State Park ★★★/$$

You can take a stroll through the grounds of this abandoned 19th-century iron smelting town. During the summer, guides will take you through the eight preserved buildings. *M-183, Garden; (906) 644-2603.*

Glass-bottom Boat Shipwreck Tour

★★★★/$$$

Wait till the kids at school hear about this. When your kids take a tour aboard the *Miss Munising*, a 60-foot Coast Guard Certified steel ship with glass viewing areas in the hull, they

FamilyFun READER'S TIP

Counting the Miles

Last summer, we set out on our first big road trip. To get us through the first long day of driving (500 miles), I strung a long string with a marble-size bead for every 25 miles we would travel. Every fourth bead was a white bead. As we completed each 25 miles, the children moved a bead to the other end of the string. Our children could visualize how far we had to go by how many beads were left. After 100 miles, the white bead was moved, signaling a treat from Mom's Bag. Every day, our kids stayed occupied counting the beads, comparing how far we had come to how far we had to go. Our first grader added the 25's and informed us often of our progress.

Jane Rice, Maple Grove, Minnesota

can see submerged shipwrecks between Grand Island and the northernmost shore of the Upper Peninsula. You'll see the wrecks of an 1880s schooner, an 1895 steam barge, a 1926 wooden steamer, and more during the two-hour tour. (Dispense medicine to those prone to seasickness before you set out.) Tours run June through October. *On Lake Superior, 60 miles from Escanaba. 1204 Commercial St., Munising; (906) 387-4477;* www.shipwrecktours.com

Manistique Breakwater Light

★★/Free

Walk out along the waterfront walkway or stroll on the beach at the site of this still functional lighthouse. *Off U.S. Hwy. 2, Manistique; (906) 341-5010.*

Palms Book State Park

MUST-SEE FamilyFun MUST-SEE **★★★★/$**

The largest spring in the state is here, 200 feet across and so clear you can easily see fish, sunken logs, and the sandy bottom. Take the self-propelled observation raft (get your kids to paddle) across the spring and watch thousands of gallons of water spurt up from cracks in the rock below. The jets of water spin the sand around in swirls that are hypnotically fascinating to watch. Don't even think about swimming—the water is 45 degrees—yes, that's Fahrenheit! *CR 149, Manistique; (906) 341-2355.*

The Circle Tour

The Lake Michigan Circle Tour is something of a tradition in Wisconsin, Illinois, Indiana, and Michigan. It's a 1,100-mile tour of all the **lighthouses edging Lake Michigan**, completed by driving the circle around the lake from Mackinac Island to the north, down along Michigan's west coast, through Indiana, along the Chicago coastline and up north through Wisconsin to Door County, back to Green Bay, up to the Upper Peninsula, and then ending at St. Ignace. There are more than 115 lighthouses on the route—some you can only see, some you can enter, and some with towers that can be climbed; 55 of the beacons are in Michigan. The tour is a great way to organize a family trip, even if you can't cover all 1,100 miles.

FamilyFun GAME

Word Stretch

Give your child a word challenge by asking her to make as many words as she can from the letters in a phrase such as "Are we there yet?" or "When will we be at the zoo?"

Pictured Rocks National Lakeshore ★★★/Free-$

For some 40 miles, the shoreline is edged with dramatic, tall sandstone rock formations, deep green forests, and sandy dunes. The maps at the park visitors' center can direct you to the trail (eight miles west of the center) that leads to the **Au Sable Lighthouse and Museum** (you can climb the lighthouse only with a guide during daily tours). There's camping, too (fee). *Between Munising and Grand Marais; (906) 387-3700).*

Soo Locks ★★★★/$$$

Kids love watching 1,000-foot-long freighters, nearly close enough to touch, being raised and lowered through one of the largest and busiest waterway traffic systems in the world. The two-hour, live-narrated **Soo Locks Boat Tour** cruises *(800/432-6301)* through the American and Canadian locks. Kids are pretty fascinated by riding up on a water "elevator" 21 feet to Lake Superior. *Sault Ste. Marie.*

Tahquamenon State Park ★★★/$$

Hundreds of acres and very wild, this park is the site of the Tahquamenon Falls, the third-largest waterfall east of the Mississippi River and the falls Longfellow was talking about in *Hiawatha.* It's actually two falls, an upper and lower. Hike with your kids through the woods to the upper falls, a 200-foot-wide sheet of streaming golden water. Four miles downstream, the lower falls splits into three cascades. It's a medium-level hike—too tough for toddlers, but grade-schoolers can handle it. You can also rent a boat and row across to an island for a better look. Or, take the 6½-hour Toonerville train and boat trip from Soo Junction. *Newberry; (888) 778-7246; (906) 492-3415.*

BUNKING DOWN

Drummond Island Yacht Haven ★★/$$

There's actually something for everyone at this lovely place. Some of the 20 waterfront cottages have fireplaces here at the island's largest marina. Good for large families, they sleep up to eight people and have full kitchens with microwaves. One cottage has two baths, the rest have one. Your kids can play on the beach, and you can rent boats. *Drummond Island; (800) 543-4743.*

Ojibway Ramada Plaza

★★/$$$

With a heated pool for kids and a sauna and whirlpool for road-weary parents, this 71-room historic hotel is a good family stop. The top-notch restaurant and the lounge are both kid-friendly and have children's menus. The rooms overlook the locks. Ask about the Agawa Canyon Tour Train package. *240 W. Portage Ave., Sault Ste. Marie; (906) 632-4100;* www.waterviewhotels.com

Sault Ste. Marie Holiday Inn Express

★★★/$$

You can get package deals for lodging and the Agawa Canyon Train Tour and Soo Locks Boat Tour here. There are 97 rooms and five suites, some with whirlpools. Kids will go for the indoor pool and complimentary breakfast bar. Parents will appreciate the guest laundry room if the suitcase is filled with dirty clothes. *1171 Riverview Way, Sault Ste. Marie; (800) 632-7879; (906) 632-3999;* www.holiday-inn.com

Straits State Park

★★★/$$

A beachside campground with electricity at each site, plus central showers and flush toilets. *St. Ignace; (800) 447-2757; (906) 643-8620.*

Woodmoore Resort

★★/$$$

Stay in the 40-room log lodge or in one of the cottages and log homes, which have from one to five bedrooms. Hotel rooms have a refrigerator, TV, and VCR. Cabins have complete kitchens and VCRs. Boat rentals, a heated pool, and a sandy beach provide entertainment here. There's a family restaurant and a gourmet waterfront restaurant, too. *Drummond Island; (800) 999-6343.*

GOOD EATS

Abner's

★/$

The buffet makes feeding kids quick and easy. They can just pick what they want out of the lineup of home-cooked food. The wood floors and fireplace give it a homey feel. *2865 I-75 Business Spur, Sault Ste. Marie; (906) 632-4221.*

Freighters

★★★/$$

This restaurant overlooks the Soo Locks, so you get a view to enjoy along with your meal. There's a children's menu, and you get a nice price break if you come early for dinner. *240 W. Portage, Sault Ste. Marie; (906) 632-4211.*

Illinois

FROM THE sights, flavors, and scents of one of the world's great cities—Chicago—to the simple country pleasures of a home-baked pie in Amish country, Illinois delivers diverse delights for every member of the family.

You'll find great history lessons here, particularly in Springfield, where memorials and museums chronicle the life and times of native son Abraham Lincoln. In Arcola and Arthur, your kids will be exposed to a different way of life as they meet Amish farm families living much as their parents, grandparents, and

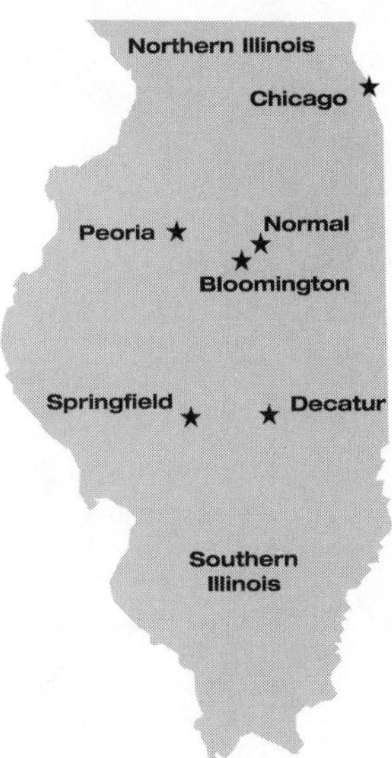

great-grandparents did. And the history of Superman is told in Metropolis, the town where the "Man of Steel" comics are set. The state's boundaries, Lake Michigan and three rivers—the Mississippi, the Ohio, and the Wabash—are both scenic and full of places to boat, hike, swim, and the like.

The cultural and fun feast to be found in Chicago is the stuff of lifelong memories: a trip to the moon (at the Adler Planetarium), a visit with Sue, the Tyrannosaurus rex (at the Field Museum), a walk through the heart of a girl named Kathy (at the Health Museum), a spin on the carousel at Lincoln Park Zoo–and, of course, the view from the Sears Tower Skydeck.

ATTRACTIONS

$	under $5
$$	$5 - $15
$$$	$15 - $25
$$$$	$25 +

HOTELS/MOTELS/CAMPGROUNDS

$	under $75
$$	$75 - $100
$$$	$100 - $140
$$$$	$140 +

RESTAURANTS

$	under $10
$$	$10 - $20
$$$	$20 - $30
$$$$	$30 +

***FAMILYFUN* RATED**

★	Fine
★★	Good
★★★	Very Good
★★★★	*FamilyFun* Recommended

Chicago's Navy Pier juts 3,300 feet into Lake Michigan and is home to a skating rink, tropical garden, ferris wheel, carousel, and more.

Chicago

GAZING AT THE SKYLINE, which has some of the tallest and most distinctive skyscrapers in the world, is a great way to introduce your kids to the nation's All-American city. The skyline and the architecture are recognized across the country as being pure "Chicago style." It's a style due, in no small part, to rebuilding after the great fire of 1871. Nearly a third of the city was destroyed, and 300 people were killed in the fire, which was long blamed on Mrs. O'Leary's cow kicking over a lantern. (The jury is still out on the cow's culpability, however: it seems that the man who fingered the bovine couldn't see the barn from his vantage point.)

There's a wealth of awesome art and architecture here. Challenge your kids to try to count the buildings. Can they find the John

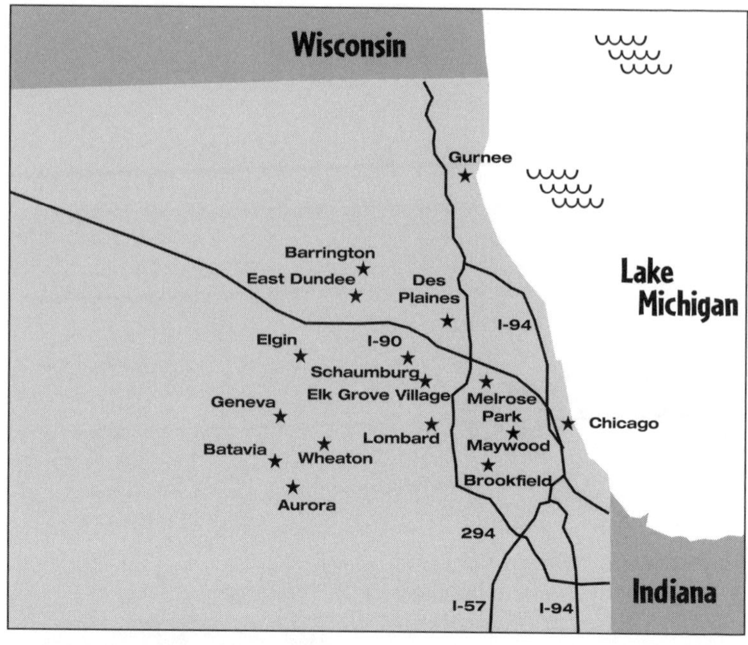

Hancock Tower? The Sears Tower? Wrigley Field? Tell them to look for sculpture, too. The works of Picasso, Claes Oldenburg, Chagall, and Calder decorate the city's plazas. In addition, many famous and infamous characters were born, lived in, or visited Chicago over the years: Abe Lincoln, Al Capone, Ernest Hemingway, Carl Sandburg, and Tokyo Rose.

There's so much to see and do in Chicago that it's not possible to do it all—don't even try. Fortunately, you can be selective. Whatever your kids' interests, they'll find a museum to match: Adler Planetarium, the Chicago Children's Museum, the Field Museum of Natural History, the Museum of Science and Industry (home to the U-505, the only German submarine captured by the United States during World War II), and Health World. One of the country's finest zoos, Brookfield Zoo, is in the area, and Lincoln Park Zoo is in the city proper.

Chicago is fun to explore with children. Its public spaces are, for the most part, clean, and the wonderful lakefront along Lake Michigan is lined with parks, a zoo, amusements, attractions, and sports fields and playing areas. The result: the whole city plays at the lakefront, walking and jogging along its paths and gathering at special events at Lincoln Park and on Navy Pier. **NOTE:** In addition to Chicago, attractions are listed in the suburban communities of Aurora, Oak Park, Brookfield, Evanston, Elk Grove Village, Glencoe, Glenview, Wilmette, and South Holland. You can reach most of these places easily by car. You can also take the "El" (elevated train—the Chicago Transit Authority rapid transit line; *312/836-7000*) out from the city to some suburban stops.

Cultural Adventures

Adler Planetarium and Astronomy Museum
★★★/$$

More than just a domed screen with stars, this place has three floors of exhibits about space exploration, telescopes, the solar system, and astronomy to capture the imaginations of star-struck kids. Hands-on activities help them to understand concepts like the phases of the moon and gravitational pull. A look at the Atwood Sphere, the 1913 planetarium that simulated a night sky using small holes punched through the roof, will help youngsters appreciate the new state-of-the art planetarium, which has a ground-level telescope and a view of Lake Michigan.

The steep escalator up to the Zeiss Sky Theater is fun, but hang on tight to any family members who aren't fond of heights—it's designed to look as if it's traveling through space. Younger kids will get a better grip on the mysteries of the cosmos from watching the cartoons in the theater, which also offers programs for preschoolers (check for schedule).

The Sky Pavilion's four galleries include the StarRider Theater, where a virtual-reality show uses flight-simulator-style technology to let your family imagine themselves as colonists on Mars. You decide together which route to take and how to create the colony. Then everybody can lie back in their chairs to experience the 3-D film projected onto the dome. **NOTE:** The SkyRider, which uses technology similar to an IMAX theater, may be too much for preschoolers. If you've got little ones, stick to the Zeiss Sky Theater. For a kid-friendly but classy lunch, try Galileo's, the planetarium restaurant. You get views of the Chicago skyline and an expanse of Lake Michigan. The kids' menu features such faves as hot dogs and pizza. *1300 S. Lake Shore Dr., Chicago; (312) 322-0300; (312) 922-7827;* www.adlerplanetarium.org

FamilyFun TIP

Q & A

Laminate a map of your route, then create question-and-answer cards keyed to highlights along the way. Play with them like flash cards.

Art Institute of Chicago

★★/$$

After you've taken the requisite snapshot of your kids and the bronze lions in front, go inside and pick up the special guidebooks for children at the Kraft Education Center and follow the exhibit route they suggest. A few favorite exhibits continue to delight young visitors. The Thorne Miniatures are 68 dollhouse-like rooms, some of which are models of very famous places, decorated with tiny furniture, books, and toys. Gunsalus Hall has walls lined with medieval suits of armor, swords, and horse equipment.

The Kraft Education Center is the most kid-friendly exhibit in the house. Using computer games, music, and works of art, it helps kids understand art better; they can even try out artistic techniques that mirror methods artists used to create some of the great works in the museum. The Family Room is a nice place to take some quiet time with toddlers, and you can usually find original children's book illustrations in gallery 16. And do have your kids at least stand in front of some of the Impressionist masterpieces and the Rodin sculptures, whether they are quite ready to appreciate them or not—they just shouldn't be missed. Kid-pleasing snacks—hot dogs and pizza—can be found at the Court Cafeteria, or in summer, have a more relaxed meal in the Garden Restaurant (but be aware that the food in these places is generally pretty pricey for what you get). No admission charge on Tuesday. *111 S. Michigan Ave., at Adams, Chicago; (312) 443-3600;* www.artic.edu

MUST-SEE FamilyFun MUST-SEE Chicago Children's Museum

★★★★/$$

This three-story interactive museum scores high on the kid-o-meter. A replica of an 1850s schooner has a real crow's nest and deck for climbing, a rope bridge, a gangplank, and a slide down to the aquarium. Preschoolers can explore the Tree House Trails and the city hospital, complete with its own ambulance. Playmaze, the news broadcast center, and the art studio are fun, too. Face to Face, an important video presentation dealing with prejudice and discrimination, is riveting. The two 50-foot towers have some awesome exhibits: one about air, the other about water. Your kids can fuel an airplane, set a propeller spinning, and pilot a plane at Terminal

2, designed to resemble part of O'Hare International Airport. There's so much more for kids to do here: pull on raincoats in the water tower, where they pump and shoot water to move waterwheels and fill streams, dig for dinosaur bones in a real excavation pit, and stop by the Inventing Lab to create their own inventions. No admission charge on Thursday evening. *On the Navy Pier, 700 E. Grand Ave., Chicago; (312) 527-1000.*

Chicago holds the world's largest **public library** with a collection of more than **2 million books!**

Chicago Historical Society ★★/$

If you want your kids to get a feel for the rich history of Chicago, head to the historical society. You can tour exhibits on the Chicago fire, pioneer life in the region, and American colonial life. No admission charge on Monday. *Clark St. at North Ave., Chicago; (312) 642-4600;* www.chicagohistory.org

Field Museum ★★★★/$$

FamilyFun MUST-SEE

Sue, the Tyrannosaurus rex that the museum worked for years to assemble, is now up and accepting visitors. Your family, no doubt, will be most pleased to meet her. This natural history museum was built in 1893 and remains one of the nation's best. It covers more than nine acres and holds more than 19 million specimens. Other kid favorites include a four-story brachiosaurus just inside the door and a life-size tomb to explore at the Inside Ancient Egypt exhibit. Your over-8 crowd will delight in the many interactive activities. (The chance to pull a three-ton stone block at the Egypt exhibit never fails to inspire some friendly sibling rivalry.) Life Over Time is another kid-pleasing exhibit—computers, light shows, and games help explain how dinosaurs evolved. Push a button to hear the huge creatures roar, another to hear their thundering footsteps, and a fun one to smell their dino bad breath (yuk!). *Roosevelt Rd. at Lakeshore Dr., Chicago; (312) 922-9410;* www.fieldmuseum.org

Health World ★★/$$

Honest, this is fun. Just inside the doors, kids meet Kelly, a 95-foot-long fiberglass Little League player lying on the floor. She's two stories high, and your family can walk around inside her to learn about human anatomy. Stroll through her heart and stop in her backpack (the Brain Theater) to see a presentation of what a child's body goes through on a typical day. It even includes some bumps and bruises. Among the exhibits in this 85,000-square-foot museum is one that lets kids practice bike safety on a virtual bike ride, and see what doctors see when they stick that thing in your ear. Kids can also check out the inside of a real ambulance. Parents will like the exhibit that shows kids the germs that live on their hands (a special lotion makes them glow under ultraviolet light); they'll stop complaining when you ask them to wash their hands before meals. *Approximately 50 miles northwest of Chicago. Take Rte. 294 north to Hwy. 90 west; take 90 to Barrington Rd. north; take Barrington Rd. to Dundee Rd.; right on Dundee for a half-mile and turn left to Grove. 1301 S. Grove Ave., Barrington; (847) 842-9100;* www.healthworldmuseum.org

Museum of Broadcast Communications ★★/Free

Your kids may be surprised to learn that televisions used to have little screens and were kept in great big furniture cabinets. And wait until they see the radios that grandma and grandpa used to gather around. The displays of vintage broadcast equipment and hands-on activities will keep your children's interest throughout this museum. Particularly amusing is an exhibit featuring award-winning commercials from around the globe; another showcases great moments in televised sports. Make sure to call ahead *(312/629-6010)* and make reservations for MBC NewsCenter, where your kids can put on blue blazers and deliver the news on camera. For a fee (a steep one!) you can take home a tape of their television debut. *Michigan Ave. at Washington St., Chicago; (312) 629-6000;* www.museum.tv

MUST-SEE FamilyFun MUST-SEE Museum of Science and Industry ★★★/$$

Set in the reconstructed Palace of Fine Arts from the 1893 Columbian Exhibition, this famed science museum encompasses 15 acres of exhibits in 75 exhibition halls. Save your energy and let your kids pull the levers, push the buttons, and work

FamilyFun READER'S TIP

It's in the Cards

My family loves to travel, and I have found a wonderful way to preserve our vacation memories. First, we buy postcards at all the different locations we visit. On the back, I jot down the highlights of the trip or funny things that happened while we were there. After we have returned home, I laminate the postcards, punch holes in the top left corners, and put them all on a ring clip. It's exciting to see all of the places we have been, and the cards are inexpensive souvenirs of our travels.

Stefanie Wirths, Camdenton, Missouri

the computers. The museum does a stellar job of converting complicated scientific concepts into interesting, well-designed exhibits accessible to most age groups.

Kids can walk through a 16-foot-high model of a human heart; explore virtual reality; take an underground train through a working coal mine; see a real World War II submarine close up. Your preschoolers will love Curiosity Place, a scaled-down, interactive exhibit designed to spark their interest in science. The Henry Crown Space Center and Omnimax Theater is a must-see for space and astronomy lovers. Examine a space station, see the real *Apollo 8* and *Aurora 7*, and watch a film on a five-story-high screen with 70 speakers. No admission charge on Thursday. *In Jackson Park, at 57th St. and Lake Shore Dr., Chicago; (773) 684-1414;* www.msichicago.org

Scitech ★★/$$

Your kids can try the more than 200 hands-on science exhibits that let them conduct experiments and learn about magnetic fields, color and light, mathematics, astronomy, heat, subatomic physics, and more. They can turn themselves into giant soap bubbles, send a balloon up in the air, look into the sun through a telescope, and stroll through a tornado. Some exhibits are created and produced by children for children. They look a bit amateurish, but they also offer a nice kid-to-kid perspective. *18 W. Benton St., Aurora; (630) 859-3434;* www.scitech.mus.il.us

Just for Fun

American Girl Place
★★/Free

If your daughter loves the popular book series and dolls, this is a must-see. The entire line of American Girl dolls and merchandise, including sometimes-hard-to-find accessories, and girl-size clothing that matches the dolls' garments is here. Dioramas for each doll/character are miniature history lessons about what everyday life was like during specific periods and locations. How did they carry books to school? (Book straps came before backpacks.) How did they dress for rain? What did they eat for lunch? What were they allowed to do? After browsing and buying, see the live musical production (fee) based on six American Girl characters and their adventures; reservations are required. *111 E. Chicago Ave., Chicago; (877) 247-5223;* www.americangirl.com

Brookfield Zoo (Chicago Zoological Park) ★★★/$$

This wonderful zoo is one of the largest in the country, with more than 2,700 animals, many from Africa and Asia, living in natural habitats that cover 216 acres.

Highlights include the Fragile Rainforest, which showcases life in the humid rain forests of Asia; the Fragile Hunters section features jaguars, Siberian tigers, African lions, Amur, and snow leopards in outdoor environments; and the Fragile Desert reveals the sometimes easily overlooked life forms that live in desert sands. These three areas make up the Fragile Kingdom, and offer a quick and effective lesson on how all species depend on one another to protect the chain of life.

In Tropic World, A Primate's Journey lets children walk right into a rain forest and see a plethora of creatures living together in the jungle. It really rains in here, but the primates, mammals, and birds (and the 50-foot-high trees) are the only things that get wet. Habitat Africa! The Savanna is a new exhibit where kids can see giraffes, birds, reptiles, and zebras gather at a water hole in a five-acre savannah.

Habitat Africa! The Forest, also new to the zoo, features animals from Africa's Itwi rain forest: okapi (a relative of the giraffe), duiker (forest antelope), forest buffalo, and a millipede that's almost a foot long!

The Living Coast: A World of Surprising Connections shows kids how sharks, sea turtles, moon jellies, penguins, bats, and birds share the coasts of Peru and Chile, out in the water and up on the shore.

The Swamp: Wonders of Our Wetlands features dramatic tupelo and cypress trees, home to egrets, salamanders, and water snakes, and an Illinois river animal neighborhood whose residents include an alligator, snapping turtle, river otters, and fish.

Salt Creek Wilderness is a nature preserve–style exhibit with a boardwalk tour through a wetland, with toads, bugs, and raccoons. Skip this one if your legs are tired or your kids cranky.

Check schedules posted throughout the zoo for times for the daily dolphin show at the Seven Seas Dolphinarium. Arrive early enough to check out the noisy sea lions, seals, and walruses outside. There's an extra charge for this show.

Take the guided tour aboard the Motor Safari tram to get an overview of the zoo. In winter, parents will appreciate the Snowball Express bus, which carries you from exhibit to exhibit and cuts down on the chills. Concession stands throughout the zoo offer burgers, hot dogs, pizza, and Mexican food. No admission

FamilyFun GAME

GUESS MOBILE

Name a guessmaster—the person who poses a guessing challenge. He or she could ask passengers to guess the color of the next passing car, or how long before you get to the next town. Or, with three clues, what it is that someone else sees.

charge Tuesday and Thursday October through March. Fee for parking. *Fourteen miles southwest of Chicago. Take Rte. 290 west to First Ave., go south and follow signs. First Ave. and 31st St., Brookfield; (708) 485-0263, ext. 267;* www.brookfieldzoo.org

Caldwell Woods ★★/Free

When your kids get tired of museums and want to get outside, bring them here. In warm weather, you can hike the trails, take the prairie and wetland walk, picnic, and try out the Whealan Aquatic Center, with a pool, water slides, and a kiddie play area with sprinklers and water sprays. In cold weather, rent a toboggan and shoot down the impressive snow and ice slides, or bring your skates (no rentals here) and execute figure eights on the outdoor rink. *6200 W. Devon Ave., Chicago; (773) 775-1666.*

Comiskey Park ★★/$$-$$$

Catch a baseball game (and maybe a high fly ball) at the home of the Chicago White Sox. If you want to bypass the concession stands, bring along some sandwiches and eat them in the family picnic areas below the bleachers. *333 W. 35th St., Chicago; (312) 674-1000;* www.whitesox.com

ESPN Zone ★★/$$

Yes, this is a sports bar, and yes, you can eat here, but to kids, this is a 33,000-square-foot play zone. They can shoot baskets and see how their performances compare with those of the NBA players who have played hoops here. Pick a family goalie and take shots at him or her on simulated ice. Try out the rock-climbing wall (it moves up and down!). See if your young gridiron fans can toss a football through the hole in the moving players. Every sports-themed arcade and video game you can imagine is here, and even the rest rooms seem to have been designed by kids—there are televisions tuned to ESPN in there! Mom and Dad will want to spend some time in the Screening Room reclining in leather chairs and watching the big game on a 16-by-13-foot—not inch—screen. When your team gets hungry, eat at the Studio Grill, where kids can look

TOP DOGS

You may have eaten hot dogs at the ballpark or a backyard barbecue, but have you ever had one Chicago style? The classic food is often served in the Windy City topped with yellow mustard, green relish, onions, a dill pickle wedge, tomato slices, celery salt, and optional sport peppers.

into a View-Master at their food choices. *43 E. Ohio St., Chicago; (312) 644-3776;* www.espnzone.com

Grant Park ★★/Free

This lakefront park is home to the **Art Institute, Adler Planetarium**, and the **Field Museum** *(see pages 191, 192, and 193)*, a rose garden, and Augustus Saint-Gaudens's *Seated Statue of Lincoln.* Kids also love Buckingham Memorial Fountain, which measures 280 feet across and shoots water 135 feet into the air. May through October, families can see special light shows at the fountain daily between 9 and 11 P.M. Be sure to walk, or at least drive, by. *East of Lake Shore Dr., between Randolph St. and Michigan Ave.; (312) 294-2493.*

The Hancock Observatory ★★★/$$

The X beams of this building are stacked to the heavens. It's 100 stories high, with 1,127 feet worth of shops, offices, and even apartments (wouldn't you love to live at the top?). Take the elevator up to the 94th floor to get a knockout eagle-eye view of the town. (The fast ride may be your kids' favorite part of this site.) Walk along the history wall to see Chicago's development from swamp to city, and check out the "soundscopes," talking telescopes that tell about the history and architecture of Chicago. For an additional fee, take your kids on a guided tour of what you're seeing below. The Skywalk lets you take an open-air stroll at 1,127 feet (it's enclosed with mesh—no danger of falling). You can even look down at fireworks shows during the summer. *875 N. Michigan Ave., Chicago; (312) 751-3681;* www.hancockobservatory.com

Jackson Park ★★/Free

This park contains the John G. Shedd Aquarium (see page 203) and Midway Plaisance, a double boulevard a mile long that was the site of the 1893 Columbian Exposition. If you're here in winter, take everybody ice-skating at the open-air rink. In summer, let your kids play at one of the three beaches, the playgrounds, or the tennis courts. *Adjoining Burnham Park to the south, bordered by Grant Park to the northwest, and by Lake Michigan to the east; accessible via Lake Shore Dr.*

Kiddieland ★★/$$

Chicago-area kids know this amusement park as a beloved tradition. Only one water coaster, the Pipeline, offers some in-the-dark thrills. Most attractions are relatively low-tech and low-terror, making this a good place to bring younger kids. Preschoolers get lots of pint-size rides, including a small-scale Ferris wheel, a tamed-down roller coaster, plus boats and cars and other things that go around in circles. The coolest thing is a delightful German carousel decorated with fairy-tale figures and cars to ride. Your kids can also try a log ride along a gentle waterway—the scariest part is the point where spectators can squirt you with water. Kids two and under are free. Closed late October to mid-April. *8400 W. North Ave., Melrose Park; (708) 343-8000;* www.kiddieland.com

Lake Shore Drive
★★/Free

Your family can join the rest of Chicago and bike, Rollerblade (see "Chicago—From All Angles" on page 205), or walk the legendary path that runs along Lake Michigan for 20 miles.

Lincoln Park ★★/Free

Chicago's largest park runs along Lake Shore Drive, north of Navy Pier. It is home to many statues, among them the Augustus Saint-Gaudens's *Standing Statue of Lincoln*, but for parents with young kids to amuse, the highlights are the playground equipment, the bird sanctuary, the beaches, and, best of all, the **Lincoln Park Zoo** *(see below). From North Ave. to Hollywood Ave.*

MUST-SEE FamilyFun MUST-SEE Lincoln Park Zoo
★★★/Free

The nation's oldest zoo is a 35-acre complex with more than 1,080 animals and entertainment—and no admission charge. Your family tour will include the Lester E. Fisher Great Ape House, with its amazing collection of primates, from chimpanzees to gorillas; smaller primates live at the Helen Brach Primate House. Kids can see animals in their natural settings at the Small Mammal-Reptile House, but they'll need to do a bit of detective work to find the spiders, snakes, and lizards—they wear good disguises. In the Penguin and Seabird House, watch the black-and-white birds swim and slide; and look in the bear area for spectacled bears, whose markings resemble designer eyeglasses.

The Pritzger Children's Zoo is a great place to see (and sometimes even pet!) baby animals and learn about different animal habitats. At the Farm-in-the-Zoo, a five-acre model of a typical Midwestern farm, you can view cows, pigs, and other barnyard animals. Kids love churning butter in the main barn. Stop at the discovery stations that are part of many exhibits, where related touchable objects—a fish scale, a porcupine quill, a feather—allow children

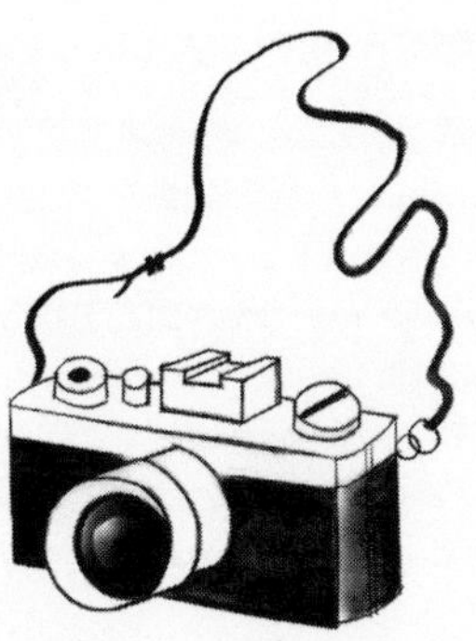

to feel some part of the animals' world. Also let your kids take a spin on the Ameritech Endangered Species Carousel, featuring 48 handcrafted wooden animals. *2200 N. Cannon Dr., Chicago; (312) 742-2000;* www.lpzoo.com

McDonald's Museum
★★/Free

Prove to your kids that there was life before McDonald's. A replica of the first Ray Kroc restaurant, built in 1955, stands here at its original site. Your kids will get a good laugh out of the cheap prices, the arches, photos, and the videotape on how it was back then, before food became "fast." Any car fans in the group will love the 1955 cars that are parked outside. Closed between Labor Day and Memorial Day. *400 N. Lee St., Des Plaines; (847) 297-5022.*

Moran Water Park ★★/$$

A sand play area and a zero-depth pool (wade in as you would into a lake) will make your kids think they're getting a day at the beach. Water slides make it even more fun. Open Memorial Day through Labor Day. *433 E. St. Charles Rd., Lombard; (630) 627-6127.*

> **FamilyFun SNACK**
>
> **Cranberry-nut Snack Mix**
>
> Measure 2 cups raw sunflower seeds; 1 cup pine nuts; 1 cup raw pumpkin seeds; 1 cup sweetened, dried cranberries; and 1 cup raisins into a mixing bowl and stir with a wooden spoon. Makes 6 cups.

Navy Pier
MUST-SEE FamilyFun MUST-SEE

★★★/Free

Smack in the center of the city, the pier is made up of 50 acres of land jutting 3,300 feet into Lake Michigan, all of it filled with fun things to do and see. Small children get a break from walking too far because most of the family attractions are at the end of the pier nearest the city. The Gateway Park fountain is at the entrance, and the Family Pavilion building is next. It holds an IMAX theater, the **Chicago Children's Museum** (see page 192), restaurants, and shops. The pond turns into an ice rink in winter, and you can take a break in the tropical garden until your kids spy the carousel.

Your white-knucklers will like the 150-foot-high Ferris wheel, which looks scary, but is very kid-friendly; instead of open buckets, riders sit in groups of six in glassed-in gondolas, so the whole family can ride together. And the wheel turns a tame revolution roughly every ten minutes—not exactly a breakneck pace.

Look to see who's appearing on the Skyline Stage—there are often free musical or dance performances. Kids will also like the mimes, jugglers, singers, and the frequent

ON ITS OPENING DAY of business in 1955, the original McDonald's in Des Plaines, Illinois, served only six items. Hamburgers cost 15 cents, cheeseburgers were 19 cents, and fries set hungry customers back a dime. Shakes were the most expensive item at 20 cents. (Sodas cost 10 and 15 cents; and coffee cost 10 cents.)

fireworks displays—also free. Or take a sight-seeing cruise off the dock. When the troops get hungry, stop at one of the street vendors along the walkways who hawk lemonade and hot dogs and snacks. There's an admission to some attractions. The Pier is open year-round; some attractions are open seasonally. *600 E. Grand Ave., Chicago; (800) 595-7437; (312) 595-7437;* www.navypier.com

Phillips Park Family Aquatic Center ★★/$$

There's a sand volleyball court where your older kids can play and a sand play area where little ones can build castles and make sand pies. Toddlers like the gentle kiddie slide and waterfall; grade-schoolers will go for the body and tube slides. Adults will want to drop into the Jacuzzi. Closed October through May. *Forty miles southwest of Chicago. Take Rte. 88 west to Farnsworth exit, take Farnsworth south to 5th Ave.; go west to Hill Ave. (Rte. 30), then north to Montgomery Rd. The center is one and a half miles on the right. 828 Montgomery Rd., Aurora; (630) 851-8686.*

Pirate's Cove/ Rainbow Falls Waterpark ★★/$$

Toddlers, preschoolers, and grade-schoolers up to age 8 will find rides at Pirate's Cove geared just for them. Let your kids try the hand-powered trains (which need a good, hard crank to get them going), ride the classic carousel, try the major-league playground with ladders and platforms, ride gentle bumper boats and a tame Jungle Cruise water ride, and test a climbing wall. Stop in the pirate ship for snacks and souvenirs.

If the troops are still feeling energetic, drive one mile to Rainbow Falls Waterpark and get wet. The turtle fountain, small slide, squirt guns, and shallow pool are perfect for toddlers and preschoolers. There's also a waterfall, lazy river, larger pool, and giant water slides for your older kids. Both Pirate's Cove and Rainbow Falls Waterpark are closed fall through spring. *Pirate's Cove: 499 Biesterfield Rd., Elk Grove Village. Rainbow Falls: Elk Grove Blvd. and Lions Dr., Elk Grove Village. Phone for both: (847) 437-9494.*

Santa's Village/ Racing Rapids Action Park ★★/$$$

What does Santa do in the summer? Apparently, he hangs out at an amusement park. This one consists of three sections: Santa's Village, where little kids can try the collection of mild-mannered rides; a petting zoo called Old McDonald's Farm; and Coney Island, where older kids will go for a more rambunctious set of coasters and scramblers. The 63-foot-tall Typhoon coaster is popular with teens, but too full of twists, turns, and loops for grade-schoolers. Next door to the amusement park is Racing Rapids Action Park, a water park with a lazy river, water slides, a kiddie area, and a fun "car wash"—your kids are the cars, and they get squirted and showered with water as they run through. A combination ticket for both attractions is available. Closed after Labor Day through May. *Rtes. 25 and 72, East Dundee; (847) 426-6753;* www.santasvillageil.com

WHITE WHALES

See if you can figure out the approximate age of beluga whales at the Shedd Aquarium. Beluga whales are born a dark gray, and as they grow and get older, their skin color changes to a creamy white. This skin coloration process helps them to blend into the background of Arctic ice, and can take between three and eight years.

MUST-SEE FamilyFun MUST-SEE Sears Tower Skydeck ★★★/$$

This is the tallest building in the United States, towering 110 stories over the city. The observation deck on the 103rd floor is the highest observatory in the world—1,353 feet up! Watch the seven-minute film, then load everyone on for the quick 55-second trip up to the observation deck on an elevator that travels at 1,600 feet per minute. (**HINT:** Have everyone chew gum. Your ears are going to pop.) The glass-enclosed observation deck has been revamped to include an indoor museum exhibit of the history of Chicago, a four-foot-tall "mini Chicago" for children to explore, state-of-the-art sound and lighting, and new telescopes. Your kids will be able to tell their friends that they saw three states from one spot—Michigan, Indiana, and Wisconsin. Expect a wait to get to the observation deck; the crowds are lightest in midweek, early in the day. The good news is that once you get up there, you can stay as long as you like. *233 S. Wacker Dr., Chicago; (312) 875-9696;* www.theskydeck.com

MUST-SEE FamilyFun MUST-SEE (John G.) Shedd Aquarium ★★★/$$

Plan to spend a day here at the world's largest indoor aquarium. Tell your kids there's enough water in its tanks to fill 100,000 bathtubs—without dirty children in them. The 90,000-gallon Caribbean reef tank is the centerpiece of the aquarium, with more than 300 types of brilliantly colored tropical fish swimming alongside spectacular coral. Try to plan your day around the 11 A.M. and 2 P.M. feedings at the tank—it's great fun to see the divers serve lunch to the sharks, sea turtles, and eels.

Another must-see: one of the world's largest indoor marine mammal exhibits, with dolphins, whales, sea otters, penguins, and seals. Lovers of the odd and ugly will want to see the huge and nearly immobile iguanas in the Animals of the Caribbean Coral Reef exhibit, and the creepily undulating electric eels in the Freshwater Animals of the Americas.

You won't regret paying the extra fee to enter the Oceanarium: this re-creation of the Pacific Northwest Coast includes a nature trail that takes you past tide pools, sea otters, dolphins, and beluga whales. A Penguin Shore gives kids a great opportunity to watch the tuxedo-clad birds perform their comedy routines—toddlers especially love their antics. Marine mammal presentations that feature whales and dolphins are held several times daily.

There's a snack bar for quick and cheap eats, but for quality cuisine and a remarkable view, spring for lunch in the elegant Soundings restaurant. Children are definitely welcome, and the quiet and relaxed atmosphere may give you all enough energy to see a few more exhibits. **NOTE:** Buy your tickets ahead of time through Ticketmaster *(312/559-0200)*; the lines can be quite long. *1200 S. Lake Shore Dr., Chicago; (312) 939-2426;* www.sheddaquarium.org

Six Flags Great America ★★★/$$$$

There are 12 roller coasters, four water rides, stage productions, theaters, shops, and restaurants for your family to choose from at this 300-acre-theme park. Plan to stay for hours—your kids will need all day to sample everything. First, everyone board the Great America Scenic Railway for a train tour of the park. You can discuss who wants to ride what ride and plan the rest of your day accordingly. The ominous names of some of the rides are a clue: preschoolers and the squeamish won't like them, and middle- and high-school kids will love them. Two of the newer thrill rides are Vertical Velocity, which will give you a jump start, going from 0 to 70-mph in two seconds, and Deja Vu, a suspended looping boomerang roller coaster, which you should ride before eating lunch. The American

Eagle wooden coaster rises 127 feet and has a double track, the Shock Wave is a steel coaster with seven loops, and the Iron Wolf delivers a standing 90-foot drop. The Viper is a wooden coaster with a 100-foot incline and an 80-mph drop. The Raging Bull goes up 20 stories—20 stories!—and then drops at 70 mph. The Batman coaster isn't exactly tame, but it's less terrifying than these big guys.

Your kids will go for Space Shuttle America, but keep them off if they're prone to motion sickness—it's a motion simulator. The water rides, Splashwater Falls and Roaring Rapids, aren't much calmer—kids who are easily rattled should skip them. Surprisingly, one of the calmest rides is one of the highest. The Sky Trek Tower ride ascends at a leisurely pace to a 285-foot rotating observation deck.

Younger kids love the double-decker Columbia Carousel—it's classic, pretty, and calm, with 88 horses and 15 other creatures to ride on. Toddlers and preschoolers get a kick out of seeing costumed characters walking around in the Camp Cartoon Network and Looney Tunes National Park, two children's areas, where four acres of attractions are reserved for children shorter than 54 inches. Be sure to give your kids a crack at the Looney Tunes Lodge, where they can shoot, toss, drop, and zing foam balls at each other.

When everybody is ready to sit still for a while, check the live performances: including Zajie, the Chinese acrobats has pyrotechnics and daring feats. Reduced rate for kids under 54 inches tall; reduced two-day rate; and kids under 3 are free. Closed November to mid-April. *About 25 miles north of Chicago on I-94, 1 mile east on Grand Ave./SR 132, Gurnee; (847) 249-1776;* www.sixflags.com

Soldier Field

★★/$$$

If you've got any football fans in the family, at least stop by this stately football field near the lake that's the home of the Chicago Bears. Tickets are hard to come by, but being here for a game is the stuff of memories.

EVERY ST. PATRICK'S DAY, the city of Chicago dyes the Chicago River green. The tradition started in 1962 when city workers dyed the river in order to trace sewage leaks; they thought that the green dye would be a unique way to commemorate the holiday. Today, the city uses 40 pounds of dye to color the river for a few hours.

CHICAGO—FROM ALL ANGLES

THERE ARE as many ways to see the city as there are things to see. By land or by sea, here are some of our favorites:

CityPass

If your family is planning on seeing all of Chicago's top attractions—the Art Institute of Chicago, the Field Museum, the Museum of Science and Industry, Adler Planetarium and Astronomy Museum, Shedd Aquarium, and the John Hancock Observatory—be sure to buy everyone a CityPass. It lets you in to all six facilities over the course of nine days at a money-saving price: $39 for adults and $29 for children 3 to 11. CityPasses are sold at all of the above attractions. Additional information can be obtained by sending an email to info@citypass.com

Getting Around Town

New to the Windy City? Take a bus tour. A narrated bus tour of Chicago lets you focus on having fun with your kids and gives you the chance to see the sights without having to negotiate traffic. There are several companies that run general guided tours that cover the main architectural and historic sites. **Gray Line** *(312/251-3107)* offers tours in deluxe coach buses and trolley buses; participants can get on and off when they like. **American Sightseeing** *(312/251-3100)* tours are in deluxe motor coaches, with scheduled stops of predetermined lengths. The **Chicago Trolley Company** *(773/648-5000)* offers an hour-long tour that includes stops at Water Tower Place, the Field Museum, and other hot spots. Or you can buy a day pass and get on and off the trolleys all day long. A day pass is $20 for adults, $10 for children 3 to 11; kids under 3 ride free.

Kids who have had their fill of culture will love **Untouchable Tours** *(773/881-1195)*, which focuses on the gangland legends of Chicago. Kids of all ages tend to like the pretend tough guys in their pinstriped suits, but the tour is really best for ages 10 and up. There's taped gunfire, and a discussion about the St. Valentine's Day Massacre. Reservations are required; call for rates.

Chicago from the Water

Ask any local: one of the best ways to see Chicago's beautiful buildings is from a boat on Lake Michigan. The following companies offer narrated sight-seeing boat tours, which

continued on next page

your kids will like even if they couldn't care less about looking at skyscrapers. **TIP:** Buy tickets early, then return in time for the tour. Tours are offered April through October, depending on weather conditions.

Mercury Cruise Lines

Ninety-minute and two-hour cruises depart daily from the southwest corner of Michigan Avenue. Tickets are $15 and up for adults; $7.50 and up for children 11 and under. *Michigan Avenue Bridge and Wacker Dr., Chicago; (312) 332-1353.*

Shoreline Sightseeing Company Harbor Tours

Based next to the Shedd Aquarium, this company offers a 30-minute narrated tour, a good bet for impatient younger children. Tickets are $9; $4 for children under 11. *Boats leave from Navy Pier, Chicago. (312) 222-9328;* www.shorelinessightseeing.com

Wendella Sightseeing Boats

Another good choice for those with short attention spans, this company has 90-minute tours. Tickets are $15; $7.50 for children 11 and under. *400 N. Michigan Ave., Chicago; (312) 337-1446.*

Chicago by Bike

An excellent way to tour Chicago, especially Lake Shore Drive is by bike. Many rental companies also offer guided tours. **Bike Chicago Rentals and Tours,** *Navy Piers, 600 E. North Avenue Beach, North Ave. and Lake Shore Dr., Chicago; (713/327-2706). Also at 63rd Street Beach, 6300 S. Lake Shore Dr., Chicago; (773/324-3400);* www.bikechicago.com

Out of town—biking outside Chicago

Walk, bike, jog, or horseback ride on the 55-mile gravel path trail called Illinois Prairie Path. It begins just outside the city in Maywood and runs west to Wheaton, where it splits into four legs to Batavia, Geneva, Aurora, and Elgin. The trail follows the historic path of the former Chicago Aurora, and Elgin Railway—an electric commuter line that until 1961 carried passengers and freight between Chicago and its western suburbs.

Try Ticketmaster (*312/559-1212;* www.Ticketmaster.com) or stand in line at Gate 1 the Thursday before a home game. *McFetridge and S. Lake Shore Drs., Chicago; (847) 615-2327;* www.soldierfield.net

Trails Entertainment's Enchanted Castle ★★/$$

Your family will really be enchanted by the miniature golf, topflight playground, laser tag, bumper cars, theater of various simulated rides and adventures, and a karaoke pizza parlor, among other distractions at this entertainment complex; just 35 miles west of Chicago. *Take Rte. 290 west, exit at Roosevelt Rd; go 5 miles west to Main St. 1103 S. Main St., Lombard; (630) 953-7860;* www.enchanted.com

United Center ★★/$$$$

Take your sports buffs to see professional hockey (the Chicago Blackhawks) and basketball (the Chicago Bulls) at the "house that Michael built." Tickets are expensive but easier to get than you might think; just walk up to the box office window. *1901 W. Madison, Chicago; (312) 455-4500;* www.unitedcenter.com

Wrigley Field ★★/$$$

The famous home of baseball's famous Chicago Cubs is a particularly kid-friendly ball stadium: it's outdoors, and most games are played in the afternoon, when it's easier for young fans to stay awake. Tickets to games can be hard to get, but worth the effort; try Ticketmaster (*312/559-1212;* www.Ticketmaster.com) or the box office. Otherwise, kids get a big kick out of the tour, which includes the press box, the Stadium Club, and even the locker room. (Call *800/THE-CUBS* for tour information and reservations.) Tours are offered on selected weekends during the season (April through September); call for the schedule. **NOTE:** Parking near the stadium is almost impossible (there's no official lot or ramp). Take a bus, a taxi, or the elevated train. *1060 W. Addison St., Chicago; (773) 404-2827;* www.chicagocubs.com

> **Lights On**
>
> **Wrigley Field was the last major league ballpark to add lights for night games. The Chicago Cubs did not play a night game at home until 1988.**

BUNKING DOWN

Best Western River North ★★/$$$

Parents will appreciate the indoor pool, and the in-room video games in the suites to distract your kids while they do a little lounging themselves or visit the sauna and exercise room. The 150 rooms also have cable TV, refrigerators, coffeemakers, and safes; suites also have refrigerators. Reserve early if you want the only two-bedroom unit. *125 W. Ohio St., Chicago; (312) 467-0800;* www.bestwestern.com

Chicago Marriott Downtown
★★/$$$$

This elegant and enormous hotel overlooks Grant Park and Lake Michigan and is close to much of what you'll want to see. Some of the 1,192 rooms adjoin, and there are two- and three-bedroom units. Rooms have coffeemakers and 24-hour room service; some rooms have a minibar. Your tired kids will appreciate the in-room movies, or if they're still raring to go, they can check out the arcade or visit the indoor/outdoor heated pool. There are whirlpools, three dining rooms, a coffee shop, gift shop, and a shopping shuttle. *540 N. Michigan Ave., Chicago; (800) 228-9290; (312) 836-0100.*

Days Inn Gold Coast
★★/$$

Walk from here to a host of Chicago attractions, including Lincoln Park, the Lincoln Park Zoo, the lakefront beaches, and the Magnificent Mile. Both rooms and suites are available, plus an on-site restaurant and a small convenience store. Parking is free. *1816 N. Park St.; (312) 664-3040.*

Days Inn—Lincoln Park North
★★/$

This historic 1918 building offers more ambience than usual budget chain motels. It's an easy walk to Wrigley Field, Lincoln Park Zoo, and the beaches. Plus it's nice to have a home base for a rest stop for tired youngsters between visiting attractions. The on-site restaurant is reasonably priced. *644 W. Diversey Pkwy., Chicago; (773) 525-7010.*

Radisson Hotel & Suites Chicago ★★/$$$

This 350-room hotel is one block off Michigan Avenue, so you won't have far to walk to shopping, museums, and the lake. Check the weekly and monthly rates for longer vacations. Rooms have nice extras, including movies, coffeemakers, cable TV, and refrigerators; some have a minibar (microwaves available on request). The heated pool is small, and there is 24-hour room service and a fitness center. *160 E. Huron St., Chicago; (800) 333-3333; (312) 787-2900;* www.radisson.com

GOOD EATS

Bubba Gump Shrimp Co.
★★/$$

If you've got any *Forrest Gump* fans in the family, do not miss this place. The menu features shrimp, shrimp, and more shrimp (remember Bubba's obsession?), plus burgers for the youngsters. For service, kids hold up a "Stop, Forrest, Stop" sign; the flip side reads "Run, Forrest, Run." Desserts change: Key lime pie, layer cakes, and cobblers are all baked the same day they're served. The movie plays continuously (the servers must have it memorized by now), and Forrest's bus bench is here, complete with his suitcase and box of chocolates. *Navy Pier, 700 E. Grand Ave., Chicago; (312) 252-GUMP;* www.bubbagump.com

Byron's Hot Dogs ★★/$

Here's a great place to introduce your kids to real Chicago-style hot dogs. The interior looks like kids have already decorated it—the walls seem to be covered with splotches of ketchup and mustard. It's really just paint. *680 N. Holster St., Chicago; (312) 266-3355.*

Ed Debevic's Short Order Deluxe ★★★/$$

Even if they've been eating sugar and riding roller coasters all day, your children will not be the noisiest things in this hoppin' joint. Every half hour, the disco ball whirls, lights flash, and some waiter or waitress jumps up on the counter and starts to sing and dance. Deejays play records and make goofy announcements ("That little girl is not eating her pickles!"). Servers hassle the patrons—warn your kids about this ahead of time—and the dress code is bizarre. Waiters wear toys, balloons,

A Travel Scrapbook

This suitcase-style scrapbook is just right for your child to pack with mementos of his vacation adventures — and it's a cinch to make.

Start with two cardboard report covers. Use one for the suitcase itself and one to cut out two U-shaped handles and two $1^1/_2$- by 18-inch straps.

Attach one handle to the front of the suitcase by gluing the ends to the inside of the upper edge. Match up the second handle with the first one and glue it to the back side. Now close the suitcase and glue on the straps. Position the strap tops on the front of the suitcase 1 inch down from the upper edge, then wrap the straps around the back of the suitcase. Finally, fold down the strap ends so that they overlap the tops and attach stick-on, Velcro-type fasteners.

For a handy photo pocket, glue a large open envelope to the inner cover Then, fill the suitcase with manila folders for storing ticket stubs, brochures, and other souvenirs.

The Earache Solution

You can often lessen ear discomfort on airplanes by nursing infants, giving tots bottles or pacifiers, and letting older kids chew gum (buy it on your way to the airport because many terminals do not sell chewing gum—workers are tired of cleaning it off floors and chairs). But if your child experiences real ear pain, you can try this funny-looking but often effective trick. Ask the attendant for two plastic cups. Fold a napkin into the bottom of each cup and pour in just enough hot water to moisten the napkins. Then, place the cups over your child's ears, making sure you hold them tightly against his head.

and outrageous hairdos. The menu is 1950s comfort food: meat loaf, burgers, and pot roast. *640 N. Wells St., Chicago; (312) 664-1707;* www.eddebevics.com

Medieval Times Dinner and Tournament ★★★/$$$$

Feast like knights and ladies in a place that looks like a medieval castle and is staffed by pseudo serfs and wenches. Kids of all ages love watching knights joust on horseback and picking who'll win the sword fights while they eat a four-course dinner—including chicken and ribs—with their hands. Well, they didn't have silverware back in those times, now, did they? For an additional charge, your kids can be officially knighted and pressed into service for the crown. Skip the dungeon, though. It's a creepy display of torture devices and will upset either your kids, you, or both. This is pricey for dinner, especially the one served here, but the entertainment is worth the cost; the fee for kids is a little more than half price. Reservations are a must. *Take the 294 Expressway west to 90W; exit on Roselle Rd. 2001 N. Roselle Rd., Schaumburg; (800) 544-2001; (847) 843-3900;* www.medievaltimes.com

Pizzeria Uno ★★/$

You can't visit Chicago and not have deep-dish pizza. Where better to enjoy it than its birthplace—the numero uno Pizzeria Uno. Come before your kids get so hungry that they're cranky—it can take 30 to 45 minutes for a deep-dish pie to cook. *29 East Ohio St., Chicago; (312) 321-1000.*

Rock 'n' Roll McDonald's ★★/$

This is a McDonald's with a twist, where your kids will discover that there was life before MTV. Travel back to the 1950s, when fast food was news, and rock and roll was king. Huge renderings of Elvis and James Dean are outside; cool '50s and '60s artifacts are inside. And you can still get a Happy Meal. *600 N. Clark St., Chicago; (312) 664-7940.*

Superdawg Drive-In ★/$

Your kids will get a kick out of trying to be the first to spot the giant hot dog statues standing on the roof. Guess what's on the menu? *6363 N. Milwaukee Ave., Chicago; (773) 763-0660.*

Souvenir Hunting

Abraham Lincoln Bookstore

If your visit to Springfield and Decatur piqued your young history buffs' interest in Lincoln, stop at this bookshop in the River North neighborhood of Chicago. In addition to selling books about the Civil War and Lincoln, the shop displays a collection of presidential manuscripts and artifacts from Lincoln's time. *357 W. Chicago Ave., Chicago; (312) 944-3085.*

FAO Schwarz

It's the mother of all toy stores, and your kids will love the displays as much as the playthings themselves. Every imaginable toy is here, from enormous stuffed animals to all the clothes and accessories Barbie could possibly need. *840 N. Michigan Ave., Chicago; (312) 587-5000;* www.fao.com

Marshall Field's

How can you say you've been to Chicago if you don't at least walk through Marshall Field's? Let your kids buy a Frango mint or an inexpensive paperweight or something else they can bring home in the green paper bag, and don't miss seeing the Tiffany dome between the sixth and seventh floors. At winter holiday time, the Marshall Field's window displays are worth a special trip. *111 N. State St., Chicago; (312) 781-1000.*

Water Tower Place

Even if your kids aren't much for shopping, they'll go for the glass elevators and crisscrossing escalators. This glamorous, six-level complex at the north end of the Magnificent Mile includes Lord & Taylor and another Marshall Field's, along with 123 other shops. *835 N. Michigan Ave., Chicago; (312) 440-3165.*

Check out the 18 canyons and 15 miles of hiking trails at Starved Rock State Park.

INTRODUCTION

Northern Illinois

THE QUIET PLEASURES OF the towns and attractions on the side of northern Illinois opposite Chicago are kind of a relief after the Windy City.

Galena, close to the northwestern tip of the state, is a picturesque town of terrific antiques stores, romantic bed-and-breakfasts, and restored 19th-century homes. Eighty-five percent of its buildings are on the National Register of Historic Places. What your kids will like is the town's renowned fudge and the great hiking and biking they can do on the rolling hills, craggy cliffs, and rugged bluffs. History buffs can go down inside a real mine to see how miners once got the lead out, while Civil War buffs can tour the home of Ulysses S. Grant in Galena and ask guides what life was like here during the Civil War.

Museums are the main draw in Rockford, 83 miles northwest of Chicago: the Burpee Museum of Natural History, the children's Discovery Center, and the Midway

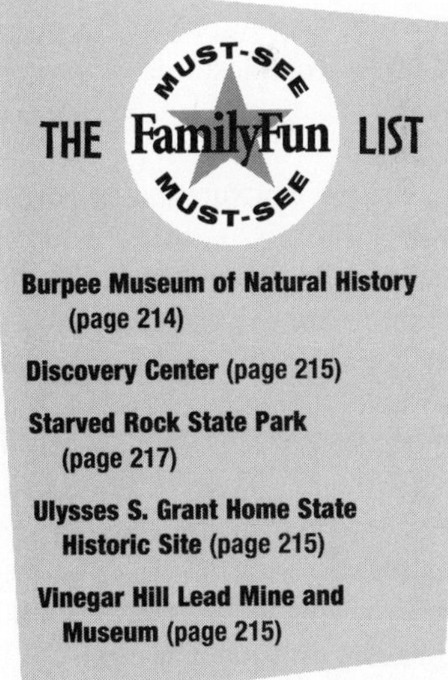

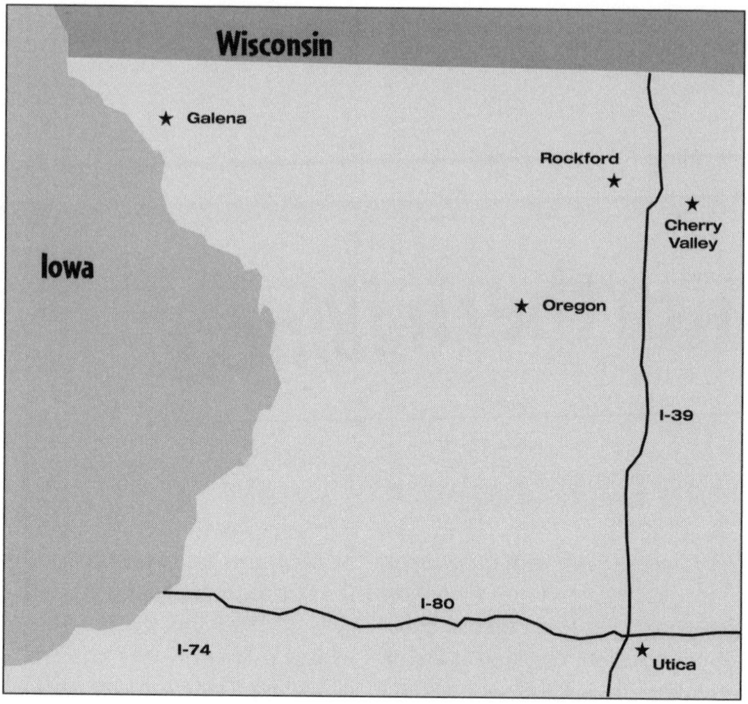

Village and Museum Center. The town of Oregon, about 15 miles southwest of Rockford, has the dramatic beauty of Castle Rock State Park.

Geneva, a picturesque Victorian town about 20 miles west of Chicago, was founded in 1833 and is known for its well-preserved historic homes and buildings. Hike and bike along the Fox River Trail there, and take in a minor league baseball game. Starved Rock State Park, well known for its scenery and its 18 canyons, is in Utica, about 60 miles south of Rockford and 90 miles southwest of Chicago.

CULTURAL ADVENTURES

Burpee Museum of Natural History

★★★/$

Your kids will probably think the full-size cast of a Tyrannosaurus rex and the realistic dioramas of Native Americans are the best parts of this museum. Fossil exhibits, mounted birds and mammals, and a coal forest (fossilized animals and trees make the coal we use today) where there are make-believe thunderstorms, are other highlights. *737 N. Main St., Rockford; (815) 965-3433;* www.burpee.org

Discovery Center

FamilyFun MUST-SEE ★★★/$

More than 180 exciting hands-on science and art exhibits and activities let your family experiment, explore, and create. The country's first outdoor science park focuses on sound, water, and weather. There's also a children's television and radio station, a playground for toddlers, and a planetarium. *711 N. Main St., Riverfront Museum Park, Rockford; (815) 963-6769;* www.discoverycenter.org

Midway Village and Museum Center ★★/$$

Even your preschoolers will understand the demonstrations and explanations of the kid-oriented guides at this re-created 19th-century village. The place covers 137 acres and has 24 historic buildings. Schedule your trip for the end of June if you have any Civil War buffs in the family—there's a Civil War reenactment the final weekend of the month. World War II students get their chance the last weekend in September, when a battle from that war is reenacted. The village is closed November through March. *6799 Guilford Rd., Rockford; (815) 397-9112;* www.midwayvillage.com

Ulysses S. Grant Home State Historic Site

FamilyFun MUST-SEE ★★★/$

Your offspring may not be dying to visit this site, but once they start talking with the costumed guides (who answer in period language) they may decide it's pretty interesting after all. Maintained as it was when Grant lived here after the Civil War, the home is a chance to walk back in time. Donation suggested. *500 Bouthillier St., Galena; (815) 777-0248;* www.state.il.us/hpa

Vinegar Hill Lead Mine and Museum

FamilyFun MUST-SEE ★★★/$$

Put on a hard hat and go down (way down) into this 200-year-old lead mine. You'll all learn where those number 2 pencils used to come from, and your kids will get an eye-opening glimpse of the hard, dangerous work that was so important to America's growth. *8885 N. Three Pines Rd., Galena; (815) 777-0855.*

WE ALL KNOW THAT Ulysses S. Grant is not "buried" in Grant's Tomb, but where is his above-ground tomb located? The tomb and memorial to the former president, who led the Union Army to victory in the Civil War, is in New York City.

JUST FOR FUN

Alice T. Virtue Memorial Pool and Water Park ★★/$

The zero-depth pool is a great place to pull up a lounge chair and watch the preschoolers wade in. (As on a beach, the water depth gradually increases from inches to feet.) Your older kids will head for the 131-foot water slide and sand volleyball court, and the smaller ones can try the playground when they're ready to dry off. Closed September through May. *Stagecoach Trail Recreation Park, Galena; (815) 777-0807.*

Castle Rock State Park
★★/Free

Climb to the top of the sandstone butte that gives this park its name. It's not hard (even 3-year-olds can do it)—there's a stairway built right into the rock. There's no camping at Castle Rock (unless you come in by boat), but the view of Rock River Valley from the top is the best in the state. *Two hours west of Chicago. 1365 W. Castle Rd., Oregon; (815) 732-7329.*

Chestnut Mountain Resort
★★/$$$$

Your kids can take skiing lessons here (reservations needed) or Mom and Dad can sign up for baby-sitting service (reservation needed) and do a little grown-up skiing. This alpine ski area has 17 runs; the biggest drop is 475 feet; the longest run is 3,500 feet. There are five chairlifts and three surface lifts. Be sure to spend some time in the Tudor-style lodge; the view of the Mississippi River is breathtaking. During the summer months you can rent bicycles, enjoy the pool, or bring a pole and go fishing. *8700 W. Chestnut Rd., Galena; (800) 397-1320; (815) 777-1320;* www.chestnutmtn.com

Family Land
★★/$$

Kids can play miniature golf, race go-carts, splash in an activity pool, and see who's fastest down the water slide. Closed October through April. *Hwy. 6, Utica; (815) 224-4130.*

Fox River Trail
★★/Free

The paved 32-mile hiking and biking trail stretches along the Fox River. *Geneva; (630) 232-6060.* For bike rentals, contact **Mill Race Cyclery,** *11 E. State St., Geneva; (630) 232-2833.*

Kane County Cougars

★★/$$

Want to show your kids what baseball was like before the players became millionaires? Take them to a minor-league game. The players aren't hardened to autograph hunters, you can get close enough to really see the action, and the atmosphere just seems to be more fun. Between innings and during breaks, your family can watch races around the bases between a child spectator and a cougar (it's just a mascot) and other silly events. The season runs April through September. *Philip B. Elfstrom Stadium, 34W002 Cherry La., Geneva; (630) 232-8811;* www.kccougars.com

Magic Waters Waterpark

★★/$$

Big kids will like the lazy river, wave pool, tube slides, and water slides, and toddlers and preschoolers can splash in the Little Lagoon at this 35-acre park. Kids can also play beach volleyball or climb up to a tree house. Mom and Dad might even get a chance to relax in a hot tub. *Bell School Rd., Cherry Valley; (800) 373-1679; (815) 332-3260;* www.magicwaterswaterpark.com

Mathiessen State Park

★★/Free

Across the street from Starved Rock State Park, this park has a five-mile trail that's good for family hikes in summer and cross-country skiing in winter. Young equestrians may prefer the horseback-riding trail (see Starved Rock Stables, *below*). You're not allowed to swim, but you can watch the waterfalls. *Rte. 71, off Illinois Hwy. 71, Utica; (815) 667-4868.*

Starved Rock Stables

★★/$$$

Rent horses to ride at either Mathiessen State Park or Starved Rock State Park. The horses know the trails even if you don't. If your kids are small, you can put them on your horse with you. Closed November through April. *Hwy. 71, west of Starved Rock State Park, Utica; (815) 677-3026.*

Starved Rock State Park

★★★/Free

Starved Rock stands 125 feet high over this park. Just think how big it would be if it had eaten something! (Try that one on your kids.) Actually, this 2,630-acre wooded park takes its name from an Indian conflict, the tale of which is best saved for older kids. (In the 1760s, a band of Illiniwek were trapped by a Potawatomi war party, on the butte, where they starved to death.) There are 18 canyons here—visit in the spring for a stunning view of the streams and springs swollen from melting snow cascading over the rock formations. Hike the 15 miles of trails through the canyons, or stick to the easy trails designed for kids. You can also take a boat ride in the Rock River; board at the dock near the main parking lot. A lodge and cabins provide overnight accommodations (see Bunking Down on page 219). *Rte. 71, off Illinois Hwy. 71, Utica; (815) 667-4906; (815) 667-4726.*

Trolley Tours
★★/$

Your family has traveled on planes and boats and in cars—now you can try trolleys; these pass by Galena's picturesque buildings and along historic Main Street. Kids who don't care about the scenery will still like the ride. The two local trolley companies offer similar tours: **Brill's Trolley Tours** *(102 N. Main St., Galena; 815/777-3121)* and **Galena Trolley Tours** *(314 S. Main St., Galena; 815/777-1248).*

Warren Cheese Plant ★★/$

For young travelers running on grilled cheese sandwiches and macaroni and cheese—here's their chance to see where the stuff comes from. See how cheese is made, from curds to whey. Tours—offering samples of Apple Jack cheese and other varieties—are held Monday mornings. *415 Jefferson St., Warren, about 30 minutes east of Galena; (815) 745-2627.*

BUNKING DOWN

Best Western Quiet House and Suites ★★/$$$$

All 42 lodgings here are suites, offering traveling families a bit more space. Standard suites have one queen-size bed and coffeemaker; executive suites have a queen-size bed in the bedroom and a sofa bed

FamilyFun READER'S TIP

Terrific Task Masters

When our family goes on vacation, we assign each of our seven children an important task for the duration of the trip, one that will make each child an active part of planning. On a trip to Orlando, Florida, these were their assignments.

Sylvia, age 15, navigator and accountant, kept track of mileage, maps, and money; TamiSue, 13, photographer, had to use two rolls of film a day; Joshua, 10, auto mechanic, pumped gas and checked oil and tire pressure; Bryan, 7, mailman, got postcards and stamps and mailed the cards kids write to themselves each day; Libby, 7, dietitian, made sure the cooler was stocked; Andrew, 6, activities coordinator and music director, was solely in charge of the tape player; and Katie, 5, referee, settled all road disputes.

Wendy Lira, Alma, Kansas

in the living area; the larger "leisure suites" have two queen-size beds or a king-size bed in the bedroom and a sofa bed in the living area. All units have cable television and in-room movies. There are specialty theme suites as well; they're usually chosen for romantic weekends, but your kids might get a kick out of staying in the Lincoln Log Cabin, Mississippi River Boat, or Roman suites. There are heated indoor and outdoor pools, and you can swim from one to the other, even in the winter. *Hwy. 20 E., Galena; (800) 528-1234; (815) 777-2577;* www.quiethouse.com

Eagle Ridge Inn and Resort ★★★/$$$$

Why will your kids love this place? Three heated pools, a playground, tennis courts, numerous trails to hike and bike, horseback riding, skiing in winter, and boating in summer should do it. Grown-ups will also appreciate the championship golf courses, beautifully manicured grounds, and gorgeous views. You can rent ski equipment, bicycles, boats, and paddleboats. The 430 rooms include many two- and three-bedroom units. They are well-appointed, with in-room movies, VCRs, coffeemakers, microwaves, and refrigerators; some units have complete kitchens. There are three on-site restaurants. Spikes and Paisanos are both casual, while the Woodlands is more elegant. All are family-friendly and offer the usual kid faves on their menus. *444 Eagle Ridge Dr., Galena; (800) 892-2269; (815) 777-2444;* www.eagleridge.com

Starved Rock Campground ★/$

There are 133 sites with electrical hookups here, plus showers and toilets. *Starved Rock State Park, Rte. 71, off Illinois Hwy. 71, Utica; (815) 667-4726.*

Starved Rock State Park Lodge and Cabins ★★/$$

Stay in one of the 72 rooms in the native stone-and-log lodge, or in one of the 18 cabins. Each of the deluxe cabins has a king-size bed, TV, and fireplace. The pioneer cabins have one king-size or two double beds, but no TV or bathtub (just a shower)—not ideal for folks traveling with little ones. The lodge's Great Hall has a beamed ceiling and a stone fireplace and is filled with eye-catching Native American artwork, rugs, and artifacts. Kids love the indoor heated pool and children's indoor wading pool; parents will like the two saunas, whirlpool, full-service restaurant, lounge, café, and gift shop. Children under 12 stay free. *Starved Rock State Park, Utica; (800) 868-7625; (815) 667-4211;* www.starvedrocklodge.com

White Pines Inn ★★/$

Cabins sleep two adults and two children in one queen-size bed and one full-size pullout trundle, and

1-2-3 FUDGE

We can't give you the secret to Galena's famous fudge, but how about this vacation-inspired rocky road recipe?

ROCKY ROAD FUDGE

Everybody knows that peanut butter and marshmallow make a great match. Add chocolate, and you've got a real trio of a treat.

- **1 12-ounce package chocolate chips**
- **1 cup crunchy peanut butter**
- **2 cups mini marshmallows**

Melt the chocolate chips in a double boiler or heavy saucepan and stir in the peanut butter until blended. Remove from the heat and fold in the marshmallows. Spread the mixture into a greased 9- by 13-inch baking pan. Cover and chill until the candy firms up (about 10 to 15 minutes). Cut into 1½-inch squares. Makes 4 dozen pieces.

CRISPED RICE CRUNCH

For a peanut-free version of this candy, simply substitute 1 cup of crisped rice cereal for the crunchy peanut butter.

all cabins have forest views. The one two-bedroom cabin has a living room, kitchen, and bath, but it is located across from the park. The renovated main lodge is a lovely spot to relax, and the log cabin restaurant hosts a dinner theater at noon during the summer or in the evenings at other times, featuring programs of interest to families. Closed January and February. *White Pines Forest State Park, 6712 W. Pines Rd., Oregon; (815) 946-3817;* www.whitepinesinn.com

GOOD EATS

American Old-Fashioned Ice-Cream Parlor ★★/$

This soda fountain is more than 150 years old, which means they ought to have perfected the ice-cream cone by now—and they have. *102 N. Main St., Galena; (815) 777-3121.*

Bing's Drive-In ★★/$

Cruise on in to this old-fashioned drive-in, where carhops take your order and deliver coneys, burgers, and onion rings to your car window. Closed October through February. *3613 S. Main, Rockford; (815) 968-8663.*

Happy Joe's Pizza and Ice-Cream Parlor ★★/$

The name says it all—two things every kid loves. *9919 Hwy. 20 W., Galena; (815) 777-1830.*

Log Cabin ★★/$

Your kids may not eat the flaming *saganaki* (a chunk of cheese finished with brandy and a squeeze of lemon) at this Greek restaurant, but they'll love it when the waiter sets it aflame and yells "*Opah!*" ("Good health to all"). For children under 12, there are plenty of kid-friendly items, including shrimp, burgers, fried chicken, and a steak sandwich. *201 N. Main St., Galena; (815) 777-0393.*

Starved Rock State Park Lodge ★★/$$

Reserve early for dinner—there aren't a lot of other dining choices in these parts, and the dining room fills up at night. No problem at breakfast or lunch, though. The children's menu features spaghetti, hamburgers, pizza, and chicken fingers; Moms and Dads can enjoy Caesar salad, Asian chicken salad, pasta primavera, prime rib, shrimp, and chicken Oscar. *Starved Rock State Park, Utica; (815) 667-4227.*

SOUVENIR HUNTING

Galena's Kandy Kitchen

Watch them make the fudge, then buy and eat the finished product. *100 N. Main St., Galena; (815) 777-0241.*

Rocky Mountain Chocolate Factory

The chocolate treats are top-notch at this shop (there's no actual factory involved). If you start craving more when you get home, use the 800 number and have some shipped to you. *207 S. Main St., Galena; (800) 235-8160; (815) 777-3200.*

Oh, how they will play in Peoria!

Peoria, Bloomington, and Normal

SAY "PEORIA" AND the first thing most people will think is "typical American town." They're right, too. Peoria is about 150 miles south of Chicago and 165 miles north of St. Louis. The drive along the Illinois River valley bluffs between Chicago and Peoria is stunningly scenic. Once in Peoria, your family can visit the Glen Oak Park and Zoo and take in a Peoria Chiefs baseball game. Young astronomy lovers will go for the Lakeview Museum of Arts and Sciences, which has the world's largest solar system model.

About 35 miles east of Peoria are the twin university towns of Bloomington and Normal. There, you and your kids will enjoy the Children's Discovery Museum, the Illinois State University Planetarium, and the Wildlife Prairie Park, where kids can see what pioneer life was like.

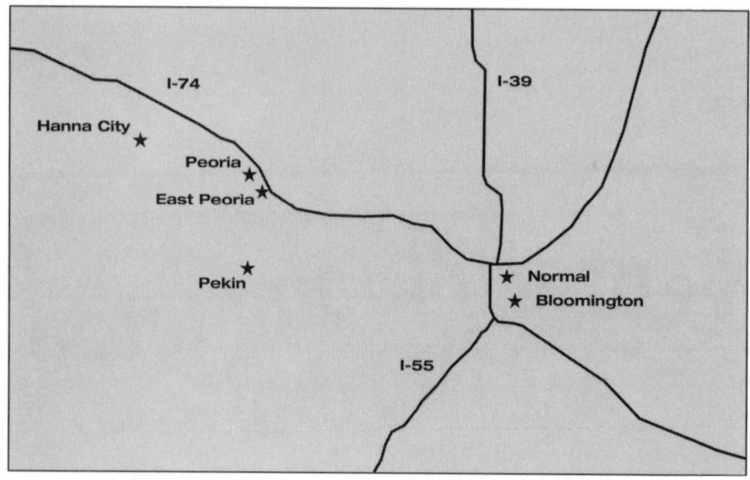

CULTURAL ADVENTURES

Children's Discovery Museum of Central Illinois★★★/$

Kids between 2 and 12 can tour the dozen exhibits at this museum and stop at each for some hands-on fun. In the process your older children might learn something new or discover a scientific principle all by themselves. Curious youngsters of all ages can step up to the microphone and become a radio announcer, take the controls of a railroad train, stop by for a visit to a pretend doctor's office, shop in a miniature grocery store, and play in a real car, parked safely indoors. *716 E. Empire St., Bloomington; (309) 829-6222;* www.cdmci.org

Illinois State University Planetarium ★★/$

Sit in the dark and learn about the constellations. More than 2,000 "stars" are projected in the planetarium sky. Skip this if your preschooler fears the dark. *School St. and College Ave., Normal; (309) 438-2496; (309) 438-8756.*

MUST-SEE FamilyFun MUST-SEE

Lakeview Museum of Arts and Sciences ★★★/$$

The world's largest solar system model starts here, then spreads out over 40 miles. The sun, 36 feet wide, is painted on the side of the museum building. The earth is six blocks away at a gas station. Saturn is at a grocery store eight miles away. Pluto is 40 miles away in a large furniture store in Kewaunee, Illinois. The model is to scale and was listed in the *Guinness Book of Records.* Though your older kids will probably be more interested in the natural sciences displays, the children's Discovery Center is a treat for everyone from 3-year-olds to grandma and grandpa. There's a planetarium, too. *1125 W. Lake Ave., Peoria; (309) 686-7000.*

Wheels o' Time Museum

★★/$

Kids don't just look at the historical exhibits here. They get to push buttons, pull knobs, try out musical instruments, play with model trains and other toys, and sit in vintage cars and tractors. The museum is set in a real firehouse, complete with an 1855 fire engine. It's easy to find—just look for the building with the train parked out front. Closed November through April. *11923 N. Knoxville Ave., Peoria; (309) 243-9020.*

Wildlife Prairie State Park

★★★/$

If your kids like to hear stories about families that moved west, they'll be fascinated by the vintage country store, one-room schoolhouse, pioneer farmstead, and museum and visitors' center. They'll also enjoy the working (and very splashy) water pump. This is also one of the country's leading wildlife parks. The 2,000 acres are home to wolves, bison, elk, cougars, bears, and bald eagles in fenced-in areas. The fences aren't obvious, and the animals roam over wide, open spaces. The setup is nice for the animals, but makes it harder for kids to actually spy any wildlife. If you want to see bison, eat lunch at the Arboretum Café, which has a good view of the bison range. Closed mid-December through February. *3826 N. Taylor Rd., Hanna City, 10 miles west of downtown Peoria; (309) 676-0998.* www.wildlifeprairiestatepark.org

JUST FOR FUN

Dragonland Water Park ★★/$

Bring toddlers and preschoolers to the zero-depth edge of the pool, where they can gradually wade in and get comfortable with the water, an inch at a time, and then climb a green dragon and slide down. Older

> **FamilyFun GAME**
>
> **What If?**
>
> Take turns answering these hypothetical questions and then invent some of your own:
>
> - If you were king or queen of a country, how would you use your power?
> - If you were stranded on a desert island and could eat only one kind of food for the rest of your life, what would it be?
> - If you could make up a holiday, what would it be and how would you celebrate it?

grade-schoolers will like the water slides, one of which they can ride on an inner tube. Kids 3 and under are free. Closed between Labor Day and Memorial Day. *1701 Court St., Mineral Springs Park, Pekin; (309) 347-4000.*

Glen Oak Park and Zoo

MUST-SEE FamilyFun MUST-SEE ★★★/$

The zoo is small, but its size is actually a plus—your family can see almost everything in 40 minutes or so. More than 250 animals are in residence, and kids can get close to a number of them, including goats, llamas, a tortoise, camels, and zebras. This 100-acre park also has a playground, tennis courts, a conservatory, and gardens. In summer, catch outdoor performances (kids love them, too) in the amphitheater. Kids under 4 free. *2218 N. Prospect Rd., Peoria; (309) 686-3365;* www.glenoakzoo.org

Grady's Golf and Games

★★/$$

What fun! Kids (and Mom and Dad) can shoot 18 holes of miniature golf, play arcade games, ride bumper boats, and work on their swing in batting cages. Younger kids will head for the amusement park with toddler-size rides. Fee for each activity. *1501½ Morrissey Dr., Bloomington; (309) 662-3332.*

Miller Park Zoo

MUST-SEE FamilyFun MUST-SEE ★★★/$

A real reindeer (with just a plain old brown nose), a wallaby, a mongoose, and a New Guinea singing dog are among the kid-pleasing and rare residents here. The big, furry Sumatran tigers, the snow leopards, and the lion are favorites with children, who also like meeting the goats and sheep in the petting zoo. This small zoo is more than 100 years old, but it still has a lot to

FamilyFun READER'S TIP

A Map of His Own

Whenever our family sets out on a road trip, my husband and I trace out the planned route for our 11-year-old son, David, and our 8-year-old daughter, Caytlin. Using AAA maps, I cut out the portion that pertains to our trip and glue it to a piece of cardboard. (Depending on how much area our journey will cover, I sometimes use both sides of the cardboard to display the map.) My husband highlights the roadways with a marker, then we cover the map with a sheet of clear Con-Tact paper. Besides being a big hit with the kids, the map is a ready reference for the driver. Although long stints in the car can be hard on kids (and adults), we have learned that when everyone is interested in following the route, the trip can be a special time spent together as a family.

Annette Payne, Santa Barbara, California

offer. The paved pathways and pretty planted beds make it easy and pleasant to get around. *1020 S. Morris Ave., Bloomington; (309) 434-2250.*

Peoria Chiefs ★★/$

The license number of the dirtiest car in the parking lot is broadcast, a child gets to race the mascot around the park, and the chicken dance is a favorite nightly event. Catch this Class-A baseball team during one of their fun and goofy summer games. The ball game is legitimate, but the hijinks on the sidelines and in the stands are especially silly and appealing to kids. Games are played at O'Brien Field Stadium April through August. *730 S.W. Jefferson St., Peoria; (309) 688-1622;* www.peoriachiefs.com

Bunking Down

Holiday Inn Bloomington-Normal ★★/$$

The attached Holidome is the lure for traveling families here at this 160-room hotel. Kids and parents both will enjoy the indoor pool, game room, and hot tub. Your basketball fans should check out the exhibition room, featuring a basketball coaches Hall of Fame, honoring high school coaches. Some rooms have coffeemakers, microwaves, and refrigerators. *8 Traders Cir., Normal; (800) 465-4329; (309) 452-8300;* www.holiday-inn.com

Teaching Your Kids How to Pack

Encourage your kids to think of mix-and-match outfits for various activities, just as they do when dressing paper dolls. (You even can have them practice by packing a doll wardrobe — trying out the different outfits — while they pack for themselves.) For example, ask a preschooler, "We're going hiking. Which of your comfortable pants do you want to wear?" After he lays these out, ask him to match them with two T-shirts (for two outfits), a sweatshirt in case it is cold, and appropriate shoes. Then, consider another vacation activity. Ask him to find two bathing suits, for instance, with a sun cover-up and a hat. Next, ask him to think about nighttime, laying out toothbrush and toothpaste, pajamas, a beloved but small stuffed animal, a bathrobe, and slippers.

Jumer's ★★/$$$$

Your older kids will remember this as the time you stayed in a castle. There are two of these very distinctive hotels in the area. Each hotel in the chain looks like a castle or Old-World lodge inside and out. Rooms are furnished with grand-scale antique reproductions. Each property interprets the Jumer's concept a little differently, but all have a royal flair. **Jumer's Castle Lodge**, in Peoria, has 175 rooms, including 30 suites, an indoor pool, and a family-friendly restaurant (see Good Eats). **Jumer's Chateau**, in Normal, has 180 rooms and suites, an indoor pool, a whirlpool, plus an on-site French restaurant. *Jumer's Castle Lodge: 117 N. Western Ave., Peoria; (800/285-8637 or 309/673-8040). Jumer's Chateau: 1601 Jumer Dr., Normal; (800/285-8637 or 309/662-2020).*

Stoney Creek Inn ★★/$$$

Kids will like swimming back and forth between the indoor and outdoor sections of the pool. This hotel has 153 charmingly decorated guest rooms complete with kitchens and decks. Some have a full-size refrigerator, microwave, and a fieldstone fireplace/TV wall. Continental breakfast is included. *101 Mariners Way, East Peoria; (800) 659-2220; (309) 694-1300;* www.stoneycreekinn.com

Wildlife Prairie Park Cabooses ★★/$

Staying overnight near the animals is fun enough, but the accommodations in a red caboose make this an extra-special treat. The four refinished train cars are not luxurious, but what they lack in comfort, they make up in novelty.

Up to six people can sleep on the bunk bed, futons, and pullout bed, and there is a small bathroom with a shower.

The most awesome feature is a button you can push that activates some sort of motor/noise machine that makes the caboose feel and sound like it's rolling along the rails. Cabooses are air-conditioned and have a small refrigerator, toaster oven, and kettle for heating water, but no plates or utensils. *3826 N. Taylor Rd., Hanna City, 10 miles west of downtown Peoria; (309) 676-0998;* www.wildlifeprairiestatepark.org

GOOD EATS

Fairview Farms Restaurant

★★/$

The service here is family style, with everybody passing the serving dishes around. The food is just like Mom makes, too. Prices are reduced for kids. *5911 Heurmann Rd., Peoria; (309) 697-4111.*

Jumer's Restaurant

★★/$$$

This amazing-looking Bavarian-style lodge is fun to just walk into, but why not stay and eat? Try soups, salads, fish sandwiches, pasta, hamburgers, and German favorites, like pork and sauerkraut, and sauerbraten. There's a children's menu featuring the usual suspects: hot dogs, burgers, grilled cheese, fish sticks, and macaroni and cheese. Be sure to leave room for one of the heavenly cinnamon rolls. *117 N. Western Ave., Peoria; (309) 673-8181.*

Lucca Grill

★★/$$

Here's a family Italian restaurant like the ones in the movies: everybody's happy, loud, and well-fed, and children are completely welcome. The menu features kid pleasers like pasta and pizza. *116 E. Market St., Bloomington; (309) 828-7521.*

Abe Lincoln's home is filled with classic Americana, including drugstores with old-fashioned soda fountains.

INTRODUCTION

Springfield and Decatur

THIS IS THE land of Lincoln. In Decatur, Abraham Lincoln's family spent a year and a rough winter in a log cabin on the Sangamon River, and 21-year-old Lincoln made his first forays into politics. He made his first public speech at Lincoln Square, and he worked as a circuit-riding attorney from his Decatur home. Statues of Lincoln decorate the town and the Millikin University Campus.

Lincoln lived in Springfield for 24 years. He married here, raised his family, buried one child before he went to Washington, and is buried here himself. Before he left, he made the moving "To this place . . . I owe everything" speech, which is immortalized in several spots in the town. Young children won't exactly be spellbound, but older kids who have started studying

Children's Museum of Illinois (page 232)

Henson-Robinson Zoo (page 234)

Lincoln Home National Historic Site (page 232)

Lincoln's Tomb State Historic Site (page 233)

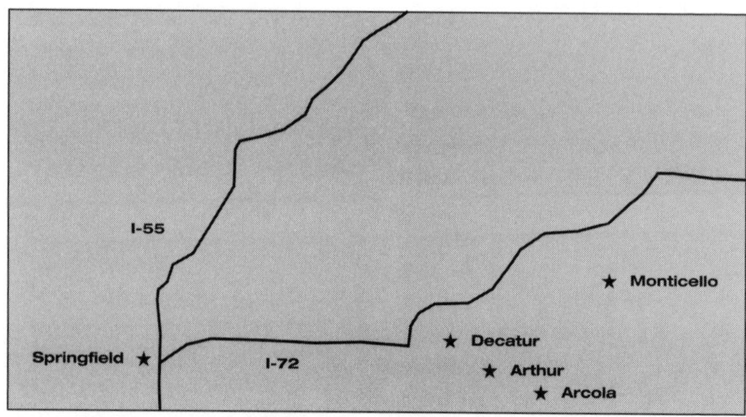

American history have a good opportunity to learn about our nation's 16th president.

Springfield is 39 miles west of Decatur, which is roughly in the center of the state. When your family tires of Lincoln-related sites, try the other attractions in the area—two zoos, a children's museum, an amusement park, and a train museum.

Cultural Adventures

Children's Museum of Illinois ★★★/$

Stop here for a large dose of imaginative, hands-on fun for all ages. Youngsters can enclose themselves in a gigantic bubble, ride a bicycle built for two, and see what it feels like to get around in a wheelchair. There's also a play town where kids can try out grown-up roles: be a banker, a newspaper reporter, or a business leader. *55 S. Country Club Rd., Decatur; (217) 423-5437.* www.cmofil.com

MUST-SEE FamilyFun Lincoln Home National Historic Site ★★★/Free

This four-block pedestrian mall, lighted with gaslights and edged with wooden sidewalks, surrounds the only home that Abraham Lincoln actually owned. It was built in 1839; he bought it in 1844, and lived there for 17 years with wife, Mary Todd Lincoln, and sons Robert, Willie, Tad, and Eddie. The area is always undergoing some restoration, but take the walking tour anyway—each house has a sign that describes some of its Lincoln-era history. The 10-and-up crowd enjoys the **Lincoln Home Visitor Center** *(426 S. Seventh St., Springfield)*, where two films on Lincoln run continuously. The whole family can take the guided tour that leaves from the center or in front of the family home, or simply walk the mall and read the plaques. *Eighth and Jackson Sts., Springfield; (217) 492-4241;* www.nps.gov/liho

Lincoln's Ledger
★★/Free

Looking for a cash machine? Choose Bank One, at East Old State Capitol Plaza, where you can also see an original ledger of Lincoln's account with the Springfield Marine and Fire Insurance Co. This glimpse into his personal finances may also help your grade-schoolers think of Lincoln as a real person. *Sixth and Washington Sts., Springfield; (217) 525-9600.*

Lincoln's Tomb State Historic Site
★★★/Free

This impressive 117-foot-tall monument marks where Abraham Lincoln, his wife, Mary Todd Lincoln, and three of their four children are buried. Lincoln's most memorable speeches—the Gettysburg Address, his farewell to Springfield, and his second inaugural address—are immortalized on bronze tablets. Your kids can rub the nose of the bronze Lincoln bust for luck. If you're in Springfield on a summer Tuesday, bring the family to the 6 P.M. stirring drill movements and retreat ceremonies by the 114th Infantry Regiment, which wears Civil War uniforms. *Oak Ridge Cemetery, 1500 Monument Ave., Springfield; (217) 782-2717.*

Monticello Railway Museum ★★/$$

About 20 miles east of Decatur, this museum is in a restored Illinois Central train depot. Train lovers of all ages enjoy walking through old cars, and looking at the exhibits within. A vintage film-reel about trains runs on screens throughout the museum. Even more exciting is taking the one-hour round-trip ride

FamilyFun READER'S TIP

Travels with Teddy

When my husband and I went to Ireland on business, our children, Lucas, age four, and Emily, six, stayed with my parents. Unbeknownst to the kids, we secretly took along one of each of their small stuffed animals. As we traveled, we took pictures of each animal "hiding" in the hotel lobbies, landscapes, castles, and so on. After we returned home and developed the film, we told the kids of our traveling companions and challenged them to locate their little friends in the pictures. The kids were excited to search the photos and learn about the places we had visited.

Lisa Reynolds, San Antonio, Texas

aboard a vintage train to the historic Wabash Depot in Monticello. Open weekends and holidays May through October. *One mile east of I-72, exit 166. Iron Horse Pl. and Access Rd., Monticello; (800) 952-3396; (217) 762-9011;* www.prairienet.org/mrm

JUST FOR FUN

Adventure Village

★★/$$

Hit this amusement park for non-spectacular but thoroughly enjoyable old-fashioned rides, including a carousel, Tilt-A-Whirl, and Ferris wheel. Your preschoolers will like the little helicopters and the ball pits. Open weekends. *Sangamon Ave. and Peoria Rd., Springfield; (217) 528-9207.*

MUST-SEE FamilyFun MUST-SEE

Henson-Robinson Zoo

★★★/$

More than 300 animals live on the 14 nicely landscaped acres of this small zoo. Little ones love visiting the zoo's monkeys (they live on a cool island), penguins, reptiles, otters, and lemurs. The zoo's new cheetah and red wolf exhibits are also highlights. Warn your preschoolers before entering the dark building where nocturnal animals believe it's night and fly, crawl, and hunt around. For a small fee, you can buy a zoo key and let the kids turn the lock at various enclosures to hear more about the animals within. Stop at the barnyard petting zoo for up-close animal experiences. *1100 E. Lake Dr., Springfield; (217) 753-6217.*

Knight's Action Park and Caribbean Adventure

★★/$$

The action park features mini golf, go-carts, batting cages, and laser tag. The Caribbean Adventure is a water park with water slides, pedal boats, swimming pools, and bumper boats. Admission is based on height (this place is best for older kids anyhow); there are additional fees for some activities. Closed November through March. *1700 Recreation Dr., Springfield; (217) 546-8881;* www.knightsactionpark.com

Scovill Zoo

★★/$

Kids can test their ability to howl like the wolves at WolfHowl; ride the ZO&O express train on a mile of track around the zoo; and meet donkeys, pigs, chicks, ducklings, and goats at the petting zoo. About 500 animals live at this small zoo—everything from kangaroos and ring-tailed lemurs to bobcats and

Log on to This

In 1916, Lincoln Logs were invented by John Lloyd Wright, the son of world-famous architect Frank Lloyd Wright. The creator of the children's classic named the toy in tribute to former President Lincoln.

prairie dogs. The herpaquarium is filled with reptiles and amphibians such as boa constrictors, lizards, salamanders, and frogs; the aquarium has exotic fish, including blind cave fish and piranha. The on-site Zoopermarket is a convenient place for lunch. Before you leave the area, stop at the playground next door with the large and nifty play structure. *71 S. Country Club Rd., Decatur; (217) 421-7435.*

BUNKING DOWN

Hilton Springfield
★★/$$

At 30 stories, this hotel is the tallest building in town. Each of the 367 rooms has a coffeemaker, microwave, and in-room movies—all of which will make Mom and Dad's life easier. You can request a refrigerator. Kids will go for the heated pool, and parents can enjoy the exercise club, too. *700 E. Adams St., Springfield; (217) 789-1530;* www.hilton.com

Holiday Inn Select Conference Hotel ★★/$$

This 383-room hotel has some very ritzy rooms. Ask for the amenities you want—most units have a microwave, a coffeemaker, and in-room movies. Refrigerators are available for an additional fee. There's an exercise room, tennis court, heated pool, playground, and a gift shop. *4191 W. Hwy. 36, Decatur; (217) 422-8800;* www.holiday-inn.com

Looking for Lincoln in Lincoln

If your family embraces the presidential legends and history, take the 35-mile interstate drive north from Springfield to Lincoln—a town named for Abraham Lincoln long before he became president. Young Lincoln helped developers draw up papers to sell the land, and in gratitude, they named the town for him. Visit the two-room Lincoln Museum in the McKinstry Memorial Library of Lincoln College *(300 Keokuk; 217/732-3155)* to see documents and memorabilia related to the president.

GOOD EATS

Gumbo Ya-Ya's ★★/$$

This restaurant is at the top of the 30-story Springfield Hilton, so the view is terrific. Parents can try Creole dishes like shrimp étouffée; kids may feel safer with the kids' menu—burgers, chicken fingers, Cajun pasta, and meatballs. But who knows? They might get hooked on gumbo. *700 E. Adams St., Springfield; (217) 789-1530.*

DAY TRIP

Amish Country: Arcola and Arthur

Illinois is home to a large community of Amish, members of a strict religious sect whose principal belief is in a simple life dedicated to God, one without modern conveniences large and small (everything from automobiles and electricity to zippers). The town of **Arcola** (which, incidentally, is the "birthplace" of Raggedy Ann and Andy) is about two hours (or 85 miles) east of Springfield, and sits at the east side of Illinois Amish country in the central heartland of the state. Many Amish farms lie within the area that stretches west from Arcola for about ten miles, including the town of **Arthur.**

Most savvy kids know that America is full of different kinds of people, but they may not realize that some of these people actively avoid certain aspects of modern life—things that your children couldn't imagine living without. A visit to Amish country is a great way to teach your kids that their must-haves are other people's must-nots—and that they should respect those choices. They'll also come away with a new appreciation of the various appliances that they've taken for granted. ("They have no TV sets?") Along the way, you'll see horse-drawn buggies traveling the roads and Amish families working their farms. (Wave, but don't take pictures—it's against the Amish peoples' religious beliefs to allow themselves to be photographed.) In Arthur, you'll find Amish-run shops where hand-built furniture, handmade quilts, and homemade pies are sold. At **Rockome Gardens** and the **Illinois Amish Interpretive Center,** you can get a close-up view of how Amish people live their lives, without invading another family's privacy. Here's how we spent the day:

9 A.M. Start the day at the **Arcola Depot Welcome Center** *(135 North Oak, Arcola; 800/336-5456).* Here you'll see a Raggedy Ann and Andy display (the dolls were invented here) and a large collection of antique brushes and brooms.

9:30 A.M. At the **Illinois Amish Interpretive Center** *(111 S. Locust, Arcola; 888/452-6474)* your family can get an overview of the Amish and their beliefs. Your kids can check out an authentic Amish farmstead and buggy. A shop sells quilts, oil lamps, wooden toys, and the like—stop by if you want to add some Amish touches to your life.

11 A.M. An absolute must-see is **Johnny Gruelle's Raggedy Ann and Andy Museum** *(110 Main St., Arcola; 217/268-4908;* www.raggedyann-museum.org). Gruelle created the popular rag doll characters and wrote a series of children's books about them, first published in 1915. This 2,000-square-foot museum is devoted to his work. Your young doll collectors will love the gift shop.

12:30 P.M. For a true Amish dining experience, have lunch at the **Dutch Kitchen Family Restaurant** *(127 E. Main St., Arcola; 217/268-3518)*. Whatever you eat, save room for pie. Amish-style home cooking (ham, fried chicken, codfish, baked steak, sausages); and a kids' menu that includes the usual—chicken nuggets, grilled cheese—fill the bill.

2 P.M. The homestead at **Rockome Gardens** *(125 N. County Rd. 425 E, Arcola; 800/549-7625; 217/268-4106;* www.rockomegardens.com) will give you and your kids an idea of how the Amish live. Volunteers demonstrate methods of quilting; your kids will get a kick out of the antique and hand-powered farm implements and tools displayed in the barn. Your little ones will like riding around the grounds in an Amish buggy. One particularly cool way to remember your visit: a child can sit atop a horse that walks in a circle to power a rotating saw blade that cuts a slice off a log. Then, he or she can take the slice to the blacksmith, who burns the child's name into the wood. It's a perfect souvenir—and great for show-and-tell. Closed November through March.

Rock 'n' Roll Hardee's

★★/$

This is fast food with an attitude. Typical Hardee's fare is served in a rock 'n' roll setting. There's a Wurlitzer jukebox, a gas pump, and other cool stuff. *2501 Stevenson Dr., Springfield; (217) 529-1331.*

Souvenir Hunting

Bachman and Keener Drug Store

Before there was Gatorade, there were Green Rivers. Get your kids to try one at this classic drugstore. *530 E. Capitol Ave., Springfield; (217) 523-2431.*

Tinsley Dry Goods

This is a trip back in time, to before megastores that sold in bulk. Your kids will get a kick out of seeing this old place, particularly its selection of penny candy. *209 S. Sixth St., Springfield; (217) 525-1825.*

Visit the one and only Metropolis–home to the one and only Superman.

INTRODUCTION

Southern Illinois

SOUTHERN ILLINOIS is as far from metropolitan Chicago as you can get and still be in Illinois. In fact, it's closer to Memphis than Chicago. In a day's outing, your family can visit three or four of the many small towns in the region, each with something you want to see or do. The drive from town to town is part of the fun, though, since the countryside is so scenic. The steep, rugged hills offer a sharp contrast to the flat farmland up north. Save some time for hiking, biking, boating, and/or fishing.

Collinsville, 12 miles from St. Louis on the Illinois side, is a town with more history than the rest of the country—a prehistoric people lived here from A.D. 700 to 1400. On the side of pop culture, Collinsville's other big attraction is a water tower that's shaped and painted like a giant catsup bottle. Effingham is in the northwest corner of southern Illinois. There, your family can cool out on the sandy beaches and campgrounds of Lake Sara. If you have any motorcycle maniacs in the family, don't miss Mount Vernon, in the center of southern Illinois, which has a motorcycle museum with

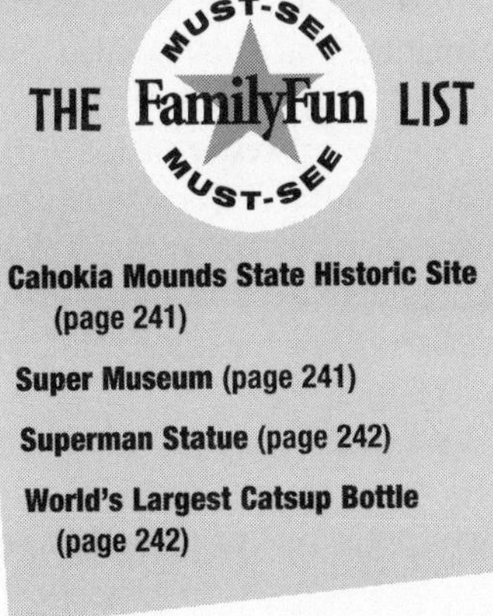

Cahokia Mounds State Historic Site (page 241)

Super Museum (page 241)

Superman Statue (page 242)

World's Largest Catsup Bottle (page 242)

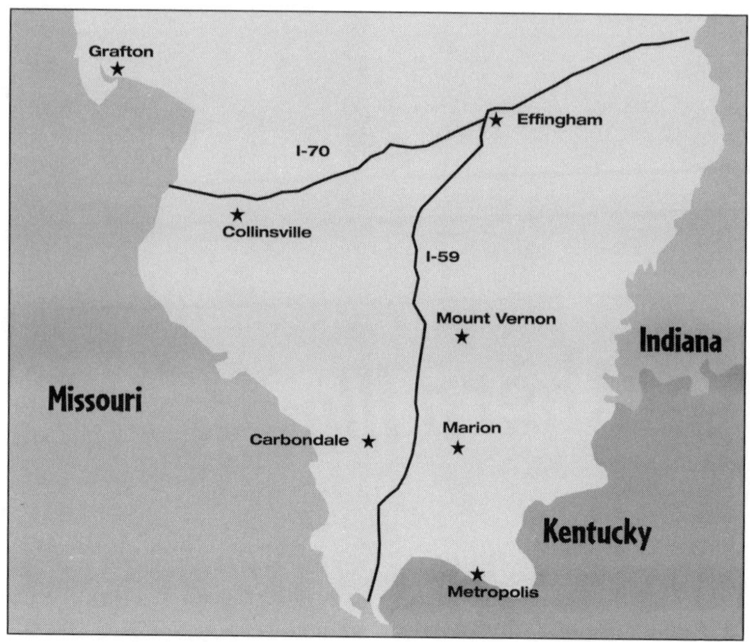

Harley-Davidsons and Evel Knievel memorabilia.

Marion, just a bit south of West Frankfort, is home to the gorgeous woodlands of the Shawnee National Forest, great for hiking and camping. Just west of Marion lies Carbondale, home to towering rock formations and 4,000 wooded acres in Giant City State Park. Grafton lies to the far western edge of the state; 8,000-acre Pere Marquette State Park is a picturesque spot along the Illinois River that offers lots of opportunities for hiking, biking, and boating.

One Southern Illinois town is known around the world. Metropolis, one of the southernmost towns in the state, was home to modest and spectacled Clark Kent, aka Superman. The town well remembers the Man of Steel, who, according to his comic book legend, fell to earth from the Planet Krypton, was lovingly raised by his adoptive human parents, and then went to work as a reporter for the city's *Daily Planet.* Metropolis makes the most of its supercitizen: his statue stands downtown, and there's a telephone booth in his honor (just try to change your clothes in there) inside the Chamber of Commerce office. Metropolis also has a lovely state park with a reconstruction of a fort from 1794. It's a great spot for picnics, too.

CULTURAL ADVENTURES

Cahokia Mounds State Historic Site

★★★/Free-$

Junior archaeologists take note: this is said to be the site of the only prehistoric Indian city north of Mexico on this continent. Prehistoric people lived on a 2,200-acre area on the banks of the Mississippi from A.D. 700 to 1400. Now a state historic site, the area is dotted with more than 65 mounds, which Native Americans used for various purposes: as living areas, sites for ceremonies, and burial plots. Take a guided tour past Monks Mound, the largest mound; it is 100 feet tall and covers 14 acres. Donations accepted. *30 Ramey St., Collinsville; (618) 346-5160.* www.cahokiamounds.com

Fort Massac State Park

★★/Free

Young history buffs enjoy the reconstruction of the 1794 timber fort that once stood on this site. The very scenic state park is on the banks of the Ohio River. The museum's displays of weapons and uniforms soldiers once used and wore here add another interesting historic touch. You can also hike trails, picnic, and camp at the park's several campgrounds. *1308 E. Fifth St., Metropolis; (618) 524-9321.*

Super Museum

★★★/$

It's a bird, it's a plane, it's . . . well, parents remember that introduction to this early superhero even if their kids don't. This super collection of Superman toys, advertising, and memorabilia is great fun for parents and kids both. Costumes worn in the Superman movies are here, plus drawings from the comic-strip creators, props from the films, and artifacts from the original television show. You can take home Superman souvenirs, too. *Superman Square, 517 Market St., Metropolis; (618) 524-5518.* www.supermancollectors.com

Wheels Through Time Museum

★★/Free

This place is a must-see for motorcycle lovers. It houses an Evel Knievel motorcycle and a 1910 Harley-Davidson, perhaps the most valuable bike in the nation. The three-wheeled prototype that Harley-Davidson created for the Army is here, too. *Rte. 1, Veterans Memorial Dr., Mount Vernon; (618) 244-4118.*

FamilyFun TIP

Shawnee Trails Wilderness Outfitters

If you get the itch to head into the countryside, come here to get whatever you need to bike, hike, fish, canoe, or kayak. *222 W. Freeman, Carbondale; (618) 529-2313.*

Just for Fun

Lake Sara ★★/Free

This lake near Effingham has more than 25 miles of shoreline. Kids can swim, slide down the water slide, play on the sandy beach, and fish. There are campgrounds *(217/868-2964)* and a bathhouse. *Five miles northwest of Effingham, off Rte. 32.*

Shawnee National Forest ★★★/$

This gorgeous forest land stretches across the state, from the Mississippi River to the Ohio River. In the many state parks within the forest, you can picnic, camp, hike, and stay in a state park lodge (see Bunking Down on page 243). Highlights include these three state parks. **Cave-in-Rock State Park,** on the banks of the Ohio River, where you can hike, fish, boat, and golf. *Southern tip of Rte. 1, Marion; (618) 289-4545.* **Giant City State Park,** named for its towering rock formations, has 4,000 wooded acres where your family can camp, hike, fish, boat, and horseback ride. There's also a lodge and an outdoor pool. *Giant City Rd., Carbondale; (618) 457-4836.* And **Pere Marquette State Park,** if your kids aren't hiked out yet, stop at these 8,000 wooded acres, where you can hike, bike, fish, horseback ride, and boat. *Hwy. 100, four miles west of Grafton; (618) 786-3323.*

MUST-SEE FamilyFun MUST-SEE Superman Statue ★★★/Free

Look! Up in the sky! It's a 15-foot-high bronze statue of Superman. (Okay, it's not actually in the sky—but it does stand tall.) *Massac County Courthouse, Superman Square, 517 Market St., Metropolis.*

MUST-SEE FamilyFun MUST-SEE World's Largest Catsup Bottle ★★/Free

Ah, now here's some culture—a 170-foot water tank and tower painted to look like a Brooks Catsup bottle. It was built in 1949, restored a few years ago, and no longer holds water—or catsup. *209 E. Main St., Collinsville; (618) 345-5598.*

KEEP A TRIP JOURNAL

On a canoe trip to a new spot, pretend that your family is recording a great expedition, in the spirit of Lewis and Clark, and imagine that you've discovered the place. Have people take turns recording their feelings, plus the weather and wildlife sightings.

BUNKING DOWN

Cave-in-Rock, a State Park Lodge ★★/$

This lodge on the banks of the Ohio River has four duplex cabins with eight suites; each one can accommodate four people. The suites have small refrigerators. The grounds offer picnic shelters and playgrounds. The family-style restaurant serves southern specialties. Try the catfish! *Cave-in-Rock State Park, Southern tip of Rte. 1, Marion; (618) 289-4545.*

Giant City, A State Park Lodge ★★/$

Constructed of rustic sandstone and white timber, the lodge has 34 cabins and an outdoor pool. Small cabins have two double beds; midsize ones have a queen-size and a double bed; and large cabins have two queen-size beds and a rollaway cot. The medium and large cabins also have refrigerators. The main lodge has a lobby, dining rooms, and a lounge. The Giant City Lodge Restaurant is a family-style restaurant, known for its fried chicken. *Giant City State Park, Giant City Rd., Carbondale; (618) 457-4921.*

Pere Marquette, A State Park Lodge ★★/$

Parents love the massive stone fireplace, a lofty beamed ceiling, rustic furniture, and woodsy feel of the lodge. Kids are more interested in the indoor pool and whirlpool, outdoor tennis courts, and playground. The 72 rooms and river cabins are all close to fishing, hiking, biking, and boating. Each cabin has two double beds but no kitchen facilities. You can eat at the on-site restaurant with such favorites as catfish, prime rib, and grilled chicken. *Pere Marquette State Park; Rte. 100, Great River Rd., Grafton; (618) 786-2331;* www.dnr.state.il.us

GOOD EATS

NOTE: The best food is in the restaurants in the lodges listed above or try:

Porter's Steakhouse ★★/$$

A cozy place for a family dinner after a day of sight-seeing, this restaurant has steaks, shrimp, pork loin, and the like; and there's a kids' menu, too. The desserts are very good, and large. Very large. *Holiday Inn, 1000 E. Port Plaza Dr., Collinsville; (618) 345-2400.*

SOUVENIR HUNTING

Pamona General Store

This general store has been around since 1876, and still honors the age-old tradition of keeping a soda fountain in back—and selling everything under the sun up front. *Poplar and Main Sts., Pamona; (618) 893-4045.*

Wisconsin

Wisconsin seems to have been constructed especially for families. First of all, it's a state filled with lakes, woods, and beaches—surefire kid pleasers all. Second, Wisconsin's passion for producing, serving, and consuming dairy products means there's a frozen custard stand on just about every block. (Frozen custard is the Wisconsin version of ice cream, with even more butterfat and creamy deliciousness added.)

And then, the state seems to have gone out of its way to create several children's paradises. Door County, a fairy-tale

land of pretty Victorian and New England architecture, has more miniature-golf courses than you can shake a miniature club at, plus pick-your-own cherry orchards and go-cart and batting-cage parks galore. Green Bay is home to the Green Bay Packers and their Hall of Fame, near-nirvana for any football-crazy kid. The Lake Geneva area is a cluster of beautiful lakes and family resorts devoted to keeping small vacationers happy. Milwaukee has children's museums, theaters, and theme restaurants. And the Wisconsin Dells is so thoroughly designed with youngsters in mind that it could very well have been dreamed up by a child. Kids think Wisconsin is cool. No wonder.

ATTRACTIONS

$	under $5
$$	$5 - $15
$$$	$15 - $25
$$$$	$25 +

HOTELS/MOTELS/CAMPGROUNDS

$	under $75
$$	$75 - $100
$$$	$100 - $140
$$$$	$140 +

RESTAURANTS

$	under $10
$$	$10 - $20
$$$	$20 - $30
$$$$	$30 +

***FAMILYFUN* RATED**

★	Fine
★★	Good
★★★	Very Good
★★★★	*FamilyFun* Recommended

The apple orchards of Door County are flanked by Green Bay and Lake Michigan.

INTRODUCTION

Door County

THE LONG, NARROW finger-shaped northeastern peninsula of Wisconsin is a beloved vacation spot for both Wisconsinites and out-of-staters. The unique scenic quality of the 75-mile-long spit of land comes from having Green Bay on one side and Lake Michigan on the other. In many places, the county is less than ten miles wide. Those dimensions make Door County seem a world apart. (They also make finding your way around here pretty simple; your 9-year-old can navigate and direct the adventures.) The county has a rather lovely trip-back-in-time feeling, with its plethora of cherry and apple orchards, raspberry patches, old Victorian inns, white picket fences, boats in every harbor, and ten lighthouses.

In fact, Door County seems to make it a mission to be as picturesque as possible. Nearly every narrow country road and property line is edged in flowers, and even the names of the villages along the coastlines are cute: Egg Harbor, Baileys Harbor, Gills Rock, and Sister Bay.

Cana Island Lighthouse (page 250)

Door County Maritime Museum (page 248)

The Farm (page 251)

Lautenbach's Orchard Country (page 252)

Peninsula State Park (page 254)

Whitefish Dunes State Park (page 259)

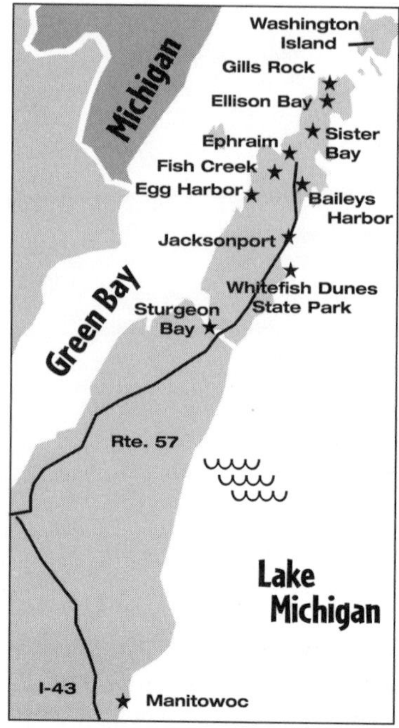

This relatively small peninsula has five state parks, each with its own particular beauty, and all with beaches and outdoor attractions. There are also 17 county parks and 250 miles of rocky shoreline.

Your family can enjoy outdoor activities and outstanding scenery year-round here. Fall brings russet and gold colors against the bright blue lake and evergreen forests. In winter, there is cross-country skiing, snowmobiling, winter hiking, and snowshoeing. In spring, cherry trees and apple trees in Wisconsin orchards are in bloom, and on the third weekend in May, all ten lighthouses are open to visitors.

But summer is the high season here. There's much for a vacationing family to do in Door County when the sun is shining and the weather is warm. Build sand castles on the park beaches. Ride a ferry out to Washington Island. Give your kids a look at a working farm or visit a petting zoo. Pick your own cherries or raspberries, compete in a cherry-pit-spitting contest, or eat a slice of fresh-baked cherry pie. Tour the two lighthouses that are open to visitors, Eagle Bluff and Cana Island. Play miniature golf, race go-carts, and eat like a native: fish boils, fudge, butter burgers (hamburgers on buttered buns), and rich frozen custard in a cone.

Cultural Adventures

Door County Historical Museum ★★/$

Exhibits here chronicle the county's unique history. Kids tend to be most interested in the pioneer firehouse and the wildlife exhibits. Closed November through April. *18 N. Fourth Ave., Sturgeon Bay; (920) 743-5809.*

MUST-SEE FamilyFun MUST-SEE Door County Maritime Museum ★★★/$

The history of the local fishing and shipping industry comes to life at this museum. Young sailors can steer a ship from the great captain's wheel, man the periscope, climb into the pilot house, and see where shipwrecks lie not far off the coast. A summer branch in Gills Rock is open from Memorial Day through Labor Day. *120 N. Madison Ave., Sturgeon Bay (920/743-5958); 12724 Hwy. 42, Gills Rock (920/854-1844);* www.dcmm.org

Wisconsin Maritime Museum ★★/$$

Touring the authentic USS *Cobia* World War II submarine is bound to be the high point of your family's visit to this, the state's largest maritime museum. The gallery of model ships is impressive, too. *75 Maritime Dr., Manitowoc; (920) 684-0218;* www.wimaritimemuseum.org

JUST FOR FUN

Ahnapee Ranch ★★/$$$

Take a trail ride, a sunset ride, or even a moonlight ride at this dude ranch, which also has several programs especially for children. The Cow Kids Adventure, for 5- to 8-year-olds, teaches youngsters how to say hello to, saddle, and lead a horse; participants also play games that encourage them to ride. The Wrangler Adventure is a riding experience for kids ages 9 to 12. Reservations are required. *6875 Tagge Rd., Sturgeon Bay; (920) 743-2715.*

The Beaches of Door County

The many Door County beaches are inviting, but if your children are accustomed to warm ocean shores, they're in for a chilly surprise. Explain to them ahead of time that the beaches here front Lake Michigan and its bay, Green Bay, which means that the water is often quite cold. While your kids may wade and play in the shallow water, Lake Michigan is rarely warm enough for actual swimming. And, when kids come out of the lake, they'll be cold and shivery: be ready with lots of towels and a cozy beach cover-up. NOTE: The beaches on the west side of Door County, the side that faces Green Bay, are more sheltered. The water there is slightly warmer and less choppy than the waters of the open lake.

Even when the water isn't warm, the sunshine is, and it's still great fun to sunbathe and build castles in the sand. The coastlines on both sides of the peninsula are gorgeous but rocky, leaving small patches of sandy beach here and there. What's fun about this topography is that your family can likely "camp" in one area for the day in relative privacy: just you, your kids, the sand, the lake, and a few dozen seagulls.

Cana Island Lighthouse ★★★/$

MUST-SEE FamilyFun MUST-SEE

Getting to this 1869 lighthouse is half the fun! When the water level is low, you can just walk right out to the island on which the lighthouse stands. When the water is high, you have to wade from the mainland on a narrow strip of often-submerged land. The water is usually only ankle-deep on a grown-up, and won't alarm children if you prepare them first and dress them in shorts or rolled-up pants.

Stats to share with your kids: The island itself is barely nine acres. The lighthouse tower is 89 feet high, the lens inside is five feet tall, and the lightbulb is 500 watts. The light can be seen for 18 miles out over the lake. Closed November through April. *Hwy. Q, about four miles northeast of Baileys Harbor; (920) 743-3958.*

Collector Showcase

★★/$

If you miss the kitschy charm of the Wisconsin Dells, drop in here to see antique cars, vintage toys, and old dolls, including thousands of Barbies. There's a gift shop of both old and new Barbies, an "old town" with a gas station (your kids won't believe that attendants used to wear uniforms and leave the building to wash windshields), and a merry-go-round. Closed November through April. *Chal-A-Motel, 3910 Hwy. 42/57, Sturgeon Bay; (920) 743-6788.*

Egg Harbor ★★/Free

How did this charming village get its odd name? The stories are many and conflicting. One says that back in 1825 two rowboat crews began throwing eggs at each other in the harbor. Invite your kids to make up their own stories—they're bound to be better than that one. Downtown streets are lined with restored historic buildings, and flowers are growing everywhere. There are no specifically kid-focused activities here, but it is a pretty little village to drive and/or walk through. In winter, take a sleigh ride through neighboring orchards; contact **Mayberry's Carriage and Sleigh Rides** *(4404 Cty. Rd. V, Egg Harbor; 920/743-2352).*

Ephraim

★★/$

In 1853, 40 Norwegian Moravians settled here. Moravian tradition favors simple white buildings, which has left the waterfront town with a restrained and elegant look. A fun way to survey the scene in summer is to take a carriage ride through town; *(see Mayberry's Carriage and Sleigh Rides, above)*. You can get a lovely view from the top of a tall wooden tower in Peninsula State Park, on the western edge of town; kids 11 and older may like the climb up the eight flights of stairs.

There are also several historic museums along Moravia Street: the restored old-fashioned **Anderson**

FamilyFun READER'S TIP

Pocket Pals

After a family car trip, my husband and I realized that we needed a way to keep our children's things from scattering all over the car. To solve this problem I made organizers that could easily hang over the backs of the seats. I sewed some old pants pockets onto two aprons and used puffy paint to label the pockets for things like pencils, tissue, and books. I used the apron ties to attach them to the seats. They keep things organized but still accessible, and the kids, Zachary, age nine, and Megan, eight, love them.

Trish Hazell, Rocklin, California

Store; **Anderson Barn Museum**, with its unusual square silo; **Pioneer Schoolhouse**, which has 1869 furnishings; and **Thomas Goodletson House**, built in 1857, one of the first permanent houses on the peninsula, now authentically restored and finished. Here, too, the **Ephraim Monument** commemorates the landing of the Moravians in 1853 *(920/854-9688)*. Most houses are closed after Labor Day to late June. On the June weekend closest to the summer solstice, a Scandinavian festival called *Fyr Bal* includes bonfires, food, music, and art; in July, there's a windsurfing regatta in the harbor. For information on these events, call the local tourism office *(920/854-4989);* www.ephraimdoorcounty.com

The Farm

MUST-SEE FamilyFun MUST-SEE

★★★/$$

Get your camera ready. You'll want a shot of your little ones petting or giving a bottle of milk to tame piglets, baby goats, and lambs. Your kids can also cuddle a kitten, gobble at a turkey, and maybe even help milk a goat. The entire family will enjoy seeing old farm machinery and walking on nature trails through woods, past a small pond, and into prairie grasslands. Five log houses give everybody a peek at what homes looked like in the pioneer days. Open between Memorial Day and Labor Day. *Hwy. 57, Sturgeon Bay; (920) 743-6666.*

Fish Creek

★★/Free

The log cabin of Asa Thorp, the founder of the town of Fish Creek, sits in **Founders Square** *(920/868-2316)*; a visit might launch an interesting family historical discussion. If you're here in-season (June to mid-October), plan on seeing the **Peninsula Players**, who perform outdoor plays in a pretty garden setting along Highway 42 between Fish Creek and Egg Harbor *(4351*

Peninsula Players Rd.; 920/868-3287). The view of Green Bay and the surrounding gardens make it a memorable evening, and kids enjoy the shows—they're brief enough to hold their interest, and they usually feature a lot of music and funny bits. Depending on the time of year, you can also rent bikes, cross-country skis, ice skates, and snowshoes at **Nor-Door Sport and Cycling** *(4007 Hwy. 42; 920/868-2275).*

Herb's Riding Stables ★★/$$$$

Longing to get in the saddle? Head for Herb's, where there are riding trails for older children and parents, and pony trails for preschoolers. *6926 Division Rd., Egg Harbor; (920) 868-3304.*

Island Clipper ★★/$$$

Get a view of the Door County shoreline during this boat ride out to Washington Island (see page 258). *The narrated cruises depart from Gills Rock; (920) 854-2972.*

Kurtz Corral Riding Stables ★★/$$$$

Give your little ones pony rides and take your inexperienced school-age kids on gentle walking or walk-trot trails. Winter rides end with cider around the fireplace. The stables are open year-round, but by appointment only September through May. *County Chunk I, Egg Harbor; (920) 743-6742;* www.kurtzcorral.com

Lautenbach's Orchard Country ★★★/$

How many cherries will make it into the bucket—and how many will get tossed into your mouth? Pick-your-own cherries are cheap food and cheap fun ($4 for ten pounds), not to mention nutritious. In addition to picking, your kids can learn how a cherry orchard operates and how apple trees grow. You can also watch cherries and apples being picked and then turned into cider and treats. Speaking of treats, stop at the on-site market for a piece of cherry pie. *Hwy. 42, half a mile south of Fish Creek; (920) 868-3479.*

Newport State Park ★★/$

This 2,400-acre park includes 11 miles of Lake Michigan shoreline for strolls, sight-seeing, and picnicking, as well as wilderness areas you can hike through on 30 miles of trails. You can bike on the hiking trails and, in the winter, cross-country ski and snowshoe (**Harbor House Inn** rents bikes—*12666 Hwy. 42, Gills Rock; 920/854-5196*). The coastline is mostly rocky, but kids can scramble around on the rocks, and there is a section of sandy beach that faces Lake Michigan (look for the signs to "Lot #3"—that's the spot). The beach here is easier for toddlers and preschoolers to reach on foot than is the Whitefish Dunes beach (see page 259). And yes, there are rest rooms here, and a picnic

PICK YOUR OWN BERRIES AND CHERRIES

DOOR COUNTY'S ROADSIDE apple and cherry orchards and raspberry patches beautify the county when the trees and bushes are in bloom, and feed visitors and locals alike when the fruit ripens.

In May, the trees blossom, coloring the countryside with pink petals. In June, the raspberry bushes bloom with white flowers. In July, cherries and raspberries are ripe, and many roadside orchards are open for pick-your-own bounty. In September and October, apples are ripe and ready for picking. *For blossom updates, call (920) 743-4456.*

The following are our favorite orchards. Call ahead to see what fruits are in season.

Hyline Orchard

Pick-your-own apples and cherries in season. Fresh-pressed apple cider, jams and jellies, maple syrup, popcorn, pumpkins, and crafts are among the other highlights. Open seven days a week, year-round. *8240 Hwy. 42, Fish Creek; (920) 868-3067.*

Lautenbach Orchard Country Winery Market

Pick-your-own cherries, apples, and raspberries. Head to the on-site market for hand-picked fruits, homemade preserves, fresh-baked pies, and a variety of homemade Door County products and gifts. Open seven days a week, year-round. *9197 Hwy. 42, Fish Creek; (920) 868-3479.*

Le Fevre Orchards

Pick-your-own cherries in season. Apples, apple and cherry ciders and pies, gift baskets, honey, jams and jellies, and maple syrup are also available. (Cherries are in season in late July through August.) *Hwy. 42-57 S., Sturgeon Bay; (920) 743-2775.*

Rocky Ridge Orchards

Pick-your-own cherries and apples in season. Take home frozen cherries, apple cider, cherry juice, jams, jellies, honey, and syrups. Closed November through May. *3482 City E., Baileys Harbor; (920) 868-3992.*

Go Play on a Lake

A visit to Door County in the summer is not complete without a marine adventure. Get your family out onto the waters of Lake Michigan with a boat or kayak rental or charter.

For paddle sports, head to **Bayshore Outdoor Store** where you can get completely outfitted with canoes, kayaks, and accessories, or schedule a guided kayak tour *(Hwy. 42 S., Sister Bay; 920/854-7598)*. To the south, **Door County Bicycle Works** also rents kayaks and gives guided tours *(20 N. Third Ave., Sturgeon Bay; 920/743-4434)*. Sign the family up for sailing class at **Ephraim Sailing Center** *(located at South Shore Pier)*. They promise you'll be on Eagle Harbor in two hours. Double kayaks are available for rent, too *(920/854-4336)*.

Or, if being pampered is more your family's speed, make for one of the area's kid-friendly charter companies: **Bella Sailing Cruises** runs two-hour sailing trips on Scuppers, a captained 26-foot, red-sailed ketch *(920/854-2628)*; **Shoreline Waterfront Motel Charters** hosts narrated cruises past bluffs, scenic islands, and lighthouses *(12747 Hwy. 42, Gills Rock; 920/854-2606)*; and **Stiletto Catamaran Sailing Cruises** has cruises, departing seven times daily from South Shore Pier in Ephraim *(920/854-7245)*.

area, too. *475 County Rd. and Newport Lane, Ellison Bay; (920) 854-2500.*

Peninsula State Park ★★★/$$

MUST-SEE FamilyFun MUST-SEE

At 3,776 acres, this park is the largest in the county, jutting out into Green Bay with six miles of shoreline. It's in Fish Creek, on the Green Bay side of the peninsula, where the water is more tranquil and slightly warmer than the water on the Lake Michigan side of Door County. There's a lot to do here—on a good-weather day you can spend hours hiking, biking, and enjoying the gorgeous views of the lake. Your kids can bike with confidence here, because hikers and bikers have their own separate trails (that also means you can hike with your kids without worrying about collisions with passing cyclists).

If your kids are experienced cyclists, rent bikes from **Edge of the Park Inc.** *(at the entrance of the park and adjacent to the trails; 920/868-3344)* and bike on Peninsula State Park Road, or **Nor-Door Sport and Cyclery** *(4007 Hwy. 42; 920/868-2275)* and take the five-mile Sunset Trail through forests, a wildflower prairie, and along the lake. You'll arrive at the **Eagle Bluff Lighthouse** *(920/839-2377)*, one of the two Door County lighthouses open to the public (May through October). Touring it gives your kids a sense of how much the ships at sea depended on these enormous night-lights; tours are given daily every 30 minutes from 10 A.M. to 4:30 P.M. The tour guide tells a tale that modern-day kids may find highly unlikely: the lighthouse keeper and his wife raised seven sons here, without electricity or running water. Climbing the light tower and seeing its Fresnel lens takes about half an hour.

The park is situated along Nicolet Bay, where **Nicolet Beach** offers sand and shore fun, and you can also rent boats and kayaks for on-the-water outings. Tiger Woods wanna-bes might enjoy the **18-hole golf course** *(920/854-5791)*, which is open May through October; in winter, the course is a great place for cross-country skiing and snowshoeing.

Park staff regularly run nature programs for kids; call for details. The park has rest rooms, showers, changing facilities, and concession stands, so it's easy to stay here all day. If you'd like to spend the night as well, there's a campground with showers and flush toilets. *Fish Creek; (920) 868-3258.*

Pine River Dairy

★★/Free

More than 130 varieties of cheese are produced here, including string cheese and cheese curds, both favorites with children. You can watch cheesemakers through the observation window. Let each person pick out his or her own favorite for a takeout cheese picnic. For more information, see "Cheese, Please" on page 306. *10115 English Lake Rd., Manitowoc; (920) 758-2233.*

Potawatomi State Park

★★/Free

A place for all seasons, this park offers year-round family fun. On the Green Bay side of the peninsula, in the town of Sturgeon Bay, this 1,178-acre state park has more than two miles of Green Bay shoreline and a sandy beach. There are also six miles of hiking trails, many bike trails, and you can camp and fish here, too. In winter the family can go snowshoeing and cross-country skiing on 13 miles of trails. *3740 Park Dr., Sturgeon Bay; (920) 746-2890.*

When It Snows

Many of Door County's attractions close down or reduce their hours of operation during the winter. But lots of people especially love visiting at this time of year, when the trees lose their leaves and allow even more expansive views of the lake. In four of the state parks, the hiking trails become cross-country ski trails; for trail conditions and a weather report, call the **Door County Chamber of Commerce** *(920/743-4456)*. There's also snowshoeing at several of the parks, downhill skiing at Potawatomi State Park, and sledding and tobogganing at Peninsula State Park.

Prof. H. H. Scott's Old Time Portraits

★★/$$

For a priceless photo, pose your kids in old-fashioned costumes in front of an old-time backdrop (a Wild West saloon, say, or Al Capone's Model A). Your portrait will be ready in ten minutes. *4201 Main St., Fish Creek; (920) 868-3309.*

Rock Island State Park

★★/$$

Forget the car—no vehicles (motorized or otherwise) are allowed on this island, off the northeastern tip of Washington Island (see page 258). Now a primitive 906-acre park that you can reach only by boat, a visit here is a bit of an adventure. But once you're here, you'll enjoy a vacation within your vacation. Your family can take the milelong self-guided nature trail, or hike or bike along the ten miles of trails. When snow is on the ground, cross-country skis and snowshoes are the main means of transportation.

There's a sandy beach on the south end of the park, and picturesque limestone bluffs on the north end. The stone buildings here were built by Chester Thordarson, an Icelandic immigrant who once owned the island. The Viking Hall and his former boathouse now dis-

DOOR COUNTY LIGHTHOUSES

THE ROCKY SHORELINES OF the Door County peninsula pose a hazard to ships sailing the waters of Lake Michigan. To alert passing vessels to the danger, 10 lighthouses were built here between the 1830s and the 1890s—more than in any other county in the country. Though only two are usually open to the public, on the third weekend in May all ten lighthouses on the peninsula open their doors to visitors for an annual event known as **Lighthouse Walk** *(for information, call 920/743-5958).*

The two lighthouses that are generally open to the public are **Eagle Bluff Lighthouse** in *Peninsula State Park (920/839-2377)* and **Cana Island Lighthouse** *(Hwy. Q, four miles northeast of Baileys Harbor; 920/743-5958).* Eagle Bluff Lighthouse, which dates to 1869, is open May through October. The lighthouse at Cana Island, which dates to 1868, is manned from May through October; the rest of the year, you can get there in low tide or by walking on the ice.

The other Door County lighthouses *(for information, call 920/743-5958)* are:

Baileys Harbor Rangelight (1869) Range lights were used at this site for

play archaeological artifacts from the site and other historical exhibits. The lighthouse here is Wisconsin's oldest, built in 1836; the interior is not open to the public.

A full day is recommended to take in the history, trails, views, and lake breezes. Bring your own food, as there is none to be had on the island. If you want to overnight here, there are 40 rustic campsites (drinking water and toilets); reserve ahead *(920/847-2235)*. The ferry runs about three times a day from May to early October, and is half-price for children. *The island is one mile north of Jackson Harbor, Washington Island; (920) 847-2235.*

Sister Bay

★★/Free

Settled in the mid-1800s by Norwegian immigrants, Sister Bay has an especially picturesque shoreline and a sandy beach right in the heart of downtown. The waterfront park is the site of summer outdoor concerts. In October, the town has an annual Fall Festival of parades, fireworks, and an arts-and-crafts fair. In winter, your family can get outfitted for snowshoeing and skiing at **Bayshore Outdoor Store** *(Hwy. 42 S.; 920/854-7598)*. An 1866 schoolhouse, the first in northern Door County, sits on the south edge of town *(Hwy. 42 and 57; 920/854-*

100 years before being replaced with a directional light.

Chambers Island Lighthouse (1858) Ships use this beacon to navigate Strawberry Channel. The lighthouse is almost an exact copy of the Eagle Bluff Light.

Pilot Lighthouse (1858) This light still helps ships coming into Ports des Morts (Death's Door Passage).

Plum Lighthouse (1895) Not actually a lighthouse, this keeper's quarters houses a set of range lights.

Potawatomi Lighthouse (1836) The oldest of all the Door County Lighthouses, it sits on Rock Island.

Range Lighthouse (1899) This lighthouse, in conjunction with the Baileys Harbor Rangelight, provides safe passage into Baileys Harbor.

Sherwood Point Lighthouse (1883) The light was guarded for 100 years until the light was automated in 1983. It is the only Door County lighthouse built with red brick.

Sturgeon Bay Ship Canal Lighthouse (1899) The first keeper guarded the light without a dwelling from 1882, living on a dredge working on the canal. The skeletal steel framework that surrounds the 78-foot tower was added in 1903 to stabilize the structure that vibrated so violently in the wind.

2812). Your kids will get a kick out of seeing the old maps, school desks, and antique portraits of Lincoln and Washington at the school, which is open daily from Memorial Day to mid-October.

Skyway Drive-In Theatre

★★/$$

Show your kids how summer nights were spent in the 1950s. The theater screens a double feature on weekend nights in summer. Stop at the concession stand for popcorn and other treats. Open weekends May through September. *Hwy. 42, between Fish Creek and Ephraim; (920) 854-9938.*

Sturgeon Bay ★★/Free

This is the largest community on the peninsula. Its roots are in lumbering, but once the canal was built linking Green Bay and Lake Michigan, shipping and commerce became the city's mainstays. The architecture is hardly picturesque, but the canal and the lake make for remarkable vistas. **Potawatomi State Park**, with its biking and hiking trails, is here, and area guides take out amateur fisherpersons daily with great success. (They say fishing over a shipwreck is a good way to catch a smallmouth bass.) Don't miss the **farmers' market** *(920/743-6246)* held downtown on Saturday morning in June through October. Let your kids pick out their favorite fruit to munch as you stroll along Main Street.

There's a self-guided historic walking or driving tour of the town's two districts that are on the National Register of Historic Places. You can see some of the historic sites in unforgettable fashion by riding in a 6- or 12-person carriage; you'll find them at Stone Harbor and at Third and Michigan streets; contact **Carriages of Door County** *(920/743-4343)* for more information. Or rent children's, adults, and tandem bikes at **Door County Bicycle Works** *(20 N. Third Ave.; 920/746-1185)*. At the eastern foot of the canal that connects Lake Michigan and Sturgeon Bay lies the **Sturgeon Bay Ship Canal and Coastguard Station Lighthouse.** The canal was built in 1882. This lighthouse and breakwater pier are perhaps the most photographed subjects in the county. For more information, see: sturgeonbay.area guides.net

Washington Island

★★/$ (for ferry)

Of the many islands off the coast of Door County, Washington is the only one where people live year-round. It's exciting to take the 30-minute **Washington Island ferry** from Northport Pier *(at the end of Hwy. 42; 800/223-2094; 920/847-2546)*. Kids love seeing canoes, cars, boats, and bicycles get loaded onto the ferry along with the passengers.

Biking is a good way to get around the island. You can rent bicycles in Gills Rock near Northport Pier (but then you have to pay to take them on the ferry) or rent them on the island at **Harbor Bike Rental** *(800/223-2094)*. If your kids are too young to cycle any distance, board the **Washington Island Cherry Train** *(920/847-2039)* for a narrated 90-minute tour. Just don't try to walk downtown—it's three miles from the ferry landing. Call **Vi's Taxis** *(920/493-2388)*; Violet gives a great tour, but be sure to call ahead.

Island attractions include the **Double K-W Ostrich Farm** *(Main Rd. and West Harbor Rd.; 920/847-3202)*, where your kids can get a good view of the huge birds, and the **Washington Island Farm Museum** *(Jackson Harbor Rd.; 920/847-3336)*, where kids can see old-fashioned farm equipment and log houses and enjoy a horse-drawn wagon ride. The **Art and Nature Center** *(920/847-2025)* is in an old schoolhouse and features the work of local watercolor painters and jewelry designers. Kids will find the coolest part is the working beehive. Young equestrians can take a trail ride on Icelandic horses at **Field Wood Farm Stables** *(West Harbor Rd., 3½ miles from the dock; 920/847-2490)*. Timid riders can double up with a sibling or parent. More experienced riders can ride with a lead line or solo. It's open Memorial Day to mid-October.

Or, just buy some fudge and go hang out at the beach. There are several: **Percy Johnson County Park** has picnic tables and a sandy stretch; **Schoolhouse Beach** has picnic spots and lots of rocky shoreline; and the **Sand Dunes Beach** has picturesque evergreens and especially clear water.

MUST-SEE FamilyFun MUST-SEE Whitefish Dunes State Park ★★★/$

Yes, midwestern Wisconsin does have sand dunes, and the highest ones in the state are at this 863-acre park. Old Baldy is the tallest

Clap, Tickle, Tug

It's the sitting—and sitting and sitting—that gets to kids on the road. Get their belted-in bodies moving with this game of competitive copycat. The first player makes an expression or a movement, such as a hand clap; the next player repeats that movement and adds another; and so on. Kids will be pulling on their ears, sticking out their tongues, tipping back their heads, holding their elbows—and smiling! When a player forgets a movement, he's out. When everyone's out, start over.

dune; get your kids to scramble up it for a great view of Lake Michigan. The beach here is really terrific, but if you've got preschoolers, skip it. The hike from the parking lot is too much for little legs to manage—and the rest room facilities are rustic at best. If your kids are older and up to the hike, pack light and teach them to whistle the *Bridge on the River Kwai* song. After about a nine-minute trek, you'll find the beach—really a sort of steep dunelike clearing in a grove of pine trees. Stop at the ranger station for a schedule of guided tours through the park. The wildflowers are notable (though not riveting points of interest for kids). There's a mile of sandy beach, two miles of rocky shoreline, nearly 15 miles of hiking and skiing trails, plus cross-country skiing, snowshoeing, swimming, and fishing, depending on the season. *3701 Clark Lake Rd., Sturgeon Bay; (920) 823-2400.*

BUNKING DOWN

Camping

Aqualand Camp Resort

★★★/$

Some sites here are wooded, and you get modern rest rooms, a heated swimming pool, picnic tables, fire rings where you can have a campfire and cook, and paddleboats. There's trout fishing, too. Closed November to mid-May. *Hwy. 57 and Hwy. Q, Sister Bay; (920) 854-4573.*

FISH STORY

GREEN BAY and the waters around Door County are great for families that fish. You can board a fishing charter boat from most of the towns on both coasts, but be warned: waters (and the ride) can be choppy and have been known to make even sturdy sailors seasick. Try motion-sickness medicine, or fish from the dock or shore. You'll need to take a charter out to catch a lake trout or walleye and northerns, but you can catch trout, bass, and panfish like sunnies from dry land. Children under 16 need no fishing license, but adults do. Any charter service can set you up with them.

The following companies offer captained and guided fishing charters:

Dawidiuk's Fishing Team Full- and half-day adventures offered. Kids and novices are very welcome. Must have a license with a salmon and trout stamp, or a two-day license. *Sturgeon Bay; (920) 746-9916.*

Baileys Bluff Campgrounds and RV Park ★★★/$
This campground is in the center of the peninsula (not near water) and offers hookups, toilets, showers, picnic tables, fire rings, a playground, fish freezing, trailer rental, and a camp store. Closed mid-October to mid-April. *2701 County EE, Baileys Harbor; (920) 839-2109.*

Baileys Grove Travel Park and Campground ★★★/$
Level, shady sites and pull-throughs, electrical hookups and sewer sites, heated bathrooms and showers, picnic tables, a playground, and a game room—this is a pretty neat campground. Another plus: there's a heated pool. *County Rd. EE just off Hwy. 57, Baileys Harbor; (920) 839-2559.*

Camp-Tel Family Campground ★★★★/$
Shady sites (nice in the hottest months), a heated pool (nice in the cooler months), TV and game rooms, playgrounds, laundry, and showers make this a family-friendly place. *8164 Hwy. 42, Egg Harbor; (920) 868-3278.*

Door County Camping Retreat ★★★/$-$$
This site is near Horseshoe Bay Beach. There are 186 campsites with water and electricity; no sewer hookup, but there is a dump station. There are also 30 basic tenting sites. Both the camp and the tent sites have access to a building with showers and toilets. Four cabins are available, too. The property has a

Fox 1 Charters Four-, six-, and eight-hour tours are generally run out of **Leathem Smith Lodge & Marina,** *1640 Memorial Drive.* The crew's 25-plus years of experience makes for a wonderful outing. Limit: four passengers. Families welcome. Must have a license with a salmon and trout stamp, or a two-day license. Open mid-May through mid-October only. *435 N. Geneva Ave., Sturgeon Bay; (920) 743-3092.*

Lynn's Charter Fishing Captain Lynn offers 20 years of charter experience and expertise about the area's ecology. Kids love learning all there is to know about the fish swimming under the boat. *10309 Old Stage Rd., Sister Bay; (920) 854-5109.*

Salmon Depot The largest charter service in the area, Salmon Depot is definitely full-service: licenses can be processed on-site; fish can be cleaned, filleted, vacuum-packed, frozen, and/or sent home. Full- and half-day trips are available for up to 13 passengers. Be aware that only snacks and beverages are offered, so you might want to bring your own lunch. Or you can prearrange to have a catered lunch. *Baileys Harbor; (800) 345-6701.*

playground, game room, volleyball court, heated pool, family movies shown on summer nights, and occasional evening naturalist presentations. You can rent bikes on-site. *4906 Court Rd., Egg Harbor; (920) 868-3151.*

Frontier Wilderness Campground
★★★/$

The sites here are large and wooded, and even on rainy days, your family will find plenty to do thanks to a large indoor heated pool, sauna and exercise domes, and a game arcade. If the weather is good, you'll enjoy the miniature-golf course and three playgrounds. Private individual washrooms and private individual shower rooms, plus laundry facilities and a store make this a rather luxurious campground. *4375 Hillside Rd., Egg Harbor; (920) 868-3349.*

Monument Point Camping
★★★/$

These sites are very private and heavily wooded. There are hookups, shower stalls and dressing rooms, flush toilets, and a dump station. Kids like the playground and game room. *5718 W. Monument Point Rd., Sturgeon Bay; (920) 743-9411.*

Path of Pines Campground
★★★/$

This is the closest campground to Peninsula State Park. It has water and electricity at all sites, plus a camp store, television lounge, rec room, laundry facilities, and a heated bathhouse. *3709 County Rd., Fish Creek; (800) 868-7802; (920) 868-3332.*

Peninsula State Park
★★/$

The park has rest rooms, showers, changing facilities, and concession stands, plus a campground with showers and flush toilets. *Fish Creek; (920) 868-3258.*

Quietwoods North Camping Resort ★★★/$

You can get to Potawatomi State Park from these campgrounds. The sites are large, and the facilities are good: heated outdoor pools, miniature golf, a game room, a camp store, laundry facilities, a dump station, and rest rooms. *3668 Grondin Rd., Sturgeon Bay; (800) 9-TO-CAMP; (920) 743-7115.*

Rock Island State Park
★★★/$

Forty primitive campsites are at this park, which is only accessible by boat. The campgrounds are open May through the end of October, but the ferry only runs until early October. After that, you have to find your own nautical transportation. *One mile north of Jackson Harbor, Washington Island; (920) 847-2235.*

Yogi Bear's Jellystone Park
★★★★/$

Some of the 286 sites at this campground are wooded, some not. Three heated pools, a game room, miniature-golf course, and a playground make it a great place for kids. There's a dump station and pump-out service, too. *3677 May Rd., Sturgeon Bay; (920) 743-9001.*

Hotels

As a picturesque and charming vacation spot, Door County has many inns that cater to couples , so be sure to choose one that is kid-friendly. Door County has a helpful Website, www.doorcountyvacations.com, that can connect you to INNLINE, a service that lets you know where there are inn and hotel vacancies. **NOTE:** Summer is high season in Door County, which means that you can save big on accommodations the rest of the year. Ask each hotel or resort what they consider to be off-season when you call.

The Alpine Resort—Inn and Cottages

★★★/$$$

This shoreline property feels like an old-time destination resort, complete with wicker-furnished porches for curling up to read and time-tested family activities like shuffleboard. Accommodations are in rooms, houses, and cottages, all with wet bars, refrigerators, and microwaves—100 units in all. Your kids can choose among swimming in the pool, frolicking on the sandy

From Wisconsin to Michigan by Car and Boat

Take a shortcut from Wisconsin to Michigan (or vice versa)—straight across Lake Michigan. The S.S. *Badger* car ferry takes four hours to cross the lake, and keeps both kids and parents entertained with movies, a video arcade, shopping, storytelling, snacks, strolls around the deck, bingo, and a gift shop. Ferry is a misnomer—it's an enormous, 410-foot ship that can carry 620 passengers and 180 vehicles. **NOTE:** You can't get to your car during the trip, so be sure your kids remove the toys, books, and food they want before you're underway. Administer the motion-sickness medicine beforehand, or pick up an acupressure sea band on board. You can rent a stateroom, which is not luxurious but your kids can nap there, for under $35. Fares are $45 per adult one way, $20 for kids 5 to 15, children under 5 free. Vehicles are $49. The ferry runs May 1 to mid-October. *For information, call (800) 841-4243;* www.ssbadger.com

THE WATER PURSE

Talk about wash and wear! This thoroughly waterproof and easy-to-make drawstring purse, crafted from an onion bag, is more than just a fashion statement. Secured to your clothing with a plastic clip, it's invaluable for carrying quarters for the pool's soda machine, holding interesting river rocks, or hauling your goggles and earplugs to the beach. Directions: Weave a length of plastic twine (or other waterproof material) around the onion bag's opening to serve as a drawstring. About halfway around the bag, weave the twine through the loop of a plastic clip, like the kind commonly sold as key chains.

beach, boating, biking, tennis, shuffleboard, fishing, and playing in the game room or at the playground. (Dad may opt for the 27-hole golf course.) Nightly activities are planned for guests and children in July and August. The Hof Restaurant (see Good Eats) serves breakfast, lunch, and dinner. If you want to picnic, they have an outdoor grill, too. Closed November through May. *Hwy. G, Egg Harbor; (920) 868-3000.*

Baileys Harbor Yacht Club Resort

★★★/$$$$

The condominium suites at this luxurious resort have whirlpools, fireplaces, and kitchens—all in all, quite comfortable homes away from home. Your family will also appreciate the indoor and outdoor pools, tennis court, whirlpool, sauna, and full-service marina. The property has walkways and a beach on the waterfront, but note that the rooms themselves are a short walk from the water, not directly on it. *8151 Ridges Rd., Baileys Harbor; (800) 927-2492; (920) 839-2336.*

Bay Shore Inn

★★/$$$

On the waterfront, this lovely resort has 37 one-, two-, and three-bedroom suites with water views. All units have kitchens and whirlpools, big pluses as far as parents are concerned. Your kids will be able to use up some excess energy at the indoor

OTHER WISCONSIN STATE PARKS

DOOR COUNTY and Northwestern Wisconsin haven't cornered the market on great state parks. Wisconsin has other attractive parks that are terrific for camping and outdoor recreation.

Amnicon Falls State Park, Superior

Imagine a river made of root beer cascading over waterfalls and rapids in a frothy foam. That's what the Amnicon River, which runs through this state park, looks like. A 36-unit campground, a playground, and picnic areas are other attractions. Closed November through April. *Park entrance is southeast of Superior, off U.S. Hwy. 2; (715) 398-3000.*

Cooper Falls State Park, Mellon

The Bad River runs through this scenic north woods park, creating gorgeous canyon views. The deep gorges and steep climbs mean challenging hiking, but Loon Lake offers fishing and swimming at the sandy beach. That big shape up in the tree that looks like a crabby old guy hunched in an overcoat is a bald eagle. Yes, they are that big, and they are regularly spotted here. Listen in the early morning and in the evening for the ululating call of the loon, and look out on the lake to see the black-and-white spotted bird family swimming in a train (kids are last in line). There are 56 campsites. *Hwy. 169, two miles northeast of Melon; (715) 274-5123.*

Harrington Beach State Park, Belgium

On the shores of Lake Michigan, this 686-acre park was once the site of limestone quarrying. Quarry Lake was created for the purpose, and you can still see the limestone rock formations around the park. Your kids will like the exhibit in the picnic area explaining how quarrying was done. There's no camping here, but you can hike nature trails, including a very easy mile-long one through the white cedar swamp. There's also fishing on Lake Michigan, Quarry Lake, and Pucketts Pond. *The park is about a half hour north of Milwaukee. Hwy. D, a half mile east of I-43, exit 107, Belgium; (262) 285-3015.*

continued on next page

Kinnickinnic State Park, River Falls

Located at the point where the St. Croix and Kinnickinnic rivers meet, this park attracts many boaters, who moor on the sand delta and come ashore for picnicking, swimming, and sunbathing. It's a gorgeous place, edged in high limestone bluffs. In late summer, ask where the wild blackberry bushes grow. The berries are the sweetest when they're dark, dark purple. *W11983 820th Ave., River Falls; (715) 425-1129.*

Roche-A-Cri State Park, Friendship

The strange, 300-foot-high sandstone outcropping here was visited often by Midwestern Native Americans, who left their carvings on the rock. Climb the stairs to the observation platform for a stunning view of the landscape, then take a nature walk and look for deer. There are three and a half miles of trails as well as picnic areas and 41 campsites. Closed November through April. *1767 Hwy. 13, Friendship; (608) 339-6881.*

Wildcat Mountain State Park, Ontario

Though Wisconsin does border Canada to the north, this Ontario isn't Canadian; it's a small town in the southwest region of the state. Wildcat is a large, 3,470-acre park with the 125-mile Kickapoo River meandering through it. The river attracts canoeists and kayakers, and if the urge strikes, you can stop at one of a number of canoe rental outlets along the river. Horseback riding excursions and camping overnight with your horse are popular here. There's a horse campsite with a corral, and a scenic 12-mile horse trail. There are also 30 campsites with no horse accommodations. *Hwy. 33, Ontario; (608) 337-4775.*

Yellowstone Lake State Park, Blanchardville

This "other Yellowstone" is a lake created by a dam in the Yellowstone River, located in the southwest part of Wisconsin. Water fun includes boating, canoeing, and windsurfing. Rowboats, canoes, paddleboats, and motorboats can be rented at the park. There's a swimming area and a large beach with a bathhouse and toilets. Of the 128 campsites, 38 have electrical hookups; reservations are required for most. *8495 Lake Rd., Blanchardville, about 55 miles southwest of Madison; (608) 523-4427.*

and outdoor pools, sandy beach, play area, basketball and tennis courts, and on bikes. *4205 Bay Shore Dr., Sturgeon Bay; (800) 556-4551; (920) 743-4551;* www.bayshore inn.net

Bridgeport Resort

★★/$$$

The big hit here is the outdoor pool with a waterfall play area. Kids also go for the game room, indoor pool, sandy beach, and tennis and basketball courts. The waterfront property, which looks like a large, modern New England-style apartment building, has 70 one-, two-, and three-bedroom suites. All have water views, kitchens, whirlpools, and fireplaces. You can fuel up on complimentary coffee and pastries in the morning, and the lakefront walkway and breakwater is just steps away. *50 W. Larch St., Sturgeon Bay; (800) 671-9190; (920) 746-9919;* www.bridgeportresort.net

Evergreen Hill Condominiums

★★★/$$$

If you're headed to Peninsula State Park, you can't get much closer than this. These two-bedroom condos sit right at the entrance, and the facilities are first-rate. Each air-conditioned unit has a complete kitchen, two bathrooms, three TV sets with cable, a VCR, a fireplace, and a deck facing the heated outdoor pool. There's also an indoor pool from fall to spring, and a laundry facility. You can bike or ski right out your door and into the park. Your kids won't want to leave—neither will you. *Fish Creek; (800) 686-6621; (920) 868-3748;* www.homestead suites.com

Landmark Resort and Conference Center

★★★★/$$$

This kid-friendly resort provides a full day of activities for children 5 and older daily from Memorial Day through Labor Day. Among the planned daily activities, kids can fish, hike, and watch a video at an evening pizza party. The 293-unit resort is on a bluff, with great views of Green Bay. Suites have one, two, or three bedrooms, along with living, dining, and kitchen areas. There are indoor and outdoor pools, five tennis courts, and a game room, plus a restaurant and lounge. *7643 Hillside Rd., Egg Harbor; (800) 273-7877; (920) 868-3205;* www.the landmarkresort.com

Sandy Bay Shores

★★/$$

This spot is great for kids. Four waterfront housekeeping units with two and three bedrooms sit on a large estate; each has a television and VCR, a grill, and a fireplace, while the grounds feature a private sandy beach, boats for guest use, fishing, and a great view. *5490 N. Alberta Ct., Sturgeon Bay; (888) 854-2368; (920) 743-1364.*

Wagon Trail Resort ★★/$$

Located on 200 wooded acres, this resort is crisscrossed with hiking and skiing trails. A sandy beach, a playground, and kayak and paddleboat rentals provide outdoor fun, while the game room and indoor pool come in handy on rainy days. All of the 40 rooms have mini refrigerators, and there are some two- and three-bedroom suites with kitchenettes. You can also choose one of six freestanding two- or three-bedroom cabins with a fully equipped kitchen, fireplace, and one or two baths. *1041 Hwy. ZZ, Ellison Bay; (800) 999-2466; (920) 854-2385;* www.wagontrail.com

GOOD EATS

Al Johnson's Restaurant ★★/$

The big draws here are the goats grazing on the grassy roof of this restaurant. Yes, they're real, and yes, they're eating the sod covering the roof. The family menu covers breakfast (flat, square Swedish pancakes with lingonberries), lunch, and dinner. The kids' menu offers pancakes, eggs, hamburgers, ribs, perch, shrimp, and chicken fingers. The wait can be long at the popular eatery, so come before your kids get ravenous. (By the way, the goats mount the roof via a ramp in back and aren't up there all the time. Al's staff puts them up there in the morning, and brings them down at night.) *700 N. Bay Shore Dr., Sister Bay; (920) 854-2626.*

The Cookery Restaurant ★★/$

Three meals a day are served at this great family spot. Breakfast specials include Door County cherry pancakes; lunch and dinner feature whitefish chowder and fish fries. There are nightly specials and a dessert tray—and a children's menu, too. The preserves and sauces sold here are made with the local produce. *Hwy. 42, Main St., Fish Creek; (920) 868-3634.*

Culvers ★★/$

Kids can order from the standard children's menu or opt for local favorites like butter burgers and frozen custard served in a fast-food restaurant atmosphere. *5581 Gordon Rd. BB, Sturgeon Bay (920/746-0870); 4601 Calumet Ave., Manitowoc (920/682-6400).*

Grandma's Swedish Restaurant & Bakery at Wagon Trail Resort ★★/$

For breakfast, grab one of the signature pecan rolls and a cup of coffee (juice for kids) and take in the view of Rowley's Bay. Come back for the Friday night Captain's Catch dinner or the famous grand Sunday brunch. There's pizza, too. *1041 Hwy. ZZ, Ellison Bay; (800) 999-2466; (920) 854-2385.*

Hof Restaurant and Lounge at the Alpine Resort

★★/$$

This family-friendly restaurant at the Alpine Resort has a great shoreline view. Breakfast choices include Swiss toast with cherries and omelettes; featured dinner items are whitefish and steak. There's a children's menu for small appetites and picky eaters. Closed November through May. *Hwy. G, Egg Harbor; (920) 868-3000.*

Natural Ovens Farm

★★/$

Don't pass up this unique organic farm where your kids can see farm animals being raised in humane surroundings! The menu includes nutrient powders mixed into fruit drinks, great granola, blueberry muffins, and whole-grain foods enhanced with nutrients like flaxseed, folic acid, and other vitamins. You even get to tour the bakery from which the heavenly smells emanate. *4300 Hwy. CR, Manitowoc; (800) 558-3535; (920) 758-2500.*

Not Licked Yet

★★★/$

Your kids can amuse themselves in the next-door play area while you walk up to the window of this legendary and cute custard stop to order burgers, floats, and ice-cream cones. Fish Creek runs right through the property. *Hwy. 42, Fish Creek; (920) 868-2617.*

Old Post Office Restaurant

★★/$

The breakfast menu here includes Door County cherry muffins and pancakes, and you can have a fish boil, barbecued ribs, or chicken at dinner. Closed November through April. *10040 Water St., Hwy. 42, Ephraim; (920) 854-4034.*

Weisgerber's Cornerstone Pub

★★/$

The Friday night fish fry is the traditional Wisconsin treat. Your children may or may not eat the tasty panfried perch (come on, try it!), but the homemade pizza that's also served here is sure to please even the most particular eater. Other kid pleasers are the video game room and the Green Bay Packer memorabilia. *8123 Hwy. 57, Baileys Harbor; (920) 839-9001.*

White Gull Inn

★★/$$

If you want to see (and taste!) a fish boil, here's the classic spot to stop. The White Gull fish boil is a famous

> **FamilyFun TIP**
>
> **Eco Etiquette**
>
> When snacking on the beach, make sure you throw away plastic bags and garbage, which can easily drift into the water. Eating garbage is one of the leading causes of death in aquatic animals.

FISH BOILS

EVERY AMERICAN REGION has its own traditional outdoor feast. Hawaii has luaus, Texas has barbecues, New England has clambakes, and Wisconsin has fish boils. As you drive around Door County, you'll notice sandwich boards set up on sidewalks and on corners advertising these festive meals.

Here's how it works: huge cauldrons are placed over open fires, and into the pot goes red-skinned new potatoes, small onions, and fresh-caught whitefish. The chef pours kerosene on the fire, the smoke flares, and the pot boils over. Not only is this a photo op and a dramatic sight, but it has a culinary purpose: the boil-over removes oils from the whitefish and leaves it light and tender.

TIP: Don't ask for tartar sauce, just eat the fish with melted butter the way the locals do. Instruct your kids to separate the fish from the bone carefully—to keep the fish from flaking apart, it's served with bones in place. A typical fish boil menu includes the whitefish, coleslaw, rye or pumpernickel bread, and fresh-baked cherry pie—made with Door County cherries, of course.

Some Door County restaurants that serve fish boils:

Grandma's Swedish Restaurant and Bakery, *Ellison Bay; (800) 99-WAGON* (see Good Eats).

Leathem Smith Lodge, *Sturgeon Bay; (920) 743-5555.*

Mill Supper Club, *Sturgeon Bay; (920) 743-5044.*

Old Post Office Restaurant, *Ephraim, (920) 854-4034* (see Good Eats).

Pelletier's Restaurant, *Fish Creek; (920) 868-3313.*

Sandpiper Restaurant, *Baileys Harbor; (920) 839-2528.*

Square Rigger Galley, *Jacksonport; (920) 823-2408.*

Summertime Restaurant, *Fish Creek; (920) 868-3738.*

Viking Grill, *Ellison Bay; (920) 854-2998.*

White Gull Inn, *Fish Creek; (920) 868-3517* (see Good Eats).

Door County tradition. The charming inn specializes in the outdoor dining event but also offers a full menu indoors. Call ahead for nights and times. *4225 Main St., Fish Creek; (920) 868-3517.*

Wilson's Restaurant and Ice Cream Parlor ★★/$

This is the spot in Ephraim for great ice-cream sundaes, cones, and home-brewed draft root beer. Tell your kids to look for a white restaurant with red-and-white-striped awnings, a pretty outdoor seating area, and a popcorn wagon by the flower boxes. *9990 Water St., Ephraim; (920) 854-2041.*

Souvenir Hunting

Dancing Bear

It's filled with fussy, gifty stuff that grown-ups like more than kids. But wait—the children's rooms are stocked with cool toys, stuffed animals, classic picture books, and lots of teddy bears. *13 N. Third Ave., Sturgeon Bay; (920) 746-5223.*

Spielman Wood Works

You can get old-fashioned wooden trains, cars, blocks, and pull-and-push toys here. They also carry toy kits and play fishing poles. *4075 Hwy. 42, Fish Creek; (920) 868-3130.*

Yes, Green Bay's got the Packers, but it's also got a fabulous children's museum, zoo, and amusement park.

Green Bay

SETTLED BY THE FRENCH, Green Bay is Wisconsin's oldest community. But it is best known for a bunch of guys wearing gold-and-green uniforms who play football in a place called Lambeau Field. If your kids love football, they'll jump at the chance to visit the Green Bay Packer Hall of Fame and see Lambeau Field, just across the street. But Green Bay isn't just about football—the town has lots of kid-pleasing things to do. The old-fashioned Bay Beach Amusement Park is one of Wisconsin's premier family attractions. Even your 1-year-old will love the Great Explorations Children's Museum, and the N.E.W. Zoo offers an intimate setting for young animal lovers to observe creatures from around the world. Buy yourself a cheese head and a brat. You're in Green Bay!

Bay Beach Amusement Park (page 276)

Great Explorations Children's Museum (page 274)

Green Bay Packer Hall of Fame and Lambeau Field (pages 275 and 277)

National Railroad Museum (page 275)

N.E.W. Zoo (page 277)

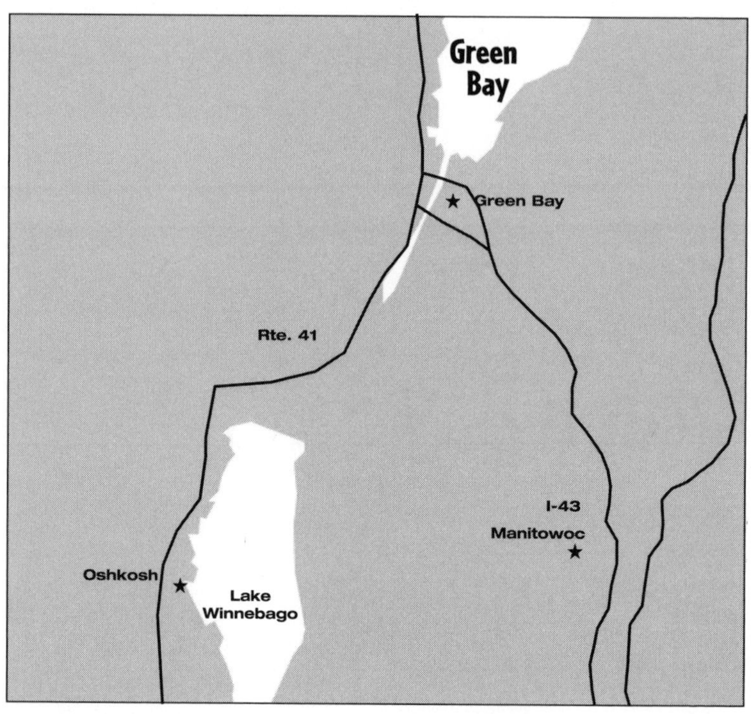

CULTURAL ADVENTURES

Experimental Aircraft Association AirVenture Museum ★★/$$

Military planes, spacecraft, and historical aircraft make up the museum's extraordinary collection. More than 90 airplanes on display range from the amazing to the unusual. Your kids will be amazed to discover that the famous Wright Flyer—a full-size replica of which is on display—required the pilot to lie across the wings in order to maneuver the plane. Other highlights include the *Baby Bird* (only 11 feet long), and an Aerocar that resembles an early Volkswagen Beetle, with wings. Don't miss the train shuttle to the outdoor exhibits. For an additional fee, you can also ride an antique plane! *3000 Poberezny Rd., Oshkosh; (920) 426-4800;* www.eaa.org

MUST-SEE FamilyFun MUST-SEE Great Explorations Children's Museum ★★★/$

The 12-and-under crowd goes crazy for the hands-on exhibits and activities at this compact facility. Kids can explore a submarine with an underwater view of Lake Michigan; take a trip through Wisconsin history with a visit to an old trading post, a pioneer school, a Depression Era kitchen, and a '50s diner; and dress up like a fire fighter and respond to an emergency dispatch. Baby's Great Adventure is a unique and stimulating playground for infants and toddlers. *320 N. Adams, Washington Commons, Green Bay; (920) 432-4397.*

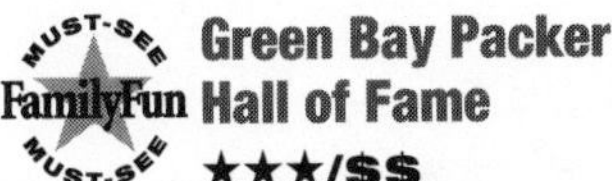

Green Bay Packer Hall of Fame

★★★/$$

Any football lover, and especially any Packer fan, must make the pilgrimage to the Hall of Fame and Lambeau Field (see page 277). The Hall of Fame is easy to spot. The overhang of the entry is supported by a column that is shaped like a football, and out front there's a gigantic statue of a football with a football player who looks like he's trying to catch it. The exhibits, shows, and memorabilia trace the singular history of this city-owned ball club. In the past, when the stars didn't have million-dollar salaries, locals sometimes drove the players home from practice in their own family cars. The gift shop sells all things green-and-gold as well as ridiculously silly foam cheese accessories. *855 Lombardi Ave., Green Bay; (888) 442-7225; (920) 499-4281;* www.packerhalloffame.com

National Railroad Museum

★★★/$

This is the great-granddaddy of all railroad museums, the country's oldest and largest. Train buffs will love the 77 pieces of railroad rolling stock (engineer talk for things with wheels that roll on the tracks). They can also take a ride behind a vintage diesel locomotive and check out the *Dwight D. Eisenhower*, a World War II train, and *Big Boy*, the world's largest steam locomotive. A 60-foot observation tower provides a great view of the museum grounds and nearby Fox River. *2285 S. Broadway St., Green Bay; (920) 437-7623;* www.nationalrrmuseum.org

THE GREEN BAY PACKERS are one of sport's most beloved teams. Fifty-six thousand fans are on the waiting list for season tickets. Unlike many professional sports teams, which are owned by one or a few individuals, the Green Bay Packers are owned by their fans. There are more than 110,000 shareholders in the team.

Bandanna Sit-upon

True camp crafts are traditionally the kind you can use in the woods—a water jug, a sling for hauling wood, a candle lantern, or this camp pillow. Made from two bandannas, the sit-upon fits into a kid's pocket, ready to fill with grasses and leaves whenever she needs a soft place to sit for a spell–on the trail, around the campfire, or in the neighborhood clubhouse.

What you'll need: Two bandannas, embroidery floss or yarn, embroidery needle, adhesive Velcro tab, and soft grasses, leaves, or moss.

How it's done: Place one bandanna on top of the other and stitch them together on three sides. On the open side, attach a Velcro tab to make a simple closure (experienced sewers might like to make a basic button-and-hole closure instead). To fill the pillow, gather the softest grasses, dead leaves, and moss you can find, carefully broken into pieces small enough that they won't pierce the fabric. At day's end, just shake out the filling and fold up the sit-upon for the next day's adventures.

Camp Crafter's Tip: You can stitch around the very edges of your bandannas or one inch in from the edges. A whip- or running stitch works fine, but if your child likes sewing, she can try a more decorative pattern or even embroider her name on one edge.

JUST FOR FUN

Batter's Box

★★/$$-$$$

Rain in the forecast? Don't despair—Green Bay has an indoor attraction your young athletes will love. There are indoor baseball and softball cages, adjustable slam-dunk basketball rooms, and a golf driving range. *1633 Western Ave., Green Bay; (920) 496-8660.*

MUST-SEE FamilyFun MUST-SEE

Bay Beach Amusement Park

★★★★/$$

An old-fashioned park, with old-fashioned prices—amazing! The setting—along the Green Bay shoreline—makes this an especially pretty amusement park, and it's small and accessible, so it won't overwhelm your kids. Other pluses: there is no admission fee, the rides are inexpensive, and there are play areas that are free. Closed October through April; open weekends only in May and September. *1313 Bay Beach Rd., Green Bay; (920) 448-3365.*

Green Bay Botanical Garden

★★/$

The formal flower gardens make for a pretty walk and the children's garden has a tree house and a frog pond. Closed November through March. *2600 Larsen Rd., Green Bay; (920) 490-9457.*

Lambeau Field

MUST-SEE FamilyFun MUST-SEE

★★★/$$$

Just across the street from the Green Bay Packer Hall of Fame is the field where the Packers play. Tickets to the games are nearly impossible to get; however, the stadium is open June through August for tours; pick up tickets at the Hall of Fame. *1265 Lombardi Ave., Green Bay; ticket office, (920) 496-5719; Tours, (920) 438-1640.*

N.E.W. Zoo ★★★/$

MUST-SEE FamilyFun MUST-SEE

Animals from around the world—including huge Galápagos tortoises as well as Wisconsin natives like the red fox—have settled at this 43-acre natural area. It's divided into Prairie Grassland, International, and Wisconsin Trail areas. Check at the visitors' center for feeding times. *4418 Reforestation Rd., Green Bay; (920) 434-7841.*

BUNKING DOWN

Best Western Washington St. Inn and Conference Center

★★/$$

This centrally located 121-room downtown hotel has an indoor pool, whirlpool, and putting green. Some of the rooms have a refrigerator and microwave. *321 S. Washington St., Green Bay; (800) 528-1234; (920) 437-8771;* www.bestwestern.com

Radisson Inn Green Bay

★★/$$

The architecture inside and out of this attractive hotel echoes the designs of Frank Lloyd Wright, but kids will care more about the indoor pool. The property has 301 rooms with in-room movies and coffeemakers; some suites have refrigerators, microwaves, and even whirlpool tubs. *2040 Airport Dr., Green Bay; (800) 333-3333; (920) 494-7300;* www.radisson.com

GOOD EATS

Kroll's

★★/$

This local institution is just west of Lambeau Field. The menu is short and sweet: fried fish, grilled chicken, and sandwiches. *1990 S. Ridge Rd., Green Bay; (920) 497-1111.*

After you've explored all the urban culture of Milwaukee, head for the lakefront and let your kids let loose.

Milwaukee

MILWAUKEE IS THE HOME of two things kids can't enjoy: Harley-Davidson motorcycles and Miller beer. But the city's many and diverse activities and attractions for children of all ages more than make up for that fact. The lakefront is a great spot for families to gather, walk, play, have an ice-cream cone, and take in a concert. One festival or another is held here nearly every summer weekend and frequently throughout the rest of the year. The port of Milwaukee and the St. Lawrence Seaway make for dramatic scenery and fun sight-seeing. Ships from all over the world deliver goods here, and watching the 730-foot-long vessels come in and out of the port is fascinating.

Milwaukee's breezy beaches, like Bradford and McKinley, along the Lake Michigan waterfront, and

many green spaces offer you and your family the opportunity to recharge your batteries. Mitchell Park features glass atria known as The Domes, with self-contained ecosystems and displays of flowers, and Veteran's Park has a dedicated area to fly kites. If your family loves sports, this is your kind of town: you'll find professional basketball and baseball, indoor soccer, hockey, and more. The cageless Milwaukee County Zoo and mind-tickling Discovery World are also top-rated family attractions.

Cultural Adventures

Betty Brinn Children's Museum ★★★/$

MUST-SEE FamilyFun MUST-SEE

This museum was specifically designed for children ages 1 to 10, and it shows. Exhibits are strictly hands-on and fun. Your kids can operate an apple orchard and make juice. They can pretend to be a red corpuscle and crawl through a giant human heart. Or they can try their hands at running a television studio, being a restaurant chef, or driving an ambulance. Betty's Busy Backyard includes a pretend garden and caterpillar sandbox for infants and toddlers. *929 E. Wisconsin Ave., Milwaukee; (414) 291-0888.*

MUST-SEE FamilyFun MUST-SEE Discovery World: The James Lovell Museum of Science, Economics & Technology ★★★/$$

If you've got a preteen in tow, he or she will be just as fascinated by this place as the preschoolers in the family are. More than 130 interactive exhibits and displays explain and demonstrate principles of physics, laws of the universe, and other cool stuff. Highlights include an Entrepreneurs Village where kids can buy and sell products, a test-pilot training center, a chance to be a weather reporter on television, and a place to play with light waves and laser beams. Your kids can also learn how electricity and magnetism work, and explore the principle of the fulcrum. And the Van de Graaf generator is always good for a giggle—have your child set a hand on the glass ball and watch the electricity make his or her hair stand on end. Stop at SPUTNIK, the Store for TechnoCats for mind-bending toys. Also here is the 275-seat **Humphrey IMAX Dome Theater** *(414/319-4629)* that presents overwhelmingly realistic sound-image movies of thrilling adventures. Combination tickets for the museum and IMAX theater are available. *815 N. James Lovell St., Milwaukee; (414) 765-9966;* www.discoveryworld.org

First Stage Milwaukee ★★/$$$

This children's theater company stages plays based on well-known children's stories, like *Peter Pan.* Performances are at the Todd Wehr Theater in the Marcus Center for the Performing Arts. Closed July and August. *929 N. Water St., Milwaukee; (414) 273-2314.*

M & W Productions Main Stage & Playhouse ★★/$$

Plays in this children's theater are based on classic stories and fairy tales. Performances are between October and May. *(414) 272-7701;* www.mandwproductions.com

MUST-SEE FamilyFun MUST-SEE Milwaukee Public Museum ★★★/$$

The world's largest dinosaur skull is at this museum and your extinct-reptile fan is not going to want to miss it. The skull

FOOTPRINTS IN THE SAND

On beach vacations, sand seems to end up everywhere, especially between the toes. The simple plaster-casting project lets your child capture that sandy barefoot feeling—and a record of his feet.

MATERIALS

- Plaster of paris
- Small bucket
- Freshwater
- 4-inch lengths of string or wire (for hangers, if desired)

Choose a site to cast your molds—the moist, hard-packed sand near (but not too near!) the water's edge works best. Have your child firmly press both feet into the sand. The prints should be about 1½ to 2 inches deep. If your child can't press down that hard, he can use his finger to dig down into the print, following its shape. Mix up the plaster according to the directions on the package so that it has a thick, creamy consistency. Pour the wet plaster gently into the footprints.

If you want to make hangers, tie a knot about a half inch from each end of your pieces of string or wire. As the plaster begins to harden, push the knotted ends into the plaster and let dry. After 20 to 25 minutes, gently dig the footprints out of the molds and brush away any excess sand. Set sole side up in the sun (away from the rising tide) for about an hour to let harden.

belongs to a Torosaurus (no, that isn't a lawn-mowing dinosaur). You can see other dinos—and hear a tyrannosaurus roar—in the Third Planet exhibit. The Old Milwaukee exhibit lets kids take a step back in time; they can walk on cobblestone streets, peer in the windows of the houses of the immigrants from many lands who settled Milwaukee, and watch an old-fashioned nickelodeon movie. If your kids are into ecology, they'll go for the rain forest exhibit. *800 W. Wells St., Milwaukee; (414) 278-2700; (414) 278-2702;* www.mpm.edu

JUST FOR FUN

Blue Max Charters

★★/$$$

What's nice about this charter company is that it rents boats by the hour, and each cruise is limited to six passengers. You can design your own excursion and go back to shore when your kids get cranky. They'll stock food and beverages on board if you ask. Reservations required. Closed November to late May. *Boats depart from 740 N. Plankinton Ave., Milwaukee; (414) 828-1094;* www.bluemaxcharters.com

Boerner Botanical Gardens/Whitnall Park

★★★/Free

Roses, wildflowers, numerous other perennials and annuals, and a waterfall are the attractions at these gardens in Whitnall Park. Kids love the bog walk and trek through a swamp-like setting, yet keep their feet dry on the walkway. Whitnall is a large county park (more than 600 acres) with a playground, golf course, and a nature center. Gardens are closed November to mid-April. *The park is a 20-minute drive from downtown Milwaukee; take I-94 to 894 West; exit 5A on Forest Home Ave. 5879 S. 92nd St., off Forest Home Ave., Hales Corners; (414) 425-1130*; www.countyparks.com/horticulture

Bradford Beach ★★/Free

The sand is more popular than the surf here: Lake Michigan is one of the Great Lakes, and the water doesn't get too warm, but just try and keep the gang from swimming in it. It's also a great place to lie around on the beach and soak up the sun. There's a bathhouse, and a concession stand sells hot dogs, burgers, and snacks. *2400 N. Lincoln Memorial Dr., Milwaukee.*

Cool Waters ★★★/$$

MUST-SEE FamilyFun MUST-SEE

Located in Greenfield Park, this family water park has wading pools, swimming pools, water slides, and other splashy fun. One of the pools lets kids wade into the water like they do at the beach—the water gradually gets deeper as they walk in. Fountains spray from the edges of giant mushrooms, and your kids will want to see who can manage the Lily Pad Walk, where you hang onto a rope and try to make it from pad to pad across the water without falling in. There's also a picnic area and sand volleyball courts. Open Memorial Day through Labor Day. *2028 S. 124th St., Milwaukee; (414) 321-7530;* www.countyparks.com/aquatics/coolwaters.html

Green Meadows Farm ★★/$$

Here's a treat for city kids—they can pet baby animals, help feed sheep and lambs, feel a goat's beard, and milk a cow. More than 300 animals live on the farm, including some odd ones, like a potbellied pig. A hayride takes you around the site, and your kids can get their questions answered by the guide, who also talks about the animals. The little guys will lobby for a pony ride. *The farm is about an hour and 15 minutes from downtown Milwaukee. 33603 High Dr., East Troy; 262-534-2891.*

The International Clown Hall of Fame ★★/$$

Some kids adore clowns; others burst into tears at the sight of one. If yours are the first kind, they'll think this place is more fun than the circus. Clowns wander around, creating balloon sculptures, doing face painting, and trying to make kids giggle. They'll teach children a few clown tricks, too. Displays

FamilyFun SNACK

Bag o' Bugs

Place a few graham crackers in a plastic bag, seal it shut, and crush the crackers into a fine sand using a large spoon. Add a few raisins and let your kids dig for bugs in the sand. Experiment with other tasty critters: dried cranberry ladybugs, chocolate- or carob-chip ants, even gummy worms.

explain a bit of clown lore. *Grand Avenue Mall, 161 W. Wisconsin Ave., Milwaukee; (414) 319-0848;* www.clownmuseum.org

Lake Park ★★/Free

The North Point Lighthouse overlooks the lake in this park. Kids love skipping along the footpath that leads to the lighthouse (closed to the public) and along a golf course, or playing on the playground. If there's a lawn bowling (bocce) game going on, stop and watch for a while. *3233 E. Kenwood Blvd., Milwaukee.*

MUST-SEE FamilyFun MUST-SEE

McKinley Marina and Beach ★★★/Free

Your family will find plenty of ways to enjoy a stop here. Get an ice-cream cone or popcorn at the snack stand and grab a bench. You can see the boats come and go at the marina and watch the windsurfers glide by. The sand here is great for building sand castles. Watch the "pros" create intricate structures, then get in there with your own shovel and pail. You can look down onto the waves from the observation area on the north side of the beach. *1750 N. Lincoln Memorial Dr., Milwaukee.*

Milwaukee Admirals ★★/$$$$

Admirals hockey is one professional sporting event you can take your kids to without dipping into their college savings. Tickets for the International Hockey League games run about $40 for a family of four, depending on where you want to sit. Buy them in advance or at the door. *Bradley Center, 1001 N. Fourth St., Milwaukee; (414) 227-0550;* www.milwaukeeadmirals.com

Milwaukee Brewers ★★★/$$$

The Brewers play National League baseball at a glorious new stadium, Miller Park. The stadium has a fan-shaped, convertible roof and holds more than 43,000 fans (or 4,655,926,995 baseballs!). Little sluggers go crazy for "Bernie Brewer," an adorable, mustached-mascot who prances, dances, and gets fans to cheer for the home team. Kids also love the antics of Klement's Racing Sausages—wieners that race at the end of the sixth inning. And, the baseball isn't bad either! Sections 217, 238, and 417 are designated for families and do not permit alcohol. Strollers are not allowed in the park, but may be checked at the gates. Arrive early if you're interested in joining the tailgating tradition. Most days you can get tickets at the box office right before game time. Children under 2 are free. *1 Brewer's Way, Milwaukee; (414) 902-4000.*

Milwaukee Bucks

★★/$$$$

Like anywhere else, it costs an arm and a leg for tickets to NBA basketball games here. If you want to see the Bucks play at Bradley Center, expect to pay about $65 each for decent seats. You can head for the upper level for a discount. Tickets are not hard to get—they're often available at the box office just before game time. *Bradley Center, 1001 N. Fourth St., Milwaukee; (414) 227-0500;* www.bucks.com

Milwaukee County Zoo

MUST-SEE FamilyFun MUST-SEE ★★★★/$$

Your kids won't feel sad for animals trapped in cages here. At this zoo, the animals, birds, and reptiles from around the world roam free in homelike environments, and the humans are separated from them by watery moats. If you have little kids, plunk down a deposit and get a stroller just inside the main entrance, then pick up a ZooKey, available at all the zoo gift shops. Use the keys to "unlock" audio recordings at various locations and learn more about the animals you're seeing.

Although feeding times may vary, try to hit the small mammal building around 2:30 P.M., and then head for either the sea lions or the feline building at 3 P.M.—you're bound to catch someone eating lunch. At the Lake Wisconsin Aquarium, your kids get an underwater peek at what (and who!) lives in Midwestern lake water. The building also houses some distinctly non-Midwestern residents: an anaconda, a Chinese alligator, and a host of reptiles. The small mammal building lets you see bats flying around because they think it's night—a little creepy, but fascinating—and you can sneak in a little science lesson about bats' importance to our ecosystem. Other favorite spots are an African water hole, where antelope, zebra, and ostriches congregate, and a working dairy farm. Kids can ride real camels

BREW CREW BUDDY

Before the Milwaukee Brewers moved into their new stadium in 2001, Bernie Brewer, the mascot, used to celebrate each team home run by slipping down a slide into a giant beer stein. The mascot now hangs out in Bernie's Dugout, high in left field.

and ponies, or the carved animals on the carousel. The Birds of Prey show is free; the outdoor sea lion shows is an additional $1. Both are held several times a day. The zoo train and zoomobile tours (additional fee) are great options when your feet hurt or little ones get tired. There's an additional parking fee. *10001 W. Blue Mound Rd., Milwaukee; (414) 771-5500;* www.milwaukeezoo.org

Milwaukee Mustangs

★★/$$$$

The Mustangs play arena football at Bradley Center, and you can get tickets at the door. *1001 N. Fourth St., Milwaukee; (414) 272-1555.*

The Milwaukee Wave ★★/$$$

Got a soccer player? Plan on attending a match at Bradley Center. The Wave, Milwaukee's professional indoor soccer team, is wildly popular with 10- to 15-year-olds, who attend their matches in droves. An afternoon here is fun for the whole family—in fact, most of the crowd is under 21. Buy tickets at the door. *Bradley Center, 1001 N. Fourth St., Milwaukee; (414) 224-9283;* www.milwaukeewave.com

Mitchell Park Horticultural Conservatory (The Domes)

★★/$

If you ask directions to the "horticultural conservatory," you might get a blank look. Locals know this trio of rounded structures as The Domes. Each dome is seven stories high, and together they hold more than 4,000 plants. One dome is always filled with tropical rain forest plants, frogs, lizards, and birds; another has a desert environment, with cactuses and palm trees. The third dome hosts special exhibits that change five times a year. Sometimes the displays are of particular interest to kids; for example, there's an annual exhibit of model trains. Mitchell Park also has a fishing lagoon, a wading pool, tennis courts, a playground, and picnic tables. There's ice-skating on the

FamilyFun READER'S TIP

Tic-Tac-Tine

While my sister Barb and I and our seven kids were waiting for dinner at a restaurant recently, my nephew Josh, age 9, surprised me with a game he invented using dinner utensils and sugar packets. He set up forks, spoons, and knives in the traditional tic-tac-toe grid and gave me the choice of being the *X*'s (regular sugar packets) or *O*'s (artificial sweetener packets).

Soon everyone at the table was pairing off to play, and it was a fun way for us to pass the time before our meal arrived.

Theresa Jung, Cincinnati, Ohio

lagoon in winter. *524 S. Layton Blvd., Milwaukee; (414) 649-9830; (414) 649-9800;* www.countyparks.com/horticulture/domes/

Riverwalk
MUST-SEE FamilyFun MUST-SEE ★★★★/Free

The Riverwalk meanders along the Milwaukee River through downtown Milwaukee, winding through the city's restaurant and pub sector. It's a fun walk for even young children, because there's so much to see: the river, boat traffic, ducks, and brazen seagulls (toss some bread their way and watch the reaction). Choose a sidewalk café for a snack and look out at the river. Or linger in Pere Marquette Park, site of a gazebo, pavilion, and boat dock where you can catch a gondola or water taxi. Or cruise the Riverwalk in a unique "car" that's really a bike that seats six people. Rent these at **High Roller Bike and Skate Rental** at *McKinley Marina (Lagoon Dr., east of Lincoln Memorial Dr.).*

Veteran's Park
MUST-SEE FamilyFun MUST-SEE ★★★/Free-$$

Want to go fly a kite? Head to Veteran's Park, where there's a special kite area set aside. If you didn't bring one from home, just sit back and watch other people do the flying; some of the kites are ultra-cool, and some of the flyers really know what they're doing. It's also fun to bike or Rollerblade along the paved Oak Leaf Trail; rent bikes or blades at **High Rollers Skate Rental,** located in the park *(N. Lincoln Memorial Dr.; 414/273-1343).* Or rent a vessel at **Juneau Park Paddleboats** *(414/217-7235)* and paddle your way around the park lagoon. *On N. Lincoln Memorial Dr. just north of the art museum, Milwaukee; (414) 257-6100.*

BUNKING DOWN

Best Western Quiet House and Suites ★★/$$$

Families large and small will find something to suit at this 55-suite hotel. "Executive" suites have a queen-size bed in the bedroom and a queen-size pullout couch in the living area; "Leisure" suites have two queen-size beds or a king-size bed in the bedroom and a queen-size pullout couch in the living area. The theme suites are usually of more interest to couples on a romantic weekend getaway, but kids might get a kick out of the Roman bath-themed suite or the vintage cabin one. All units have cable television and in-room movies. After a day of sight-seeing, kids are happy to head for the heated indoor and outdoor pools—you can swim from one to the other, even in winter. *Less than 15 miles from Milwaukee; take I-43 to the Mequon Rd./Hwy. 67 West exit. Port Washington Rd. S., Mequon; (800) 528-1234; (262) 241-3677;* www.bestwestern.com

Hilton Milwaukee City Center ★★/$$

Even young kids are impressed by the lavish interior of this 1928 historic hotel. It's very Art Deco, although kids just think the marble floors, lush floral walls and ornate railings are impressive. Each of the 554 rooms has cable TV and in-room movies. Two whirlpool rooms, a coffee shop, a gift shop, and a steak restaurant are also on the premises. The real kid-draw here, though, is Paradise Landing, an indoor water park with water slides and a lily pad walk. *509 W. Wisconsin Ave., Milwaukee; (800)-HILTONS; (414) 271-7250;* www.hilton.com

Hotel Radisson Mayfair ★★/$$

The Mission-style furnishings will please Mom and Dad, if not the kids, in this 151-room hotel. What they'll like is the cable TV and pay-per-view movies—and the indoor pool. Suites have a separate living and dining areas. The restaurant offers a kids' menu. *The hotel is in Wauwatosa, a suburb about 10 minutes from downtown; take I-94 west to Rte. 45 north to Mayfair Rd. 2303 North Mayfair Rd., Wauwatosa; (800) 333-3333; (414) 257-3400;* www.radisson.com

GOOD EATS

Ed Debevic's ★★★/$

This place is a riot, though not for the faint-hearted. Waiters and waitresses tease customers, steal food off their plates, and spin Hula Hoops while they talk to you. They'll be far naughtier than your kids! So if you think your crew can take the abuse, don't miss this family tradition. The bill of fare has all things American from meat loaf to chicken-fried steak. Kids love the burgers, fries, and yummy desserts. *780 N. Jefferson St., Milwaukee; (414) 226-2200;* www.eddebevics.com

Gilles Frozen Custard Drive-In ★★/$

This was the first custard stand in Milwaukee, opened in 1938. It's still good. The menu offers roast beef sandwiches, hamburgers, grilled chicken, sloppy joes, fries, hot dogs, and a fish fry on Fridays. Closed Christmas to mid-January. *7515 W. Blue Mound Rd., Wauwatosa; (414) 453-4875.*

Kopp's Frozen Custard ★★/$

A plain custard cone or dish is okay, but why not try one of the elaborate sundaes at this Milwaukee tradition. They also serve delicious burgers but they're huge so plan on sharing. There are three suburban Milwaukee locations. *5373 N. Port Washington Rd., Glendale (414/961-3288); 18880 W. Bluemound Rd., Brookfield (262/789-9490); 7631 W. Layton Ave., Greenfield (414/282-4312).*

Mader's German Restaurant

★★★/$$

In a restaurant that looks like a German castle, you can dine on Oktoberfest fare plus delectable desserts. Be sure to check out the huge collection of medieval armor and weapons. *1037 N. Old World 3rd St., Milwaukee; (414) 271-3377.*

Mel's Diner

★★/$

This classic 1950s-style diner serves kid meals in cardboard convertibles. *3232 S. 27th St., Milwaukee; (414) 389-9555.*

Miss Katie's Diner

★★/$

Get a grilled cheese, a burger, fries, and a malt. Former president Clinton did when he visited here. Or try the other traditional diner fare. *1900 W. Clybourn St., Milwaukee; (414) 344-0044.*

Solid Gold McDonald's

★★/$

This is not your everyday Golden Arches. This McDonald's is decorated like a Hard Rock Cafe. There's a real motorcycle up on a counter (it roars every now and then) and a guitar-player mannequin. *It's about 10 miles from downtown; take I-94 south to the 894 bypass, exit at 76th Street. 5040 S. 76th St., Greenfield; (414) 282-6480.*

Souvenir Hunting

Harry W. Schwartz Bookshops

There are five in the area, and each has story hours and children's programs. *10976 N. Port Washington Rd., Mequon (414/241-6220); 17145 W. Bluemound Rd., Brookfield (414/797-6140); 4093 N. Oakland Ave., Shorewood (414/963-3111); 2559 N. Downer Ave., Milwaukee (414/332-1181). In Racine (30 miles south of Milwaukee) at 430 Main St. (262/633-7340);* www.schwartzbooks.com

Northern Chocolates

This store's hours of operation are erratic, but the chocolate sold here is utterly excellent. The resident chocolatier mixes his own chocolate and collects antique chocolate molds from around the world. His Door County cherries dipped in chocolate, available only during cherry season, are extraordinary. *2036 N. Dr. Martin L. King (Old World Third) Dr., Milwaukee; (414) 372-1885.*

Kettle Moraine State Forest offers families 80 miles of groomed trails for summer hiking and biking or winter skiing.

The Lake Geneva Area

THE TOWN OF Lake Geneva and the surrounding towns of Delavan, Fontana on Geneva Lake, and Williams Bay are in southeastern Wisconsin, south of Madison and Milwaukee. Millions of years ago, a glacier came through here, carving out a stunning landscape. There are rolling green hills, woodlands that turn gold and red in autumn, and three lakes: Delavan Lake, Lake Como, and the largest, Lake Geneva, 7.6 miles long and 2.1 miles wide.

The lovely natural setting makes this a perfect place for an outdoor family getaway. With its gently mounded hills, Kettle Moraine State Forest to the north is a gorgeous site for hiking, biking, and camping. The lakes offer boat tours, sailing, swimming, and sheer beauty. A 20-plus-mile path completely circles Lake Geneva, the modern equivalent of the ancient trails that once linked Native American camps surrounding the lake, where your family can hike or bike.

From the 1870s, when the railroad came through, up until about 1920,

Geneva Lake Cruise Line (page 292)

Kettle Moraine State Forest (page 294)

Paradise Golf Park (page 295)

Walk, Talk & Gawk (page 295)

Williams Bay Beach (page 295)

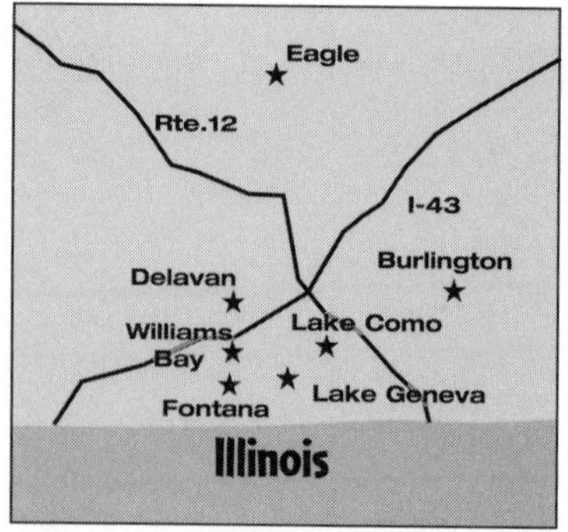

the crystal-clear waters of Lake Geneva attracted high-society folk like the Wrigleys, Swifts, and Maytags, who built enormous and elegant mansions along its shores. Today, the area still caters to visitors, offering resorts, spas, water sports, golf, and cute towns with gift shopping. You'll find none of the commercial whiz-bang attitude of the Wisconsin Dells here. What's celebrated around Lake Geneva is a love of being outdoors.

JUST FOR FUN

Big Foot Beach State Park

★★★/$

Kids may be disappointed to learn that this 272-acre park was not named for the publicity-shy woodland monster, but rather for Chief Big Foot of the Potawatomi Tribe, who left this area in 1836. They'll get over it when they see the wonderful beach. Pack a picnic to eat on the sand, but keep in mind that you can't bring glass onto the beach. Also note that lifeguards are on duty on weekends only from July 4 to Labor Day. The park also has five miles of hiking trails that pass lagoons, wooded areas, marshlands, and open meadows. There's camping, too (free; parking fee). Closed November to Memorial Day. *1550 S. Lakeshore Drive (Hwy. 120), Lake Geneva; (262) 248-2528. For camping reservations: (888) 947-2757.*

Fontana Beach

★★★/$

This beach has a large swimming and lounging area (bring your own beach chairs, none are available here) with changing rooms and lifeguards between 9 A.M. and 6 P.M. You may bring in small food items like a bag of chips or a single drink, but you can't set out a large picnic spread because it attracts great numbers of bold seagulls that leave a mess behind. There's a parking lot nearby, but you'll need quarters for the meters. Admission fees are discounted if you arrive after 5 P.M.; the beach is only open until 7 P.M. Open between Memorial Day and Labor Day. *Fontana Blvd., Fontana; (262) 275-6136.*

Geneva Lake Cruise Line

★★★★/$$$

This cruise line's boat tours are an ideal way to show your kids the elaborate mansions of Lake Geneva, once owned by such wealthy families as the Wrigleys, the Swifts, and the Maytags. Take a one- or two-hour tour, or a tour with a meal: lunch, brunch, dinner, and ice-cream-social cruises are offered. If your kids can last through a two-and-a-half-hour meal tour on the U.S. mailboat *Walworth II*, they'll see an interesting show. The mail carriers must leap from the moving boat onto the docks of summer homes, drop the mail in the dockside boxes, and then jump back onto the moving boat again. Cruises depart from the Riviera, an elegant 1933 building where Tommy Dorsey, Louis Armstrong, and the big bands of the swing era once played. The cruises run from late April to early November. *Riviera Docks, Wrigley Drive, Lake Geneva; (800) 558-5911; (262) 248-6206;* www.cruiselakegeneva.com

Kettle Moraine Ranch

★★★/$$$

It's fun to explore the scenic hills and "kettles"—geologic depressions—of Kettle Moraine State Forest (see page 294) on horseback. Your kids must be at least 8 to ride alone; younger children can ride double with parents. If little ones would rather not ride, they can pet the horses and ride the ponies instead. Reservations are required for trail rides. Closed December through March. *W379 S9446 Hwy. S., Eagle; (262) 594-2122.*

GIDDYAP!

WHETHER YOUR KIDS are experienced equestrians or toddlers who just want to pet the ponies, you can find just the right kind of horsey fun in Lake Geneva. Horseback, pony, carriage, and hayrides are available at various sites throughout the area. Be sure to call ahead for reservations.

Fantasy Hills Ranch offers the best horseback riding in the area for experienced riders. Gallop through 68 acres of rolling, wooded hills, plus a petting zoo and pony rides. *4978 Town Hall Rd., Delavan; (262) 728-1773.*

Grand Geneva Resort & Spa has trail rides and pony rides appropriate for all levels for resort guests and visitors. *Junction of Hwy. 50 and Hwy. 12 E., Lake Geneva; (262) 248-8811.*

Kane's Circle K runs carriage rides through downtown Lake Geneva, as well as hayrides and sleigh rides. *27535 Ketterhagen Rd., Burlington; (262) 534-2771.*

Kettle Moraine Ranch (at left).

FamilyFun MUST-SEE Kettle Moraine State Forest ★★★★/$$

If your kids can grasp the notion of huge, moving mountains of ice, they'll be fascinated by the natural history of this 18,000-acre state forest, where two great glaciers collided thousands of years ago. The 100 miles of countryside that they passed over are dotted with hundreds of hills called drumlins. In between, the hollows, known as kettles, are now filled by marshes or lakes. The glaciers cut narrow ridges, called eskers, through the hillsides, and dropped moraines (isolated boulders) everywhere. The state forest has 80 miles of groomed and marked forest trails for hiking, biking, and, in winter, cross-country skiing. (You can rent cross-country skis in the park's Southern Unit, along the Scuppernong Trail, or on the McMiller Trail.) Your family can camp and fish here, too. Kettle Moraine is a huge park—start at park headquarters to get maps and other information. A state park sticker is required and can be purchased on site. *Forest Headquarters, State Hwy. 59, three miles west of Eagle; (262) 594-6200.*

Lake Geneva Beach ★★★/$$

This is one long stretch of sand near the historic Riviera Docks. The gen-

FESTIVALS ON THE LAKE

Although Lake Geneva is a year-round vacation destination, two seasonal festivals bring even more entertainment and activities with family appeal.

Oktoberfest Pony rides, face painting, hayrides, sing-alongs, and a Great Pumpkin Giveaway are part of the Columbus Day weekend fun, which culminates in a street dance on Sunday. There's also a farmers' market and craft fair.

Winterfest This outdoor lakefront celebration takes place the first weekend in February. The highlight: a snow-sculpting competition that results in amazing mythological and realistic figures that sit like giant white marble statues in the center of all the fun. Street entertainers, helicopter rides, lots of concession-style food, a Torchlight Parade, and fireworks are all part of the festivities.

tle water and soft sand make this an ideal spot for kids of all ages to play. Parents will appreciate the bathhouse with showers and the lifeguards on duty daily from 9 A.M. to 6 P.M. Bring a picnic, but be sure to leave glass containers behind. Open between Memorial Day and Labor Day. *Wrigley Dr., Lake Geneva; (262) 248-3673.*

FamilyFun GAME

I Spy

Someone says "I spy with my little eye something green." Whoever guesses correctly goes next. Limit the items to what's in the vehicle. Or, get tricky and play I Spied, selecting items that you've already passed.

Lake Geneva Horse Park & Petting Zoo ★★★/$

Toddlers will be delighted with the pony rides and the petting zoo, the older kids will go for the tour of the working horse farm, and everyone will like taking a ride in a horse-drawn wagon. Call for current schedule of shows and tours. Closed November through April. *Hwy. 50 and Hwy. 67, Lake Geneva; (262) 245-0770;* www.lakegenevapettingzoo.com

MUST-SEE FamilyFun MUST-SEE

Paradise Golf Park ★★★/$

This is a pretty cool miniature-golf course, with deluxe landscaping—there are even cascading waterfalls. Kids love it, and even parents who golf find it challenging. *511 Wells St., Lake Geneva; (262) 248-3456.*

MUST-SEE FamilyFun MUST-SEE

Walk, Talk & Gawk ★★★/Free

This 20-plus mile path encircles Lake Geneva. Made up of ancient trails that linked the Native American camps that once surrounded the lake, the path is now a favorite hiking trail. Unless your family has some serious hikers, you won't want to complete the circuit with kids in tow, but you can choose a short segment to walk. Pick up the local *Walk, Talk, & Gawk* guide ($6) at almost any local shop. It breaks down the trail into seven (two- to three-and-a-half-mile) segments. The guide also includes a map and information on parking, the condition of the path, and points of interest along the way.

MUST-SEE FamilyFun MUST-SEE

Williams Bay Beach ★★★★/$

This pretty little cove is less populated than Lake Geneva Beach. And unlike Geneva Beach, there's some shade, a welcome respite on a sunny summer day. The bathhouse has showers, and lifeguards are on duty daily 9 A.M. to 5 P.M. Food is permitted, but don't bring anything in glass jugs or bottles. *East of Edgewater Park, Geneva St., Williams Bay; (262) 245-2700.*

Sand City

A family day at the shore wouldn't be complete without trying your hand at sand sculpting. Here are a few tips for creating a whole city of sand buildings and cobblestone streets. For each skyscraper, select a shallow, broad-bottomed container, such as a baking pan or bin, to serve as a mold for the ground story. Pack the mold with damp sand, invert it onto a flat section of beach, then lift off the pan.

To erect a second story, use a craft knife to cut off the top and bottom of a cardboard milk carton (adults only) and set it upright atop the first story. Fill the mold halfway with sand, then slowly pour in enough water to dampen it. Fill the rest of the carton with sand and again dampen it with water. Then remove the mold.

For a finishing touch, top off the building with a sand dome (use a small funnel) or a stone "roof." Press on stick "windows" and a driftwood "door" or "awning."

Bunking Down

The Abbey Resort

★★★/$$$

Great dining and a beautiful site set this resort apart. Your kids will probably be more interested in the indoor and outdoor pools, game arcade, and biking and water sports in summer, cross-country skiing and skating in winter. Kids and parents both love the resort's supervised programs: Kids Kapades and Kids Night Out. With Kids Kapades, children 4 to 12 can learn how to hula hoop, play "parachute" games, and generally have a great time. Kids Night Out affords kids of all ages a pizza, game, and movie night. The 344 rooms include some suites with fireplaces, plus 140 villas with kitchens. The Waterfront Cafe is the most casual of the resort's restaurants, but kids are also seen (and fed) in the more formal Monaco Dining Room, which has a great view of Fontana Harbor. *Fontana; (800) 558-2405; (262) 275-6811;* www.theabbeyresort.com

The Cove of Lake Geneva

★★★/$$$

The pools at this resort hotel will be a hit with your kids. The two outdoor pools are heated, and surrounded by a patio with umbrella tables and deck chairs, and a large heated indoor pool is great when the weather turns cloudy. All 200 guest quarters feel like a home away from home. The well-equipped suites have a full kitchen with full-size refrigerator, microwave, and stove/range, two televisions, a VCR, a fireplace, and a Jacuzzi. A sauna, fitness center, and tennis courts are also on the premises. Houlihan's, a family-friendly chain restaurant, is attached to the hotel. *111 Center St.,*

Lake Geneva; (800) 221-0031; (262) 249-9460. www.cove-lake-geneva.com

Grand Geneva Resort and Spa

★★★★/$$$$

There is no trace of this spot's former tenants. This ex–Playboy Club has completely transformed itself into a family resort of some elegance. The setting is Wisconsin at its most bucolic, with views of a lake, rolling hills, and green grass and trees. (Ask for a room with a view, or you might overlook the parking lot.) There are 355 hotel rooms, including 41 suites and 30 resort villas. The villas have one, two, or three bedrooms, a fully stocked kitchen, and a washer and dryer. Your family can simply stay put and enjoy the facilities; most everything you'll need is here. The resort has its own private lake that guests use for paddleboating, canoeing, swimming, rowing, and touring on the *Lady of the Lake*, a reproduction paddle wheeler excursion boat. Your kids will go for the indoor and outdoor pools, a lap pool, and trails through the woods. Grand Geneva is a great vacation spot in winter, too. It has its own "mountain" (in Wisconsin terms) and snowmaking facilities for 12 downhill slopes and 10 kilometers of cross-country skiing trails. There's even a separate snowboarding hill. The Grand Adventure Kids Club (fee) offers daily activities (such as swimming, tennis, arts and crafts, and treasure hunts) year-round for children 4 to 12. The resort has three restaurants and two cocktail lounges. *7036 Grand Geneva Way, Lake Geneva; (800) 558-3417; (262) 248-8811;* www.grandgeneva.com

Interlaken Resort & Country Spa

★★★/$$$

On Lake Como, about three miles west of Lake Geneva, this property has a variety of resort facilities, including three pools, tennis courts, and a spa. The resort has activities (such as art projects, making and sending personalized postcards, water games, and scavenger hunts)

What's the Catch?

Go out on Lake Geneva with an experienced fishing guide and you're almost sure to catch something wet, flopping, and feisty. **Lake Geneva Fishing Guide Service** *(262/248-3905; 262/791-0733)* provides tackle, equipment, and live bait; in winter, it rents icehouses for ice fishing. **Robert's Guide Service** *(262/763-2520)* rents fishing boats and tackle—and guarantees you'll catch a fish! Your kids can fish without a license; those over 16 need one. You can get a license at the local **Wal-Mart** *(201 Edwards Blvd.; 262/248-2266)*. Rates for nonresidents start at $15 for an individual for four days.

for children ages 5 to 12 (for a fee) on weekends year-round and daily in the summer; parents must stay on the premises while kids participate. There are 144 hotel rooms, some with whirlpools. Or you can splurge on a villa with a fireplace with full kitchen, in-room movies, and VCRs. Your video-game addicts can hang out at the video arcade. The Lake Bluff dining room offers great food and terrific views of Lake Como. The Friday evening fish fry and Sunday country brunch are family favorites. *Hwy. 50 W, Lake Geneva; (800) 225-5558; (262) 248-9121;* www.interlakenresort.com

GOOD EATS

Annie's Ice-Cream Parlor & Restaurant ★★★/$

Hefty burgers plus thick, creamy malts big enough to share equal happy kids. This old-fashioned ice-cream parlor has bentwood parlor chairs, wall-to-wall antique bric-a-brac, and a classic menu of soda-fountain treats. There's even a children's menu. *712 Main St., Lake Geneva; (262) 248-2463.*

Cocoa's ★★/$

Stop here for a light lunch or afternoon treat when you're strolling through town. Cocoa's serves café food and delectable pastries and chocolates. It's in a preserved historic landmark building, and the outdoor seating is especially picturesque. *727 Geneva St., Lake Geneva; (262) 348-0508.*

Culver's Frozen Custard & Butterburgers ★★/$

Think of this as a fast-food chain with first-rate ice cream. The burgers are comparable to what you get at McDonald's (the butter is on the bun, not on the burger itself). But the sundaes, dishes of custard, and cones are top-notch. *151 Wells St., Lake Geneva; (262) 248-6730.*

Popeye's on Lake Geneva ★★★/$$

A fun menu and a great view are

Fun on the Lakes

Your family won't lack for fun on Lake Geneva and the other area lakes. You can ride personal watercraft or pontoon boats; board a chartered cruise; or even try a little parasailing. **Gordy's Boat Rentals** rents ski boats and gives classes; **Jerry's** rents personal watercraft and pontoons. Both have several locations where the water is: *on the Waterfront at* **Fontana on the Lake** *(262/275-2163, 262/275-5222); on Lake Delavan at* **Lake Lawn Resort** *(262/728-7950); on Lake Geneva at* **The Abbey Resort** *(262/275-2163); and on Lake Como at* **Interlaken Resort** *(262/275-5222).*

the draws here. From Easter through October, this casual restaurant runs an open-flame barbecue where chicken, lamb, and pork are cooked. The spectacle is entertaining, and the aroma is enticing. You might even get your kids to eat their vegetables here—the broccoli cheese soup is delicious. Save room for dessert—Popeye's is famous for award-winning homemade pies, baked fresh each day. *811 Wrigley Dr., Lake Geneva; (262) 248-4381.*

Speedo's Harborside Cafe

★★★/$

Come early (it opens at 6:30 A.M.) for waffles and pancakes, have burgers and pizza for lunch, and steaks for dinner. The children's menu includes chicken strips, a fish sandwich, grilled cheese, and a hamburger. Save room for ice-cream sundaes—this casual dining spot has full soda-fountain service. *100 Broad St., Lake Geneva; (262) 248-3835.*

UP, UP, AND AWAY

Let your family see the gorgeous Lake Geneva, with its manicured shoreline and historic mansions, from among the clouds in a hot-air balloon. Sunbird Balloons *(2493 Crest Dr., Lake Geneva; 262/249-0660)* offers sunrise and sunset rides May through October.

Souvenir Hunting

Aerial Stunt Kites

Don't fly just any kite. Get a screamingly cutting-edge sports model and wow the other kids at the beach. The store also stocks fun puzzles and brain games, plus some unusual toys. *121 Wrigley Dr., Lake Geneva; (262) 249-0631.*

Allison Wonderland

The high-quality playthings sold here are educational, but your kids will just think they're fun. Look for American Girl books and crafts, Playmobil toys, Brio train accessories, and more. *720 Main St., Lake Geneva; (262) 248-6500.*

Goof off at Governor Dodge State Park after touring the amazing grown-up's tree fort, The House on the Rock.

Spring Green

Wisconsin's coastline towns are so beautiful that it seems as though inland towns must be less scenic. Not so. The Spring Green countryside in southwestern Wisconsin is so verdant and rolling that its most famous native, Frank Lloyd Wright, returned here to build his home and create an architecture school that's still in operation. The entire area has adopted Wright's approach to architecture, and even modest public buildings and businesses evidence Prairie School principles.

If your children are not wowed by architecture, limit your Wright-related activities to having breakfast or lunch at the restaurant at Taliesin, Wright's famous home and school. It's a painless way to give kids a glimpse at the Prairie School style. An area site that will hold your children's interest is the fanciful House on the Rock. The most-visited tourist attraction in the state, it's a sort of tree house museum created by an eclectic collector with an abundant imagination.

Governor Dodge State Park (page 305)

The House on the Rock (page 302)

Taliesin (page 304)

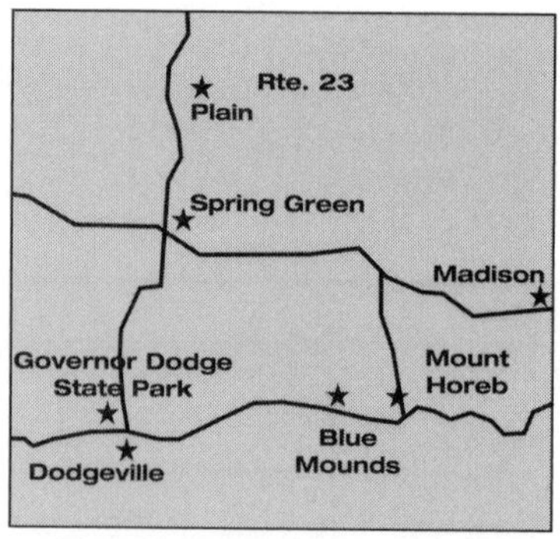

CULTURAL ADVENTURES

The House on the Rock

MUST-SEE FamilyFun MUST-SEE ★★★★/$$$

This is not a great place to take preschoolers or younger tots. The entire tour is about three miles long, and it's a fairly challenging hike, filled with stairs and ramps of varying grades. Strollers aren't allowed inside, although baby carriers are available for use on-site. But older kids will be spellbound by this strange, oddball place that's also the biggest single tourist attraction in Wisconsin, drawing half a million people a year. The "house" was never lived in by anyone. Alex Jordan, the controversial character who built most of the place, began constructing what amounted to a grown-up's tree house on this site in the 1940s. He hired local craftsmen to create reproduction "jewels," antiques, and calliopes, then mixed them in with legitimate collectors' items and showcased them in rooms added haphazardly to his original plan. The result is a l-o-n-g (four hours, if you take in everything) tour of a complicated and illogical—but magical—structure.

Start your House on the Rock tour at the scenic overlook off Highway 23 between Dodgeville and Spring Green. Park the car and take the short walk to the dead end. Then look left to see an incredible sight. A thin needle of windows and wood seems to grow 218 feet out of a rock and hang, suspended over the great valley 156 feet below. What you're seeing is the Infinity Room of the House on the Rock. If your kids see it this way first, they'll be even more impressed when they stand in the incredible room later.

The entrance to the House on the Rock is on Highway 23. Before you enter, prepare your kids for what's ahead: a series of rooms that are dark, claustrophobic, and even a little creepy, rather like a carnival fun house. If you are concerned about claustrophobia and/or acrophobia, ask the staff for an abbreviated tour that avoids some trouble areas.

The self-guided tour includes boring rooms and cool ones. After moving through the first womblike rooms, you'll be in a cool one: the Infinity Room. The 218-foot-long room features 3,264 panes of glass built into floor-to-ceiling windows; it's truly a marvel. Kids will also like the bizarre and remarkable Heritage of the Sea room, with a 200-foot fiberglass structure of a whale-cum-dinosaur sea creature fighting with an octopus. The titanic sea being is longer than the Statue of Liberty is tall.

The way the house is constructed, it's hard to go back or return to a room you've left, so when you hit the Pizza Atrium and Rozino's Pizza, sit down and eat something. (The same rule applies for passing a rest room; when you see one, use it.)

The World's Largest Carousel is a festival of 20,000 lights and 269 animals (not a single horse, though), but it can't be ridden, and the walls and ceiling of the room are covered with near-naked mannequins dressed like angels wearing bad wigs. After visiting the house, make sure to stroll around the 14-building complex that includes other displays such as the new Spirit of Aviation, where kids can see a busy 1940s airfield packed with radio-controlled airplanes and helicopters. Closed Oct. 29 for one week to decorate for the holidays; also closed January 7 to mid-March. *5754 Hwy. 23, Spring Green; (800) 947-2799; (608) 935-3639;* www.thehouseontherock.com

Little Norway ★★/$$

The Norwegian heritage of Wisconsin is celebrated in this pioneer settlement peopled by historical reenactors and costumed guides. Original cabins from an 1856 Norwegian settlement have been

Trolling for Trolls in Mount Horeb

Between Spring Green and Madison lies the little town of Mount Horeb, which boasts an unusual, kid-pleasing feature. Its Main Street harbors a dozen carved wooden trolls—an attraction known as the Trollway. It takes a bit of hunting and patience to find the carved creatures, who are part of Norse folklore. Drive up and down Main Street slowly—every few houses or businesses, you'll see one. The Trollway is better driven than covered on foot—the trolls are too few and far between to make a walk fun.

After tracking down the trolls, take a stroll in this quaint and charming town. Stop at **Schubert's Old-Fashioned Cafe and Bakery** *(126 E. Main St., Mt. Horeb; 608/437-3393)* for a meal or a treat—the place is a small-town hoot, and the bakery case is tempting. The spot is famous for its Swedish rye bread. It also sells the Norwegian flat potato pancake called *lefse*, which tastes best spread with butter, sprinkled with sugar, and then rolled up (what doesn't taste better that way?). Then cross the street to see the **Mount Horeb Mustard Museum** *(100 W. Main St., Mt. Horeb; 608/437-3986)*. If your kids know only the bright yellow kind, they will be amazed by the world's largest collection of mustards, with nearly 3,000 varieties of which you can sample or purchase any of 500. There's even a Mustardpiece Theater with a nonspicy film about how mustard is made.

preserved and filled with authentic Norse antiques and crafts. Some even have sod rooftops. In the *stabbur*, or storage house, food is stored on a raised foundation to keep out moisture and rodents (who apparently can't climb). The Norway Building, built in Norway for Chicago's Columbian Exposition of 1893, shows the *stavkirke* construction of 12th-century Norwegian churches. Kids will be amused—or scared—by the trolls carved out of tree stumps and logs all around the grounds. Guided tours last 45 minutes. Closed November through April. *3576 Cty. JG, Blue Mounds, about 25 miles southeast of Spring Green; (608) 437-8211.*

Museum of Minerals and Crystals ★★/$

Cool giant rocks are the stars here: a 90-pound quartz crystal, a 315-pound Brazilian agate, and a 215-pound geode filled with amethysts, to name a few. Kids find the fossils intriguing, likewise the collection of glow-in-the-dark fluorescent rocks and minerals. *Hwy. 23, across from Governor Dodge State Park; (608) 935-5205.*

MUST-SEE FamilyFun MUST-SEE Taliesin ★★★/$$$

This is a campus of buildings designed by and lived in by Frank Lloyd Wright. Kids won't find much here of interest to them, but they may appreciate at least a stop at the café and a visit to the gift

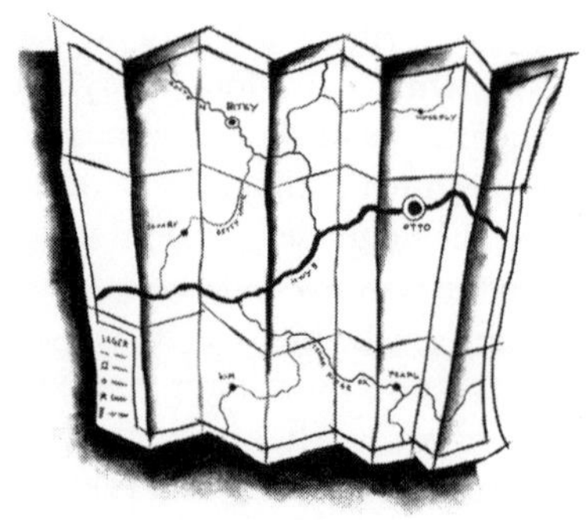

shop. The Riverview Terrace Cafe has a quintessential Frank Lloyd Wright view of the Wisconsin River (see Good Eats). It's next to the gift shop, which stocks related books, magnet sets, building blocks, coloring books, and building kits for kids—along with a lot of breakables. Three tours are offered, and two are too long for young children. Try the one-hour Hillside Studio and Theater Tour. Or, if your 8-and-up kids are game, take the guided two-hour, two-mile walking tour to see the whimsical Romeo and Juliet Windmill (tours of the house or estate require reservations). Even the drive up the driveway into the grounds yields remarkable vistas and examples of Wright-inspired attention to lighting and signage details. As you drive away, catch a glimpse of the Midway Farm, certainly the best-designed barn in America. Closed November through April. *At the junction of Hwy. 23 and Hwy. C, Spring Green; (608) 588-7900;* www.taliesinpreservation.org

JUST FOR FUN

Don Q Inn ★★/Free

In the goofball, white-elephant spirit of the House on the Rock (see page 302), this unique hotel makes a fun drive-by and lobby visit. Its rather amateurishly rendered FantaSuite theme rooms are more for romantic couples than families, however. You truly can't miss the place—the steeple of a church is attached to the end of the hotel, and there's an enormous Boeing C-97 airplane parked permanently outside. The lobby is fun to see because barber and dentist chairs are placed all around the circular hearth. *Hwy. 23 N., Dodgeville; (608) 935-2321.*

MUST-SEE FamilyFun MUST-SEE Governor Dodge State Park ★★★/$$

Outdoors never looked so good. Three miles north of Dodgeville, this park has 5,000 acres of rugged terrain, including steep hills, deep crevices, and sandstone bluffs—all of which make for challenging hiking on the two trails. Boats or canoes can be rented at the Cox Hollow Beach concessions stand, which also sells drinks, ice cream, pizza, and ice and charcoal for campers (open Memorial Day through Labor Day). Two man-made lakes in the park offer fishing for bass, muskie, panfish, and walleye; fishing licenses are sold at the park office. You can also swim at both lakes, but there are no lifeguards. During the summer months, the park naturalist leads free nature walks. In the winter, try the 35 miles of maintained and marked snowmobile and cross-country ski trails. There are 267 campsites, too (see Bunking Down). *4175 Hwy. 23, three miles north of Dodgeville; (608) 935-2315.*

BUNKING DOWN

Best Western Quiet House and Suites ★★/$$

Perhaps the best choice here for families is the American Suite, with a separate bedroom, generous living room, and mini kitchen, though all units have cable television and in-room movies. The 40-room property has rooms, suites, and even specialty theme suites (they're designed for romantic weekends, but a couple of them are appropriate for kids, like the Roman Bath and the vintage cabin suites). Kids love the two heated pools, one

FamilyFun GAME

Playing the Numbers

Two players take turns counting to twenty. On each turn, a player can say one or two numbers. (If the first says "One," the second might say "Two, three.") Try to force your opponent to reach 20 first.

Cheese, Please

Wisconsin takes its reputation as America's Dairyland very seriously. Restaurants serve butter, not margarine, and cream, not nondairy creamer. Along any interstate or county road, the plethora of cheese-shop signs proclaim that the art of cheesemaking is thriving in these rolling hills. A stop at a cheese shop can be a fun side trip for kids. Some show how cheese is made, some shops sell silly cow souvenirs (including a chocolate-and-nuts candy bar facetiously named a cow pie), and all offer samples of dozens of rich, creamy cheeses, including Swiss, Muenster, Limburger, cheddar, provolone, mozzarella, and much more. The Wisconsin icon of all cheeses is something called a cheese curd—a chunk of fresh, young, unprocessed cheddar cheese that is sometimes served deep-fried, and that is said to squeak when you bite it. Try a bag, or try a half pound of sharp aged cheddar. Stop at the Cedar Grove Cheese shop *in Plain (608/546-5284)* for traditional and specialty cheeses made without artificial growth hormones or animal enzymes. *It's on Highway 23, just north of Spring Green.*

indoor and one outdoor, and swim from one to the other—even in the winter! Dodgeville is the hometown of Lands' End, so visit the Lands' End outlet while you're in town (see Souvenir Hunting). *1130 N. Johns Ave., Dodgeville; (800) 528-1234; (608) 935-7739;* www.bestwestern.com

Governor Dodge State Park
★★★/$

The park has 269 campsites in two campgrounds. Twin Valley Campground has 77 electrical sites, but no water or sewer hookup; there's a shower building. Cox Hollow Campground has no hookups or electricity, but a shower building and flush toilets. Both have dump and fill stations. Reservations are recommended. *4175 Hwy. 23, three miles north of Dodgeville; (608) 935-2315.*

House on the Rock Resort
★★/$$$$

Though it's named after the circusy House on the Rock, it's the spirit of Frank Lloyd Wright's Taliesin that touches everything in this attractive, sprawling resort complex. The 80 guest rooms and two condos are nicely appointed in Wright-inspired furnishings, and all are family-friendly two-room suites with a living room, a mini refrigerator, a microwave, and a coffeemaker, plus cable TV. There's also a large, attractive indoor pool with whirlpool; tennis, racquetball, and volleyball courts; and hiking and biking trails. The resort is closed from January through April. The two restaurants offer casual daytime meals and a dressier dinner atmosphere as well as room service. *400 Springs Dr., Spring Green; (800) 822-7774; (608) 588-7000.*

Usonian Inn
★★/$$

This 11-unit motel is an example of Frank Lloyd Wright's Usonian style of architecture. More important to families, the price is right and the landscape of intensely green, rolling hills is as stunning as nearby Taliesin's. All rooms have cable TV; some have refrigerators and microwaves, too. You can start the day with the free continental breakfast. *Hwy. 14 and Hwy. 23 S., Spring Green; (877) 876-6426; (608) 588-2323;* www.usonianinn.com

Good Eats

Riverview Terrace Cafe
★★/$

After a tour of Taliesin buildings or a visit to its gift shop, order breakfast or lunch at the counter in this beautiful café. Grab a window seat with a great view of the river and the woods. The menu is simple, and the setting elegant. Try the breakfast pancakes or a bagel and yogurt; lunch offerings include turkey sandwiches and pizza. Open for breakfast and lunch only. *Hwy. 23 and County Road C, Spring Green; (608) 588-7937.*

Round Barn ★★/$

This 1904 dairy-barn-turned-restaurant now serves Wisconsin favorites: steak, prime rib, and a famous seafood buffet on Friday nights. Breakfasts are hearty, with omelettes, pancakes, and waffles. *Hwy. 14, Spring Green; (608) 588-2568.*

Rumbleseats ★★/$

There's nothing like a real old-fashioned, outdoor drive-in to make fast food seem special. Drive up under the roof and wait for a carhop to deliver burgers, corn dogs, and root-beer floats. May be closed from November through March. *Hwy. 14, Spring Green; (608) 588-2924.*

Spring Green Cafe and General Store ★★/$

This converted cheese warehouse is now a great spot for tasty continental breakfasts and lunches. The menu includes vegetarian and daily specials. *137 S. Albany St., Spring Green; (608) 588-7070.*

Souvenir Hunting

Lands' End Outlet

Catalog stuff, including clothes for kids, is sold at discounts of up to 40 percent. *113 N. Iowa St., Dodgeville; (608) 935-9341.*

You can't visit Wisconsin without seeing the Dells. And you can't visit the Dells without taking in the Tommy Bartlett Thrill Show.

Wisconsin Dells

WHAT STARTED OUT 150 years ago as the site of genteel boat rides past the Wisconsin River's spectacular sandstone cliffs has become a summer family tourist mecca of epic proportions. Today the Wisconsin Dells area is a somewhat tacky yet entirely fun-filled vacation destination, and a profoundly child-friendly one at that. Here is a place in which most restaurants have a kids' menu, most attractions have a kids' rate, and most tourists have offspring.

The Wisconsin Dells area (or the Dells as it is called) is made up of two communities, the city of Wisconsin Dells and the village of Lake Delton. The region in south central Wisconsin was given its name by the *voyageurs*, the first Europeans to see the cliffs, deep, narrow gorges, and unusual rock formations created by

Canyon Creek Riding Stable (page 313)

Circus World Museum (page 311)

Dells Boat Tours (page 313)

Dells Duck Tours/The Original Wisconsin Ducks (page 314)

Family Land/Bay of Dreams Indoor Waterpark (page 315)

Noah's Ark Family Park (page 316)

Pirate's Cove Adventure Golf (page 317)

Tommy Bartlett's Robot World and Exploratory (page 319)

Tommy Bartlett Thrill Show (page 319)

Wisconsin Deer Park (page 320)

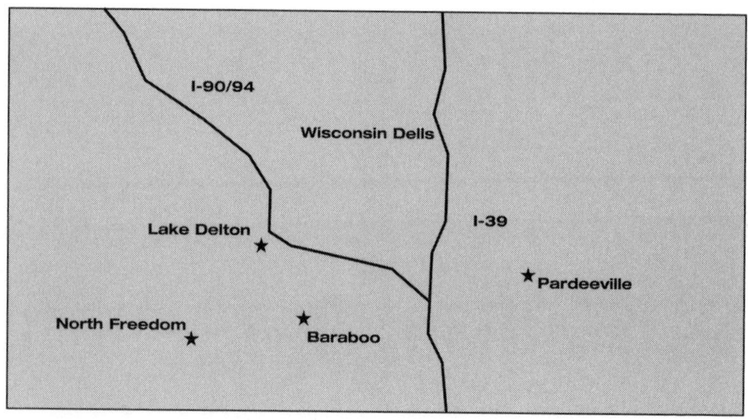

the melting of glacial Lake Wisconsin. "Dells" comes from the French word *dalles*, which means paving stone. It may refer to the rock formations around the waterways in the area—though, in truth, none particularly looks like patio material.

Today, the long-skirted ladies and suited gentlemen are gone, but you can still tour the river on boats or ducks (amphibious World War II vehicles). And there's lots of action off the river, too. The area boasts 7,000 hotel rooms, 3,000 campsites, and 77 attractions, including multiple theme parks, a nationally known water-skiing show, several miniature-golf courses, helicopter rides, a magic show, a wax museum, and a circus museum, as well as the usual north woods resort activities such as fishing, swimming, and jet skiing.

The Dells is a water-play paradise, with many freestanding destination water parks, including the gigantic Noah's Ark Family Park. But keep in mind that many resort hotels have created their own water parks, and some are quite spectacular. Staying at a hotel with a water park can make a lot of sense. Though the nightly rate at such places is generally higher than at a standard hotel, it's still less than a hotel room plus a water park admission fee—and having the park close to your room makes for easier nap and mealtime transitions. Hotel water parks are less crowded, too.

In short, the Dells is kid nirvana, and as such it attracts families from all over the Midwest, many of whom make an annual pilgrimage here. Grown-ups less enamored of water slides and wax museums will be relieved to hear that much of the natural beauty of the region and the river remains unspoiled by the surrounding tourist hoopla. Most families will find they need to stay at least two or three days to see and do everything the Dells has to offer.

Wisconsin Dells's location, almost equidistant from Chicago (188 miles southeast) and the Twin Cities (230 miles northwest), adds to its popularity. It's about 115 miles west of Milwaukee and about 50 miles north of Madison. Because the town is conveniently located just off Interstate Highway 94 and offers so much for families to do, it has become an increasingly popular family reunion destination as well. **NOTE:** This is strictly a summer destination. Before Memorial Day and after Labor Day, most attractions are closed and it's hard to find even a roadside hot dog stand.

CULTURAL ADVENTURES

American UFO and Sci-Fi Museum ★★/$$

Take a photo of your kids with E.T. See models of aliens from movies such as *Planet of the Apes*, *Star Trek*, *Mars Attacks*, *Star Wars*, and *Alien*. (Steer monster-fearing preschoolers away from the latter—it's pretty scary.) This just-for-fun collection of special effects is an enjoyable stop for movie lovers, Trekkies, and those who use the Force. Also visit the Galactic Gift Shop. Closed November through March. *740 Eddy St., Wisconsin Dells; (608) 253-5055;* www.ufomuseum.com

MUST-SEE FamilyFun MUST-SEE Circus World Museum ★★★/$$

Have your kids ever been to the circus? If they haven't, now is the time. And if they have, they'll still like it here. Unlikely as it seems, the tiny town of Baraboo was once home to two circuses, including the Ringling Brothers. Today, the Wisconsin State Historical Society runs a unique circus museum here that's far from stodgy but isn't exactly circusy, either. Set in a quiet, residential neighborhood and dotted with shaded picnic tables, it's a green and breezy relief after the clamor of the Dells strip. The museum's manageable scale means your family can do the whole thing in a single morning, perfect for preschoolers who still need a midday nap. In season, two daily shows, with trapeze artists and performing Pekignese dogs, are held under the Big Top, but the tent is actually small enough so that all spectators get a good view. There are pony and elephant rides, too, and more than 200 circus wagons housed in several different buildings. Daily

FamilyFun TIP

Essentials

The Magellan's catalog (800-962-4943) has inflatable pillows (saving graces on long trips) and a variety of light, durable travel essentials, such as hair dryers, luggage straps, alarms, adapter plugs, and clothing organizers.

A Fun Fishing Trip: Guaranteed

Fishing is rarely a sure thing. Which can make for some disappointed little anglers at the end of the day. But "fee fishing" stacks the odds in the favor of junior fisherpersons. Three spots in the Dells are privately owned fish hatcheries that let you fish in their rearing ponds for a fee. Depending on the hatchery you choose, you'll be fishing for bass, pike, sunfish, salmon, or trout. Just show up and pay your fee. The hatchery will provide you with all the necessary gear: rods, reels, bait. You won't need a fishing license, since the ponds are privately owned. These ponds are heavily stocked and the fish will be biting, which means that you're bound to catch something. Most fee fishing sites will also clean your catch, and even freeze it and mail it to your home. NOTE: Ask how the fees are structured. Some sites charge by the inch, some by the pound. Either way, it's hard to predict what you'll be paying until you reel them in. Try B&H Trout Fishing & Bait *(3640 Hwy. 13 N., Wisconsin Dells; 608/254-7280)*, Beaver Springs Fishing Park *(600 Trout Rd., Wisconsin Dells; 608/254-2735)*, or Wisconsin Dells Trout Farm & Canoe Trips *(Hwy. 13 & K, Wisconsin Dells; 608/589-5353)*.

special events and demonstrations add to the backstage atmosphere and answer such questions as "How do you load the animals on a train?" and "Where does circus music come from?" Don't miss the afternoon parade, once a mainstay of small-town life. One word of warning: timid younger kids may be frightened by the speedy merry-go-round. Exhibits open year-round; daily shows May to Labor Day. *From the Dells, head 10 miles down Hwy. 12 to Baraboo. 550 Water St., Baraboo; (866) 693-1500; (608) 356-0800;* www.circusworldmuseum.com

LaReau's World of Miniature Buildings ★★/$$

This spot takes dollhouse miniatures to new heights—or, more accurately, lows. Wonders of the world, architectural landmarks, and fairy tale kingdoms are replicated here on a small scale. The fascinating collection of miniatures includes the White House, the pyramids of Egypt, and the Eiffel Tower. The more than 100 (and counting) mostly Styrofoam structures are displayed in a parklike setting along a garden path. Little signs tell how long each miniature took the LaReau's to build—the impressive U.S. Capitol required 1,487 hours. Goodness gracious! Closed October to Memorial Day. *The site is 25 miles from the Dells; take Hwy. 16 south to Hwy. 33 east to Hwy. 22. Pardeeville; (608) 429-2848.*

JUST FOR FUN

Big Sky Twin Drive-In Theatres
★★/$$

Give your kids an old-fashioned treat. Put on their jammies and pile them into the car for a night at the movies. (They may not even believe that movies were ever shown outdoors—with the audience sitting in cars?) Each night, four films are shown on two screens here. There's a concession stand, of course. (Remember the old ads with the dancing hot dogs?) The show starts at dusk. Closed October through March. *Hwy. 16 E., one mile south of Wisconsin Dells; (608) 254-8025.*

MUST-SEE FamilyFun Canyon Creek Riding Stable ★★★★/$$

On these one-hour guided tours, children under 7 ride free with an adult. Follow trails that edge babbling brooks, a waterfall, wildflower prairies, and wind through covered bridges. You might even see a deer. At Boot Hill Cemetery, the Tombstone sherriff tells tall tales of the history of the town. And if wildlife sightings are slight (or not happening), there's always the petting zoo at the stables at the end of the trail. *60 Hillman Rd.; Lake Delton; (608) 253-6942;* www.dells.com/horses/canyoncreek

MUST-SEE FamilyFun Dells Boat Tours ★★★/$$

If you've got a kid too queasy to travel on an amphibious "duck" *(see page 314)*, these boat tours will do just fine. The scenery is stunning: walls of butterscotch-colored rock and emerald evergreens rise dramatically out of dark water. Some of the rock formations are positively eerie, looking like sets out of a science-fiction movie. The hour-long tour explores the Lower Dells and is just long enough to entertain without boring preschoolers (who ride free, by the way). Older kids can handle the two-hour trip, which

FamilyFun READER'S TIP

Fledgling Photographers

Last summer, I put an extra flash in our vacation. Instead of having grown-ups be the only photographers, I bought each of our five children, whose ages range from 7 to 19, a 24-exposure disposable camera and let them snap their own pictures. The kids loved it, and we were able to see our vacation through their eyes. Plus, since they were inexpensive cameras, I didn't worry about them being dropped or lost. For very little money, these simple cameras brought our family a lot of smiles.

Kathi Kanuk, Chardon, Ohio

navigates the more spectacular rock formations of the Upper Dells. The longer trip also includes shore landings at Stand Rock and Witches Gulch, where walkways bring you even closer to the weird rock "sculptures" created by the wind and rain. The corny commentary from the tour guide during the first hour may make you roll your eyes, but 8-year-olds will giggle. The second hour is blessedly silent; the captain, as he puts it, lets "the river and rocks and trees tell their own story." Tell your kids to watch for prehistoric-size ferns, turtles sunning themselves on river rocks, and pine martens darting into the woods.

The unique call of the **whooping crane** can be heard up to two miles away.

The highlight of the tour: the daring dog leap at Stand Rock. The famous rock is j-u-s-t far enough from the canyon wall to make a leap seem death-defying. (Actually, the dog has a net, so not to worry.) For the more adventurous, there is now a 30-minute jetboat adventure tour. Closed mid-November through February. *11 Broadway, Wisconsin Dells; (608) 254-8555; (608) 254-7227;* www.dellsboattours.com

FamilyFun MUST-SEE Dells Duck Tours/ The Original Wisconsin Ducks

★★★★/$$-$$$

One of these tours will likely be the highlight of the trip—from your kids' point of view, anyhow. The "ducks" are amphibious World War II vehicles; part hovercraft and part tank, they ride over hill, dale, and right through the water! (The family car will be so boring after this.) Two companies offer the hour-long land and water tours of the Wisconsin River. The ride is a good way to introduce youngsters to the natural beauty of the Dells, but don't expect them to be moved by the gorgeous scenery—they'll focus on the duck's moves into and out of water, up and down the banks of the waterways. Kids also will love the silly jokes and puns Ducks' drivers are famous for. Sit in the middle of the duck to stay dry, in the back to avoid some of the diesel fuel smell. The ducks have a roof, but bring along the sunscreen anyway. Got a kid especially prone to motion sickness? Try a calmer boat ride instead. Closed November through April. No reservations needed. *Dells Duck Tours: 1550 Wisconsin Dells Pkwy., Wisconsin Dells; (608) 254-6080. Original Wisconsin Ducks: 1890 Wisconsin Dells Pkwy., Wisconsin Dells; (608) 254-8751.*

The Dells Experience Jet Boats

★★/$$$

These open-air, 40-passenger boats zip through the Dells with more pep than the lumbering "ducks." The 16-mile trip takes an hour and a half.

The sights along the way are gorgeous, and grade-schoolers may enjoy the relative speed, but the tour is too long for kids under 6 to sit without squirming. You'll be out in the sun the entire trip, so wear hats with brims and slather on the sunblock. Bringing along bottled water is a good idea, too. Closed November through April. *Cty. Rd. N., five miles outside the Dells; (608) 254-8246;* www.dellsjetboats.com

Devils Lake State Park ★★/$$
You'll think you're in the Rocky Mountains or at a miniature Grand Canyon—this site just doesn't look like the Midwest. Fifteen minutes south of the Dells, the state park has camping, hiking, swimming, and spectacular overlooks from the stunning bluffs. In autumn, drive the five-mile South Shore Road/South Lake Road, which winds through the park and along 500-foot bluffs; the blue, blue lake contrasts with the gold and red leaves, creating memorable views. *S. 5975 Park Rd., south of Baraboo on Hwy. 123; (608) 356-8301.*

MUST-SEE FamilyFun MUST-SEE **Family Land/Bay of Dreams Indoor Waterpark ★★★/$$$**
Rain or shine, this place is great fun. It's two attractions in one, offering splashy play both indoors and out. Family Land is a 35-acre outdoor water park, with 29 water slides, two raging rivers, a tidal wave pool, an adventure river, bumper boats, three kiddie water play areas, kiddie bumper boats, miniature golf, bumper cars, a picnic area, a gift shop, and more. Whew! The adjacent Bay of Dreams is the country's largest indoor water park. It has 1,500 feet of water slides, including 52-foot and 32-foot tube slides. There are five slides for younger children, two body slides, a 400-foot river, a leisure pool with water basketball, two whirlpools with waterfalls, a children's pool with a 35-foot interactive pirate ship with five water slides, and a game room. Even on sunny days, the indoor park has its charms—kids can play in the water without worrying about getting sunburned. Guests of Treasure Island Waterpark Resort (see Bunking Down) get in free. One admission covers both indoor and outdoor parks. *1701 Wisconsin Dells Pkwy., Wisconsin Dells; (608) 254-7766;* www.familylandwaterpark.com *or* www.bayofdreams.com

International Crane Foundation ★★/$$

The world's most complete collection of cranes is exhibited in ways that let kids get a close-up look. Some of the big birds are fenced in, and others just whoop it up outdoors. There are 15 species in all, including whooping cranes in a wetland exhibit. An audiovisual presentation will help your kids understand the importance of ecology and of preserving these birds. There's a gift shop and a picnic area. Closed November through April. *E-11376 Shady Lane Rd., five miles north of Baraboo off Hwy. 12; (608) 356-9462;* www.savingcranes.org

Lost Canyon Tours ★★/$$

Sit behind a team of horses and relax—there's no hiking on this canyon tour. The half-hour excursion by horse-drawn carriage covers about a mile, and trots past geologic wonders and a scenic, sandstone canyon. Each carriage can accommodate up to 15 passengers. Carriages depart every 10 to 15 minutes. Closed October through April. *720 Canyon Rd., Wisconsin Dells; (608) 254-8757.*

Mid-Continent Railway ★★/$$

All aboard! Travel by train is back in style at this railroad museum. You and your kids can climb aboard and take a ride on an authentic, steam-powered locomotive. In season, four trips depart daily from the 1894 depot for a seven-mile, 50-minute ride. Closed mid-October through April. *E. 8948 Diamond Hill Rd., North Freedom; (608) 522-4261.*

MUST-SEE FamilyFun MUST-SEE Noah's Ark Family Park ★★★/$$$$

Sure to make a splash with your kids, this is one of the biggest attractions in the Dells. The 70 acres of water activities include 36 slides, two wave pools, two "endless rivers" where you can float in inner tubes, and four kiddie areas.

One of the most popular attractions is a water roller coaster called Flash Flood—walls of water surround you as you hurtle up and down the tracks. The Stingray is a skateboard style ride that goes back and forth between two slopes. For more adventurous riders, The Point of No Return is, as the name might indicate, a very steep slide. Popular with the grade-school set: Slide Winders, huge curvy slides with no tubes or mats needed, and Black Thunder, a tube slide in which riders find themselves in a black tunnel illuminated by pinpricks of light.

More than 4,000 strategically placed lounge chairs allow grown-ups to dry out and/or rest their feet. Smart parents buy a "neck safe," a waterproof pouch to store keys, money, and other necessities, for sale at kiosks on the grounds. That way you can store backpacks, purses, and extra gear in the lockers.

There are a dozen different restaurants or fast-food eateries plus candy shops to keep the energy levels sky-high. Or save money by bringing your own lunch and eating at one of the many picnic areas scattered throughout the grounds. The park is most crowded between July 4 and mid-August; in June, the crowds are smaller but the weather can be iffy. Other less-crowded times: Sunday, Wednesday, and Thursday. Come early and stay late; the lines are much shorter after 5 P.M. Closed after Labor Day to mid-May. *1410 Wisconsin Dells Pkwy., Wisconsin Dells; (608) 254-6351;* www.noahsarkwaterpark.com

MUST-SEE FamilyFun MUST-SEE Pirate's Cove Adventure Golf ★★★/$$

This miniature-golf extravaganza is huge. There's a giant waterfall cascading through it, and five 18-hole courses. (Whatever you do, don't tell your kids they can play all 90 holes.) They'll especially like playing behind and over the 17 waterfalls; the grown-ups will enjoy a scenic overlook of the Dells themselves. *At the intersection of Hwys. 12, 13, 16, and 23, Wisconsin Dells; (608) 254-7500.*

Ripley's Believe It or Not ★★/$$

Just the kind of creepy, gross-out, bizarre, and funky facts and figures that kids think are c-o-o-l! There are eight galleries, two sit-down the-

Life on the Mississippi

Take a historic riverboat cruise on a modern-day replica of the grand paddle wheelers that traveled up and down the Mississippi in the early 1900s. The *La Crosse Queen* departs from the town of La Crosse, located in the southwestern corner of Wisconsin. Several types of cruises are available, but the Captain's Brunch on Sunday mornings may be the best choice for families ($$$). The two-hour cruise includes a meal, and, if river conditions permit, features the fascinating process of "locking through" Lock and Dam #7. It's a lesson in river power, dams, and the laws of physics that the children won't soon forget. The sightseeing cruise ($$) is another good choice for kids, because it is only 90 minutes long. It includes an explanation, but not a demonstration, of the lock and dam. The weekend dinner cruises are more for adults, and the three-hour cruise is just too long for most children. Cruises run May through October; reservations are necessary *(608/784-2893).*

If you plan to stay overnight in La Crosse, check into the Radisson Hotel La Crosse *(corner of 2nd St. and Main St., La Crosse; 608/784-6680; 800/333-3333)*, a hotel that celebrates its city's river heritage with a striking and enormous lobby mural of the *La Crosse Queen* riverboat. The hotel has 169 rooms that overlook the Mississippi River or downtown La Crosse. Facilities include an indoor pool, poolside whirlpool, and an exercise room.

aters, and seven video presentations, plus mannequin exhibits demonstrating some weird human oddities (like the woman with the longest neck, or the guy who could fit the most golf balls in his mouth). *115 Broadway, Wisconsin Dells; (608) 253-7556;* www.ripleys.com

Riverside and Great Northern Railway ★★/$$

Take a three-mile trip on a model train powered by a steam locomotive. During the half-hour ride, the train travels through the woods and along the rock formations lining the Wisconsin River. The cars have roofs to keep out the sun, but are smaller than the real railroad cars of yesteryear. Trains depart every 45 minutes. There's also ice cream to be had at the depot. Closed mid-October to mid-May. *N115 Cty. N., Wisconsin Dells; (608) 254-6367.*

Riverview Park and Waterworld ★★★/$$-$$$

This water park/amusement park combo features 760 feet of water slides and 30 different water activities, plus many rides that children can drive themselves, like kiddie go-carts. One of the newest attractions here is The Hurricane, a water coaster/raft ride that three people can ride together. It travels through two flumes, one a dark tunnel that might be scary for young children. But families can ride together wearing street clothes (you'll hardly get wet) so you can be right there to reassure the young ones. There are also dry amusement park rides like a roller coaster, as well as a glass fun house and miniature golf. Closed between Labor Day and Memorial Day. *Hwy. 12, Wisconsin Dells; (608) 254-2608;* www.riverviewpark.com

Sandstone Reptiles ★★/$$

For some strange reason, some kids often have soft spots in their hearts for snakes, lizards, and other slithery, scaly critters. If your child does, be sure to visit this reptile zoo, with its white albino alligators and enormous anaconda. Kids can get a photograph with a snake or a gator to show their friends back home. *1425 Wisconsin Dells Pkwy., Wisconsin Dells; (608) 253-3200.*

Shipwreck Lagoon ★★/$$

There are 54 holes in all at three miniature-golf courses. A pirate ship,

WHO AM I? Do an impression of someone whom everyone else in the car knows. It could be a neighbor with an accent or a movie character. The first person to guess correctly gets the next turn at trying an impersonation.

streams, waterfalls, and natural obstacles make the game more interesting. Little Leaguers will want to head for the baseball and softball batting cages. Closed November through March. *1450 Wisconsin Dells Pkwy., Wisconsin Dells; (608) 253-7772.*

Storybook Gardens
★★/$$

Toddlers and preschoolers will encounter live storybook characters in this land of "once upon a time." They can meet Bo Peep, accompanied by two real sheep, and see Pocahontas in the woods. They'll like the tame rides, too, like a merry-go-round and a small train, plus there are animals to feed and live stage performances. Stroll the gardens and stop at the Gingerbread House for lunch. Closed mid-October to mid-April. *1500 Wisconsin Dells Pkwy., Wisconsin Dells; (608) 253-2391;* www.dells.com/storybook/

Timber Falls Adventure Golf
★★/$$

What's nice about this attraction is that it hugs the shoreline of the Wisconsin River. There are five 18-hole miniature-golf courses, and when your kids have had enough of pretending to be Tiger Woods you can all head for the Timber Wolf Log Ride. It's a fun trip through caves and waterfalls (you won't get too wet) and past an "active" volcano. If you think you'll want to play a few rounds and take the log ride, too, buy the all-day pass and save. Closed November through March. *Broadway and Stand Rock Rd., Wisconsin Dells; (608) 254-8414.*

MUST-SEE FamilyFun MUST-SEE Tommy Bartlett's Robot World and Exploratory ★★★/$$

The original Russian Mir space station has docked here, and can be toured by junior astronauts. There are 100 hands-on exhibits where the whole family can learn about magnetic and electric fields and space-age robotics. Kids love creating art with lasers and experimenting with static electricity. Be sure to try the virtual-reality exhibit that puts you into outer space. *560 Wisconsin Dells Pkwy., Wisconsin Dells; (608) 254-2525;* www.tommybartlett.com

Tommy Bartlett Thrill Show ★★★★/$$$

Even kids used to the taped thrills of cable television will grow wide-eyed with amazement at this beloved and renowned water-ski show. Speedboats, acrobats, and water-skiers zoom in, around, and between each other in synchronized (and noisy!) water ballets. Expect to see pyramids of water-skiers stacked on each other's shoulders, and lots of other exciting daredevil water-skiing moves, plus juggling and daring stunts on the stage, too. This is a popular summer attraction, but it's not hard to get a ticket and there's plenty of seating space in the open-air shaded stands. Lots of snack bars and many roving vendors will keep youngsters fed and happy. Preschoolers will fare best at the afternoon performance; the evening show starts late so it can end with a bang, literally—there's a fireworks show. Shows daily at 4:30 and 8:30 P.M., rain or shine, plus a midsummer 1 P.M. show in July and August. Memorial Day to Labor Day. *560 Wisconsin Dells Pkwy., Wisconsin Dells; (608) 254-2525;* www.tommybartlett.com

Wax World of the Stars ★★/$$

Experience an Elvis sighting. Look into Julia Roberts's big brown eyes. See *Ah*-nold's gap-toothed grin. More than 100 personalities made of wax are so lifelike your kids will do double takes. Closed mid-October through April. *105 Broadway, Wisconsin Dells; (608) 254-2184;* www.conceptattractions.com

MUST-SEE FamilyFun MUST-SEE

Wisconsin Deer Park ★★★/$$

The more than 100 tame deer that live on this 28-acre wooded site are happy to be hand-fed, patted, and photographed. Buy a handful of deer treats and then just try to walk 10 feet without getting panhandled by Bambi. You can take great photos here of your kids feeding the deer. There are buffalo, game birds, and elk to see, too. Closed November through April. *583 Wisconsin Dells Pkwy., Wisconsin Dells; (608) 253-2041.*

Wonder Spot ★★/$

Is this an oddity of nature or a silly fun-house amusement? Folks aren't telling, but kids will enjoy it, whichever it is. On this site, it seems like you're always standing at an angle on which water runs uphill, and that gravity doesn't work quite the way it's supposed to. You can't change the laws of physics. Or can you? Closed between Labor Day and Memorial Day. *Hwy. 12, Wisconsin Dells; (608) 254-4224.*

BUNKING DOWN

Camping

Baraboo Hills Campground ★★/$

This modern campground has 157 wooded sites, an outdoor pool, and attractive bathrooms. Miniature golf, fishing, a game room, playground, basketball, and horseshoes will satisfy even the most energetic of kids. *E10545 Terrytown Rd., Baraboo; (800) 226-7242; (608) 356-8505.*

Yogi Bear's Jellystone Park and Cindy's Cabins and Yogi's Bungalows ★★/$

Your kids are too young to have caught Yogi and friends the first time around, but chances are they've met him on reruns on the Cartoon Network. Well, they can meet him in person here at this 400-camping site playground. The resort has a daily organized program of kids' activities, including treasure hunts, face painting, arts and crafts, shuffleboard, and sand volleyball. And Yogi cartoons are screened each night. Sites here are primitive, with no hookups; others have water and electrical hookups; and some sites have water, electricity, and sewer hookups. Cabins sleep four and have one room (no bathroom), and are equipped with a refrigerator and an outdoor grill. Bungalows are larger versions of the cabins; each sleeps six and has two rooms (no bathroom); they also have refrigerators, microwaves, air-conditioning, and heat. Kids like the two pools, two playgrounds, 18-hole miniature-golf course, golf carts for getting around, and boats for rent. The resort has a daily organized program of kids' activities. There are dances and live music on Saturday nights. Closed mid-October to mid-April. *Corner of Grasser Rd. and Ishnala Rd. in Lake Dalton, Wisconsin Dells; (800) 462-9644; (608) 254-2568;* www.dells.com/yogibear

Hotels

Given that water parks are a main (kids might say *the* main) attraction here, cost-conscious families can take one of two approaches to lodging in Wisconsin Dells. You can stay at a budget hotel and pay admission each day to a water park, or stay in a much more expensive hotel with its own water park facility. The water parks in hotels are not necessarily less extensive than the larger freestanding parks, and the $150- to $200-a-night price tag is actually a good deal if you look at it as a lodging/entertainment package. With a terrific water park steps away from your room, you may not need to hit any other water parks on your trip. And thanks to the ubiquitous in-room refrigerators and microwaves at the more expensive hotels, you won't need to eat out much, either. Rates vary greatly according to season, so check when you call to find out the date when the rates drop or rise. Dells hotels cater to families, so most properties can accommodate a range of combina-

tions of children and adults. Rates vary according to the number of beds and how much living space you need, so ask what the options are.

Howard Johnson Antiqua Bay Resort

★★★/$$$

This property has organized activities for adults and children like those typically found on cruise ships—ice-cream socials, volleyball tournaments, kids' treasure hunts, and the like. The water theme starts at the drive-up entry, where there is a 14-foot waterfall, and continues with Caribbean accents inside the hotel. The two indoor water-fun areas have water slides: the 3,000-square-foot Dolphin Isle and the 10,000-square-foot Aqua Dome. The splashy fun continues outside, with two pools and activity areas edged with picnic tables and deck chairs. There's also a sauna and an indoor whirlpool, game room, a board-game library of games you can check out, the Green Mill Restaurant (known for its deep-dish Chicago-style pizza), a café, and a gift shop. Each of the 228 rooms has a refrigerator, and cable TV with HBO and Disney; cribs are available at no additional charge. Kids under 18 stay free in their parents' room. *655 Frontage Rd., Wisconsin Dells; (800) 54-DELLS; (608) 254-8306;* www.hojo.com

Great Wolf Lodge

★★★/$$$$

Stay in a log cabin—a big, big log cabin. This 230,000-square-foot lodge, set on 35 scenic acres, has a gorgeous lobby with golden logs, natural stone walls, and an immense antler chandelier. But within this rustic setting is a decidedly modern attraction: a large (40,000 square feet) indoor water park complete with pools, slides, a lazy river, and a six-story tree house. Each of the 300 guest rooms has cable TV, a refrigerator, and a microwave. Some units have a whirlpool and a fireplace. The lodge is attentive to its young guests, offering story time (tales about wolves and other animals are favored) and "Wolf Walks" through the lodge, during which kids learn about wolves in particular and nature in general. The Loose Moose Bar and Grill offers a casual, family dining experience, and a children's menu with grilled cheese, burgers, chicken strips, pizza, and hot dogs.

Tour Guides on Tape

Ride With Me tapes (800-752-3195) are cassettes keyed to common roadways. Put in a tape at the prescribed mile marker, and it's like having a guide versed in history, geography, and trivia along as you drive through a state. (But you won't have to give up an extra seat or share your lunch.)

1400 Great Wolf Dr., Wisconsin Dells; (800) 559-9653; (608) 253-2222; www.greatwolflodge.com

The Polynesian Resort Hotel & Suites

★★★/$$$$

The first big water park/hotel in the Dells, the Polynesian remains a favorite, especially with younger children. Warm pools and plenty of hot tubs will keep even the skinniest kids from shivering. The 232 hotel rooms offer welcome amenities: a kitchen area with a refrigerator and microwave, and cable TV. Some units have whirlpools, and suites and theme rooms are available. The water park fun is included in the rate. *857 N. Frontage Rd., Wisconsin Dells; (800) 272-5642; (608) 254-2883;* www.dellspolynesian.com

Treasure Island Waterpark Resort ★★★/$$$$

Attached via skyway to the Family Land water park (see Just for Fun), this resort is also within walking distance of many other Dells attractions, including the Ducks. There are 240 rooms, all with satellite TV, refrigerators, microwaves, and whirlpools; some suites are available. Tickets to Family Land/Bay of Dreams are included in the room rate. *1701 Wisconsin Dells Pkwy., Wisconsin Dells; (800) 800-4997; (608) 254-8560;* www.wisdelltreasureisland.com

FamilyFun GAME

One Minute of Words

Everybody gets a pencil and paper. Someone has to be the timekeeper. The timekeeper picks a letter, tells it to everyone else, and shouts "Go!" Players write as many words as possible that start with that letter. When a minute is up, the timekeeper says "Stop!" and all the players put down their pencils. Whoever has the most legitimate words wins. Decide in advance whether you can finish writing a word you've already started when the game ends. Now, give yourself one more minute to write a sentence with as many of the words as you can.

The Wilderness Hotel & Golf Resort ★★★/$$$$

If your kids want water fun—and lots of it—stay here. You can skip the area's other water attractions and just enjoy the indoor 150,000-square-foot water park on the premises. There are two tube slides, one 400 feet long and 40 feet high. A lazy river for floating down in inner tubes meanders 600 feet through an outdoor sundeck, and the two-person figure-eight-shaped tubes make it easy for a parent to double up with a young child. The spray play here is imaginative: children can swim under waterfalls, slide under giant mushrooms that rain, ride a gentle toddler-size water slide shaped like a giant butterfly, and play in a Wilderness Fort that's part playground, part water park. Special areas and wading pools just for little ones let preschoolers play without getting splashed or scared by bigger kids. There are six pools and hot springs, water basketball, a separate kiddie pool, and even large video screens so you and your kids can swim and watch sports. The entire water park area is filled with tables, chairs, and deck chairs, so parents can easily keep an eye on your kids. If they ever agree to dry off, kids can play in ersatz tree houses and rock formations on the resort grounds, and grown-up golfers will love the championship course. The resort has 309 rooms, suites, and villas. Some rooms have fireplaces with televisions built in above them. All rooms have refrigerator, microwave, and cable TV. Rooms face the gigantic pool and water-park area, so you can see the fun from your balcony (you can hear it, too, which can be a downside when you're trying to sleep). **NOTE:** Rent the vacation villa with another family and get a full kitchen, whirlpool, gas fireplaces, and more space than most people have at home. *511 E. Adams St., Wisconsin Dells; (800) 867-9453; (608) 253-9729;* www.wildernessresort.com

Wintergreen Resort & Conference Center ★★/$$$

The small indoor/outdoor water park here is just fine for preschoolers, and the rooms here cost less than those at resorts with bigger water attractions. Rooms have microwaves, refrigerators, in-room movies, and cable TV. There's a family-friendly restaurant (see Good Eats) and a game room for kids. *60 Gasser Rd., Lake Delton; (608) 254-2285.* www.wintergreen-resort.com

GOOD EATS

Black Bart's Stagecoach Buffet ★★★/$$

It's part theater, part dining experience—but then again, when was the last time you had a meal with your children that wasn't? Reasons kids love this place: the buffet means instant food they can choose themselves; they can sit at picnic tables to eat; the bar stools are miniature horses with saddles; and every now and then the sheriff races through to catch Black Bart and throw him in jail. The food is meat-and-potatoes basic, with enough variety to satisfy picky eaters. Outside, there's a campfire where kids can roast marshmallows and have a sing-along. *420 State Hwy. 13, Wisconsin Dells; (608) 253-2278.*

Culvers ★★/$

This Wisconsin-based chain of hamburger/frozen custard restaurants is a relaxing alternative to conventional fast-food places. You place your order at the counter, but sit and wait for your food at your table. Kids' meals include custard cups that don't arrive until the milk and burger are finished. *312 Broadway, Wisconsin Dells; (608) 253-9080.*

Monk's Bar & Grill
★★★/$

Seasoned Dells visitors return again and again for the famous burgers. It's a sports bar-type restaurant, but kids are very welcome. Along with burgers and fries, you can get other sandwiches and treats; there's a children's menu, too. *220 Broadway, Wisconsin Dells; (608) 254-2955.*

Paul Bunyan's Cook Shanty
★★/$

Enjoy hearty breakfasts, lunches, and dinners served lumberjack-style on tables covered with red-checkered cloths. The bill of fare at breakfast includes flapjacks, of course; the lunch and dinner menu features camp-fried chicken, potato pancakes, pot roast, barbecue ribs, and prime rib. *Hwy. 13, exit 87, just off I-90/94; (608) 254-8717. Also Hwy. 51, Minocqua; (715) 356-6270* (see page 335).

Pizza Pub ★★/$

After an exhausting day on the water slides, you might prefer collapsing in your hotel to braving the restaurant scene with your waterlogged wee ones. No problem: call the Pizza Pub. They deliver, right to your room. Already had pizza three times this week? Order fried chicken, or try the ribs, salad, or burgers. You can also dine in the restaurant, which is conveniently located right across the street from Noah's Ark. *1455 Wisconsin Dells Pkwy., Wisconsin Dells; (608) 254-7877.*

Wintergreen Grille ★★/$$

Located in the Wintergreen Resort, this low-key family restaurant specializes in ribs but also offers a nightly pizza buffet that kids will love. On Fridays, try the classic Wisconsin fish-fry special. *60 Gaser Rd., Lake Delton; (608) 254-7686.*

Souvenir Hunting

Corner on Wisconsin

The signature treasures of Wisconsin are all gathered in this one store: cheese, Amish crafts, and more. *532 Oak St., Baraboo; (608) 356-3852.*

Market Square Cheese

Visit the Swiss chalet–style cheese house for homemade fudge and cheese, cheese, cheese. *1150 Wisconsin Dells Pkwy. S., Lake Delton; (608) 254-8388.*

Kids go wild over Jim Peck's, where they can pet and feed deer and llamas.

Northern Wisconsin

WHAT DO Midwesterners do on their vacations? They head for the woods and lakes, of course. In Wisconsin, that means traveling north. Northern Wisconsin is known for its natural beauty, more than 3,000 lakes, and its family resorts. But keep in mind that here, "resort" is a word applied to a wide variety of accommodations, most of them rustic to semi-rustic. Rarely are woodland resorts large, luxurious properties with four-star restaurants. However, the simple family pleasures of a sandy beach, a basic cabin, and a shady clump of trees under which to picnic are here in abundance. In winter, snowmobilers explore this entire region on maintained trails, and cross-country skiing and snowshoeing are popular.

Circle M Corral Family Fun Park (page 329)

Jim Peck's Wildwood (page 330)

Lac du Flambeau Fish Hatchery (page 330)

The Lumberjack Special (page 330)

Million Dollar Penny (page 331)

Scheer's Lumberjack Show (page 333)

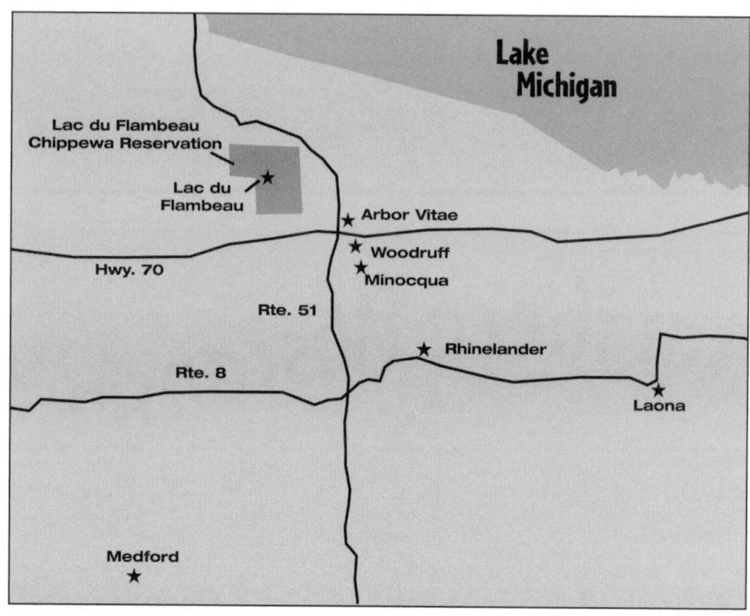

CULTURAL ADVENTURES

George W. Brown, Jr., Ojibwe Museum and Cultural Center ★★/$

What better place for kids to learn about Native American culture than at this museum on the Lac du Flambeau Chippewa Indian Reservation. Among the exhibits are an authentic dugout canoe, birch-bark canoes, Chippewa clothing, and ceremonial drums. Lac du Flambeau (Flaming Lake) was named by French fur traders who saw Chippewa Indians fishing on it in canoes by torchlight. The museum and center are south of the Indian Bowl, a large outdoor space where powwows are held. *Peace Pipe Rd., Lac du Flambeau; (715) 588-3333.*

Rhinelander Logging Museum ★★/Free

Learn about logging in a Wisconsin town where logging camps were once the main business. Kids can play at being lumberjacks in a replica of an 1870s lumber camp that even has a blacksmith shop built of pine logs and an old-fashioned train station. Old photos of huge trees and the teams of rough-and-ready men who felled them will kindle your kids' imaginations. *Pioneer Park, off Business Rte. 8, Rhinelander; (715) 369-5004.*

JUST FOR FUN

Bearskin State Park Trail

★★/Free

This wilderness trail runs 18 miles, from just above the Lincoln and Oneida county line north to just behind the Minocqua post office. It's built on a former railroad grade, with 13 trestles along its length. The trestles have been converted to wooden walkways, and are safe, but there are steep inclines off the edges of parts of the trail, so keep a close eye on little ones. The trail makes for a pleasant family excursion, with fishing spots and a pretty crossing over Beaver Creek. **NOTE:** Young children and those who fear heights won't like crossing the creek on the railroad trestles. You may want to turn the walk into a loop and head back at that point. *(715) 453-1263.*

Chequamegon National Forest

★★/Free

The 850,000 acres of this protected area are filled with lakes, rivers, streams, and hardwood and pine trees, making it a great place for your family to hike, fish, boat, and (in winter) cross-country ski. There are campgrounds, too (see Chippewa Campground in Bunking Down). *North of Medford for four miles on Hwy. 13; west on Cty. Rd. M for 24 miles to Lou Forest Rd.*

Chequamegon Wilderness Adventures

★★/$$$$

This outfitter will set up a custom canoe or kayak trip just for your family. Or you can choose a guided day trip on any one of several Wisconsin rivers. In winter, the company leads snowshoe and dogsled adventures. Open June through October for trips; store is open April through December. *443 E. Chicago Ave., Minocqua; (715) 356-1618;* www.paddlethenorthwoods.com

Circle M Corral Family Fun Park

★★★/$$

Kids will be in for a pleasant surprise when you run into this amusement park in the midst of the wilderness.

WHAT'S A HODAG?

Do dragons live in Wisconsin? Legend has it that an odd dragon-like animal, dubbed a "hodag," was photographed back in 1896 by a lumberman who said he discovered the creature in a cave. That story was obviously a hoax, but today you can find hodags aplenty in gift shops all around Rhinelander.

Make An Underwater Scope

If your kids want to check out the critters and plants in Wisconsin's lakes, why not do it from a fish's-eye view with an underwater scope?

Unfortunately, most of the really cool stuff that lives underwater is too small, too slimy, and too delicate to capture alive—or to capture at all. This easy-to-make underwater scope makes catching the little critters irrelevant. Poke it in the water and look through for a clear, enlarged view of life beneath the surface. In creeks and streams, that might mean the creepy nymphs and insects that attach themselves to rocks (neat!); in the pool, that might mean Dad's hairy toes. (Yuk!)

DIRECTIONS: You'll need a food storage tub with a snap-on lid (like the kind yogurt comes in) and some plastic wrap. Cut off the tub's bottom and cut the center out of the tub's lid so that only the rim remains. Stretch the plastic wrap over the tub's top and snap the rim over it to secure it in place. Insert the plastic-wrapped end into the water and look through the top.

WHY IT WORKS: When you stick the scope into the water, the water pressure pushes the plastic wrap into a concave magnifying lens.

It has water slides, kiddie rides, bumper boats, train rides, go-carts, pony rides, horseback riding, miniature golf, batting cages, and video games. There are individual fees for each activity or $20 for unlimited rides, not including the ponies/horses. *Hwy. 70 W., 2½ miles west of U.S. 51; (715) 356-4441;* www.circlemcorral.com

MUST-SEE FamilyFun MUST-SEE Jim Peck's Wildwood ★★★/$

Kids can feed deer, pet a llama, and see a real porcupine waddle around. The family can also enjoy boat rides and a nature walk on this 30-acre property. *Hwy. 70, two miles west of Hwy. 51; (715) 356-5588.*

MUST-SEE FamilyFun MUST-SEE Lac du Flambeau Fish Hatchery ★★★/$

Looking to introduce your kids to the joys of fishing while you're on vacation? This place makes it easy. You don't need a license or gear; the hatchery will set you up with poles and point you toward the fishing pond. Better yet, you pay only for the trout you catch (only about $2 a fish). *Lac du Flambeau Chippewa Reservation, Hwy. 47; (715) 588-3307.*

MUST-SEE FamilyFun MUST-SEE The Lumberjack Special ★★★/$

Board this old-fashioned steam train for a trip back in time to a 19th-century logging camp. The old Laona and Northern Railway train departs from the Laona Depot and heads for the Camp Five Museum Complex. It's the only way to reach the complex, where your kids will see active blacksmith and harness shops, a logging museum, an animal corral, and a nature center. You can take a pontoon boat ride through a water-covered wild rice field for an additional fee. The train runs from mid-June to late August, departing Monday through Saturday at 11 A.M., 12 noon, and 1 and 2 P.M. (Call to confirm schedule.) *Hwy. 8 and 32, one third mile west of Laona; (800) 774-3414; (715) 674-3414;* www.camp5museum.org

MUST-SEE FamilyFun MUST-SEE Million Dollar Penny ★★★/Free

It's the biggest penny in the world! Kids will like the story behind this humongous coin. Many years ago, Arbor Vitae-Woodruff grade-school children collected one million pennies for a fund drive to build Lakeland Memorial Hospital. The town constructed the huge penny to honor the kids' contributions. Made of concrete and colored copper, the "coin" is as big as two adults. *Arbor Vitae-Woodruff School, Hemlock St. and Third Ave., one block off Hwy. 51.*

Minocqua ★★/Free

This small town is a good base if you're planning to explore the nearby woodlands of Chequamegon National Forest (see page 329) and Northern Highland American Legion State Forest (see page 332). If you're in town between mid-June and mid-August, don't miss the Min-Aqua Bats water-skiing show *(715/356-5266)*. The free show, performed at the downtown Aqua Bowl on Wednesday, Friday, and Sunday nights (7 P.M.), is thrilling. Human pyramids and other hot dog water-skiing hijinks are performed by amateurs. Hey, kids—just don't try these stunts at the next water park you visit! *Off Hwy. 51.*

Minocqua Winter Park ★★/$$

Head here when it snows. The 75 kilometers of groomed cross-country ski trails include special trails groomed especially for small children. A ski shop rents cross-country skiing and snowshoeing equipment, and there's a certified ski school if lessons are in order. A day lodge provides child care on

FamilyFun SNACK

Gobbledy Gook

4 cups oat or crispy rice cereal, 1 cup chopped peanuts, 1 cup raisins or chopped, dried prunes or apricots, 1 cup sunflower seeds, 1 cup chopped pretzels, 3 tablespoons melted butter (optional).

Place all ingredients in a 2-quart plastic bag, seal, and shake until well mixed.

Tuesday, weekends, and holidays. *12375 Scotchman Lake Rd., Minocqua; (715) 356-3309;* www.skimwp.org

Northern Highland American Legion State Forest

★★/$$

This is an idyllic spot for camping and fishing. About 10 miles from Minocqua, the deep-green forest stretches across 222,000 acres and includes 900 lakes. The nine unsupervised beach and picnic areas provide plenty of places to picnic, swim, and canoe, and there are nature and hiking trails to explore, too. There's a campground for those who'd like to stay a while. Head to the Woodruff ranger station for advice and maps. *8770 County Rd. J; (715) 385-2727.*

Northwood Wildlife Center

★★/$

Would-be veterinarians will be interested in seeing the eagles, deer, and other wild animals that are nursed back to health here. *8683 Blumstein Rd., Minocqua; (715) 356-7400;* www.nwc.bfm.org

BAYFIELD, MADELINE ISLAND, AND THE APOSTLE ISLANDS

IN A STATE rich in picturesque fishing and maritime villages, **Bayfield**, at the northernmost tip of the state on Lake Superior, is among the most charming. The streets are lined with stately Victorian mansions, many converted into bed-and-breakfasts. This harbor town is a popular vacation destination, particularly in the months of July and August. **Big Bay State Park** *(715/747-6425)* has rock formations along the water for climbing, beaches for walking and swimming, and campsites. And Bayfield is the gateway to the **Apostle Islands National Lakeshore**—22 coastal islands with lighthouses, caves, hiking trails, and sailing.

If you're visiting in the summer, take in a concert or show under the huge circus tent of **Lake Superior Big Top Chautauqua** *(top of Ski Hill Rd., Bayfield; 888/244-8368)*; performances are staged June through September. Autumn is a particularly scenic time here, with brilliant fall colors usually peaking in mid-to-late September. If you're here in the fall, drive south along Highway 13 from Superior to Ashland for a spectacular view of the gold and red woodlands and the blue Brule River.

Cruise in and around the **Apostle Islands**, which lie offshore of Bayfield and north of Ashland. The **Apostle**

Scheer's Lumberjack Show ★★★/$$

FamilyFun MUST-SEE

Revisit Wisconsin's logging days in Woodruff. Modern-day lumberjacks and historical reenactors demonstrate skills that kids won't have seen before: log rolling, climbing up high poles, chopping, and sawing. Evening shows start at 7:30 P.M. on Tuesday, Thursday, and Saturday; 2 P.M. matinees are on Wednesday, Friday, and Sunday. Closed September to mid-June. *Hwy. 47, Woodruff; (715) 356-4050;* www.scheerslumberjackshow.com

Torpy Park ★★/Free

This park in downtown Minocqua has a beach on Lake Minocqua with roped-off swimming areas and lifeguards. Other features include kids' dock, tennis courts, and grills near picnic tables. *Hwy. 51, Minocqua.*

Wa-Swa-Goning ★★/$$

The name of this 20-acre re-created Native American village is Ojibwe for "the place where they spearfish by torchlight." Here, kids get a glimpse of Native American life when they view fish traps, birch-bark bas-

Islands Cruise Service *(Bayfield City Dock, Bayfield; 715/779-3925; 800/323-7619)* offers a captained, two-and-a-half-hour cruise on the 54-foot wooden schooner *Zeeto.* An active family can rent kayaks (**Trek & Trail**, *Washington Ave., Bayfield; 800/354-8735*).

Madeline Island, just three miles from Bayfield, is the most-visited of the Apostle Islands. Take the **Madeline Island Ferry Line** *(Madeline Island, La Point; 715/747-2051)*. On the island, visit the **Madeline Island Historical Museum** *(715/747-2415)*, located on the historic site of the former American Fur Company trading post.

The rocky Apostles Islands made lighthouses a nautical necessity here, and several still stand on the islands. Five are open for tours given by National Park Service volunteers. Many of the cruises out of Bayfield go near or stop at these sites, which are all open from mid-June to Labor Day. The **Devil's Island Lighthouse** *(715/779-3397)* was built in 1898 and has two Queen Anne keeper residences. The **Michigan Island Lighthouse** *(715/779-3397)* was built in 1857, and a 112-foot tower was added in 1929. The **Outer Island Lighthouse** (no phone) was constructed in 1874 with a 90-foot tower. **Raspberry Island Lighthouse** *(715/779-3397)* was built in 1863. **Sand Island Lighthouse** *(715/779-3397)* was built in 1881, with a 44-foot tower built of locally quarried brownstone. Once you dock here, there's a two-mile hike to the lighthouse, so it's the least kid-friendly of the tours. For cruises, call the **Apostle Island Cruise Service** *(800/323-7619)*.

kets, real handmade bows and arrows, and wigwams. Closed October through April. *Take Hwy. 51 to Hwy. 47 to Hwy. H; (715) 588-2615.*

Bunking Down

Chippewa Campground, Chequamegon National Forest ★★/$

There are 24 campgrounds in the national forest, but only this one has showers and flush toilets. Reservations are required. *1417 Forest Rd., north of Medford; (877) 444-6777;* www.reserveusa.com

New Concord Inn ★★/$$

This downtown Minocqua inn is in a convenient location—across the street from Torpy Park Beach and within walking distance of the water-ski show. The 54 units include two two-bedroom suites and six whirlpool rooms. All have refrigerators, in-room movies, and VCRs. A whirlpool, an indoor pool, and a game room will keep the family happy when you're not exploring the nearby woodlands. *Hwy. 51, Minocqua; (715) 356-1800;* www.newconcordinn.com

The Pointe Hotel & Conference Center ★★/$$

Right on Lake Minocqua, this property offers plenty of places for kids—and Mom and Dad—to play. The resort has a heated pool, sauna, whirlpool, tennis court, playground, and boat dock. The 69 studios and suites include 9 two-bedroom units; 57 units with full kitchens; and a dozen efficiency units with a king-size bed, a full bed, and a kitchenette with everything but a stove (microwave included). All rooms have cable TV, and you can rent a VCR. *8269 Hwy. 51S, Minocqua; (715) 356-4431;* www.thepointeresort.com

CHEESEHEADS

Wisconsin is the leading cheese-producing state in the nation; America's Dairyland makes 29% of the cheese in the country. Packer fans are particularly enthusiastic about the state staple. They are nick-named "cheeseheads" and often wear foam cheese-wedge–shaped hats to celebrate the team.

Good Eats

MaMa's Supper Club ★/$

This family-style Italian restaurant, which overlooks Curtis Lake, has been part of the Lakeland landscape for more than 40 years. The grown-ups have their choice of scrumptious Sicilian dishes (try the Tilapia Parmesan!), while your kids can feast on Mama's homemade pizza. There's a children's menu, too, and you can get takeout. *10486 Hwy. 70, Minocqua; (715) 356-5070.*

Paul Bunyan's Northwoods Cook Shanty ★★/$

You can't miss the sign for this rustic restaurant—it features a 30-foot-tall Bunyan and Babe, his blue ox! The logging camp breakfast of flapjacks, eggs, and Canadian bacon is a hit with kids. They also love making their own choices at the lunch and dinner buffets. Stop in at the bakery on your way out. Yum! *8653 Hwy. 51 N., Minocqua; (715) 356-6270.*

Souvenir Hunting

Dan's Minocqua Fudge Shop

Choose from lots of varieties of this sweet treat. On a hot day, put it in a box, not a bag, or you'll end up with gloppy goo in a sack. Still tastes good, though. *521 Oneida St., Minocqua; (715) 356-2662.*

Backseat Games

In the privacy of your own car, you can laugh as loud as you want or shout out the answers to questions. So don't hold back when you play these games — laugh, yell, or sing your hearts out. The ideas are well suited to driving, as they don't involve writing.

THE CAR NEXT DOOR

Invent stories about people in the car next to yours. What do you think they do for work? What's their favorite food? Where do they go on vacation? Get into lots of details, such as whether they snore loudly or are afraid of spiders. Give them names, hobbies, pets, and so on.

BUZZ

This is a team effort to try to reach 100 without making a mistake. Take turns counting, beginning with one. Every time you get to a number that's divisible by seven (7, 14, 21, . . .) or has a seven in it (17), say "Buzz" instead of the number. If one person forgets to say "Buzz," everyone has to start over. If this is too hard, say "Buzz" for every number divisible by 5. If you want a real challenge, try Fuzz Buzz. Say "Fuzz" for every number with a three in it or that's divisible by three, and "Buzz" for every number with a seven in it or that's divisible by seven.

Minnesota

KIDS LOVE this state. In the winter, Minnesotans celebrate the season in citywide carnivals by sculpting ice castles and snow monsters. In the summer, the more than 10,000 lakes scattered across the state—created by glaciers or by the footprints of mythic Paul Bunyan's blue ox, Babe—offer plenty of spots for canoeing, swimming, fishing, and water-skiing (invented here!). Any time of year, the humongous Mall of America delivers a screamingly exciting indoor amusement park (Knott's Camp Snoopy), an educational and fun walk-through aquarium,

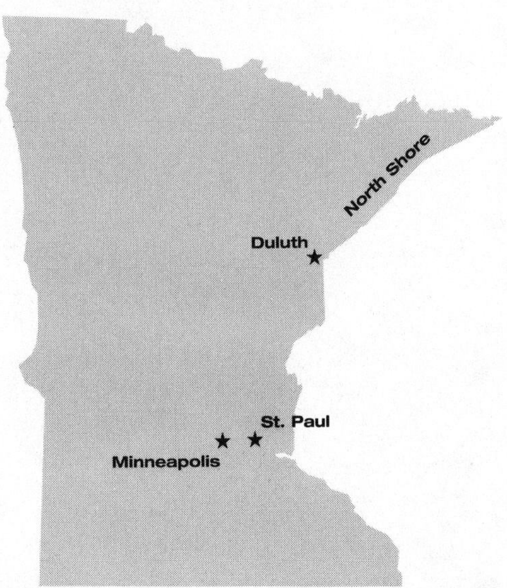

exceptionally entertaining shopping, a 14-theater complex, a miniature-golf course, and dozens of food options.

Minnesota also boasts kid-friendly museums, like the Bakken Museum, the Bell Museum of Natural History, and the Children's Museum, and theme parks like Valley Fair and Knott's Camp Snoopy. And although it is indeed cold in winter, there are so many keep-moving things for your family to do that you adjust quickly. Although many attractions in Minnesota are open year-round, some close in the late fall, winter, and early spring (roughly Labor Day through Memorial Day), and others close in summer. Call ahead to confirm dates and hours.

ATTRACTIONS

$	under $5
$$	$5 - $15
$$$	$15 - $25
$$$$	$25 +

HOTELS/MOTELS/CAMPGROUNDS

$	under $75
$$	$75 - $100
$$$	$100 - $140
$$$$	$140 +

RESTAURANTS

$	under $10
$$	$10 - $20
$$$	$20 - $30
$$$$	$30 +

***FAMILYFUN* RATED**

★	Fine
★★	Good
★★★	Very Good
★★★★	*FamilyFun* Recommended

Minneapolis is a big city with an easy-going, family-friendly feel.

INTRODUCTION

Minneapolis

THE TWIN CITIES of Minneapolis and St. Paul are just across the Mississippi River from each another and are geographically connected in one seamless metropolis. (The residents, though, definitely consider them places with distinct identities.) You can easily stay in either city and visit sites on the other side of the river within minutes. In fact, you should.

Of the two twin cities, Minneapolis has the bigger skyline and a more urban atmosphere. Stay at a downtown hotel on the five miles of "skyway" system—your kids will get a big charge out of dashing around the city without ever setting foot outdoors. And for parents, it's a lot easier than bundling and unbundling winter jackets, mittens, and the like. You can walk nearly anywhere in a 65-block area—to

Bakken Library and Museum (page 341)

Chain of Lakes (page 346)

The Children's Theatre Company (page 342)

Heart of the Beast Puppet Theater (page 343)

Minneapolis Sculpture Garden (page 347)

Minnesota Zoo (page 352)

The Original Baseball Hall of Fame Museum of Minnesota (page 345)

The Stone Arch Bridge, the Locks, and the Minneapolis/River City Trolley Ride (page 354)

Valleyfair Amusement Park (page 354)

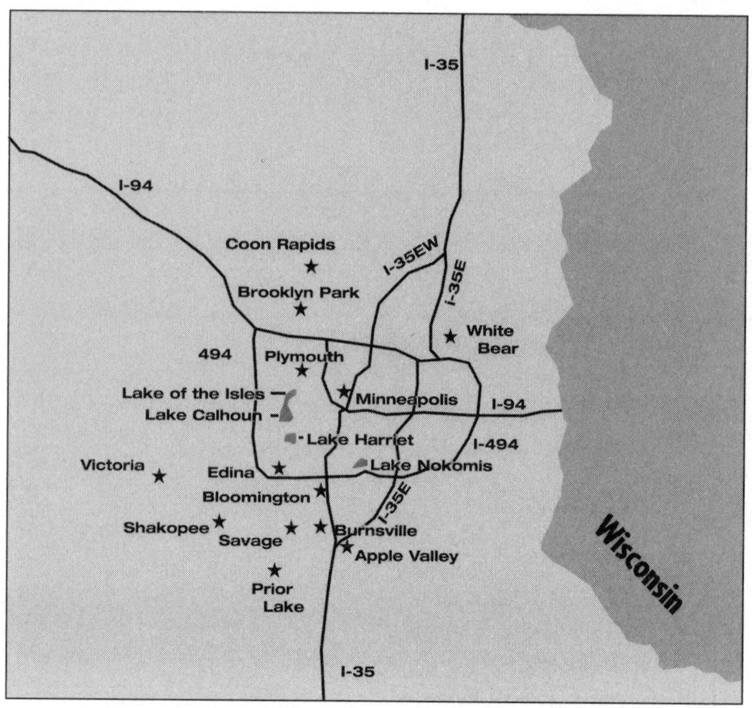

shopping, dining, and big-league sporting events—without wearing a coat or stepping outside.

Just south of downtown, the Chain of Lakes is an urban oasis of waterfront. Your family can take trolley rides and paddleboats, stroll on beaches, ride bikes (no rentals available, however), and snack on popcorn and ice cream. The lakes are also near the Children's Theatre Company, the Heart of the Beast Puppet Theater, museums, a sculpture garden, and more kid pleasers. To the east, the University of Minnesota has a museum or two that particularly delight youngsters. If your family likes to bike, you'll love the paths that crisscross the city and reach out into the suburbs and nature preserves. Not far from the city are several historical farms, complete with actors dressed in period clothing who will convince you that they are living in a different century. The historic St. Anthony neighborhood in downtown Minneapolis along the Mississippi River offers a walk across a stone bridge built by railroad tycoon James J. Hill and a look into the fascinating workings of the river locks and dams.

Minneapolis is a city where you need a car. You can easily reach places you want to visit in Minneapolis suburbs, usually in less than half an hour. Don't depend on public transportation or even taxis—public transport is limited to buses, and kids will tire on the long routes. As for taxis, in the Twin Cities you phone ahead for one and then wait at least half an hour for the cab to arrive. **NOTE:** For information about skiing, see "Winter Sports in Minnesota" on page 398; for acres of kid-friendly activities, see "The Mall of America" on page 348.

Cultural Adventures

American Swedish Institute ★★★/$

The former home of Swedish newspaper publisher Swan Turnblad resembles a castle—a sure hit with kids. The Institute's 33 rooms are filled with turn-of-the-century treasures. "American Girls" fans and other young history buffs will enjoy seeing the books, toys, and tools that Swedish immigrants brought to this country nearly a century ago. If your kids get antsy, take a detour to the coffee shop; they'll perk up after sampling the various Swedish pastries. The museum also hosts concerts, films, recitals, and festivals, so check to see if there are any special events planned for the day you're visiting. *2600 Park Ave., Minneapolis; (612) 871-4907;* www.americanswedishinst.org

Bakken Library and Museum ★★★★/$

MUST-SEE FamilyFun MUST-SEE

Don't let the "library" in the title fool you—this museum is as lively as they come. The Bakken focuses on electromagnetism, and kids love the zany experiments used to demonstrate principles of electricity. You and your kids can form a human chain and feel slight electric currents run from hand to hand (safe for toddlers, too), or touch a glowing ball that makes your hair stand on end. Older science buffs will be fascinated by the museum's more than 10,000 books, 2,000 artifacts, and scientific instruments. *3537 Zenith Ave. S., Minneapolis; (612) 927-6508;* www.thebakken.org

IF YOU VISIT DURING DECEMBER, be sure to be in the skyways along Nicollet Mall for great views of the nightly Holidazzle illuminated parade. At the late July Aquatennial, you can catch the torchlight parade. Check the Website http://www.downtownmpls.com/ for dates and hours.

What to Do When It's Too Rainy (or Snowy or Cold) to Go Outdoors

Stroll through downtown Minneapolis without setting a foot outside! Throughout downtown, glass-enclosed walkways, known as skyways, link buildings on the second-story level, crossing over city streets. The extensive system (65 city blocks and nearly 100 buildings are connected by more than five miles of skyway) not only makes it easy to get from one building to another, it is an attraction in its own right.

An entire city-above-the-city has formed along the skyway: coffeehouses, mini grocery stores, convenience stores, restaurants, and shops line the hallways within the buildings on the skyway level.

Grab a map or a copy of *Skyway News* (both are free and available in most downtown buildings) and explore downtown Minneapolis one story above the street. It's a great way to spend the day when the weather is less than ideal. (No coats, no boots, no hats, no umbrellas—need we say more?)

Bell Museum of Natural History ★★/$

You can safely skip the musty exhibits of stuffed bears and dioramas of nesting loons at this museum on the University of Minnesota campus. Kids used to Internet graphics won't be too impressed. But the Touch and See Room lets them do things a computer can't: rub a beaver pelt, touch an antler rack, see animal skeletons up close. Knowledgeable, friendly staff members will answer all the questions that parents can't. Reduced rate for children; kids under 3 free. *University Ave. S.E. and 17th St., Minneapolis; (612) 624-7083;* www.umn.edu/bellmuse

MUST-SEE FamilyFun MUST-SEE

The Children's Theatre Company ★★★★/$$-$$$

Fairy tales, Dr. Seuss stories, and beloved children's books are all brought to life by the largest professional children's theater company in the nation. Company productions are known for their high quality and imaginative staging. What's especially nice is that whatever your kids' ages, they'll enjoy the shows, most of which are designed to entertain toddlers to teens. Check to see if the production will feature a question-and-answer session at the end—kids love the opportunity to ask the child actors questions. *2400 Third Ave. S., Minneapolis; (612) 874-0400;* www.childrenstheatre.org

Fort Snelling ★★/$

This 1827 military outpost offers hours of fun for kids. Little ones like the wide-open space and the courtyard, but the historic re-creations are wasted on them. The 10-and-over set will enjoy the historical re-creation at the camp. Volunteer actors dress and speak like military camp folk of the period. Soldiers spin yarns about their experiences with Native American tribes in the area, bonnet-clad wives demonstrate what keeping house entailed (watch your kids' reaction as they contemplate life without a television or stove!), and craftsmen display their skills (kids love the working blacksmith). Take a break from the action and treat the family to old-fashioned treats like rock candy and maple-sugar sticks. They're a far cry from the Bubble Tape and Nerds your kids are used to. Closed November through April. *Intersection of Hwys. 5 and 55, Minneapolis; (612) 725-2413.*

MUST-SEE FamilyFun MUST-SEE Heart of the Beast Puppet Theater ★★★★/$$

These puppets aren't miniaturized handheld creatures—they're enormous! Wildly colorful 15-foot-high puppets and exotic creatures controlled by sticks dance and act out stories on stage. Children are spellbound and grown-ups enchanted by these one-of-a-kind productions. If you happen to be in town on the Sunday nearest May Day, head for Powderhorn Park, where the tall puppets make an annual parade like you've never seen before. *Bloomington Ave. S., near E. Lake St. and 15th Ave. S., Minneapolis; (612) 721-2535;* www.hobt.org

Minneapolis Institute of Arts ★★/Free

You might not usually take a toddler or grade-schooler to an art museum, but this one is attached to the Children's Theatre. If you're going to a play, arrive a little early and pop into the museum (there's no admission charge) to see the 2,000-year-old mummy and the suits of armor, surefire pleasers for kids over 5 (preschoolers won't enjoy much here). Older children will marvel at the huge block of jade, intricately carved with trees, steps, and tiny figures, and at glass artist Dale Chihuly's brilliant blown-glass sunburst overhead. If your kids are more adult in their taste in foods, you can lunch at an upstairs restaurant; otherwise, skip it, it may be too gourmet for

young tastes. The institute also offers family programs, so call ahead to see what's happening. You might be able to enjoy a Children's Theatre production and a family activity at the museum on the same day. Closed Monday. *2400 Third Ave. S., Minneapolis; (612) 870-3131. Children's Theatre: (612) 874-0400;* www.artsmia.org

Minnesota Orchestra Young People's Concerts and Adventures in Music ★★★/$$

The Nutcracker told in rhyme by Godfather Drosslemeier, a tale about green eggs and ham, and a conversation with Beethoven, who lives upstairs—the young people's concerts at Orchestra Hall feature world-class music from one of the best orchestras in the country performed in kid-friendly ways. Conductors, musicians, and performers give easy-to-understand commentary and guidance before, during, or after the concerts. Before the concert and during intermission, check out the lobby, where sometimes kids can pass the time making paper puppets, coloring posters, and playing listening games. Stroll along the outside of the hall to show your kids the enormous, bright blue air-exchange pipes designed to adorn the exterior of the building rather than to be hidden inside the walls as they normally would be. *1111 Nicollet Mall, Minneapolis; (612) 371-5656; (800) 292-4141;* www.minnesotaorchestra.org

Murphy's Landing ★★/$$

Travel back in time (and teach your kids what life was like before

A DAY IN DOWNTOWN MINNEAPOLIS

START WITH BREAKFAST AT **Basil's** overlooking the Crystal Court (ask for Mary Tyler Moore's table). If your children are too young to sit and wait for eggs, ride the escalator down into the Crystal Court to **Au Bon Pain** for instant breakfast: croissants, rolls, and breakfast pastries. In summer, stop on the **Nicollet Mall**, a pedestrian walkway (only taxis and buses are allowed) just outside the Crystal Court, where street vendors sell produce, bakery treats, and flowers. Or stop in at **Barnes & Noble** across the street—it has a great children's books corner. If it's baseball season and the Minnesota Twins are in town, take in a day game at the Metrodome and stop for souvenirs at the **Original Baseball Hall of Fame**. (If it's not baseball season, consider taking in a basketball game at the **Target Center** tonight. Two professional teams, the Minnesota Timberwolves and the Minnesota Lynx, a women's team, play at the

computer games). This reconstructed 19th-century village is near the Minnesota Zoo, and makes a good excursion after a zoo tour if you and your kids have another hour's worth of energy. Stroll or ride a trolley through the small community; kids can talk to the cast of characters (in period costumes) as they pretend to be residents of the time who cook, weave, and do chores; and then see how the schoolhouse is run—your kids will be amazed at the small desks and antique writing instruments.

Also explore the nearby Native American burial mounds; 16 of these small hills are visible in the surrounding countryside. (There's nothing to see but the hills themselves—but the idea that they're Indian burial places is pretty cool to older kids.) Open weekends only. Closed early September (after Labor Day) to Memorial Day. *The village is in Shakopee, about 16 miles south of Minneapolis. Take 35W south to Hwy. 13 west. 2187 Rte. 101 E., Shakopee; (952) 445-6900.*

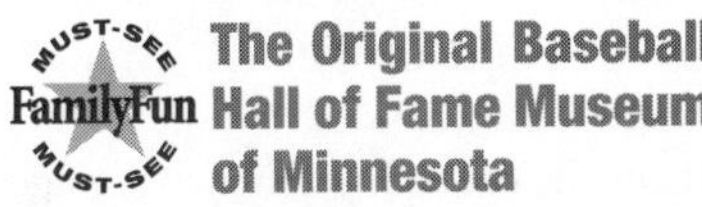

The Original Baseball Hall of Fame Museum of Minnesota

★★★★/Free

Baseball aficionados of all ages—whether they're fans of the Minnesota Twins or not—will dig this nifty display of Twins pictures, uniforms, baseball cards, bats, and autographs. It's a mini history of baseball, with a cool exhibit about how baseballs and bats are made. (Didn't you always wonder what was inside a baseball?) *910 Third St. S., Minneapolis; (612) 375-9707;* www.domeplus.com/museum

center and you can usually get tickets easily.)

Have lunch at the **Skyroom** or **Oak Grill** on the 12th floor of **Dayton's**, the city's venerable department store. If it's Christmastime, don't miss the fantastic holiday exhibit in the eighth-floor auditorium (other marvelous exhibits, like the spring Flower Show, are held here throughout the year). Then take the elevator down to the second floor, and just stroll the skyway for a while. Although you may pass the odd musician along the way (there's a cellist who hangs out there often), the main attractions of the skyway are the ease of traveling from building to building in inclement weather, and the fun of crossing busy roadways in an enclosed "bridge."

If it's winter holiday season, linger in the skyways over **Nicollet Mall** at 5:30 P.M. to get a good spot for viewing the amazing Holidazzle parade. Each dark winter night, a parade of fairy-tale characters dressed in strings of lights marches down the mall. You-know-who (Ho, ho, ho!) brings up the rear.

JUST FOR FUN

Brooklyn Park Historical Farm

★★/$$

This lively historical farm re-creates rural Minnesota in the 1900s. Little kids love the farm animals, hayrides, hoop-rolling, and dance performances. In the fall, grade-school-age kids can check out the pioneer crafts demonstrations. Closed January through April. *The farm is about 10 miles north of Minneapolis in the suburb of Brooklyn Park; 4345 101st Ave. N., Brooklyn Park; (763) 493-4604.*

Bunker Hills Wave Pool

★★★★/$

This 25,000-square-foot pseudo-ocean is a good bet for the whole family, though the "swells" can reach four feet in height, so keep your little ones toward the shallow end while older kids bodysurf. Kids can also ride the waves in style on the inflatable tubes available for rent. The waves run for 15 minutes, then stop for a 10-minute break to let the surfers catch their breath. Dress your kids in bright swimwear so you can spot them easily; the pool is popular and usually packed. Closed January through April. *The pool is about 15 miles north of downtown Minneapolis, within the Bunker Lake Regional Park in the suburb of Coon Rapids. Bunker Lake Blvd., Coon Rapids; (763) 767-2895.*

FamilyFun GAME

Car Scavenger Hunt

Hand your kids a pack of index cards and ask them to write or draw pictures of 50 things they might see on a trip. Keep the cards for scavenger hunts when players vie to match the cards with what they see.

Chain of Lakes

MUST-SEE FamilyFun MUST-SEE

★★★★/Free

Rollerblade, fish, canoe, paddleboat, walk, run, and/or just people-watch: there is no better way to spend a sunny afternoon than wandering the paths around the series of linked lakes that cut through the heart of Minneapolis. Lake Harriet, Lake of the Isles, and Lake Calhoun form a recreation web with lots for young ones to do. All three lakes have supervised beaches and the water is relatively clean, although by early August your kids will emerge from the lake dripping with seaweed. During the summer, the lakes are lined with anglers looking to catch pan fish, and the large docks provide a perfect learning spot for young fisherfolk. You can rent canoes at all three lakes for a small fee. Try the route from Lake Calhoun to Lake of the Isles—you paddle right under a picturesque arched bridge and a busy street. Or take a cool land trip: line up near the tracks along the lake and wait for the historic old trolley car to arrive. (There's

A Splash Bash!

For 11 days in mid-July, Minneapolis celebrates its lakes, rivers, and streams with more than 30 water-themed events. The annual **Aquatennial** features boating, swimming, diving, water-skiing, and other sporting competitions; a sand-castle contest at Calhoun Beach; fireworks; and crafts shows. But kids like two events best: a race of boats made from (believe it or not) milk cartons on Lake Nokomis, and a flotilla of 20,000 rubber ducks released on the Mississippi River. Youngsters will also like staying up late for the Torchlight Parade, with illuminated floats and special lighting effects. The schedule of events changes each year. Many events are free, and some are covered by the purchase of an Aquatennial button. *For more information, call (612) 338-3807;* www.aquatennial.org

a small fee.) The open-air car travels along the lake, through the woods, and even through a tunnel. Kids will find the antique advertising signs inside the car a hoot. If your preteens complain that it sounds boring, try to talk them into going anyway—they'll like it. After the trolley ride, buy ice cream or popcorn at the band shell and take a bench seat for an outdoor concert—many daytime and evening concerts are scheduled throughout the summer.

The Metrodome ★★/$$

It looks like a giant marshmallow perched at the end of downtown. The white fabric roof of this sports arena has partially collapsed once or twice over the years, but barring that unlikely event, the real fun is inside: the Minnesota Twins baseball team in summer and the Minnesota Vikings in the fall and winter. (If the pro-ball tickets are too pricey, try seats to a University of Minnesota Gophers football game instead.) On nongame weekends, the dome is sometimes open to in-line skaters. The two extra-wide, smooth, enclosed hallways on the first and second levels become blading tracks (one for grown-ups, one for kids and families). See if your kids can explain the rush of air as you exit the dome, which is held up by air pressure (you're moving from a pressurized dome through revolving doors to the outside). *900 S. Fifth St., Minneapolis; (612) 332-0386;* www.msfc.com

MUST-SEE FamilyFun MUST-SEE Minneapolis Sculpture Garden ★★★★/Free

The quirky sculptures and casual hands-on attitude of this 11-acre garden make this a great place for an afternoon excursion. Children love the giant spoon-and-cherry sculpture that squirts water (up, not at the kids). There's a glass

continued on page 352

THE MALL OF AMERICA

THIS IS ONE shopping trip your kids will beg for. That's because for them it isn't just a mall, it's an experience. There are more than 20 restaurants, numerous fast-food outlets, 14 movie screens, a theme park, an underwater walk-through aquarium, a bowling alley with a high-tech game room, and an 18-hole miniature-golf course. Oh, yes, don't forget the stores—more than 500 of them.

Mom and Dad: It's a bit intimidating for your children (and you) to figure out the best strategy for making your way around this 4.2 million-square-foot space. Not to worry—what follows is our totally kid-friendly guide to the best places to play, eat, shop—and even spend the night!

Before we get to the attractions, here are a few survival tips: Be prepared for a racket. There's a theme park smack in the middle of the mall, so expect screams, giggles, and a roller coaster rattling by now and then. But remember the quiet spots—food courts, benches along the hallways—where you and the children can grab a soft drink and rest your feet. The humongous space is more than a toddler in tennis shoes can comfortably navigate without whining, so stop at one of the guest service centers at each of the four mall entrances on Level 1 to borrow a stroller. Rent a locker for your gear, hit the rest rooms, pick up free coupon books and shopping bags, and start your day. **NOTE:** Avoid the guest services center on the mall's east side—that's where the big tours are dropped off and picked up and it's always extremely busy, with long lines.

The Mall of America is just outside Minneapolis proper, in Bloomington, three miles south of Minneapolis/St. Paul International Airport and about a half hour's drive from either of the Twin Cities; (952) 883-8800; www. mallofamerica.com

Adventures to Try

Knott's Camp Snoopy

★★★★/$$$

No need to get gloomy if the weather doesn't cooperate. Come wintry blusters or summer showers, the weather at this seven-acre theme park is always sunny: it's completely enclosed inside the Mall of America. Set in the expansive center of the mall, the park still has an outdoor feeling, thanks to hundreds of tall trees, thousands of live plants, and real birds who took up residence in the trees during mall construction. The park has 20 rides, several shops, four entertainment stages, and some kid-pleasing eateries, plus strolling vendors who draw

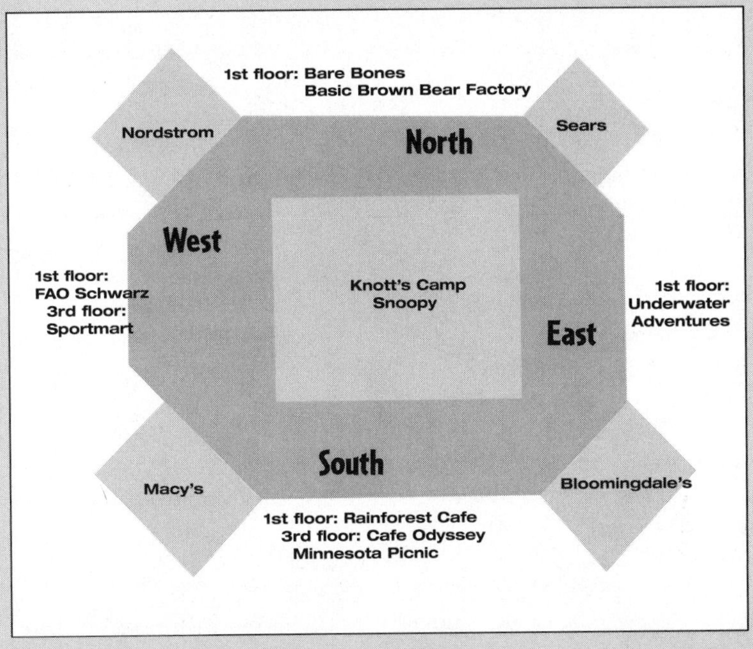

caricatures, paint faces, play carnival games, sell ice cream, and delight children in the process. You can enter the park from nine points throughout the mall, but make it easy on yourself and head for the giant Snoopy (it's a great spot to designate as your meeting place, should anyone get lost). Admission is free, but rides cost between three and five "points" (each point is 75 cents). Stop at a vending machine to buy point cards, which are electronically scanned at each ride. If you don't use all your points, save your card—it's good for a year. If the kids have their sights set on many rides, buy an all-day wristband for unlimited riding fun. Start at the Snoopy Bounce, where little ones can toss a coin in the beloved beagle's big red food dish and bounce in the trampolinelike middle of the giant pooch while you sit on a dog-bone-shaped bench and watch. Tots will also love the Americana Carousel and the big yellow Camp Bus, which "flies" through the air. The Pepsi Ripsaw Roller Coaster and the Skyscraper Ferris Wheel are thrills for bigger kids. Climbers may want to work their way up the 24-foot Rock N' Wall while the less adventurous visit the arcade. There's also a petting zoo where ducks, chicks, and rabbits make the mall their home. *In the Mall of America; (952) 883-8600;* www.campsnoopy.com

Underwater Adventures Aquarium ★★★★/$
Imagine walking through a tunnel made of see-through underwater walls with fish swimming above and all around you. This attraction is a bit pricey, but worth it for aquarium lovers and kids needing a break from the spins and flips of Camp Snoopy rides or from a long day strolling the mall stores. The aquarium is divided into four main exhibits: a Minnesota Lake, the Mississippi River, a shark cove, and a Caribbean Reef. Visitors are ushered into the tunnels by a conveyor belt much like those found at the airport. Be sure to step off the moving walkway once in a while to enjoy the spectacular fish to the fullest. Traveling through the tunnels is a thrill—like scuba diving without all the equipment. The Shark Cove is the hands-down kid favorite, so be sure to linger here. A touch pool allows children to feel the skin of sharks and stingrays. Reduced rate for children ages 3 to 12; kids under 3 free. *In Mall of America, East entrance, level 1, 120 E. Broadway; (952) 883-0202;* www.underwateradventures.net

The Mall of America employs more than 12,000 people.

Where to Stay

Comfort Inn/Bloomington ★/$$
Children will like the pool and video games at this 275-room hotel; adults will appreciate the comfortable lobby with a fireplace and sofas, and the free mall and airport shuttles. King-size units have a recliner (nice for breastfeeding an infant); standard rooms are pretty basic. An on-site restaurant serves steak, chicken, and pasta. *1321 78th St. E., Bloomington; (800) 221-2222; (952) 854-3400;* www.choicehotels.com

Embassy Suites ★★/$$$$
This chain hotel is like its relatives: multiple levels organized around a central atrium lobby. Each of the 310 guest rooms is actually a suite, with a master bedroom connected to a living space with a sofa bed, wet bar, refrigerator, microwave, and coffeemaker. Suites have two televisions, so you and the kids can watch different shows, and their TV is equipped with Nintendo. The restaurant is no great shakes, but the complimentary breakfast in the atrium, including eggs and bacon made to order, will fuel the family before you set off for the mall. *7901 34th Ave. S., Bloomington; (800) EMBASSY; (952) 854-1000;* www.embassysuites.com

Holiday Inn International Airport ★★/$$$
With 431 rooms, an Olympic-size pool, fitness center, full-service laundry, and transportation to the mall and airport, this is a family-friend-

ly choice. There are two restaurants on-site. *3 Appletree Sq., Bloomington; (800) 465-4329; (952) 854-9000;* www.holiday-inn.com

Where to Eat

Cafe Odyssey

★/$

This lively theme restaurant has three dining areas sure to interest your family. Eat in the lost city of Atlantis, Machu Pichu, or the plains of the Serengeti. The Atlantis room offers the most engaging scenery, with computer-generated fish and sea creatures projected on the walls. Good eats, too, including award-winning Pacific Rim lo mein, plus a kids' menu. *3rd Floor, Mall of America; (952) 854-9400;* www.cafe odyssey.com

Minnesota Picnic

★/$

This food-court eatery is great for two reasons. First, its menu is perfect for kids. Midwest favorites such as battered cheese curds (a sort of deep-fried chunk of cheese) and corn dogs fit perfectly into little hands, and the familiar tastes will keep complaints at bay. Secondly, the prices here are reasonable, which you'll appreciate after a day of shopping and a visit to Camp Snoopy. *Food Court, Mall of America; (952) 858-9950.*

Rainforest Cafe

★★/$$

If you don't have reservations, expect a wait—but this restaurant is worth it. Best bet: call ahead for reservations. Second best: stop here first when you arrive at the mall in the morning and make lunch reservations for later in the day. The food is only average, but the atmosphere is pure fun. The kids won't be bored between ordering and eating. They'll be watching jungle creatures: live parrots, pretend alligators, and enormous aquariums of real tropical fish, plus real rain, indoors! You'll be happy with the ribs and steak; the kids will like the burgers and pizza. *S102 next to Bloomingdale's, Mall of America; (952) 854-7500;* www.rain forestcafe.com

conservatory with an immense (as big as a house) glass fish designed by architect Frank Gehry. (Be aware that the kids aren't allowed to pick the tiny oranges that hang temptingly from miniature trees inside the Cowles Conservatory, and for good reason—they're sprayed with pesticides.) Then cross the pretty, wrought-iron blue-and-yellow Irene Hixon Whitney Bridge. Depending on whether your children like or detest heights, this crossing is cool or scary—you can watch the traffic pass under your feet. Challenge older kids to read the poem that is written on the sides of the bridge and stretches from one end of the span to the other. On the other side of the bridge, you'll hit Loring Park, with two playgrounds, a pond teeming with ducks, and frequent summer music and events. *Vineland Place, Minneapolis; (612) 375-7622.*

Minnesota is known throughout the country as the **"Land of 10,000 Lakes,"** but the nickname is actually a bit of a misnomer. Minnesota actually has over 12,000 lakes within its boundaries.

Minnehaha Falls ★★★★/Free
Henry Wadsworth Longfellow never even visited these falls, but his poem *Song of Hiawatha* immortalized them. The statue of the Native American warrior and maiden makes for a great photo op. Young climbers love the trails above the falls and below, with a stretch of embankments. (Adventuresome ones may be tempted to explore the area behind the falls, but heed the warning signs—the rocks are extremely slippery behind the rushing water.) Bring a Frisbee or softball to toss around—the main lower trail leads to a beautiful green meadow perfect for family frolicking. The historic Minnehaha Depot near the falls sells snacks in the summer and provides a spot to sit and eat them. *Minnehaha Park, Hiawatha Ave. and Godfrey Pkwy., Minneapolis; (612) 370-4939.*

MUST-SEE FamilyFun MUST-SEE **Minnesota Zoo ★★★★/$$**
Plan to spend a whole day wandering the 500 acres of this zoo, home to more than 2,800 living creatures. Kids will find the exhibits intriguing, and parents will appreciate the many spots to take a break, eat, and even change diapers. The animals live in environments that mimic their natural habitats, which is great for the creatures but means your kids might need to look pretty hard to see them. Break up your treks through the natural exhibits with time at indoor attractions and on the monorail, which provide better animal-spotting opportunities. Don't miss the nocturnal exhibit along the Tropics Trail, but be warned: it does get very dark inside.

It happens gradually, so prepare your kids, then hold hands and let them walk in slowly to get used to the dark. Soon their eyes will be adjusted enough to see the glowing eyes of night creatures as they climb trees, crawl through leaves, and hang upside down on the ceiling (yes, there are bats!). The dolphin show in the Discovery Bay building is another must-see. Check for show times at the start of your day and plan your itinerary around it. Your smaller kids will like the playground at the Children's Zoo, which also has easy access to real animals. For kids who can manage a mild (but a bit long—three-quarters of a mile) hike, the Northern Trail is a great place to see bigger animals like camels, moose, and bison. Take a break at the IMAX theater for a show—it gives you a chance to sit down, and the 3-D effects are stunning. (You may want to skip it, though, if anyone in your group gets motion sickness; the action can seem too real to some.) It's best to bring your own picnic lunch and snacks—the zoo has only fast food, with high prices and long lines. There are several scenic sites where picnicking is encouraged. *The zoo is in Apple Valley, a suburb about 14 miles south of downtown Minneapolis and 10 minutes south of the Mall of America. Take 35W south to 62 Crosstown E. to 770/Cedar S. and follow the signs. 13000 Zoo Blvd., Apple Valley; (952) 431-9500;* www.mnzoo.org

DAY TRIP

Fun in the Southern Suburbs

Three major children's attractions—**Valleyfair Amusement Park**, the **Minnesota Zoo**, and **Murphy's Landing** historical village—are far enough south of the city that, once you're down there, you'll probably want to see them all. Valleyfair and the zoo each deserve a full day, so the easiest approach is to book a room in a Burnsville-area hotel. Otherwise, plan for the half-hour drive back up to Minneapolis at the end of one long and very tiring day.

The Valleyfair amusement park is filled with wild rides, but toddler-friendly attractions abound (as do benches for grateful parents). Older kids will want a full day here, but little ones will be ready to leave at noon; parents may want to plan a split shift. After everyone has had their fill of thrills, drop in on Murphy's Landing for a brief look at what life was like before electricity and roller coasters. Toddlers won't be enthralled, but video game–loving older kids will enjoy the peek at life before Sega Genesis. The next day, head east on Highway 13 (follow the signs) to the Minnesota Zoo.

MANY CLASSIC AMERICAN CANDY BARS were created during the 1920s and 1930s. At a Minneapolis factory, Frank C. Mars introduced the Milky Way bar in 1923. After the instant success, he later created Snickers and 3 Musketeers.

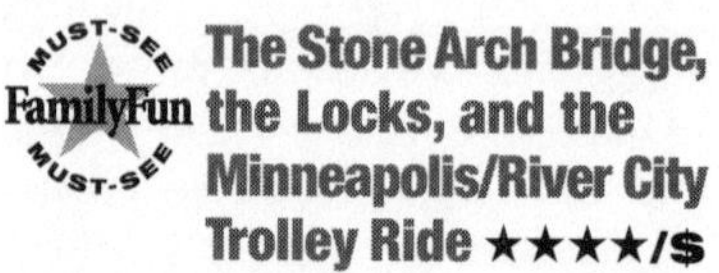

The Stone Arch Bridge, the Locks, and the Minneapolis/River City Trolley Ride ★★★★/$

Railroad tycoon James J. Hill built the picturesque Stone Arch Bridge across the river during the 1870s after several failed attempts and much local ridicule. Today, it's the best spot from which to observe the fascinating operation of the lock and dam system along the Mississippi River. Your kids will love to watch barges pass through the system and see the compartments fill with water to lift the boats into the channel. Then, hop aboard a historic-looking "trolley" on four wheels for a one-hour tour of the city's roots—in flour milling, lumber, and river trade. *Departs from the St. Anthony complex on Main St., Minneapolis. For more information, call the Mn. CUB at (612) 661-4700.*

Target Center ★★★/$$$

The home of the Minnesota Timberwolves in the NBA (men) and the Minnesota Lynx in the WNBA (women) professional basketball teams, this arena also hosts a number of events and concerts. Check with the ticket office to see if *Sesame Street Live* or the Harlem Globetrotters happen to be in town. Tickets to basketball games are usually available at the box office on short notice if you're looking for something to do in the evening. Parking nearby is scarce, but large parking garages just blocks away are linked to the center by enclosed skyways. *600 First Ave. N., Minneapolis; (612) 673-0900;* www.targetcenter.com

Valleyfair Amusement Park ★★★★/$$$$

All winter long, kids in Minnesota dream about Valleyfair, the largest amusement park in the Upper Midwest. The entrance fee is steep, but you don't have to pay for individual rides or the water park, which has an array of water slides and river rides. (Lockers and changing rooms are available for a fee.) The amusement park boasts more than 75 rides and attractions, although not all are suitable for young children. Older kids will delight in the thrills of the 250-foot Power Tower—rather like bungee jumping with seats and without the bounce—and the breathtaking drop of the Wild Thing

OUTDOOR FUN IN MINNEAPOLIS

Minnesotans like to play outside, no matter what the weather. It's easy to rent whatever equipment you and your family might need to play along with the natives.

BIKING

The paved trails around the Chain of Lakes are popular family biking routes. You can circle all the lakes, or just pick one, depending on the stamina of your little cyclers. You can rent helmets, bikes, and even kiddie pull-carts at various shops Uptown and around the lakes. Try **Calhoun Rental** *(Lake St. and James St.; 612/827-8231)*.

BOATING AND CANOEING

The Chain of Lakes is really one connected waterway, making for great canoeing. Boat-rental information is available from the **Minneapolis Park and Recreation Board** *(400 Fourth St. S.; 612/661-4875)*.

FISHING

In the city proper, fish off the docks on Lake Calhoun or offshore on the other lakes in the Chain of Lakes. Visiting in winter? No problem—they fish here all year long. Rent an icehouse and pretend you're in the movie *Grumpy Old Men*. If you're willing to travel a little bit, take the 20-minute drive to Lake Minnetonka, an immense lake in the tony western Minneapolis suburb of Minnetonka and a popular fishing spot. Call **Wayzata Bait and Tackle** *(15748 Wayzata Blvd.; 952/473-2227)* for advice on lucky fishing spots and gear. For information on fishing licenses, regulations, and other good locations, call the **Department of Natural Resources** *(651/296-6157)*.

ICE-SKATING

Hockey and figure skating are big here in the land of more than 10,000 lakes. To skate outdoors in winter, rent skates at **Aarcee Rental** *(2910 Lyndale Ave. S.; 612/827-5746)* and head for the picturesque Lake of the Isles. For more outdoor spots close to skate-rental sites, call the **Minneapolis Park and Recreation Board** *(612/661-4875)*. Numerous neighborhood enclosed arenas also have public skating and skate rental year-round. Two especially kid-friendly rinks: **St. Louis Park Rec Center** *(3700 Montery Dr.; 952/924-2540)* and **Brooklyn Park Arena** *(5600 85th Ave. N., Brooklyn Park; 763/493-8363)*.

roller coaster. Younger kids can have tamer fun in the tot areas. The water park offers a good alternative to the stomach-wrenching twists of the larger coasters. The lazy raft ride in the water park, and the games at the park's midway area are good options for family time together. To escape the midafternoon heat, check out the silly, high-energy, cabaret-style shows at the Red Garter Saloon. Closed October through April. *The park is in Shakopee, about 16 miles south of Minneapolis; take 35W south to Hwy. 13/101 west. 1 Valleyfair Dr., Shakopee; (952) 445-7600;* www.valleyfair.com

BUNKING DOWN

Downtown

If your family plans to spend a lot of time downtown, it's worth the higher prices to choose a hotel on the skyway system. These enclosed, above-street walkways link downtown buildings and make walking around town warm and cozy during the winter and cooler during the summer. Leave the jackets in your hotel room, stroll in climate-controlled comfort to shops and lunch, and return to your hotel without once having to walk outside. Kids love standing in the glass-enclosed walkways that hang over the streets and watching the traffic pass under their feet.

Hyatt Regency ★★★/$$$

Near Orchestra Hall and the Convention Center, this hotel has 532 rooms and 21 suites, cable TV, and a health club and swimming pool. The skyway (second) level houses topflight grown-up restaurants, but kids will like Spike's sports bar downstairs, where shoes of famous athletes are nailed to the walls and golf and batting cages are tucked in between the booths. (You won't want to bring youngsters to

BROTHERS Scott and Brennan Olson of Minneapolis, Minnesota, are recognized as having invented the first in-line roller skates. As hockey players, they were looking for a way to practice in their off-season. In 1979, they found a pair of early roller skates with in-line wheels, as opposed to the four-wheel parallel design. They redesigned the skates with modern materials, attaching them to ice-hockey boots and adding a rubber toe. In 1983, Scott Olson founded Rollerblade, Inc.

Spike's during prime beer-guzzling times, like Friday nights, however.) *1300 Nicollet Mall, Minneapolis; (800) 233-1234; (612) 370-1234;* www.hyatt.com

Marquette ★★★/$$$

If your kids are fans of vintage TV, they'll maybe even recognize that this is the place where Mary Tyler Moore rides down the escalator at the show's start. It's in the 51-story IDS Building, architect Philip Johnson's masterpiece, where the staggered sides of the building make each of the 278 rooms a corner room with a view. There's no pool, but the central location—right on the Crystal Court of the IDS—puts you at the heart of the skyway system. Kid-friendly Basil's Restaurant inside the hotel has a balcony that overlooks the indoor Crystal Court of the IDS Building—Mary Tyler Moore ate here, too. Kids will love the view—and the banana-bread French toast for breakfast. *Seventh St. and Marquette Ave., Minneapolis; (800) 445-8667; (612) 332-2351;* www.marquettehotel.com

Minneapolis Hilton Hotel and Towers ★★★★/$$$

Near Orchestra Hall and the Convention Center, the Hilton has 814 rooms and 51 suites that larger families appreciate, plus a health club and a swimming pool. There's a kid-friendly restaurant (Harmony's, home of a breakfast buffet). *10001 Marquette Ave., Minneapolis; (800) 445-8667; (612) 376-1000;* www.hilton.com

Minneapolis Marriott ★★★/$$$

The draws here are the proximity to downtown shopping and skyway access. This large hotel (584 rooms and suites) is above the big downtown mall, City Center. As malls go, this one doesn't offer unique shopping—it has all the stores typical of city malls—but all skyways lead to the City Center, so you can get anywhere you want to be. There's no pool or arcade room, either. *30 S. Seventh St., Minneapolis; (800) 228 9290; (612) 349-4000;* www.marriott.com

In Burnsville

If you're planning on visiting several attractions in the southern suburbs (Valleyfair Amusement Park, Minnesota Zoo, Murphy's Landing), consider a hotel in Burnsville or Bloomington (for Bloomington hotels, see "The Mall of America" on page 348). There along I-35, you're centrally located near the enormous Burnsville Center and a cluster of dependable chain family restaurants, both fast food and sit-down. Special family summer packages are sometimes available; call the **Burnsville Convention and Visitors Bureau** *(800/521-6055)* for current information.

LINDEN HILLS AND LAKE HARRIET

THE FUN AND funky Minneapolis neighborhood known as Linden Hills is a charming, family-friendly spot. It runs along the edge of Lake Harriet on the Chain of Lakes, so it's a perfect place to spend a day. Stroll around and visit the child-pleasing shops in the morning, have lunch at one of the neighborhood eateries, and then head for the lake and its quaint, colorful playground. The whole shopping district is an L of only a few blocks *(along Sheridan Ave. S. from 42nd St. W. to 44th St. W., and then down 44th St. W. from Sheridan to France Ave. S.)*, and you can see most every shop just by standing on one corner and looking around.

If you'd like to start out with a snack, buy fresh bread at **Great Harvest Bread Company** *(4314 Upton Ave. S.; 612/929-2899)*—most kids will love the plain white rolls. More goodies, including organic ones, are across the street at the **Linden Hills Co-op** grocery store *(2813 W. 43rd St.; 612/922-1159)*. Then head for **Wild Rumpus** *(2720 W. 43rd St.; 612/920-5005)*, a bookstore your kids will never forget. A rabbit, cats, and a few birds might be hopping, running, or flying around inside. Look through a "hole" in the floor to see a pet rat, and through the "hole" in the ceiling to see the cloud paintings. Pint-size furniture invites little ones to settle in and page through a favorite book, and there might even be a famous author waiting to read aloud. **Creative Kidstuff** *(4313 Upton Ave. S.; 612/927-0653)* down the street is a wild and wacky toy store that encourages hands-on exploration. The **Bibelot Shop** *(4315 Upton Ave. S.; 612/925-3175)* sells stuffed animals, hair trinkets, and other trendy kids goodies.

When lunchtime rolls around, your group has lots of choices. **Famous Dave's** *(4264 Upton Ave. S.; 612/929-1200)* is a great place. **Turtle Bread Company** *(3421 W. 44th St.; 612/ 924-6013)* is a bakery, coffeehouse, cafe, and takeout deli that serves sandwiches, soups, roasted chicken, terrific pie, and luscious pastries. Outdoor seating makes for fun people-watching in summer. The buckwheat and wild rice pancakes at **Zumbro Cafe** *(4302 Upton Ave. S.; 612/929-4742)* have a devoted following; the homemade soups and handcrafted sandwiches are delicious, too.

After lunch, walk one long block east to **Lake Harriet**. The playground *(east along W. Lake Harriet Blvd., toward William Berry Pkwy.)* has all the usual equipment and plenty of spots for grown-ups to sit and relax while your kids frolic. Summer evenings, take in one of the frequent free concerts in the nearby band shell. In spring, summer, and fall—provided, of course, that the weather cooperates—you can rent a canoe and paddle through several of the lakes and back, or rent paddleboats and pedal your way up and down the beach. Fish from a long dock (there are real fish in these waters—even muskies). Ride the trolley. Have an ice cream at the band shell (and catch a concert, if someone's playing). Sit outside along the water and toss bread to the ducks. In winter, the paths around the lake are cleared for runners and walkers.

Nature lovers take note: **Lake Calhoun**, which is less than a mile north of Lake Harriet by walking trail, and **Lake of the Isles**, north of Calhoun, are also good outdoorsy spots. Once the ice is frozen thick enough in winter—and it doesn't take that long in Minnesota—you can skate on the Lake of the Isles's large, cleared outdoor skating area. You'll have it to yourself on a weekday morning, but come the weekend, the spot teems with kids and families.

Comfort Inn
★/$$

Ten minutes from Valleyfair, this straightforward hotel is nothing fancy, but it has a pool and hot tub; continental breakfast is included in the rate; and kids stay free. *4601 West Hwy. 13, Savage; (952) 894-6124;* www.choicehotels.com

Mystic Lake Casino Hotel
★★/$$

This hotel isn't a four-star luxury retreat, but when it comes to kid-friendly amenities, it delivers: there's an indoor/outdoor pool, plus Playworks filled with computer and video games. You'll also find a fitness center, and a gift shop. Kids stay free. About 20 minutes south of the Twin Cities, it's connected to a casino—and two round-the-clock restaurants. (Children are welcome in any casino restaurant between 10 A.M. and 10 P.M.) *2400 Mystic Lake Blvd., Prior Lake; (952) 445-9000; (952) 445-9000*; www.mysticlake.com

GOOD EATS

Basil's ★★★/$

Mary Tyler Moore ate here on her show, but you may be more excited about this than your children, unless they're into reruns. It's inside the famed IDS Building; ask for a table at the edge of the open balcony, which overlooks the Crystal Court. Stick to burgers; the menu isn't par-

FamilyFun GAME

Crazy Menu

On a paper restaurant menu, take turns crossing out key words. Then have your kids read aloud the new and often grotesque combinations they've created. Anyone for Pepperoni Cake with Strawberry Lettuce?

ticularly kid-friendly. But views of the foot traffic below, the amazingly complicated see-through ceiling of glass pyramids above, and the fountain of falling water should amuse your kids while you wait for your food to arrive. *Above the IDS Crystal Court, in the Marquette Hotel, 710 Marquette Ave., Minneapolis; (612) 376-7404.*

Birchwood Café ★/$

If you find yourself near the Seward neighborhood (along I-94 and Franklin Avenue), stop in at this funky, casual, very kid-friendly eatery. Small patrons can point to foods they like in the deli case. The food isn't junk food, either. Healthy, fresh ingredients (and terrific desserts!) are the rule. *3311 E. 25th St., Minneapolis; (612) 722-4474.*

Convention Grill
★★/$

Food from the '50s sits well with kids: burgers, fries, and malts are always popular. It's cheap eats, and no one minds if your kids stand on the benches of the old-fashioned wooden booths to eat. The waitress might even call you "honey." *3912 Sunnyside Rd., Edina; (952) 920-6881.*

Famous Dave's
★★/$$

It's all finger food: BBQ on a bun, a pint-sized cob of corn, and great corn bread, served in a paper-lined basket. You can't get more kid-friendly than that. This local chain is always friendly, fast, and accommodating. The branch in the Linden Hills neighborhood (about five minutes south of downtown) has a big screened-in porch and is within walking distance of a kid's toy store and a terrific children's bookstore (see "Linden Hills and Lake Harriet" on page 358). *4264 Upton Ave. S., Minneapolis; (612) 929-1200.*

Malt Shop
★★/$

The kid appeal here includes wooden booths, tall, frosty shakes, big burgers on homemade buns, and lots of fries. Squirt the ketchup, load up the pickles, and listen to the piano player play a few tunes. It's just a short drive from Lake Harriet. *50th St. at Bryant Ave. S., Minneapolis; (612) 824-1352.*

Murray's ★/$$$

For a little girl who loves tea parties, this endearingly dated pink-satin-lined holdover from the 1940s serves a fun afternoon tea from 2 to 4 P.M. Monday through Saturday. You'll start with a truly delicious scone, move on to pretty finger sandwiches, and end with miniature desserts. *26 S. Sixth St., Minneapolis; (612) 339-0909.*

Oak Grill ★★/$$

Lunch on the 12th floor of Dayton's is a traditional part of a downtown shopping excursion. The dark-paneled, spacious, clubby room has white tablecloths, comfy leather chairs, and soft tabletop lighting. Don't be fooled by the decor, though; this is a family-friendly, if quiet, spot. The prices aren't astronomical, and they have a kids' menu, plus a paper sack of lunch activities to keep them busy until the burgers and hot dogs arrive. Grown-ups can order trendy entrées or favorite comfort foods (the meat loaf with garlic mashed potatoes is terrific). *Dayton's, 700 Nicollet Mall, Minneapolis; (612) 375-2938.*

Skyroom ★/$

If you're at Dayton's and want a faster, brighter lunch than you find at the Oak Grill, walk a few steps farther down the hall on the 12th floor to this sun-splashed, wide-open, bright-white spot with incredible views of downtown. Buffets and food court-style counters offer healthier choices than the typical food court. Kids can opt for gourmet pizza, sandwiches, grilled fare, salads, and pasta. It's good for picky, finicky eaters—they can select just what they want from the buffets with no surprises, and can even ask the piano player to play a favorite tune on that shiny white grand piano (but don't expect him to know the latest by 'N Sync). *Dayton's, 700 Nicollet Mall, Minneapolis; (612) 375-6936.*

Souvenir Hunting

The downtown stores, all on the skyway, have kid appeal. The Linden Hills neighborhood also has a few special children's stores (see "Linden Hills and Lake Harriet" on page 358). Then there's Mall of America, the biggest mall in the country—and probably one of the most interesting for youngsters. It's just a half-hour's drive south (see page 348).

Call Ahead

Besides scouting resources at your library, call or write to city chambers of commerce and state tourism boards for information about your destination. Let your kids make lists of the things they hope to see and let each child pick one activity to do each day (parents have veto power over monster truck rallies, of course).

Gaviidae Common

Anchored by Saks on one end and Neiman Marcus on the other, this mall has several levels of luxury shops in between. Older kids go for the window shopping, and preteen girls love the fashions and upscale trendy shops. If littler ones get bored, take them to the second-level fountain where the water "skips" from pool to pool. When your crowd gets cranky, stop at the Caribou coffee shop (one on the first level and another on the second) for reindeer shortbread cookies and hot chocolate. *651 Nicollet Mall, Minneapolis; (612) 372-1222.*

Marshall Field's

The chain is a Midwest institution, and this is the flagship store: 12 floors of upscale shopping in old-fashioned department-store style. Kid's clothes are on the third floor, but there aren't many toys, other than stuffed animals. If the family gets hungry while shopping, there's the Marketplace, on the lowest level, with ready-to-go gourmet entrées, salads, fresh fruit, bottled juice, good coffee, chocolates, and bakery desserts. *700 Nicollet Mall, Seventh St. and Nicollet Ave., Minneapolis; (612) 375-2200.* www.marshallfields.com

BACK TO NATURE

MINNESOTA'S city, county, and state park systems are excellent, and preserve environments that range from rolling farm country to dramatic bluffs and untouched wilderness. Near the Twin Cities, nature centers in many parks and nature preserves have programs designed specifically to acquaint kids with local wildlife, and to answer the kinds of parent-baffling questions about the universe that only kids can ask. Most programs are free, but some parks and preserves charge a modest fee for admission and/or parking.

Chutes and Ladders

This tangle of slides and ladders is a cool, real-life counterpart to the popular board game. The chutes are high—40- and 50-foot enclosed slides. The playground is in Hyland Park and makes a great place to picnic after a day of outdoor fun or shopping at the Mall of America. *Hyland Lake Park Reserve, 1014 S. Bush Lake Rd., Bloomington; (952) 941-4362.*

French Regional Park

This nature center hugs Medicine Lake in the western suburbs and offers a nice sandy beach where your kids can swim under the supervision of a lifeguard. Rent a canoe and explore the lake, or go for a hike on the park's easygoing trails. *12605 County Rd. 9, Plymouth; (763) 559-8891.*

Lowry Nature Center

The coolest of all nature centers, Lowry's has an amazing Habitats exhibit, though the center itself will be most interesting to your grade-schoolers rather than older sibs. Kids can pretend they're a part of the movie *Honey, I Shrunk the Kids* as they peer through large dragonfly eyes and slip down slides designed to look like huge vines. Your city kids will also learn that maple syrup comes from trees, not Aunt Jemima, and learn how to make it, as well as how to find constellations in the summer sky. Regular family programs make the most of the 450-acre park of marsh, forest, and meadows. Older siblings can get their chance at a larger reserve, like Minnesota Valley. *Half an hour west of Minneapolis. Parking fee. 7025 Victoria Dr., Victoria; (952) 472-4911.*

Minnesota Valley Wildlife Refuge

Children of all ages enjoy the many interactive exhibits at this 8,000-acre wildlife refuge bordering the Minnesota River. The U.S. Fish and Wildlife Service proves that not all slide shows are boring with its no-holds-barred 12-projector presentation. The other programs are good, too. *3815 E. 80th St., Bloomington; (952) 854-5900;* www.midwest.fws.gov/minnesotavalley

Tamarack Nature Center

This nature center is a good bet for younger children who aren't up for major treks through the woods to search for animals. Families can take part in programs—from snowshoeing to nature hikes—throughout the year. *The center is in White Bear, a suburb about 20 minutes northeast of Minneapolis. 5287 Otter Lake Rd., White Bear Township; (651) 407-5351;* www.co.ramsey.mn.us/parks/tamarack

St. Paul has a European feel to it, with a park or square every few blocks.

St. Paul

ST. PAUL MAY not be as cosmopolitan as Minneapolis, but it has many special attractions for kids and a character that's quite distinct from that of its twin. There's the Minnesota Children's Museum (crawl through a kid-size anthill), the Science Museum (see dinosaurs and a gigantic outdoor iguana sculpture), the modern Minnesota History Center (watch videos, push buttons, interact with exhibits), a new hockey arena, and a riverfront parkway. There's even a historic downtown building that looks like a fairy-tale castle (there are no kid-friendly attractions inside, but it does give the city a festive air). St. Paul has neat forms of transportation, too: brightly painted historic-looking modern trolleys circulate the city, and horse-drawn carriages trot through town even in winter.

Como Park Zoo (page 369)

Gabbert Raptor Center (page 367)

Gibbs Farm Museum (page 369)

Great American History Theater (page 367)

Minnesota Children's Museum (page 368)

Minnesota History Center (page 368)

St. Paul Saints at Midway Stadium (page 370)

Science Museum of Minnesota (page 368)

Trains at Bandana/Twin City Model Railroad Museum (page 371)

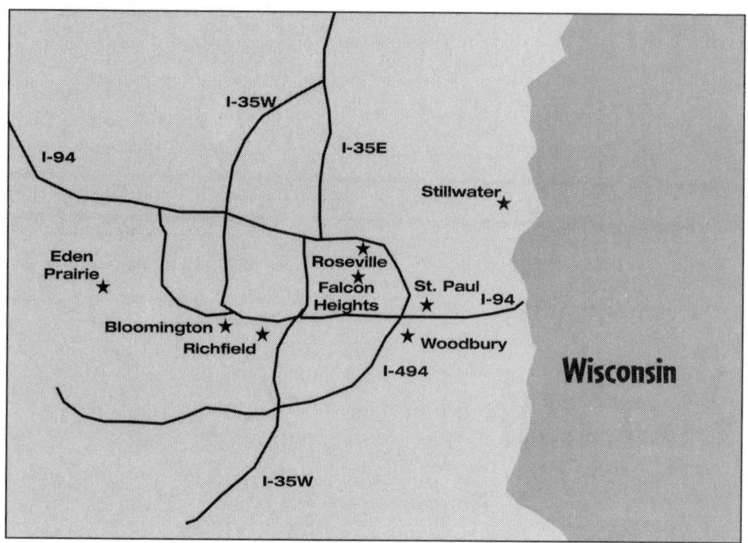

As in many European cities, St. Paul has a square or park every few blocks, offering a picturesque spot to stop, have an ice-cream cone, and let off steam. The city has a downtown skyway system, but it is not as modern, clearly marked, or extensive as the one in Minneapolis. Though downtown parking spots fill up fast, there's a parking garage near most major attractions. (In busy times, expect a hike of a block or two.)

Just north of downtown lies a refurbished railroad yard, home of a cool train museum (big ones to climb on, miniatures to watch). Nearby are the state fairgrounds, where the Minnesota State Fair is held August through Labor Day each year; the traditional farming festival features horses, cows, sheep, a children's barnyard, carnival rides, and delicious junk food. Close to the fairgrounds are the Como Park Zoo and the historic Gibbs Farm Museum, where kids can see how great-grandpa farmed. On the University of Minnesota–St. Paul campus grounds (just east of Como Park and also north of downtown) is Gabbert Raptor Center, where wounded birds of prey are treated and released, and where children can get a close-up view of hawks and eagles. If you've got baseball lovers in tow, take them to a St. Paul Saints game at Midway Stadium. The minor-league ball games are leavened with child-pleasing silliness: a pig carries fresh balls out to the pitcher; an announcer reads the license plate number of the dirtiest car in the parking lot. Comedian Bill Murray is a co-owner of the team and sometimes shows up at the games. **NOTE:** For information about skiing, see "Winter Sports in Minnesota" on page 398; for acres of kid-friendly activities, see "The Mall of America" on page 348.

CULTURAL ADVENTURES

Gabbert Raptor Center ★★/$

Eagles and hawks get sick, too. When birds of prey get hurt, they are brought here to special bird doctors who help heal them—and then release them. Run by the folks at the University of Minnesota, this is the world's largest medical center devoted to the care and treatment of birds of prey. Kids have lots of opportunities to see and learn about the falcons, eagles, hawks, and owls inside. The center offers group and individual tours on Saturdays at 10 A.M. and 2 P.M. that include educational exhibits, indoor flight pens, and medical treatment areas. *1920 Fitch Ave., St. Paul; (612) 624-4745;* www.raptor.cvm.umn.edu

Great American History Theater ★★/$$

Save this one for your older kids, 9 and up—little guys would just fidget their way through the performance. This theater company

A Winter Wonderland

The largest winter celebration in the nation was created in response to a *New York Times* reporter who in an 1885 story likened St. Paul to the chilly tundras of Siberia. Eager to prove him wrong, the hearty residents created **Winter Carnival**, which continues to be held annually at the end of January and the beginning of February. Early carnival planners created a legend that pits a cold-loving King Boreas against the Fire King, Volcanus Rex. Each year, Volcanus Rex defeats King Boreas to signal the arrival of spring. There is a lot to do and see during the 11-day festival, but the fair is scattered throughout the city, so study your carnival guide closely. A $3 Winter Carnival button is your ticket to most of the events, and your kids will thank you for getting them—lots of kid pleasers here. Both the Grande Day, featuring costumed revelers and festive floats, and the nighttime Torchlight Parades are fun. (Just beware of members of the Vulcan Crew during parades and other weeklong activities—they love to kiss your cheeks and leave you smeared with black greasepaint.) Be sure to walk around downtown's Rice Park; ice sculptors from far and wide arrive here in January to carve amazing creatures and sculptures out of ice. And—hurrah!—there's usually a mini-doughnut vendor nearby. For more information, contact the **St. Paul Festival and Heritage Foundation** *(800/488-4023; 651/223-4700).*

specializes in bringing national and Minnesota history to life, with plays based on famous historical novels, stories of American pioneers, or the lives of great leaders. The performances are fascinating, entertaining, and educational. *30 E. 10th St., St. Paul; (651) 292-4323.*

Minnesota Children's Museum
★★★★/$$

What kid could pass up the opportunity to get nose to beak with a turtle, shop for groceries at a neighborhood market, or play in a life-size anthill? They can do these things and more at the Children's Museum galleries. At the World Works Gallery, kids can splash around the wild water table or operate a giant crane. The Earth World Gallery is a forest environment and a giant anthill complete with ant costumes. (But watch your little ones in the busy hill—the tangle of hidden coves can be confusing, and worried Moms can often be seen calling to lost children inside.) One of the museum's best features is the Habitot Gallery, a wonderful space where little ones can explore in age-appropriate environments (the pond and cave are favorites) without any older children to intrude or take over. The age limit for this room is 4 years old, no exceptions. Be sure to bring the camera; a picture of your 3-year-old perched on a lily pad is priceless. The museum is wonderful for kids under 10, but older ones might scoff at some of the childish themes. *10 W. Seventh St., St. Paul; (651) 225-6000;* www.mcm.org

Minnesota History Center
★★/$

History isn't ho-hum here! This enormous, very modern facility uses video, interactive exhibits, quizzes, buzzers, and graphics to bring the past to life. Programs like History Hijinks help kids understand history through interactive presentations, crafts, classes, plays, and cool exhibits that "talk" and showcase everyday Minnesota life. Check with the museum about the program schedule. The on-site cafeteria is open for lunch and has good food and lots of room. *345 W. Kellogg Blvd., St. Paul; (651) 296-6126;* www.mnhs.org

MUST-SEE FamilyFun MUST-SEE

Science Museum of Minnesota
★★★★/$

Kids can make their own tidal waves in a see-through Plexiglas tank by manipulating Nintendo-like levers. Overhead, sparkly red fluid flows through clear pipes, vividly demonstrating how blood circulates through the body. A cluster of dinosaur skeletons built from casts taken from a site in Wyoming are assembled here, too. The museum's seven-story, 350,000-square-foot state-of-the-art building along the

Riverfront takes full advantage of its location: you can see wildlife from its many balconies and windows overlooking the river. Keep a lookout for eagles! *120 W. Kellogg Blvd., St. Paul; (651) 221-9444;* www.smm.org

JUST FOR FUN

Como Park Zoo

MUST-SEE FamilyFun MUST-SEE

★★★★/Free

The absence of an admission fee makes this community zoo a popular place. Unlike at the larger and more modern Minnesota Zoo, where animals roam in natural surroundings, here kids can easily see the animals, since they are caged in traditional zoo fashion. (No admission fees also means no revenue with which to build modern habitats.) The short walking distances between displays are a plus, too. Grab seats for the Sparky-the-Seal Show, a silly program featuring a lively seal. Kids love to buy paper cups of chopped fish and toss bits to the barking seals housed outdoors in the summer. For a great way to end the day, step inside the Como Park Conservatory (fee). Room after room of lush tropical plants transform one of the country's few remaining glass conservatories into a wonderland (especially in midwinter). The water-lily-covered koi ponds in the Japanese garden are a kid favorite. The nearby park also has paddleboats, canoes, bikes, and in-line skates for rent. *Midway Pkwy. and Kaufman Dr., St. Paul; (651) 487-8201.*

Gibbs Farm Museum

MUST-SEE FamilyFun MUST-SEE

★★★/$

Kids and animals go together like peanut butter and jelly, so your kids are bound to love this authentic 1900s–era farm. Children can pet or just watch (up close) ducks, pigs, geese, turkeys, lambs, goats, and other farm animals. Older

DAY TRIP

Museums and More in Downtown St. Paul

You'll find more than a day of kid-pleasing activities in St. Paul's downtown area. One possibility is to tour the exhibits at the **Minnesota History Center** *(345 W. Kellogg Blvd.; 651/296-6126)* and then catch a matinee at the **Great American History Theater** *(30 E. 10th St.; 651/292-4323)*. Or spend a few hours in the new **Science Museum of Minnesota**—don't miss the gigantic climb-on-me metal iguana out front *(120 W. Kellogg Blvd.; 651/221-9444)*. Then let your kids crawl through a kid-size anthill and operate a giant crane at the **Minnesota Children's Museum** *(10 W. Seventh St.; 651/225-6000)*.

Fair Games

If you're in the Twin Cities with children **in late August**, there's really no question—you must attend the **Minnesota State Fair**. One of the largest agricultural fairs in the country, it offers plenty of less pricey, kid-pleasing things to do:

- Stroll through the horse barn and check out all the varieties of exotic chickens and guinea pigs.
- Visit the state's largest hog (maybe you'll see piglets!).
- Watch silly people bungee jump.
- Look into the outdoor aquarium of the state's game fish.
- Watch the free nightly outdoor amateur talent contest.
- Look down at the crowds from the Space Needle and the gondola rides.
- Watch rodeos and horse shows in the Hippodrome.
- Pet farm animals in the kiddie barn.

And through it all—eat! Like any fair, this one has junk-food snacks everywhere. (If you want a square meal, choose one of the many church-sponsored dining halls where chicken, mashed potatoes, and veggies are served.) Otherwise, fill up on corn dogs, snow cones, and caramel apples like everyone else. A peculiar Minnesota State Fair attraction: food on a stick, including watermelon on a stick, walleye on a stick, and pickles on a stick. If you stay late, you can see fireworks. *Main entrance at Midway Parkway and Snelling Ave.; (651) 642-2200.*

kids will be interested in the Dakota-style tepees and remnants of the original sod house that once stood on the land. The museum is run by the Ramsey County Historical Society, and kids with a historical bent will find plenty to explore. Closed November through April. *2097 W. Larpenteur Ave., Falcon Heights; (651) 646-8629;* www.rchs.com

Harriet Island Park

★★/Free

As renovations and new construction rejuvenate this park, it is becoming a wonderful family spot: there are concerts in the gazebo, picnic areas, and stairs down to the river. Drive here, following signs from downtown to Harriet Island—the way can be confusing, but the signage is being improved and simplified. From the top of the hill in the park, the view of the Mississippi River and of downtown St. Paul is terrific. *Entrance is off Plato Blvd.; boundaries are Wabasha St., Smith Ave., W. Water St., and the river.*

St. Paul Saints at Midway Stadium

★★★★/$$

This outdoor stadium is the home of the St. Paul Saints, a minor-league AA baseball team whose games have become the hottest tickets in town during the summer months. The team is co-owned by comedian Bill Murray and Mike Veek, son of former White Sox owner Bill Veek. In addition to baseball fun, the games offer a wide variety of zany antics to entertain fans of all ages. A pig brings game balls out to the umpires, and inning breaks are often devoted to sumo wrestling matches or competitive relays between ticket holders. Vendors offering haircuts and neck messages in the stands are common sights. Come early to buy tickets, and you'll see a Midwestern tradition called tailgating: spectators in the parking lot grilling burgers and hot dogs and picnicking out of the backs of their pickup trucks, minivans, and SUVs. Given the demand for tickets, call ahead to reserve. *1771 Energy Park Dr., St. Paul; (651) 644-6659;* www.saintsbaseball.com

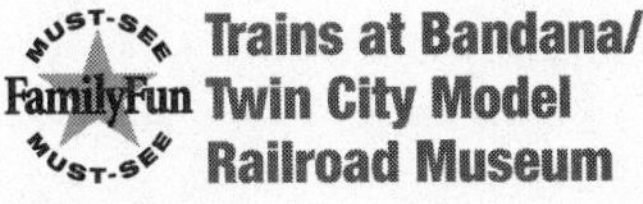

Trains at Bandana/ Twin City Model Railroad Museum

★★★★/$

It's a train lover's dream. Bandana Square, now a mellow (not very busy) shopping complex, used to be a railroad repair warehouse, and the Twin City Model Railroad Museum has preserved the legacy by setting up an immense model railroad on the mall's second floor. The trains are modeled after Twin Cities passenger trains, freight trains, and trolley cars from the 1930s to the 1950s. Look for such local landmarks as the Minneapolis Stone Arch Bridge and the Great Northern Station among the models. Also check out the real locomotive displayed near the southern entrance to Bandana Square. Kids under 4 free. *1021 E. Bandana Blvd., St. Paul; (651) 647-9628.*

BUNKING DOWN

Embassy Suites St. Paul-Downtown

★★/$$$

All rooms are suites and so good for families at this 210-unit hotel. Like the rest of the chain, each has a bedroom and living room/dining room/work space with a pullout sofa bed. Other pluses for families: each unit also has a wet bar, a refrigerator, a microwave, two TVs, and a table and chairs. On-site extras include an indoor pool, a sauna, a whirlpool, laundry service, and a restaurant with a children's menu. *175 E. 10th St., St. Paul; (800) EMBASSY (362-2779); (651) 224-5400;* www.embassysuites.com

Holiday Inn Express

★★★/$$

If you have a child (or a spouse!) who loves trains, stay here. The 109 rooms and suites were created inside an old railroad-car-repair shop. The overall effect here is a bit like getting off the train at an old-fashioned small town. The interior walls are brick and yellow clapboard, as though you were outside, and rooms are large, with wooden beams and other period details. The two-story lobby is a faithfully reproduced train depot, lit by lanterns. Located next to Bandana Square (and its train museum), the hotel is convenient to Como Park Zoo, Midway Stadium, and the state fairgrounds. *1010 W. Bandana Blvd., St. Paul; (800) 465-4329; (651) 647-1637;* www.holiday-inn.com

Radisson Riverfront Hotel Saint Paul

★★★/$$$

The draw here is the gorgeous view of the Mississippi and the proximity to riverfront attractions. The 475 guest rooms and suites are equipped

OUTDOOR FUN IN ST. PAUL

BALLOONING

The best local spot for hot-air ballooning is the St. Croix River Valley, about a half-mile east of St. Paul. Call **Stillwater Balloons** *(14791 60th St. N., Stillwater; 651/439-1800).*

CROSS-COUNTRY SKIING

The **Como Park Ski Center** *(651/266-6445)* offers trails for cross-country skiers and a couple of downhill slopes for snow skaters. There are also great trails open all winter at the **Minnesota Zoo** *(13000 Zoo Blvd.; 952/432-9000).*

ICE-SKATING

The following indoor rinks, within 15 minutes of downtown, are especially kid-friendly: **Woodbury Ice Arena** *(4125 Tower Dr., Woodbury; 651/458-3301)* and **Roseville Skating Center** *(Coney Rd. between Hamlin and Lexington Aves., Roseville; 651/415-2160).*

ST. PAUL SKYWAYS

They're not lined with convenience shops and eateries like the ones in Minneapolis, but St. Paul does have a system of skyways (enclosed walkways) and tunnels that connect many of the major attractions. Some 66 buildings and 37 city blocks are linked by nearly five miles of skyway, so you can walk to the riverfront, the arena, the Science Museum, the Children's Museum, and numerous shops and restaurants without being exposed to the elements.

BALD EAGLES do not develop their most distinctive features until they are 4 or 5 years old. The dark-colored features of young raptors mature into the white head, white tail, yellow beak, yellow eyes of an adult eagle.

with hair dryers, irons, and ironing boards, and the hotel has an indoor pool. There's a kid-pleasing, revolving restaurant. *11 E. Kellogg Blvd., St. Paul; (800) 333-3333; (651) 292-1900;* www.radisson.com

GOOD EATS

Boca Chica Mexican Restaurante

★★/$

The Guillermo and Gloria Frias family serves authentic Mexican food in a warm, cozy adobe-style building. Wall murals offer Mexican history lessons, and any kid who loves cheese, rice, and chicken will find a treat on the menu. *11 Concord St., St. Paul; (651) 222-8499.*

Buca de Beppo

★★★/$$

This unique and funky local restaurant chain offers family-style dining at its best. The atmosphere is fun and relaxed, and portions are large: listen to the waitstaff when it comes time to order—they know how much food your family will need. *1204 Harmon Pl., St. Paul (651/638-2225); 2728 Gannon Rd., St. Paul (651/722-4388); 14300 Burnhaven Dr., Burnsville, (952/892-7272); 7711 Mitchell Rd., Eden Prairie (612/724-7266).*

Cafe da Vinci

★★★/$$

Introduce your kids to the other Leonardo (not DiCaprio)—and to great pasta. This beautiful restaurant features enormous murals of Leonardo da Vinci masterworks on the walls, and the high ceilings support a full-scale model of the artist's flying machine. The food at the ready-to-eat pasta bar quiets hungry children instantly. *Inside Park Square Court, 400 Sibley St., St. Paul; (651) 222-4050.*

Cafe Latté

★★★/$

There's a reason all the families in the neighborhood dine at this upscale cafeteria. The food is healthful, the service is as fast as at the hamburger chains, the seating is plentiful, and the desserts are to die for. The lines can get long at lunch and dinner times—go a bit early or a bit late, and you'll be fine. *In Victoria Crossing Mall, Grand Ave. at S. Victoria St., St. Paul; (651) 224-5687.*

Carousel ★★/$$
This is a grown-up place to eat, but it's kid-friendly, too, and kids get a kick out of the revolving dining room. They'll also think the views of the city and riverfront from the 22nd floor are pretty cool. Breakfast and lunch up here are cheaper and more kid-appropriate than is dinner. But an early dinner off the appetizer menu is affordable and allows a great view of the city and river. *In the Radisson Riverfront Hotel Saint Paul, 11 E. Kellogg Blvd., St. Paul; (651) 292-0408.*

Dayton's ★★/$
The two restaurants at Dayton's are both kid-friendly, though in different ways. The Marketplace sells ready-to-microwave gourmet entrées, packaged salads, fruit, juices, and bottled water for making a picnic or bringing back to your hotel room. The River Room is fancy (Waterford crystal chandeliers) but still serves kid-friendly entrées—and everything comes with an oven-fresh popover. *411 Cedar St., St. Paul; (651) 292-5174 (River Room).*

Grand Old Creamery ★★★/$
Stop along Grand Avenue for a designer ice-cream cone. More than 30 flavors of ice cream (brownie, pumpkin, mint, along with all the usual favorites) are served in home-made waffle cones and sundaes. *750 Grand Ave., St. Paul; (651) 293-1655.*

Khan's Mongolian Barbecue ★★★/$
Here, the price of kids' meals is based on their height. The incredible buffet offers a great selection of raw meat and veggies (kids can pass by what they don't like). Bring your selection to the enormous black grill and the chefs will toss and flip your meal to a sizzling perfection before your eyes. Tip the cooks and they'll let your kids ring the huge gong with a big paddle. *500 E. 78th St., Richfield (612/861-7991); 2720 Snelling Ave., Roseville (651/631-3398).*

DAY TRIP

Creatures Featured: Como Park Zoo and St. Anthony Park

Begin the day at the **Como Conservatory** for a walk through tropical greenhouse gardens. Then feed the seals and watch the monkeys at **Como Park Zoo**. For more wildlife, head for the nearby **Gabbert Raptor Center** at the University of Minnesota-St. Paul, where you can get a close-up look at recovering birds of prey. From there, drive down Como Avenue to the charming St. Anthony Park neighborhood. The **St. Anthony Park Library** *(2245 Como Ave.; 651/642-0411)* has recently expanded and provides many delightful places to sit and read your children's favorite books.

Mickey's Diner ★★/$

No, your eyes aren't deceiving you. A train-style dining car is sitting smack-dab in the middle of downtown St. Paul. It's not spacious, but it's plenty funky and makes for a fun stop for a hot dog or burger during the day. At night it becomes the haunt of very grown-up and somewhat edgy folk, so skip it after dark. *36 W. Seventh St., St. Paul; (651) 222-5633.*

Taste of Scandinavia Deli and Bakery ★★★★/$

In a charming section of St. Paul called St. Anthony Park (west of the University of Minnesota-St. Paul campus and Como Park Zoo), this bakery and deli sits in the center of Milton Square, a collection of Tudor-style shops and restaurants right across from the picturesque old Carnegie Library. In addition to delectable bakery goods, it serves wholesome and healthy soups, entrées, and simple sandwiches to eat in or take back to your hotel. Dine at cute café tables topped with blue-and-white-checked cloths, or take your selections out onto the patio in sunny weather. *2264 Como Ave., St. Paul; (651) 645-9181.*

Souvenir Hunting

Creative Kidstuff

No electronic, put-your-brain-on-hold toys here. Instead, find wood-carved wonders, hands-on learning aids, and educational games. All ages, all price brackets are embraced—and the store is just plain enjoyable to walk through. *1074 Grand Ave., St. Paul; (651) 222-2472.*

Paint Your Plate

Kids old enough to sit without squirming for the better part of an hour enjoy decorating their own ceramics in this shop. Choose a piece of unfinished pottery, then sit

If your kids are old enough to tolerate a fairly grown-up menu, have lunch outside on the deck across the street at **Muffuletta** *(2260 Como Ave.; 651/644-9116)*. Or enter the delightfully European **Milton Square shops**—gingerbread-trimmed buildings with flower-filled courtyards. The **Taste of Scandinavia Deli and Bakery** *(2264 Como Ave.; 651/645-9181)* is totally kid-friendly. They'll feel like they're going underground to an enchanted cave, and the soups are nutritious and the pastries heavenly. Need a full lunch? Try **Manning's** *(2200 Como Ave.; 612/331-1053)*, where Elvis is on the radio and burgers are on the menu. Pop into the **Bibelot Shop** *(2276 Como Ave.; 651/646-5651)* for fun and funky toys, stuffed animals, and fun trinkets and gifts.

MINNESOTA'S STATE PARKS

MINNESOTA is known for its well-organized, visitor-friendly, and quite extensive park system. Throughout the state, 68 parks preserve stunning scenery and natural landmarks like waterfalls, gorges, riverbanks, and big hills (Minnesotans call them "mountains," but no one else would). Most state parks have picnic areas, hiking trails, campgrounds, cross-country ski trails, and nature programs led by park rangers.

When you see a brown-and-white road sign pointing to an entrance to a state park, it's well worth turning off the road to explore. Usually, you pay a modest fee of a few dollars to park overnight or camp, but you may be able to just drive through and look for free. Driving through won't get you to the best lookouts and coolest sights, though—for those, you have to get out and walk. Just inside the entrance of most of the parks is a ranger station. Stop in, pay the fee, ask questions, get information, and pick up a few maps of the area.

If you've got half an hour and an antsy preschooler, the ranger on duty can likely recommend a quick hike that a youngster can manage, and warn you off of more challenging trails you shouldn't try. You can often also buy firewood and a few necessary items at these stations, although they are a far cry from a convenience store.

Parks clear and maintain summer trails, winter trails, footpaths, and trails for cross-country skiing and snowmobiling.

The state park day fee is $4 per vehicle, and a yearlong sticker for unlimited park use is $20. If you're planning to camp, call ahead for reservations; the parks fill up quickly, especially in the summer and around holidays. You can make reservations on-line, www.state.mnparks.com, or by phone *(866/857-2757)*. The parks leave some campsites open for those who didn't make reservations, but they're available on a first-come, first-served basis.

Blue Mounds

This park looks like it came straight out of an episode of *Little House on the Prairie*. There are windswept grasslands and a swimming hole just like the ones where Laura Ingalls played. Kids like the 100-foot Sioux quartzite cliff. If you're lucky, you'll catch a glimpse of the bison herd that grazes the park. *Luverne; (507) 283-1307.*

St. Croix

An hour's drive from the Twin Cities metro area, this park keeps you close to more citified attractions. The family-friendly place has a great swimming beach and fun trails along the picturesque St. Croix River. If your kids are into canoeing, you can rent one here. Otherwise, explore the easy-to-hike river trails for a little outdoor adventure. The campsites aren't exactly tucked into the woods, but the trade-off is worth it—they're close to the bathrooms, a plus when your little ones want company on their way to the potty in the middle of the night. *Hinckley; (320) 384-6591.*

Tettegouche

More than 9,000 acres, this enormous park is ideal for kids. There are trout lakes for fishing and great trails of varying degrees of difficulty for hiking. If they like waterfalls, visit thundering Gooseberry Falls, a gorgeous and awe-inspiring sight, only a 20-minute drive south. Gooseberry is a must-see, but avoid camping at that park—the crowds are thick during the summer months. Better to stay here, where you'll have more breathing room and can enjoy Tettegouche's own set of beautiful trails and waterfalls. *5707 Hwy. 61, Silver Bay; (218) 226-6365.*

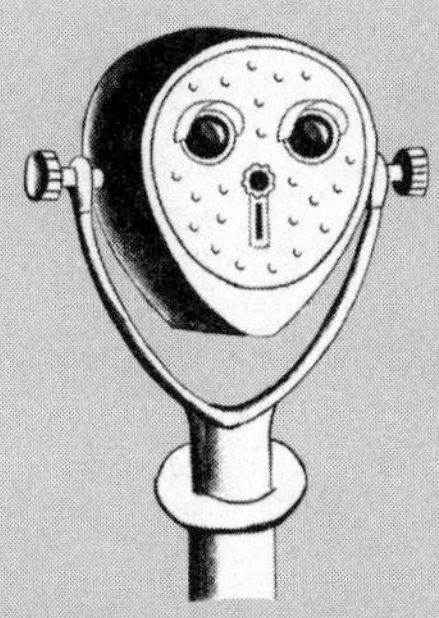

together at tables and paint. The cost is figured per piece and per hour of time. They'll put it in a kiln for you and you can return later to pick up your finished masterpiece. Some items take several days to fire, but they'll ship finished ceramics to you at home. *1106 Grand Ave., St. Paul; (651) 225-8034.*

Play It Again Sports

Used and new hockey, snowboarding, in-line skating, basketball, baseball, football, and other sporting gear is sold at easy-on-the-pocket prices. *53 S. Cleveland Ave., at Grand Ave., St. Paul; (651) 698-3773.*

Red Balloon Bookshop

The carved wooden bears outside are a hint: this is a children's place. Find your child's favorite books here and enjoy the regular readings by visiting authors. *891 Grand Ave., St. Paul; (651) 224-8320.*

Ruminator Bookstore

Known in the past as the Hungry Mind, this beloved bookstore hosts storytelling sessions for children on Saturday mornings. *1648 Grand Ave., St. Paul; (651) 699-0587.*

Wet Paint, Inc.

Got an artist in the family? This bright, friendly shop is filled with displays of paints, brushes, handmade paper, and art supplies—plus fun kits for creative kids. *1684 Grand Ave., St. Paul; (651) 698-6431.*

Stroll out to a Lake Superior lighthouse from Duluth's town square.

Duluth

THE SCENERY during the two-and-a-half-hour hour drive north from the Twin Cities into Duluth is not terribly interesting at first. There's nothing to see but flat rural landscapes and woodlands. Then suddenly, the interstate lifts, turns, and dips and there it is: Lake Superior, stretching so far to the horizon that it looks like the ocean.

This port is one fun city for kids. The sheer scale of the enormous lake and the climbing hills bordering it are amazing, and Canal Park gets young visitors up close to the phenomenally large cargo ships coming in and out of harbor. The permanently docked SS *William A. Irvine* lets youngsters climb up and walk around inside a real Great Lakes cargo ship. There's also a children's museum, a zoo, a train museum, and an OMNIMAX theater. Natural

The Depot/St. Louis County Heritage and Arts Center (page 380)

Great Lakes Aquarium and Freshwater Discovery Center (page 382)

Lake Superior Zoological Gardens (page 382)

Lakewalk (page 383)

SS *William A. Irvine* Ore Boat (page 381)

Vista Fleet Harbor Cruises (page 384)

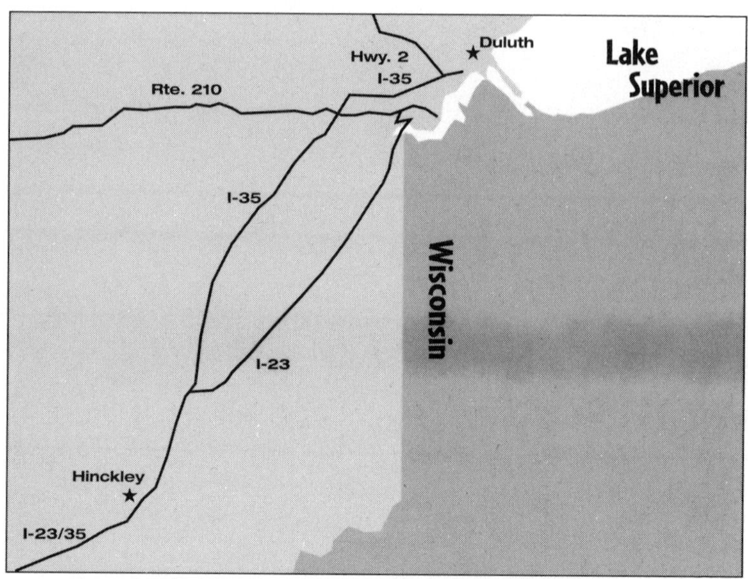

wonders are fun, here, too: the rocky lakeshore is great for exploring, Lake Superior agates are treasures for junior rock hounds to discover, and the Skyline Drive offers breathtaking views of the harbor, area wildflowers, and the surrounding hillside. Stop along the way at the frequent overlook sites for great photos and perspectives of gigantic boats traveling the shipping lanes. Everyone in the family will enjoy an evening at Lakewalk, the town square of Duluth. There you can walk out to a lighthouse, see ore boats up close as they move through a narrow canal, and watch the lift bridge rise to let boats through. **NOTE:** For more information about skiing, see "Winter Sports in Minnesota" on page 398.

CULTURAL ADVENTURES

The Depot/St. Louis County Heritage and Arts Center ★★★★/$

The picturesque green-roofed turrets make this one-time train depot look like a castle. Two of the four museums under this one roof are particularly fun for children, and one fee covers admission to all. A vintage railroad also operates out of the station; there's an additional fee for tickets. *506 W. Michigan St., Duluth.*

Duluth Children's Museum

This smallish museum, which focuses on world cultures and natural history, is best suited to children 8 years old and younger. Toddler Town provides hands-on exhibits and activities for the busy 3-and-under crowd. The International Marketplace lets older children explore the world's natural and cultural resources. *The Depot, 506 W. Michigan St., Duluth; (218) 727-8025;* www.duluthchildrensmuseum.org

Lake Superior Railroad Museum

Your kids can climb in, on, around, and under a real caboose, a train engine, and passenger cars; get a close-up look at enormous, historic, and modern trains; sit in the engineer's seat of the *Mallet,* one of the world's largest locomotives; or explore the cupola of a caboose. They can also peruse the engines and train exhibits in one of the Midwest's largest train collections. Closed on major holidays. *The Depot, 506 W. Michigan St., Duluth; (218) 733-7590.* www.lsrm.org

North Shore Scenic Railroad

Buy a ticket and ride the Lakefront Line aboard a vintage train. You'll travel over tall trestles and through the north woods during the narrated trip. The best bet for family fun is the Pizza Train, a dinner excursion designed for families. Open May through October. *506 W. Michigan St., Duluth; (800) 423-1273; (218) 722-1273.*

Lake Superior Maritime Visitor Center ★★/Free

Your kids can play with the life-size navigational wheel and controls as they look out over the immense lake. Near the lift bridge, the Lake Superior Maritime Visitor Center houses two floors of nautical memorabilia about the shipping center's history. *600 Lake Ave. S., Duluth; (218) 727-2497.*

MUST-SEE FamilyFun MUST-SEE **SS *William A. Irvine* Ore Boat ★★★★/$$**

This floating museum is just plain cool. Once the flagship of the USS Great Lakes Fleet, the *William A. Irvine* is now permanently docked near the OMNIMAX Theater. Your kids will be amazed by its sheer size even before they climb the gangplank and take the tour through its giant hull. If you're in the area around Halloween, check out the haunted boat tour—it's an original spin on the typical haunted house. Tours depart at scheduled times. Closed November through April. *350 Harbor Dr., Duluth; (218) 722-7876;* www.williamairvine.com

Just for Fun

Duluth OMNIMAX Theater

★★★/$$

This impressive theater captivates kids of all ages with smart, interesting films shown on a huge domed screen. The movies are pricey, but a great option for cold or rainy days. *301 Harbor Dr., Duluth; (218) 727-0022.*

Great Lakes Aquarium and Freshwater Discovery Center

★★★★/$$

Your kids will love the 24-foot-high water wall in the entrance, and the interactive exhibits that let them touch a live lamprey eel and guide a virtual 1,000-foot ore boat through the canal under the Aerial Lift Bridge. This new $33.8-million structure is the nation's only all-freshwater aquarium. It showcases wildlife found in and near Lake Superior and other large lakes of the world—and more than just fish: birds, snakes, salamanders, turtles, frogs, crayfish, and river otters. There's also a virtual reality submarine that "sinks" to the bottom of the lake to explore shipwrecks and sealife. Young children love crawling through a beaver lodge and bear den, and maneuvering toy boats through a water table shaped like the chain of Great Lakes. *353 Harbor Dr., Duluth; (218) 740-3474;* www.glaquarium.com

Lake Superior Zoological Gardens

★★★★/$

A beautiful natural setting is an added bonus at this zoo. A waterfall near the Australian Connection area creates a creek that winds through the entire property. Kids especially

Go For It

Want more action? Duluth has plenty of options.

BICYCLING

Rent mountain bikes and explore the area's many hiking and snowmobile trails. **Willard Munger Inn Adventure Rides** *(7408 Grand Ave.; 218/624-4814)* rents bikes and gives suggested routes. If you reserve early, they'll provide a free shuttle to a great starting point—that way the kids can't crab about its being b-o-r-i-n-g.

FLYING

Orville Air, Inc. *(Sky Harbor Airport; 218/733-0078)* offers scenic seaplane rides over Lake Superior. A 20-minute trip costs $30 per person.

KAYAKING

There's no room in a kayak for infants or

like the Polar Shores exhibit with active seals and polar bears. Also check out the Primate Conservation Center—endangered primates are on display, and exhibits discuss animal conservation efforts. Younger kids gravitate to the free-range peacocks that strut their stuff throughout the grounds. *7210 Fremont St., Duluth; (218) 733-3777; (218) 723-3748;* www.lszoo.org

Lakewalk

MUST-SEE FamilyFun MUST-SEE ★★★★/Free

This two-mile-long walk by the edge of Lake Superior has become the town square of Duluth. It starts at the Aerial Lift Bridge and follows the shoreline to the replica of the Viking ship in Leif Erickson Park. The giant bridge is a wonder of century-old trusses and counterweights that raise the center span 70 feet to allow tall ships and ore and grain boats to fit under as they pass through the canal. Shiphands wave to kids, who love the thunderous horn blasts (one long, two short) from the captain to the bridge-keeper. Take a stroll on the wide walkway out to a lighthouse (it's also a smooth ride for a stroller); and the mimes, street musicians, and vendors along the path make it extra fun. If the troops are hungry after that walk, popcorn and hot dog vendors sell snacks. *Between Canal Park and Leif Ericson Park, Duluth.*

Skyline Drive ★★★/Free

Head up the hill out of downtown, and when you hit Skyline Drive, turn either left or right. The drive twists and turns from Duluth up along the hills overlooking the harbor. The scenery is stunning, and there are many spots along the way designed to let you pull over and

toddlers. Your older kids—8 and up—will love the feeling of sitting low in the water. **Sea Kayak Tours** at the University of Minnesota Duluth *(1216 Ordean Ct.; 218/726-6533)* offers several tours including an excursion that lets you paddle close to anchored ocean freighters and the Aerial Lift Bridge.

SAILING

Charter a boat and captain to sail the lake. For details and reservations, call **Synergy Sails, Inc.** *(Harbor Cove Marina, 11th St. and Minnesota Ave., across the Aerial Lift Bridge; 218/348-3048;* www.synergysales.com).

SKIING

In winter, rent snowshoes or cross-country skis and get expert advice on where to use them at **Twin Ports Cyclery** *(2914 W. Third St.; 218/624-4008)* or **Snowflake Nordic Ski Center** *(4348 Rice Lake Rd., one quarter mile north of Arrowhead Rd.; 218/726-1550).* Snowflake also has camping in the summer months.

enjoy the wildflowers and gorgeous views. Bring a picnic lunch, and when your kids spot an ore boat making its way into the harbor, that's the time to stop to eat while you chart its progress.

MUST-SEE FamilyFun MUST-SEE Vista Fleet Harbor Cruises ★★★★/$$

Explore the gray waters of Lake Superior aboard one of the Vista Fleet boats. Kids love the narrated sight-seeing cruises, which cover the Aerial Lift Bridge—you get to ride right under it!—and the harbor area. If you're lucky, you'll pass a huge lake freighter. If your children get seasick, skip this—the water can be choppy. Closed November through April. *323 Harbor Dr., Duluth; (218) 722-6218;* www.visitduluth.com/vista

Breakfast with a Bird's-eye View

Start your day at the Radisson Hotel Duluth—Harborview. Though the hotel restaurant touts itself as a fancy dinner destination, the real fun (and the cheaper menu) is during the day, when you can see the ships coming and going in the harbor and get a bird's-eye view of the entire city. Arrive at breakfast time and get a table by the window on the revolving "carousel" floor—the entire room rotates slowly about once an hour. From your table, you'll get a 360-degree view of the harbor and city. The historic and current photos on the walls will help the kids identify which buildings they're looking at. This is a great spot to plan your day.

Wade Stadium ★★/$$

This lively outdoor stadium is the home of the Duluth-Superior Dukes, an AA minor-league baseball team that draws thousands of cheering fans each summer. Tickets are cheap (buy them at the stadium before the game). Kids enjoy the spirited atmosphere, whether they are baseball fans or not. *34th Ave. W., at Grand Ave., Duluth; (218) 727-4525;* www.dsdukes.com

BUNKING DOWN

Canal Park Inn ★★/$

Count the ore boats passing through the canal and see when the lift bridge is about to rise, all from your window at this 144-room hotel. You can walk to Lakewalk attractions: hot dogs and popcorn, Grandma's restaurant, the arcade. The complimentary, full, hot breakfast is especially good fuel for your active day ahead. And yes, there's an indoor pool. *250 Canal Park Dr., Duluth; (800) 777-8560; (218) 727-8821.*

Comfort Suites ★★/$$

The 81 one-room suites in this two-

Are We There Yet?

Midway between the Twin Cities and Duluth is a halfway stop that travelers consider nearly a sacred tradition. Pull into Tobies *(I-35 and Hwy. 48, Hinckley; 320/384-6175)* for doughnuts—and much more. Once a diner-size shop, Tobies has grown into a cluster of buildings and is now practically a destination in itself. There are round-the-clock and convenience stores, an ice-cream shop, and a full-service restaurant, as well as a shop selling bakery goods. Try the homemade caramel rolls.

story hotel come equipped with some handy extras like a refrigerator and a sofa bed. Add in the free continental breakfast, a pool, two whirlpools, and in-room movies, and you've got a solid lodging choice for families. *Near Lakewalk on the lakeshore. 408 Canal Park Dr., Duluth; (800) 228-5150; (218) 727-1378;* www.comfortsuites.com

Inn on Lake Superior ★★/$$

This family-style hotel has 101 rooms and is right on the lake near Lakewalk; for a view, ask for a lakeside room with a balcony. Your kids will like the pool and the complimentary continental breakfast. *350 Canal Park Dr., Duluth; (888) 668-4352; (218) 726-1111;* www.zmchotels.com

Radisson Hotel Duluth—Harborview ★★★/$$

This 16-floor, 268-room downtown hotel is a three-minute drive to Canal Park and the Lakewalk, and the higher your room is, the better your view of the harbor, the big boats, the downtown Depot, and the docked *William A. Irvine* ship. The hotel is round, and the Carousel restaurant on the top floor offers a breathtaking and ever-revolving view of the town and harbor. An indoor pool, whirlpool, and sundeck complete the family picture. *505 W. Superior St., Duluth; (800) 333-3333; (218) 727-8981;* www.radisson.com

GOOD EATS

Black Woods Grill & Bar on the Lake ★/$$

You get prime rib, the kids get lots to choose from off the children's menu. *2525 London Rd., Duluth; (218) 724-1612.*

Grandma's ★★★/$$

You'll see the old-fashioned "Grandma" logo nearly everywhere you go in Duluth. Grandma's is a big name here, and the restaurant and bar sponsors a nationally recognized running marathon each year. This is a great place for a family meal. Big burgers, thick sandwiches, and thin-crust pizzas are served in a noisy, high-energy environment kids can feel comfortable in. There are three Grandma's in Duluth (and one in Minneapolis), but natives view the original site in Canal Park as the "real" one. The **Grandma's Sports Garden Bar & Grill** includes lots of video arcade games and serves pizzas and burgers. *425 Lake Ave. S., Duluth; (218) 722-4724.* The original Grandma's: *522 Lake Ave. S., Duluth; (218) 727-4192.* Another Grandma's site: *2202 Maple Grove Rd., Duluth; (218) 722-9313.*

Radisson Hotel Duluth Top of the Harbor ★★/$$-$$$

This revolving restaurant has 360 degrees of windowside tables and the best view in town. Bring the kids here for breakfast and a great perspective from which to plan your day—you can see everything you'll visit later. At night, it's romantic, but the dinner menu isn't especially kid-friendly, and the view is better with sunlight. *505 W. Superior St., Duluth; (218) 727-8981.*

SOUVENIR HUNTING

DeWitt-Seitz Marketplace

This historic building in Canal Park near the Aerial Lift Bridge is now an eclectic mall, with 11 shops, a bakery, and two restaurants. **J. Skylark Company** *(218/722-3794)* delivers some real kid-friendly stuff: cool kites, stuffed animals, unusual toys, and games and puzzles. The chocolaty sweet scents emanating from **Hepzibah's Sweet Shoppe** *(218/722-5049)* and the chocolate ore boats are

Duluth Delights

Begin a nautical day taking a ride up **Skyline Drive**, which winds you up the face of what Duluthians call The Hill. You'll get a terrific view of the entire harbor, the city, the industry, and of any ore or grain boats heading in to dock. In fact, from almost any point in Duluth, you can look out on the lake and see the next big boat heading in. Once you spy one that's approaching the **Aerial Lift Bridge**, head for Canal Park. Park the car in one of the free lots and scoot the kids down to the bridge for a real treat.

As a boat approaches, parkgoers line up along the concrete canal wall for a chance to see a huge ship up close—and to hear the clanging of the bridge as it signals that it's going to lift. Traffic stops on either side of the bridge, and the entire center span lifts to allow the boat to pass underneath. The boat horn toots (loudly) to the bridge operator (maybe the captain's way of saying "thank you"), and slowly passes under.

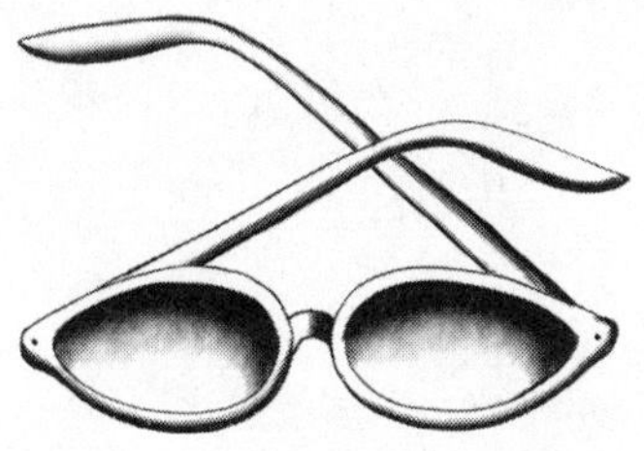

the draw here. **Blue Heron Trading Co.** *(218/722-8799)* sells kitchen gadgets of no interest to kids, but some of the regional specialty foods—local jams, jellies, and treats—along with loon-shaped suckers and the like may be fun. *Canal Park, 394 Lake Ave. S., Duluth; (218) 722-0047.* www.dewitt-seitz.com

Fitger's Brewery Complex

The 1885 historic brewery has been renovated into a hotel-restaurant-shopping complex-museum space that your kids will get a kick out of walking through. The **Bookstore at Fitger's** *(218/727-9077)* carries children's books at a discount and kids' toys. **Torke Weihnachten Christmas & Chocolates** *(218/723-1225)* has holiday ornaments kids won't care about, but they'll think that the hundreds of nutcrackers are really cool. Restaurants include **Chi-Chi's** *(218/727-0979)*, one of the national chain but with great views of the lake, and **Fitger's Brewhouse Brewery and Grille** *(218/726-1392). 600 E. Superior St., Duluth; (218) 722-8826.*

The Stamping Post, Inc.

If you have crafts-minded kids, don't miss this great spot filled with 15,000 rubber stamps, wonderful papers, stickers, and album supplies. *5705 Grand Ave., Duluth; (218) 624-4722.*

In the **Maritime Museum** next to the bridge, pick up the schedule that lists boat arrival times. The museum isn't large, and you can take the kids on a quick but fun stroll through it. They'll love the captain's nest up top; it has a real ship's wheel, so they can take turns at the helm.

Then stroll the length of the canal walkway—you'll probably see mimes, musicians, and maybe a magician. At the end of the walkway there's a real lighthouse. You can't go inside, but your kids will like being up close.

Walk back to the park and get a hot dog and popcorn at the colorful vendor wagon, or stop in **Grandma's** for burgers and an atmosphere of happy, noisy commotion that young ones love. On your way back to the car, stop at **Grand Slam Family Fun Center** for video games and cool virtual activities, like the ski machine that shows a big-screen snowy mountainside that you "ski" down, standing on ski-shaped pedals. Your 10-year-old will consider it the perfect end to a perfect day.

Factor in lots of stops-along-the-way time during your North Shore Drive—stops to marvel at the craggy shoreline, explore lighthouses, and eat diner desserts.

North Shore

THE DRIVE FROM DULUTH farther north along the shore of Lake Superior is one of the most gorgeous in the entire country. It's like an oceanside drive—Lake Superior is so large you can't see the other side, and the craggy, rocky beaches are dramatic and beautiful. The drive is also dotted with family-friendly stopping points such as state parks, lighthouses, and great places to eat pie.

This is an easy trip to navigate: simply head north out of Duluth on London Road/Highway 61/Scenic 61. When signs offer the option of taking the expressway, stick to the route marked "scenic." (Don't be confused by its many descriptive monikers, among them "Scenic Drive" and "North Shore Drive.") Keep Lake Superior on your right, and you'll be fine.

Just a few miles outside of Duluth, the scenery becomes downright stupendous. Take advantage of the many scenic lookouts and pull the car over to enjoy views of the lake.

Venture up as far north along Highway 61 as you like. Grand

Gooseberry Falls State Park Waterfalls (page 390)

Grand Marais (page 391)

Lutsen Resort (for views of the lake and lunch) (page 396)

Split Rock Lighthouse State Park and Historic Site (page 392)

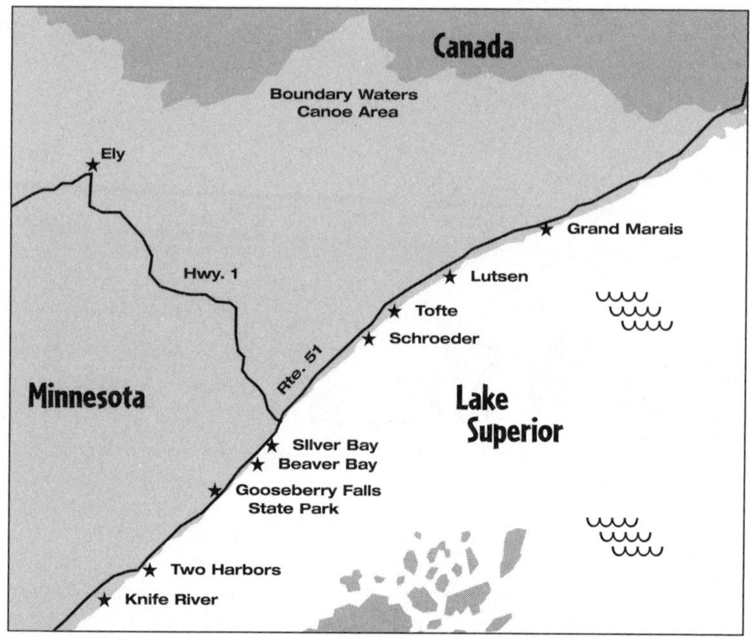

Marais, about two and a half hours from Duluth, is a popular place to visit. There's no easy circle route back to Duluth—you pretty much turn around and head back the way you came, so you may want to save a few stops and attractions for the way home.

Your family will definitely enjoy the scenic ride more in sunlight, so get an early start and head back south well before sunset. Remind your kids to keep their eyes open for deer, moose, beaver, eagles, and hawks—there is an abundance of interesting wildlife along the way.

If you want to stay overnight, there are lodges, resorts, and hotels along the way.

JUST FOR FUN

Cascade River State Park

★★★★/$

Paths you can walk here in winter or summer make the most of the Cascade River's tumbling route through the rocks. The park also has a fishing site and hiking and cross-country ski trails. *It's about nine miles north of the ski area. 3481 W. Hwy. 61, Lutsen; (218) 387-5053.*

Gooseberry Falls State Park Waterfalls

★★★★/$

About eight miles north of Silver Creek, the Gooseberry River drops

100 feet to the lake in a stunning series of waterfalls. The state park has picnic grounds, foot trails, and cross-country ski trails. In summer your family can take part in one of the naturalist-led educational programs (ask at the ranger station for details). *3206 Hwy. 61E, Two Harbors; (218) 834-3855.*

Grand Marais ★★★★/Free

MUST-SEE FamilyFun MUST-SEE

About nine miles beyond Cascade River, you'll arrive at a picturesque coastal village that's a pure delight. It's wrapped around a harbor, with a Coast Guard station and lighthouse standing watch. Park anywhere and just walk around the tiny town. There are notable spots to eat, stay, and shop. Town outfitters can set you up for canoeing, fishing, kayaking, and camping trips from here. The Gunflint Trail heads straight up the hill from town and deep into wild forest country. Drive up the trail for several miles to show your kids a real logging operation at a working lumber mill: tell them to look carefully as you drive along—you might spy the guy who lives in a hut in the woods and uses his horse to haul logs. In summer, **World's Best Donuts** down by the water is open—you know what to do. *(888) 922-5000.*

Knife River ★★★/Free

Give your kids a taste of smoked lake trout (they may not like it enough to make it a meal) at **Russ Kendall's Smoked Fish House** *(Scenic Hwy. 61, Knife River; 218/834-5995).*

Lutsen Mountains Ski Area ★★★/$$$

Yes, there is downhill skiing in Minnesota. About nine miles north of Temperance River, there are four mountains of beginner-to-expert trails and a 1,000-foot drop. A gondola lift system takes you where you want to go, and a half-mile alpine slide makes use of the mountain in summer. *Hwy. 61, Lutsen; (218) 663-7281.*

Silver Creek Cliff Tunnels ★★★★/$

If your kids are asleep, wake them up before you drive through these two amazing tunnels—about seven miles north of Two Harbors—hewn out of the rocky cliffs of the Sawtooth Mountain Range that edges the lake. If you look fast as you enter the first tunnel, you'll see where the old road ran outside the

> **FamilyFun TIP**
>
> **Stone Search**
>
> Pull over to one of the scenic overlooks on the lake side of the road to hunt for Lake Superior agates on the beach. (They look gray and bumpy on the outside edge, and have gorgeous red-and-gold striations inside. Wet them with lake water to see the full effect of the colors.)

Lake Superior Statistics

Your kids are bound to ask. Here's what you need to know:

Lake Superior is the world's largest freshwater lake by surface area: 31,820 square miles. It holds 10 percent of the world's fresh surface water. It is 383 by 160 miles in size, and holds three quadrillion gallons of water. It's cold, averaging about 40°F, and it's deep—an average of 489 feet, and 1,333 feet at its deepest point. It is 602 feet above sea level, and has 2,980 miles of shoreline, including the islands that dot the lake. It takes 400 to 500 years for the lake to "flush"—change over—its water content totally. One drop of water stays in the lake nearly 200 years. The lake is calmest in summer months, but the fall months of October and November are known for storms (the highest wave ever recorded here was 31 feet) and shipwrecks (a total of 350, with more than 1,000 lives lost).

tunnel mouth closer to the lake—and you'll see how the falling rocks were a danger.

Split Rock Lighthouse State Park and Historic Site ★★★★/$

Once you're past Gooseberry Falls, tell your kids to start looking out along the lakeshore: way before you come to the lighthouse park entrance (about seven miles north of Gooseberry), you can see this yellow landmark perched at the edge of a cliff 168 feet above the lake. During some storms, the waves have reached up to the lighthouse. In service for 60 years, the lighthouse is no longer in use, but it's open for tours May through October; you can walk to the top of the lighthouse, see the lightkeeper's dwelling, and watch a 20-minute film. If you arrive in the off-season, drive into the park and walk around the outside of the lighthouse, anyway; the views are amazing, and your kids will take away vivid memories of watching the winter ice break up. (If you hear what sounds like small explosions and gunshots near the lake in winter, it's probably ice cracking and breaking.) The park has campsites, foot trails, cross-country ski trails, and picnic areas. If you pay admission to the historic site, the park fee is waived. Reduced rates for children and families; kids under 6 free. *3713 Split Rock Lighthouse Rd., Two Harbors; (218) 226-6372;* www.mnhs.org/splitrock

Superior Hiking Trail

★★★★/Free

This 235-plus-mile hiking trail runs from Duluth northeast to the very tip of Minnesota at the Canadian border. Along Highway 61, you'll see signs with a leaf-shaped logo that indicate points to get on and off the trail. Obviously, you can't walk the entire trail, but it roughly follows the shoreline of the lake and allows easy parking and on-and-off access.

The trail is broken up into four mapped sections. You can pick up maps at many convenience stores along Highway 61, or stop at a state park ranger station or visitor information center.

Weather conditions dictate what's accessible on this trail; your best bet is to ask someone at the state park station to recommend a hike your family can handle, or call the **Superior Hiking Trail Association in Two Harbors** *(731 Seventh Ave.; 218/834-4436;* www.shta.org).

Temperance River State Park

★★★★/$

Rich in waterfalls, rocky gorges, and pine forests, this park, 23 miles north of Tettegouche, also has a fishing stream, foot trails, and cross-country ski trails, plus beautiful scenery. *Hwy. 61, Schroeder; (218) 663-7476.*

Tettegouche State Park

★★★★/$

Twelve miles north of Split Rock, the picturesque Baptism River flows through this park, creating some of the highest waterfalls in the state. Walk up the trail to Shore Point, a scenic overlook 170 feet above the lake. *5702 Hwy. 61E, Silver Bay; (218) 226-6365.*

Tom's Logging Camp

★★★/$

In the summer, visit this authentic replica of a logging camp. Eight museum buildings house historic logging artifacts, and your kids can see and pet llamas, pygmy goats, and bunnies. Closed November through April. *5797 North Shore Scenic Dr., Two Harbors; (218) 525-4120;* www.tomsloggingcamp.com

Two Harbors ★★★★/Free

Five miles north of Knife River lies this little town, which, like many

BEAVERS USE THEIR TAILS for a variety of purposes. While the animal swims, the tail acts as a rudder. If a beaver senses danger, he slaps his tail on the water to warn other animals. When the creature stands on its hind legs, the tail provides body support.

settlements up here, has its roots in the early days of the iron-ore industry. Enormous ore carriers still take on loads of taconite in the harbor here. Stop at Paul Van Hoven Park, between the highway and the lake, and walk out on the breakwater for a great lake view.

BUNKING DOWN

NOTE: All the state parks listed above offer camping facilities.

Bluefin Bay

★★★★/$$-$$$$

This modern development in Tofte, north of Temperance River and south of Lutsen, resembles a cluster of attractive New England town homes and shops, painted blue and white and perched on opposite sides of a lakeside bay. Choose from hotel-style rooms (some with whirlpools, all with great views), condominiums, and town house-style accommodations. Most units have fireplaces. The three restaurants here

Northern Exposure:

A TRIP TO THE WILDERNESS BOUNDARY WATERS CANOE AREA

WAY UP NORTH, along the Canadian border, is a beloved and pristine Minnesota wilderness: the Boundary Waters Canoe Area. Note the word "canoe"—you need one to get around these parts, where motorized vehicles are not permitted. This is the most heavily used wilderness in the nation, but you won't see any crowds. In fact, you might not even see another person! There are 1,200 miles of canoe routes to explore, but unless everyone in your group is an experienced camper and canoeist, you'll just want to venture in for a day trip. The isolation of the campsites may frighten young children, and even the older ones will balk at carrying canoes over long portages. Talk to the folks at the BWCA Reservation Office about which routes best suit your family. Although visits here require a lot of physical effort, the wildlife and exotic plant life in the area make the daylong paddles worthwhile. Local outfitters can supply your family with the food and equipment you'll need for your voyage. Be forewarned: the rule here is that you must carry out everything that you carry in;

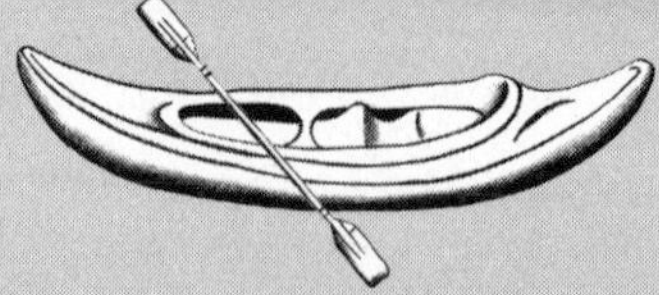

have fabulous views and terrific food, and it's a full-service resort with lots of amenities: a pool, tennis courts, and satellite TV make this a stay-put vacation spot, ideal for families. *Tofte; (800) 258-3346; (218) 663-7296;* www.bluefinbay.com

Bob's Cabins

★★★/$$

If you're seeking an old-fashioned family lakeside vacation, book a cabin here. The cabins are clean but not fancy, sleep two to four adults (a few cabins sleep six), and are close to the rocky shoreline and accessible beach. Open May to mid-October. *664 Old North Shore Rd., near Two Harbors; (218) 834-4583.*

Eagle Ridge Condominiums

★★★/$-$$$

These condos are great for a family skiing vacation. Each unit has a full kitchen, and you can ski right out the door onto trails of the Lutsen Mountains Ski Area. *County Rd. 5, Lutsen; (800) 360-7666.*

make peace with the idea of schlepping your garbage around in your backpack. Pick up a BWCA permit (about $9) at the Permit Center, and choose an outfitter near the entry point you've chosen.

TRAVEL TIMES

Weekends are busiest here. Arrive midweek to avoid crowds of people trying to launch on the same day. Once you're launched, you'll soon separate from others and get the true feeling of being "in the wild."

GROUP SIZE

No more than nine people and four watercraft are allowed in any one group. Most campsites fit two tents, so kids can sleep in their own den—if you or they are willing to carry the weight of an extra tent.

MAPS

Don't skimp. Accurate maps are a must-have. Most lakes look fairly similar, and it's easy to get disoriented once the marks of civilization are gone. Maps are available at the Permit Center and from outfitters.

PACKING

You'll need a good backpack and lots of plastic bags to cover things in the rain. Whatever you bring with you, you'll have to carry over rugged portages between lakes, so don't overdo it. Ask your outfitter to help you determine how much food and supplies you'll need.

OUTFITTERS

You can find a number of outfitters in Ely, Tofte, and Grand Marais. The Website Canoecountry.com has a helpful list of resources. *Or call the BWCA (877/550-6777).*

East Bay Hotel, Restaurant, and Lounge ★★★/$-$$

A terrific family spot, this quirky hotel is part historic building and part new additions. The older side has smaller rooms with narrower windows, but the lakeside views are great and the furnishings are charming. A few of the older rooms share bathrooms, so you'll want to check and be sure you have facilities of your own. On the new side of the hotel, rooms are generously oversized. Second- and third-floor rooms have balconies overlooking the lake, and first-floor rooms have private patios where you can walk right out to the beach and the lake. The restaurant is as good as it gets in Grand Marais, though, and well worth more than one meal here. *1 Wisconsin St., Grand Marais; (800) 414-2807; (218) 387-2800;* www.eastbayhotel.com

Moose are named for an Algonquin word that means "eater of twigs."

Lutsen Sea Villas and Lutsen Resort ★★/$-$$$$

The resort is a beloved North Shore timber-and-rock lodge, designed by noted architect Edwin Lundie. The Sea Villas are condominiums near the shore; most are privately owned, so the style and amenities vary from unit to unit. If you don't stay here, at least come for dinner, enjoy the lake view and charming architecture, have a great piece of pie, and show your kids the real stuffed bear in the glass case outside the dining room. After dinner, walk the path along the lake and cross the small footbridge over the creek—and look for deer. In winter, this is a popular destination among skiers. *Hwy. 61E, Lutsen; (800) 2-LUTSEN; (218) 663-7212;* www.lutsenresort.com

Superior Shores Resort & Conference Center ★★★★/$$-$$$$

You won't be roughing it here. This resort is known for its lovely lakefront site surrounded by natural woodlands and attractive landscaping. The 144 rooms are like those at any modern hotel, the public spaces are comfortable and well appointed, and the food is great. Choose one- or two-bedroom suites with a fireplace, Jacuzzi, and king-size bed, or one of the town houses on the shore that has a fireplace and sleep two to eight people. All units have a gas barbecue grill, TV, VCR, and a kitchen complete with microwave, coffeemaker, toaster, and stove. A restaurant (with a kids' menu), indoor and outdoor pools, Jacuzzis, tennis courts, and trails for snowmobiles, cross-country skiing, and hiking should keep your kids happy. *1521 Superior Shores Dr., Two Harbors; (800) 242-1988; (218) 834-5671;* www.superiorshores.com

Good Eats

Betty's Pies ★★/$

Good pie, burgers, and fries will make your hungry lunchers happy. But save room for pie at the Scenic Café and Rustic Inn Café, too *(see below). 215 Hwy. 61 E., Two Harbors; (218) 834-3367.*

The Pie Place ★★★/$

This charming restaurant is on your left just as you enter Grand Marais. The menu features vegetarian soups, inventive salads, sandwiches, and terrific pies. There's no kids' menu, but the staff will customize an order to please little eaters. *2017 W. Hwy. 61, Grand Marais; (218) 387-1513.*

Rustic Inn Café ★★★★/$

Pie is the main draw at this homey, log-cabin café. Try the seven-layer chocolate pie or the "angel pie" of sweet lemon and meringue. But first, order a hearty soup, sandwich, or grilled lake trout. There's a kids' menu, too. *Hwy. 61, north of Silver Creek and south of Gooseberry Falls State Park; (218) 834-2488.*

Scenic Café
★★★★/$

This little building on the west side of the highway is a real treat, with a gourmet kitchen and an unbelievable view of Lake Superior from the dining room. There's a kids' menu, but save room for dessert: the pies,

Fly Time Scavenger Hunts

You end up with a lot of idle time when you travel by air. Scavenger hunts are an easy way to spend those hours calmly.

IN THE AIRPORT

You don't want anyone lost in the crowd, so set off in parent-child teams to find the following:

- ♦ A child holding a doll
- ♦ A person carrying four pieces of luggage
- ♦ An abandoned sports section of *USA Today*
- ♦ 4 pilots
- ♦ 2 courtesy carts

ON THE AIRPLANE

Find these items individually or together:

- ♦ Cars
- ♦ Railroad tracks
- ♦ A cloud
- ♦ Another airplane
- ♦ A mountain range below
- ♦ Someone speaking in a foreign language
- ♦ A father holding a baby
- ♦ A person in an apron
- ♦ Somebody sleeping
- ♦ A laptop computer
- ♦ A mustache
- ♦ A briefcase
- ♦ A Walkman radio
- ♦ A pillow and blanket
- ♦ Candy
- ♦ A blue tie

crusty with sugar and brimming with fresh fruit, are among the best on the North Shore. *5461 North Shore Dr., a few miles north of Duluth and south of Knife River; (218) 525-6274.*

SOUVENIR HUNTING

Beaver Bay Agate Shop

If you haven't found striated red-and-gold-colored agates on the beaches, buy one here. *1003 Main St., Beaver Bay; (218) 226-4847.*

Joynes Department Store & Ben Franklin

Kids just love it. So will you. The narrow aisles are piled high with everything folks need to get through the seasons in the Northland. In winter, the place is packed with flannel, fleece, fur, boots, and snowshoes. In summer, plenty of lanterns, fishing gear, swimsuits, and mos-

Schussing and Sliding:

WINTER SPORTS IN MINNESOTA

Skiing

Afton Alps

★★★/$$

This is the closest thing to great skiing you're going to find close to the metro area (about a half hour from St. Paul). There are 37 scenic ski runs here, with enough variety to satisfy all ages and skill levels. Got a beginner wobbling around the slopes? Sign up for ski lessons, or do supervised runs on the bunny hill. For more advanced skiers, there are plenty of "blue square" and "black diamond" trails. Vertical drop is 350 feet. *6600 Peller Ave. S., Hastings; (651) 436-5245.*

Buck Hill ★★/$$

This ski area is along I-35 W, south of the Twin Cities near the Burnsville Center mall. It's an easy drive from the metro area (30 to 40 minutes). It has fewer slopes than Afton Alps, but it offers a little more help to beginners. The Sports Learning Center has ski lessons for all ages and abilities, so take advantage of the staff's vast knowledge. There are 11 runs here, and management promises 100-percent snow coverage throughout the ski season. Vertical drop is 306 feet. *15400 Buck Hill Rd., Burnsville; (952) 435-7187.*

Lutsen Mountains Ski Area

★★★★/$$$$

If you and your kids love skiing, this is the place to go; be aware, however, that it's a bit of a drive. Lutsen is north of Duluth, along the breathtakingly beautiful north shore of

quito repellent are in stock. Like an old-fashioned general store, it's great fun to poke around in. *205 Wisconsin St., Grand Marais; (218) 387-2233.*

Lake Superior Trading Post

Your children will be intrigued by the split-log staircase and the log-cabin feel of this elegant, upscale Northwoods store. They'll like the toys, books, and other fun kid stuff. *16 First Ave. S., right on the lake, Grand Marais; (218) 387-2020.*

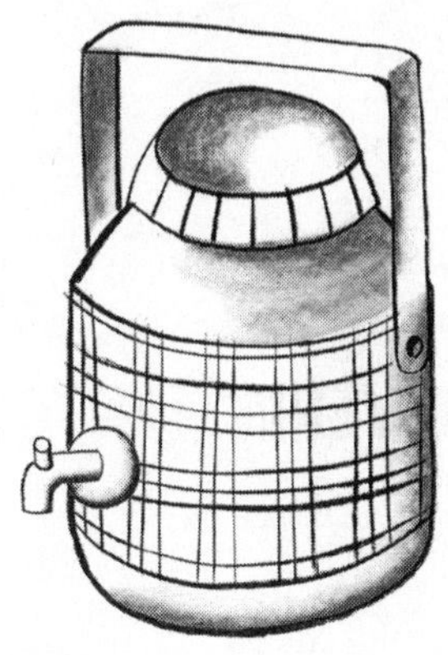

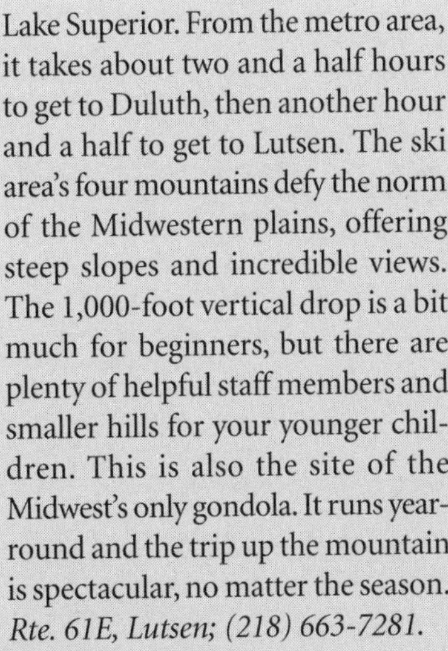

Lake Superior. From the metro area, it takes about two and a half hours to get to Duluth, then another hour and a half to get to Lutsen. The ski area's four mountains defy the norm of the Midwestern plains, offering steep slopes and incredible views. The 1,000-foot vertical drop is a bit much for beginners, but there are plenty of helpful staff members and smaller hills for your younger children. This is also the site of the Midwest's only gondola. It runs year-round and the trip up the mountain is spectacular, no matter the season. *Rte. 61E, Lutsen; (218) 663-7281.*

Snow Tubing

Snow tubing is a great way to spend a chilly winter day, and it doesn't require the balance and skills that skiing demands. Even if your kids aren't used to the sport (or to snow) they'll master the basics quickly—hang on!

Eko Bakken

★★/$$

There are great hills here, and they're all well lighted and well staffed. Watch your younger kids closely on their first couple of tries with the towing system—the swiftly moving ropes can give you a nasty burn. *22570 Manning Trail, Scandia; (651) 433-2422.*

Green Acres Recreation

★★/$$

Here's a good place to learn the ropes of snow tubing. This smallish facility is great for the whole family, but especially welcoming to younger kids who aren't yet confident on big hills. Family members can keep each other in sight on the facility's two hills. If it gets too chilly, enjoy some hot cocoa in the warming chalet. *8989 55th St. N., at Demontriville Trail, Lake Elmo; (651) 770-6060;* www.greenacresrec.com

Index

O

P

R

S

U

V

W

PHOTO CREDITS

Cover *(from top to bottom)*:
Sandra Baker
T. Nowotz/Folio, Inc.
Team Russell
Rob Atkins

Inside:
Ryan McVay/ Getty Images, page 4
Colin Barker/ Getty Images, page 10
Courtesy of Neil Armstrong Museum, page 42
Courtesy of Cedar Point Amusement Park/Resort, page 52
Hans Teensma, page 62
Ryan McVay/ Getty Images, page 74
S. Soulum/ Getty Images, page 82
Courtesy of Columbus Zoo and Aquarium, page 88
Peter Pearson/ Getty Images, page 98
Jonathan Skow/ Getty Images, page 110
Courtesy of Detroit Metro Convention & Visitors Bureau, page 120
Tamara Reynolds/ Getty Images, page 132
Eyewire Collection/ Getty Images, page 140
Vito Palmisano/ Getty Images, page 146
Werner Bokelberg/ Getty Images, page 152
EyeWire Collection/ Getty Images, page 164
Stewart Cohen/ Getty Images, page 170
Chris Sanders/ Getty Images, page 178
Peter Pearson/ Getty Images, page 188
Courtesy of Illinois Department of Natural Resources, page 212
Dave Nagel/ Getty Images, page 222
Ty Allison/ Getty Images, page 230
Courtesy of Southernmost Illinois Tourism Bureau, page 238
Peter Cade/ Getty Images, page 246
Digital Vision/ Getty Images, page 272
Anne Menke/ Getty Images, page 278
Eyewire Collection/ Getty Images, page 290
Anne Menke/ Getty Images, page 300
Courtesy of Wisconsin Dells Visitor & Convention Bureau, page 308
Courtesy of Peck's Wildwood Wildlife Park, page 326
Donna Day/ Getty Images, page 338
Christian Lantry/ Getty Images, page 364
Phil Boorman/ Getty Images, page 378
Anne Menke/ Getty Images, page 388

Also from FamilyFun

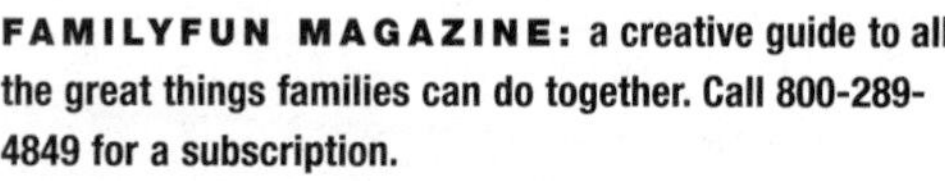

FAMILYFUN MAGAZINE: a creative guide to all the great things families can do together. Call 800-289-4849 for a subscription.

FAMILYFUN.COM: visit us at www.familyfun.com and search our extensive archives for games, crafts, recipes, and holiday projects.

FAMILYFUN COOKBOOK: a collection of more than 250 irresistible recipes for you and your kids, from healthy snacks to birthday cakes to dinners everyone in the family can enjoy (Disney Editions, 256 pages; $24.95).

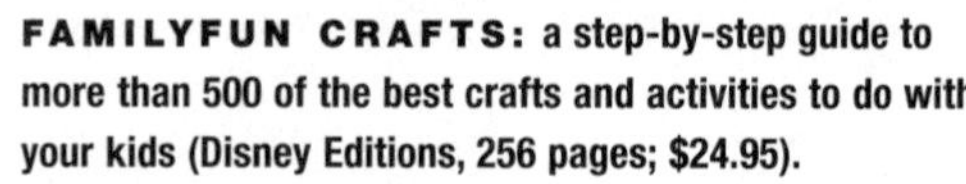

FAMILYFUN CRAFTS: a step-by-step guide to more than 500 of the best crafts and activities to do with your kids (Disney Editions, 256 pages; $24.95).

FAMILYFUN PARTIES: a complete party planner featuring 100 celebrations for birthdays, holidays, and every day (Disney Editions, 224 pages; $24.95).

FAMILYFUN COOKIES FOR CHRISTMAS: a batch of 50 recipes for creative holiday treats (Disney Editions, 64 pages; $9.95).

FAMILYFUN TRICKS AND TREATS: a collection of wickedly easy crafts, costumes, party plans, and recipes for Halloween (Disney Editions, 98 pages; $14.95).

FAMILYFUN BOREDOM BUSTERS: a collection of 365 activities, from instant fun and after-school crafts to kitchen projects and learning games (Disney Editions, 224 pages; $24.95).

FAMILYFUN HOMEMADE HOLIDAYS: A collection of 150 holiday activities, from festive decorations and family traditions to holiday recipes and gifts kids can make (Disney Editions, 96 pages; $14.95).